I
N
T
E
R
A
C
T
I
V
E

T
E
X
T

Foundations in Accountancy

FA2

MAINTAINING FINANCIAL RECORDS

BPP Learning Media is an **ACCA Approved Content Provider** for the Foundations In Accountancy qualification. This means we work closely with ACCA to ensure this Interactive Text contains the information you need to pass your exam.

In this Interactive Text, which has been reviewed by the **ACCA examining team**, we:

- **Highlight** the **most important elements** in the syllabus and the **key skills** you need

- **Signpost** how each chapter links to the syllabus and the study guide

- **Provide** lots of **exam focus points** demonstrating what the examining team will want you to do

- **Emphasise key points** in regular **fast forward summaries**

- **Test your knowledge** in **quick quizzes**

- **Examine your understanding** in our **practice question bank**

- **Reference all the important topics** in our full index

BPP's **Practice & Revision Kit** also supports the FA2 syllabus.

FOR EXAMS FROM 1 SEPTEMBER 2021 TO 31 AUGUST 2022

First edition November 2011
Tenth edition March 2021

ISBN 9781 5097 3776 5
(Previous ISBN) 9781 5097 3038 4
e-ISBN 9781 5097 3827 4

British Library Cataloguing-in-Publication Data
A catalogue record for this book
is available from the British Library

Published by

BPP Learning Media Ltd
BPP House, Aldine Place
London W12 8AA

www.bpp.com/learningmedia

Printed in the United Kingdom

Your learning materials, published by BPP Learning
Media Ltd, are printed on paper obtained from
traceable sustainable sources.

BPP Learning Media is grateful to the IASB for
permission to reproduce extracts from the International
Financial Reporting Standards including all
International Accounting Standards, SIC and IFRIC
Interpretations (the Standards). The Standards together
with their accompanying documents are issued by:

The International Accounting Standards Board (IASB)
30 Cannon Street, London, EC4M 6XH, United
Kingdom. Email: info@ifrs.org Web: www.ifrs.org

Disclaimer: The IASB, the International Financial
Reporting Standards (IFRS) Foundation, the authors
and the publishers do not accept responsibility for any
loss caused by acting or refraining from acting in
reliance on the material in this publication, whether
such loss is caused by negligence or otherwise to the
maximum extent permitted by law.

BPP
LEARNING MEDIA

Contents

Helping you to pass

BPP Learning Media – ACCA Approved Content Provider

As an ACCA **Approved Content Provider**, BPP Learning Media gives you the **opportunity** to use study materials reviewed by the ACCA examining team. By incorporating the examining team's comments and suggestions regarding the depth and breadth of syllabus coverage, the BPP Learning Media Interactive Text provides excellent, **ACCA-approved** support for your studies.

These materials are reviewed by the ACCA examining team. The objective of the review is to ensure that the material properly covers the syllabus and study guide outcomes, used by the examining team in setting the exams, in the appropriate breadth and depth. The review does not ensure that every eventuality, combination or application of examinable topics is addressed by the ACCA Approved Content. Nor does the review comprise a detailed technical check of the content as the Approved Content Provider has its own quality assurance processes in place in this respect.

BPP Learning Media do everything possible to ensure the material is accurate and up to date when sending to print. In the event that any errors are found after the print date, they are uploaded to the following website: www.bpp.com/learningmedia/Errata.

The PER alert!

To become a Certified Accounting Technician or qualify as an ACCA member, you not only have to pass all your exams but also fulfil a **practical experience requirement** (PER).To help you to recognise areas of the syllabus that you might be able to apply in the workplace to achieve different performance objectives, we have introduced the '**PER alert**' feature. You will find this feature throughout the Interactive Text to remind you that what you are **learning in order to pass** your Foundations In Accountancy and ACCA exams is **equally useful to the fulfilment of the PER requirement**.

Tackling studying

Studying can be a daunting prospect, particularly when you have lots of other commitments. The **different features** of the Interactive Text, the **purposes** of which are explained fully on the **Chapter features** page, will help you whilst studying and improve your chances of **exam success**.

Developing exam awareness

Our Interactive Texts are completely **focused** on helping you pass your exam.

Our advice on **Studying FA2** outlines the **content** of the exam, the **recommended approach to studying** and any **brought forward knowledge** you are expected to have.

Exam focus points are included within the chapters to highlight when and how specific topics might be examined.

Testing what you can do

Testing yourself helps you develop the skills you need to pass the exam and also confirms that you can recall what you have learnt.

We include **Questions** – lots of them – both within chapters and in the **Practice Question Bank**, as well as **Quick Quizzes** at the end of each chapter to test your knowledge of the chapter content.

Chapter features

Each chapter contains a number of helpful features to guide you through each topic.

Topic list	Tells you what you will be studying in this chapter and the relevant section numbers, together with ACCA syllabus references.
Introduction	Puts the chapter content in the context of the syllabus as a whole.
Study Guide	Links the chapter content with ACCA guidance.
Fast Forward	Summarises the content of main chapter headings, allowing you to preview and review each section easily.
EXAMPLE	Demonstrates how to apply key knowledge and techniques.
Key Term	Definitions of important concepts that can often earn you easy marks in exams.
Exam Focus Point	Tell you how specific topics may be examined.
π **Formula**	Formulae which have to be learnt.
(PER) Alert	This feature gives you a useful indication of syllabus areas that closely relate to performance objectives in your Practical Experience Requirement (PER).
Question	Gives you essential practice of techniques covered in the chapter.
Chapter Roundup	A full list of the Fast Forwards included in the chapter, providing an easy source of review.
Quick Quiz	A quick test of your knowledge of the main topics in the chapter.
Practice Question Bank	Found at the back of the Interactive Text with more exam-style chapter questions. Cross referenced for easy navigation.

Studying FA2

How to Use this Interactive Text

Aim of this Interactive Text

To provide the knowledge and practice to help you succeed in the examination for FA2 *Maintaining Financial Records*.

To pass the examination you need a thorough understanding in all areas covered by the syllabus and teaching guide.

Recommended approach

(a) To pass you need to be able to answer questions on **everything** specified by the syllabus and teaching guide. Read the Interactive Text very carefully and do not skip any of it.

(b) Learning is an **active** process. Do **all** the questions as you work through the Text so you can be sure you really understand what you have read.

(c) After you have covered the material in the Interactive Text, work through the **Practice Question Bank**, checking your answers carefully against the **Practice Answer Bank**.

(d) Before you take the exam, check that you still remember the material using the following quick revision plan.

   (i) Read through the **chapter topic list** at the beginning of each chapter. Are there any gaps in your knowledge? If so, study the section again.

   (ii) Read and learn the **key terms**.

   (iii) Look at the **exam focus points**. These show the ways in which topics might be examined.

   (iv) Read the **chapter roundups**, which are a summary of the **fast forwards** in each chapter.

   (v) Do the **quick quizzes** again. If you know what you're doing, they shouldn't take long.

This approach is only a suggestion. You or your college may well adapt it to suit your needs. Remember this is a **practical** course.

(a) Try to relate the material to your experience in the workplace or any other work experience you may have had.

(b) Try to make as many links as you can to other exams at the Introductory and Intermediate levels.

For practice and revision use BPP Learning Media's Practice & Revision Kit and Passcards.

What FA2 is about

The aim of this syllabus is to develop knowledge and understanding of the underlying principles and concepts relating to Maintaining Financial Records and technical proficiency in the use of double-entry accounting techniques including the preparation of basic financial statements.

Brought forward knowledge

You will need to have a good knowledge of recording financial transactions from FA1 *Recording Financial Transactions.* The examining team will assume you know this material and it may form part of an exam question.

Approach to examining the syllabus

FA2 is a two-hour computer-based exam. The questions in the computer based examination are objective test questions – multiple choice, number entry and multiple response. (See page x for frequently asked questions about computer-based examinations.)

The written examination is structured as follows:

	Marks
50 compulsory objective test questions of two marks each	100

Syllabus and Study Guide

The complete FA2 syllabus and study guide can be found by visiting the exam resource finder on the ACCA website.

BPP LEARNING MEDIA

The computer-based examination

Computer-based examinations (CBEs) are available for the Foundations In Accountancy exams. The CBE exams for the first seven modules can be taken at any time; these are referred to as 'exams on demand'. The Option exams can be sat in June and December each year; these are referred to as 'exams on sitting'.

Computer-based examinations must be taken at an ACCA CBE Licensed Centre.

How do CBEs work?

- Questions are displayed on a monitor

- Candidates enter their answer directly onto the computer

- Candidates have two hours to complete the examination

- Candidates are provided with a Provisional Result Notification showing their results before leaving the examination room

- The CBE Licensed Centre uploads the results to the ACCA (as proof of the candidate's performance) within 72 hours

- Candidates sitting the Option exams will receive their results approximately five weeks after the exam sitting once they have been expert marked

- Candidates can check their exam status on the ACCA website by logging into myACCA

Benefits

- **Flexibility** – the first seven modules, exams on demand, can be sat at any time

- **Resits** for the first seven modules can also be taken at any time and there is no restriction on the number of times a candidate can sit a CBE

- **Instant feedback** for the exams on demand as the computer displays the results at the end of the CBE

For more information on computer-based exams, visit the ACCA website.

Tackling multiple choice questions

MCQs are part of all Foundations In Accountancy exams.

The MCQs in your exam contain up to four possible answers. **You have to select the single correct answer to the question**. The incorrect options are called distracters. There is a skill in answering MCQs quickly and correctly. By practising MCQs you can develop this skill, giving you a better chance of passing the exam.

You may wish to follow the approach outlined below, or you may prefer to adapt it.

Step 1	Read the question **thoroughly**. You may prefer to work out the answer before looking at the options, or you may prefer to look at the options at the beginning. Adopt the method that works best for you.

Step 2	Read the four options and see if one matches your own answer. Be careful with numerical questions as the distracters are designed to match answers that incorporate common errors. Check that your calculation is correct. Have you followed the requirement exactly? Have you included every stage of the calculation?

Step 3	You may find that none of the options match your answer. • Re-read the question to ensure that you understand it and are answering the requirement • Eliminate any obviously wrong answers • Consider which of the remaining answers is the most likely to be correct and select the option

Step 4	If you are still unsure make a note and continue to the next question

Step 5	Revisit unanswered questions. When you come back to a question after a break you often find you are able to answer it correctly straight away. If you are still unsure, have a guess. You are not penalised for incorrect answers, so **never leave a question unanswered!**

After extensive practice and revision of MCQs, you may find that you recognise a question when you sit the exam. Be aware that the detail and/or requirement may be different. If the question seems familiar read the requirement and options carefully – do not assume that it is identical.

Tempting though it might be, don't try to predict where the correct answers might fall based on any kind of pattern you think you might perceive in this section. The distribution of the correct answers do not follow any predictable pattern in this exam!

part

A

Basic bookkeeping

This chapter introduces the fundamentals of accounting.

It is important that a business is treated separately from its owners and this is known as the **business entity concept**.

When a business is started up, the proprietor injects their own funds as **capital**. As the business trades it will build up **assets** and **liabilities** and hopefully it will make a **profit** which is added to the proprietor's capital.

At any point in time the assets less the liabilities will equal the capital of the business. This rule forms the basis of the **accounting equation** and, as long as the **double entry bookkeeping** system is used, the accounting equation will remain balanced.

Assets, liabilities and the accounting equation

TOPIC LIST	SYLLABUS REFERENCE
1 Introduction: accounting fundamentals	B1(b)
2 What is a business?	B1(b)
3 Asset and liabilities	B1(b)
4 A business is separate from its owner(s): the business entity concept	A1(a)
5 The accounting equation	B1(a), D7(a), D7(b)
6 The business equation	B1(a), D7(b)
7 Accounts payable and accounts receivable	B1(b)
8 Double entry bookkeeping	A1(a), C1(a)

Study Guide	Intellectual level
A **Generally accepted accounting principles and concepts**	
1 **The key accounting principles and characteristics**	
(a) Explain the principles of accounting	K
(iv) Double entry	
(v) Business entity concept	
B **The principles and process of basic bookkeeping**	
1 **The elements of the financial statements**	
(a) Explain the meaning of the accounting equation	K
(b) Describe the meaning of assets, liabilities and capital in an accounting context	K
C **The preparation of journals and ledger accounts**	
1 **Preparation of journals from the books of prime entry**	
(a) Explain and illustrate the dual aspect convention	S
D **Recording transactions and events**	
7 **Capital and finance costs**	
(a) Distinguish between capital injected by the business owner(s) and third parties for an unincorporated business	K
(b) Explain the accounting equation including the impact of changes in capital.	K

1   Introduction: accounting fundamentals

In order to pass this exam it is vital that you acquire a thorough understanding of the **principles of double entry bookkeeping** outlined in this chapter and developed in Chapters 3 and 4.

The purpose of Chapters 1 to 4 of this Interactive Text is to introduce the **fundamentals of accounting**, particularly the principles of **double entry bookkeeping**.

Accounting practice is based on a number of key accounting principles which are set out in the *Conceptual Framework for Financial Reporting* (often referred to as '*the Conceptual Framework*'). How these principles, as well as the qualitative characteristics of accounting, are applied is explained in a number of International Financial Reporting Standards (IFRS). The Framework and the standards are published by the International Accounting Standards Board. The extent to which these documents are examinable will be explained throughout this text, with Chapter 5 in particular providing guidance on this.

EXAM FOCUS POINT

The material in these first few chapters is very important. Many of the topics are mentioned specifically in the Study Guide.

2 What is a business?

A **business** may be defined in various ways. Its purpose is to make a **profit** for its owner(s).

Profit is the excess of income over expenditure.

Before tackling the nuts and bolts of accounting, it is worth considering what we mean when we talk about a **business**.

- A business is a commercial or industrial concern which exists to deal in the manufacture, resale or **supply of goods and services**.
- A business is an organisation which uses **economic resources** to create goods or services which customers will buy.
- A business is an organisation **providing jobs** for people to work in.
- A business invests money in resources (eg it buys buildings, machinery etc; it pays employees) in order to make even **more money for its owners.**

This last definition – **investing money to make more money** – introduces the important idea of **profit**. Business entities vary in character, size and complexity. They range from very small businesses (the local shopkeeper or plumber) to very large multinationals. But the **objective of earning profit** is common to all of them.

Profit is the excess of income over expenditure. When expenditure exceeds income, the business is running at a **loss**.

One of the jobs of an accountant is to **measure** income, expenditure and profit. This is not always straightforward: it can be an inexact science, although the **accounting fundamentals** of **double entry bookkeeping** make sure that there is a firm set of principles underlying everything an accountant does.

Learning how to account for a business involves building up a clear picture of what a business consists of. We shall start with what a business **owns** and what it **owes** – its **assets** and **liabilities.**

3 Assets and liabilities

A business **owns assets** and **owes liabilities**.

Assets are items belonging to a business and used in the running of the business. They may be **non-current** (machinery, office premises) or **current** (inventory, receivables, cash).

Liabilities are sums of money owed by a business to outsiders such as a bank or a supplier.

3.1 Assets

The definition of an asset is set out in the IASB's *Conceptual Framework*, but it is essentially the ability to access a resource; it may be physical (such as cash or a van) or a 'right' to receive these physical assets (such as trade receivable). The access to a resource (an economic resource) arises as a result of a transaction that has already been completed, for example, the sale of goods to a third party means that the business will have either cash (a physical asset) or the right to receive cash (a trade receivable)

An **asset** is a present economic resource controlled by the entity as a result of past events. An economic resource is a right that has the potential to produce economic benefits.

(Conceptual Framework, para.4.3–4.4)

3.1.1 Non-current and current assets

Some assets are held and used in operations for a **long time**. An office building might be occupied by administrative staff for years; similarly, a machine might have a productive life of many years before it wears out. These are usually referred to as **non-current assets**.

Other assets are held for only a **short time**. The owner of a newsagent's shop, for example, will have to sell their newspapers on the same day that they get them, and weekly newspapers and monthly magazines also have a short shelf life. The more quickly a business can sell the goods it has in store, the more profit it is likely to make. We usually call these **current assets.**

3.2 Liabilities

A liability is something which is owed to somebody else as a result of a past event. These can include payments owed to suppliers, loans from banks or third parties, including leased assets.

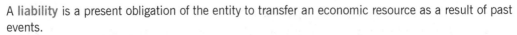

A liability is a present obligation of the entity to transfer an economic resource as a result of past events.

(Conceptual Framework, para.4.26)

'**Liabilities**' is the accounting term for the debts of a business. Debts are owed to **other parties**. Here are some examples of liabilities.

Liability	Description
A **bank loan** or **bank overdraft**	The **liability** is the amount which must eventually be repaid to the **bank**. Note that an overdraft **facility** means that the bank has agreed that the business account may be overdrawn by up to a set limit, but does not mean that the account has an overdrawn balance.
Amounts owed to **suppliers** for goods purchased but not yet paid for	A boat builder might buy some timber on credit from a **timber merchant**, which means that the boat builder does not have to pay for the timber until some time after it has been delivered. Until the boat builder pays what they owe, the timber merchant will be their **liability** (or payable) for the amount owed. The balance is often referred to as an 'account payable' or 'trade payable'.
Taxation owed to the **government**	A business pays tax on its profits but there is a gap in time between when a business earns its profits and becomes liable to pay tax and the time when the tax bill must eventually be paid. While tax is due but unpaid, it is a **liability**.

4   A business is separate from its owner(s): the business entity concept

For accounting purposes it is important to keep business assets and liabilities **separate** from the personal assets and liabilities of the proprietor(s).

A business is always treated as a separate entity from its owners for accounting purposes. This is known as the business entity concept.

So far we have spoken of assets and liabilities 'of a business'. We shall see that, in accounting terms, a business is **always a separate entity from its owner(s)**, but there are two aspects to this question: the strict legal position and the convention adopted by accountants. The law recognises a company as a separate legal entity, but recognises no distinction between a business carried on as either a sole trader or partnership and the owner(s) of the business.

BPP
LEARNING MEDIA

Suppose that Fiona Smith sets herself up in business as a hairdresser trading under the business name 'Hair by Fiona'. The law recognises no distinction between Fiona, the individual, and the business known as 'Hair by Fiona'. Any debts of the business which cannot be met from business assets must be met from Fiona's private resources.

In many countries, the law recognises no distinction between the business of a sole trader or partnership and its owner(s).

QUESTION
Terms

Distinguish between the terms 'entity', 'business', 'company' and 'firm'.

ANSWER

An **entity** is the most general term, referring to just about any organisation in which people join together to achieve a common end. In the context of accounting it can refer to a multinational conglomerate, a small club, a local authority and so on.

A **business** is also a very general term, but it does not extend as widely as the term 'entity': for example, it would not include a charity or a local authority. But any organisation existing to trade and make a profit could be called a business.

A **company** is an entity constituted in a particular legal form, usually involving limited liability for its members. Companies need not be businesses; for example, many charities are constituted as companies.

A **firm** is a much vaguer term. It is sometimes used loosely in the sense of a business or a company. Some writers, more usefully, try to restrict its meaning to that of an unincorporated business (ie a business not constituted as a company, for example a partnership).

EXAM FOCUS POINT

You will not be asked in the exam about the accounts of limited companies. Your syllabus only covers sole traders and partnerships. Accounting standards are obligatory for incorporated entities, but their use is also recommended for unincorporated entities and therefore are examinable in this exam.

4.1 Accounting using the business entity concept

The crucial point to grasp, however, is that **a business must always be treated as a separate entity from its owners when preparing accounts**. This applies whether or not the business is recognised in law as a separate entity, so it applies whether the business is carried on by a company, a sole trader or by a partnership.

QUESTION
Separate entity

Fill in the missing words to make sure you understand the concept of the business as a separate entity and how the law differs from accounting practice.

A business is a .... entity, distinct from its .... This applies to .... businesses. However, the law only recognises a .... as a legal entity separate from its .... The liability of shareholders to the company is .... to the amount the company asks them to pay for their shares.

ANSWER

The missing words are:

separate; owners; all; company; owners; limited.

5 The accounting equation

Assets = Capital + Liabilities is the accounting equation.

Since a business is a separate entity from its owners, it follows that:

(a)   The business can owe money to, or be owed money by, its owners.

(b)   The assets and liabilities of the business are separate from the assets and liabilities of the owners.

This is the basis of a fundamental rule of accounting, which is that **the assets and the aggregate of the capital and the liabilities of a business must always be equal (the accounting equation)**. Let's demonstrate this with an example, which we will build up during this chapter.

5.1 Example: The accounting equation

On 1 September 20X8, Courtney Wilder decides to open up a stall in the market, to sell West Indian fruit and vegetables. He has saved up some money and has $1,000 to put into his business.

When the business is set up, an 'accountant's picture' can be drawn of what it **owns** and what it **owes**. The business begins by **owning** the cash that Courtney has put into it, $1,000. But does it **owe** anything? The answer is **yes**.

The business is a separate entity in accounting terms. It has obtained its **assets**, in this example cash, from its owner, Courtney Wilder. **It therefore owes this amount of money to its owner.** If Courtney changed his mind and decided not to go into business after all, the business would be dissolved by the 'repayment' of the cash by the business to Courtney.

The money put into a business by its owners is **capital**. As long as that money is invested, **accountants will treat the capital as money owed to the proprietor by the business**.

Capital is an investment of money (funds) with the intention of earning a return. A business proprietor invests capital with the intention of earning **profit**. The business owes the capital and the profit to the proprietor.

Capital invested is an amount owed by the business. Adapting this to the idea that the amounts that a business owes and owns are always equal, we can state the accounting equation as follows.

FORMULA TO LEARN

The accounting equation 1

Assets = Capital + Liabilities

The capital invested into a business from its owners is distinct from other funding to the business from third parties. Funds coming into the business from third parties are treated as loans rather than investments of capital and as such are liabilities of the business.

For Courtney Wilder, as at 1 July 20X8:

Assets	=	Capital	+	Liabilities
$1,000 cash		$1,000 owed to Courtney		$0

5.2 Example continued: different assets

Courtney Wilder uses some of the money invested to purchase a market stall from George Sobers, who is retiring from his fruit and vegetables business. The cost of the stall is $600.

He also purchases some fruit and vegetables from a trader in the wholesale market, at a cost of $340.

This leaves $60 in cash, after paying for the stall and goods for resale, out of the original $1,000. Courtney keeps $30 in the bank and draws out $30 in small change. He is now ready for his first day of market trading on 3 September 20X8. How does the accounting equation look now?

Solution

The assets and liabilities of the business have now altered, and at 3 September, before trading begins, the state of his business is as follows.

Assets		=	Capital	+	Liabilities
	$		$1,000		$0
Stall	600				
Fruit and veg	340				
Cash at bank	30				
Cash in hand	30				
	1,000				

5.3 Example continued: Profit explained

Let us now suppose that on 3 September Courtney has a very successful day. He is able to sell all of his fruit and vegetables, for $500 cash.

Since Courtney has sold goods costing $340 to earn revenue of $500, we can say that he has earned a **profit** of $(500 – 340) = $160 on the day's trading. How do we reflect this in the accounting equation?

Solution

Profit, like capital, belongs to the owners of a business: it's why they invested in the first place. In this case, the $160 belongs to Courtney Wilder. However, so long as the **business retains the profits, and does not pay anything out to its owners, the retained profits are accounted for as an addition to the proprietor's capital:** they become part of that capital.

Assets		=	Capital		+	Liabilities
	$			$		
Stall	600		Capital			
Fruit and vegetables	0		introduced	1,000		
Cash in hand and			Retained			
at bank $(30 + 30 + 500)	560		profit	160		
	1,160			1,160		$0

So we could expand the accounting equation as follows.

FORMULA TO LEARN

The accounting equation 2

Assets = (Capital introduced + Retained profits) + Liabilities

5.4 Increase in net assets

Net assets = Total assets – Total liabilities

We can rearrange the accounting equation to help us to calculate the total capital balance, which we have seen is the sum of capital introduced plus retained profit.

Assets – Liabilities	=	Capital
Net assets	=	Capital

At the beginning and then at the end of 3 September 20X8 Courtney Wilder's financial position was as follows.

		Net assets	=		Capital
(a)	At the beginning of the day:	$(1,000 – 0)	=		$1,000
(b)	At the end of the day:	$(1,160 – 0)	=		$1,160
	Increase in net assets	160	=	Retained profit for day	160

We can now state various principles.

- At any point in time, a business's **net assets** represent the **capital introduced** by the owner plus the business's **retained profit** to that point in time.

- At a later point in time, the **increase** in the business's net assets represents the additional **profit made** in the intervening period.

- **Total** net assets at that later point represent the capital introduced by the owner plus the business's **increased** retained profit.

For example:

		$m			$m			$m
1 Jan	Net assets	170	=	Capital introduced	20	+	Retained profit	150
1 Jan–31 Dec	Increase	34	=				Profit made in year	34
31 Dec	Total net assets	204	=	Capital introduced	20	+	Total retained profit	184

5.5 Drawings

Drawings are amounts of money taken out of a business by its owner.

5.6 Example continued: drawings

Since Courtney Wilder has made a profit of $160 from his first day's work, he might well feel fully justified in drawing some of the profits out of the business. After all, business owners, like everyone else, need income for living expenses. We will suppose that Courtney decides to pay himself $100, in what he thinks of as 'wages', as a fair reward for his day's work.

But because he is the business's **owner,** the $100 is **not** an expense to be deducted before the figure of profit is arrived at. In other words, it would be **incorrect** to calculate the profit earned by the business as follows.

	$
Profit on sale of fruit and vegetables	160
Less 'wages' paid to Courtney as drawings	(100)
Profit earned by business (incorrect)	60

This is because **any amounts paid by a business to its proprietor are treated by accountants as withdrawals of profit (drawings)**, and not as expenses incurred by the business. In the case of Courtney's business, the true position is that the profit **earned** is the $160 surplus on sale of fruit and vegetables, but the profit **retained** in the business is $(160 – 100) = $60.

	$
Profit earned by business	160
Less profit withdrawn by Courtney	(100)
Profit retained in the business	60

The drawings are taken in cash, and so the business loses $100 of its cash assets. After the drawings have been made, the accounting equation would be restated.

Assets		=	Capital		+	Liabilities
	$			$		
Stall	600		Capital introduced	1,000		
Fruit and vegetables	0		Profit earned	160		
Cash $(560 – 100)	460		Less drawings	(100)		
	1,060			1,060		$0

BPP LEARNING MEDIA

The increase in net assets since trading operations began is now only $(1,060 − 1,000) = $60, which is the amount of the retained profits.

So profits are capital as long as they are retained in the business. When they are paid out as drawings, the business suffers a reduction in capital.

We can therefore restate the accounting equation again.

FORMULA TO LEARN

The accounting equation 3

Assets = Capital introduced + (Earned profit − Drawings) + Liabilities

These examples have illustrated that the basic equation (Assets = Capital + Liabilities) always holds good. Any transaction affecting the business has a **dual effect** as shown in the table below.

	Asset	=	Capital	+	Liabilities
	Increase		Increase		
or	Increase				Increase
or			Increase		Decrease
or			Decrease		Increase
or	Decrease		Decrease		
or	Decrease				Decrease

QUESTION

Transactions

Consider each of the transactions below, and mark on the grid which area will be increased and which decreased by the transaction. We have done the first one for you.

(a)   The bank tells the business it no longer owes the bank $100 in bank charges.
(b)   The business finds it has been overcharged $50 for some furniture it bought on credit.
(c)   A gas bill of $200 is received by the business.
(d)   The owner withdraws $500 from the business.
(e)   Cash is introduced into the business by its owner.
(f)   A car is bought by the business, for payment in 1 month's time.

Transaction	=	Assets	=	Capital	+	Liabilities
(a)				Increase		Decrease
(b)						
(c)						
(d)						
(e)						
(f)						

ANSWER

Transaction	Assets	=	Capital	+	Liabilities
(a)			Increase		Decrease
(b)	Decrease				Decrease
(c)			Decrease		Increase
(d)	Decrease		Decrease		
(e)	Increase		Increase		
(f)	Increase				Increase

6 The business equation

P = I + D – C is the business equation.

Where

P	=	Profit earned in current period
I	=	Increase/decrease in net assets in current period
D	=	Drawings in current period
C	=	Capital introduced in current period

The business equation is a further elaboration of the accounting equation which gives a definition of profits earned. The example of Courtney Wilder has shown that **the amount of profit earned in a time period can be related to the increase in the net assets of the business, the drawings of profits by the proprietor** and **the introduction of new capital**.

We know that: *Accounting equation*

Assets	=	Capital	+	Liabilities	1

which is the same as:

Assets	=	Capital introduced + Retained profits	+	Liabilities	2

which is the same as:

Assets	=	Capital introduced + Profit earned – Drawings	+	Liabilities	3

As time goes on, **retained profit** (shown as profit earned less drawings) builds up the amount of capital in the business – it becomes **part of the opening balance of capital**. As we proceed through another period of trading, additional profit will (hopefully) be earned. So we should restate the accounting equation again:

FORMULA TO LEARN

The accounting equation 4

Assets =	Capital introduced + Profit retained in previous periods + Profit earned in current period – Drawings	+	Liabilities

Let's see how this works in the case of Courtney Wilder.

6.1 Example continued: more profit earned

The next market day is on 10 September, and Courtney gets ready by purchasing more fruit and vegetables for cash, at a cost of $400. He had a family party to attend during the day, however, and so he decided to accept the offer of help for the day from his aunt, Sheila, whom he agrees to pay a wage of $50 at the end of the day.

Trading on 10 September is again very brisk, and Courtney and Sheila sell all their goods for $760 cash. Courtney pays Sheila her wage of $50 and draws out $150 for himself. How do these transactions affect Courtney's capital?

Solution

The accounting equation before trading begins on 10 September, and after trading ends on 10 September, can be set out as follows.

(a) *Before trading begins*

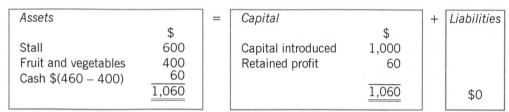

Assets	$	=	Capital	$	+	Liabilities
Stall	600		Capital introduced	1,000		
Fruit and vegetables	400		Retained profit	60		
Cash $(460 – 400)	60					
	1,060			1,060		$0

(b) *After trading ends*

On 10 September, all the goods are sold for $760 cash, and Sheila is paid $50. The profit for the day is $310, computed as follows.

	$	$
Sales		760
Less: cost of goods sold	400	
Sheila's wage	50	
		(450)
Profit		310

Courtney withdraws $150 of this profit for his personal use.

Assets	$	=	Capital	$	+	Liabilities
Stall	600		At beginning of 10 Sept	1,060		
Fruit and vegetables	0		Profits earned on 10 Sept	310		
Cash $(60 + 760			Less drawings	(150)		
– 50 – 150)	620					
	1,220			1,220		$0

6.2 More capital introduced

When a business is going well, the owner is very likely to **invest more money** in it in the expectation of generating even more profit. We need to include this in our accounting equation too: in doing so, we will arrive at the **business equation**, which allows us to compute profit from analysing the increase in net assets of the business, drawings and new capital introduced.

6.3 Example: more capital introduced

Suppose on 10 September, in addition to all the other transactions, Courtney decides to hire a van at a cost of $30 to transport the fruit and vegetables, paying for the hire out of cash from his own pocket. How would this affect the accounting equation at the end of 10 September?

Solution

After trading ends

On 10 September, all the goods are sold for $760 cash, Sheila is paid $50 and the van cost $30. Profit for the day is $280:

	$	$
Sales		760
Less: Cost of goods sold	400	
Sheila's wage	50	
Van hire	30	
		(480)
		280

Courtney withdraws $200 for his personal use.

Assets		=	Capital		+	Liabilities
	$			$		
Stall	600		At start of trading	1,060		
Goods	0		Capital introduced	30		
Cash $(60 + 760 + 30 – 50			Profit earned 10 Sep	280		
– 30 – 150)	620		Drawings	(150)		
	__1,220__			__1,220__		$0

So new capital introduced should also be brought into the accounting equation.

 FORMULA TO LEARN

The accounting equation 5

Assets = Capital introduced in previous periods + Liabilities
+ Profit retained in previous periods
+ Profit earned in current period
+ Capital introduced in current period
– Drawings in current period

If we put Courtney Wilder's figures from Paragraph 6.1 into this, we get:

	$			$		$
Assets	1,220	= Capital introduced in previous periods		1,000	+	0
		+ Profit retained in previous periods		60		
		+ Profit earned in current period		280		
		+ Capital introduced in current period		30		
		– Drawings in current period		(150)		
	__1,220__			__1,220__		__0__

6.4 The business equation

We are now ready to see how profit earned in a period can be expressed simply in terms of transactions within the period.

PREVIOUS PERIODS	Assets at start of period	=	Capital introduced in previous periods + Profit retained in previous periods	+	Liabilities at start of period
	+				
CURRENT PERIOD	Increase/decrease in assets (I)*	=	Profit earned in current period (P) + Capital introduced in current period (C) – Drawings in current period (D)	+	Increase/decrease in liabilities (I)*
	* Together these represent the increase/decrease in net assets in current period				
	=				
END OF CURRENT PERIOD	Total assets at end of period	=	Total capital at end of period	+	Liabilities at end of period

Concentrating on the current period box above, we can state the business equation as follows.

FORMULA TO LEARN

The business equation

Profit earned in current period = Increase/decrease + Drawings − Capital
in net assets in   in current   introduced
current period*   period   in current
period

$$P = I + D - C$$

*This is the net figure of the increase/decrease in assets less the increase/decrease in liabilities.

Let's see how Courtney's figures for 10 September plug into this equation.

Profit = Increase in net assets + Drawings − Capital introduced
= \$(1,220 − 1,060) + \$150 − \$30
= \$280

You may be a little concerned about why the **capital introduced in the period** is a **negative figure** in the equation. This is because when a business is given new capital, perhaps in the form of extra money paid in by the proprietor herself, there will be an increase in the net assets of the business without any profits being earned. This means, say, that if a proprietor puts an extra \$5,000 into his business the profit from the transaction, according to the business equation, would be P = \$5,000 + 0 − \$5,000 = \$0.

Similarly we saw with Courtney Wilder that the \$30 cash introduced was added to assets (cash) in the accounting equation in Paragraph 6.3 but was also added to capital:

P = \$30 + 0 − 30 = 0

7   Accounts payable and accounts receivable

7.1 Credit transactions

So far we have been concentrating on **capital** (including profits) and certain types of **asset** (cash, goods for resale, non-current assets). We now look at two important items which arise when goods and services are purchased or sold as part of a **credit transaction: accounts payable and accounts receivable, often referred to as payables and receivables.**

A **credit transaction** is a sale or a purchase which occurs some time **earlier** than cash is received or paid.

Sales and purchases occur in two different ways, by cash or on credit.

(a)   A **sale** takes place at one of two points in time.

    (i)   **Cash sales**. If the sale is for cash, the sale occurs when goods or services are given in exchange for immediate payment, in notes and coins, or by cheque or plastic card.

    (ii)   **Credit sales** (goods are ordered and delivered before payment is received). If it is on credit, the sale occurs when the business sends out an invoice for the goods or services supplied; cash is received later.

(b)   A **purchase** also takes place at one of two points in time.

    (i)   **Purchases for cash**. If the goods are paid for in cash then the purchase occurs when the goods and cash exchange hands.

    (ii)   **Purchases on credit**. If the goods are bought on credit, the purchase normally occurs when the business receives the goods, accompanied by an invoice from the supplier. Cash is paid later.

With credit transactions, the point in time when a sale or purchase is recognised in the accounts of the business is **not** the same as the point in time when cash is eventually received or paid for the sale or purchase. There is a gap in time between the sale or purchase and the eventual cash settlement. (It is possible that something might happen during that time which results in the amount of cash eventually paid (if any) being different from the original value of the sale or purchase on the invoice.)

For companies, there is an international accounting standard, IFRS 15 *Revenue from Contracts with Customers*, which sets out rules for when a sale is recognised (we look at international accounting standards in Chapter 5). One of the rules is that the sale of goods is not recognised until the **risks and rewards of ownership** of the goods have been transferred to the customer. This ties in with what was discussed above, because the credit sales are recorded when the goods are delivered and an invoice has been issued, even if they have not been paid for. This is because the risks and rewards are with the customer when they have received the goods.

7.2 Accounts payable

An **account payable** results from the purchase by a business of items for later payment. An account payable is a **liability** of the business.

A **trade account payable** is a balance owing for debts incurred in the course of trading operations. The term might refer to debts still outstanding which arise from the purchase from suppliers of goods for resale.

It is a common business practice to make purchases on **credit terms**, with a promise to pay within 30 days, or 2 or 3 months of the date of the purchase. For example, if Jackson buys goods costing $5,000 on credit from Millie, Millie might send Jackson an invoice for $5,000, dated say 1 June, with credit terms that payment must be made within 30 days. If Jackson then delays payment until 30 June, Millie's balance of $5,000 is an **account payable** in the records of Jackson between 1 and 30 June.

We will be looking at **invoices** in more detail in Chapter 3.

7.3 Accounts receivable

An **account receivable** results from the sale by a business of items for later payment. An account receivable is an **asset** of a business (the right to receive payment is owned by the business).

A **trade account receivable** is a balance owing to the business for debts incurred in the course of trading operations ie because the business has sold its goods or services.

Just as a business might buy goods on credit, so too might it sell goods to customers on credit. For example, suppose that Parker sells goods on credit to Rogers for $4,300 on terms that the debt must be settled within two months of the invoice date, 1 March. If Rogers does not pay the $4,300 until 30 April, the $4,300 balance is an **account receivable** in the records of Parker from 1 March to 30 April.

This should serve as a useful summary.

CREDIT TRANSACTIONS	
SALES by the business to a customer	PURCHASES by the business from a supplier
↓ creates an ACCOUNT RECEIVABLE a customer who owes money to the business	↓ creates an ACCOUNT PAYABLE a supplier who is owed money by the business
↓ recorded as an ASSET of the business	↓ recorded as a LIABILITY of the business
↓ settled when the business RECEIVES CASH	↓ settled when the business PAYS CASH

BPP
LEARNING MEDIA

7.4 Example continued: receivables and payables

The example of Courtney Wilder's market stall will be continued further, by looking at the consequences of the following transactions in the week to 17 September 20X8.

(a)   Courtney realises that he is going to need even more money in the business and so he makes the following arrangements:

   (i)   He invests immediately a further $200 of his own capital.
   (ii)   He persuades his cousin Gary to lend him $400 immediately. Gary tells him that he can repay the loan whenever he likes, but in the meantime he must pay him interest of $3 per week each week at the end of the market day. They agree that it will probably be quite a long time before the loan is eventually repaid.

(b)   Courtney is very pleased with the progress of his business, and decides that he can afford to buy a second-hand van to pick up fruit and vegetables from his supplier and bring them to his stall in the market. He finds a car dealer, Carrie Carver, who agrees to sell him a van on credit for $550. Courtney agrees to pay for the van after 30 days' trial use.

(c)   During the week before the next market day (which is on 17 September), Courtney's Uncle Viv telephones him to ask whether he would be interested in selling him some special West Indian spices and equipment for his kitchen. Courtney tells him that he will look for a supplier. After some investigations, he buys what Uncle Viv has asked for, paying $250 in cash to the supplier. Uncle Viv accepts delivery of the goods and agrees to pay $320 at a later date.

(d)   The next market day approaches, and Courtney buys fruit and vegetables costing $650. Of these purchases $550 are paid in cash, with the remaining $100 on 14 days' credit. Courtney decides to use his aunt Sheila's services again as an assistant on market day, at an agreed wage of $50.

(e)   For the third market day running, on 17 September, Courtney sells all his goods, earning $1,050 (all in cash). He decides to take out drawings of $200 for his week's work. He also pays Sheila $50 in cash. He decides to make the interest payment to his cousin Gary the next time he sees him.

(f)   There were no van expenses.

First of all we want to state the accounting equations:

(a)   After Courtney and his cousin Gary have put more money into the business.
(b)   After the purchase of the van.
(c)   After the sale of goods to Uncle Viv.
(d)   After the purchase of goods for the weekly market.
(e)   At the end of the day's trading on 17 September, and after drawings have been withdrawn from profit.

Then we are going to state the business equation showing profit earned during the week ended 17 September.

Solution

There are a number of different transactions to deal with here. This solution deals with them one at a time in chronological order, highlighting the numbers that change each time in **bold type**. (In practice, it would be possible to do one set of calculations which combines the results of all the transactions, but we shall come to this 'shortcut' method later.)

(a)   The addition of Courtney's extra capital and his cousin Gary's loan.

   Cousin Gary's loan is for the long term, but he is not an owner of the business, even though he has made an investment of a loan to it. He would only become an owner if Courtney offered him a partnership in the business, and he has not done so. To the business, his cousin Gary is a long-term **liability** of the business – it is not business capital.

The accounting equation after $(200 + 400) = $600 cash is put into the business will be:

Assets		=	Capital		+	Liabilities	
	$			$			$
Stall	600		As at end of 10 Sept	1,220		Loan	**400**
Goods	0		Additional capital	**200**			
Cash $(620 + **600**)	**1,220**						
	1,820			1,420			400

(b)   The purchase of the van (cost $550) is on credit, so Courtney doesn't have to pay until later.

Assets		=	Capital		+	Liabilities	
	$			$			$
Stall	600		As at end of 10 Sept	1,220		Loan	400
Van	**550**		Additional capital	200		Payable	**550**
Cash	1,220						
	2,370			1,420			950

(c)   The sale of goods to Uncle Viv is on credit ($320), the cost to the business being $250 (cash paid). Uncle Viv, because he is paying later, is shown as a receivable.

Assets		=	Capital		+	Liabilities	
	$			$			$
Stall	600		As at end of 10 Sept	1,220		Loan	400
Van	550		Additional capital	200		Payable	550
Receivable	**320**		Profit on sale to				
Cash $(1,220 − **250**)	**970**		Uncle Viv	**70**			
	2,440			1,490			950

(d)   After the purchase of goods for the weekly market ($550 paid in cash and $100 of purchases on credit) we have:

Assets		=	Capital		+	Liabilities	
	$			$			$
Stall	600		As at end of 10 Sept	1,220		Loan	400
Van	550		Additional capital	200		Payable for van	550
Goods	**650**		Profit on sale to			Payable for	
Receivable	320		Uncle Viv	70		goods	**100**
Cash $(970 − **550**)	**420**						
	2,540			1,490			1,050

(e)   After market trading on 17 September. Sales of goods costing $650 earned revenues of $1,050. Sheila's wages were $50 (paid), Courtney's cousin Gary's interest charge is $3 (not paid yet) and drawings out of profits were $200 (paid). The profit for 17 September may be calculated as follows, taking the full $3 of interest as a cost on that day.

	$	$
Sales		1,050
Cost of goods sold	650	
Wages	50	
Interest	3	
		(703)
Profits earned on 17 September		347
Profit on sale of goods to Uncle Viv		70
Total profit for the week		417

Assets		=	Capital		+	Liabilities	
	$			$			$
Stall	600		As at end of 10 Sept	1,220		Loan	400
Van	550		Additional capital	200		Payable for van	550
Goods	0		Profit on sale to			Payable for	
Receivable	320		Uncle Viv	70		goods	100
Cash $(420 +**1,050**			Profit for week	**347**		Liability for	
– 50 – 200)	**1,220**		Drawings	**(200)**		interest	**3**
	2,690			1,637			1,053

The increase in the net assets of the business during the week was as follows.

	$
Net assets as at the end of 17 September $(2,690 – 1,053)	1,637
Net assets as at the end of 10 September	1,220
Increase in net assets in week	417

The business equation for the week ended 17 September is as follows. (Remember that extra capital of $200 was invested by Courtney.)

P   =   I + D – C
    = $417 + $200 – $200
    = $417

This confirms the calculation of total profit.

QUESTION

Liza Doolittle

Liza Doolittle has $2,500 invested in her business. Of this, only $1,750 has been provided by herself, the balance being provided by a loan of $750 from Professor Higgins. What are the implications of this for the accounting equation?

Hint. The answer is not necessarily clear cut. There are different ways of looking at the Professor's investment.

ANSWER

We have assets of $2,500 (cash), balanced by liabilities of $2,500 (the amounts owed by the business to Liza and the Professor).

- The $1,750 owed to Liza clearly falls into the special category of liability labelled **capital**, because it is a sum owed to the proprietor of the business.

- To classify the $750 owed to the Professor, we would need to know more about the **terms of his agreement** with Liza.

- If they have effectively gone into **partnership**, sharing the risks and rewards of the business, then the Professor is a proprietor too and the $750 is 'capital' in the sense that Liza's $1,750 is.

- If the professor has no share in the profits of the business, and can expect only a repayment of his 'loan' plus some interest, the amount of $750 should be classified under **liabilities**.

8 Double entry bookkeeping

Double entry bookkeeping requires that every transaction has two accounting entries, a **debit** and a **credit**.

EXAM FOCUS POINT

You will **always** be asked to demonstrate your knowledge of double entry bookkeeping in the exam, so you must be clear about the principles involved.

8.1 Dual aspect convention (Duality)

In accounting every transaction has two aspects. We know that, since the **total of liabilities plus capital is always equal to total assets**, any transaction has a **dual effect** – if it changes the amount of total assets it also changes the total liabilities plus capital, and *vice versa*. For example, if a business buys plant and equipment for cash, the non-current asset plant and equipment increases and the current asset cash decreases. Similarly, if a business pays $500 in cash for some goods, its total assets will be unchanged, but as the amount of cash falls by $500, the value of goods in inventory rises by $500.

We can say then that there are two sides to every business transaction. Out of this concept has developed the system of accounting known as the 'double entry' system of bookkeeping, which reflects the dual aspect convention, so called because every transaction is recorded twice in the accounts.

Double entry bookkeeping is the system of accounting which reflects the fact that:

Every financial transaction affects the entity in two ways and gives rise to two accounting entries, one a debit and the other a credit

The total value of **debit entries** is therefore always equal at any time to the total value of **credit entries**.

Each asset, liability, item of expense or item of income has a **ledger account** in which debits and credits are made. (We shall see a great deal more about these in Chapter 4.) Which account receives the credit entry and which receives the debit depends on the nature of the transaction.

Below is a summary. We shall look again in detail at double entry in Chapter 4.

DEBIT To own/have ↓	CREDIT To owe ↓
AN ASSET INCREASES eg new office furniture	AN ASSET DECREASES eg pay out cash
CAPITAL/ A LIABILITY DECREASES eg pay a supplier	CAPITAL/A LIABILITY INCREASES eg buy goods on credit
INCOME DECREASES eg cancel a sale	INCOME INCREASES eg make a sale
AN EXPENSE INCREASES eg incur advertising costs	AN EXPENSE DECREASES eg cancel a purchase
Left hand side	Right hand side

QUESTION

Dual effects

Try to explain the dual effects of each of the following transactions.

(a)   A business receives a loan of $5,000 from its bank
(b)   A business pays $800 cash to purchase goods for resale
(c)   The proprietor of a business removes $50 from the till to buy her husband a birthday present
(d)   A business sells goods costing $300 at a profit of $140
(e)   A business repays a $5,000 bank loan, plus interest of $270

ANSWER

(a)   Assets (cash) increase by $5,000; liabilities (amount owed to the bank) increase by $5,000

(b)   Assets (cash) decrease by $800; assets (inventory) increase by $800

(c)   Assets (cash) decrease by $50; capital decreases by $50 (the proprietor has taken $50 drawings for her personal use; in effect, the business has repaid her part of the amount it owed)

(d)   Assets (cash) increase by $440; assets (inventory) decrease by $300; capital (the profit earned for the proprietor) increases by $140

(e)   Assets (cash) decrease by $5,270; liabilities (the bank loan) decrease by $5,000; capital decreases by $270 (the proprietor has made a 'loss' of $270 on the transaction)

EXAM FOCUS POINT

We have highlighted key terms throughout this chapter. These are important definitions: go back and reread them now. You should do this at the end of each chapter of this Interactive Text.

CHAPTER ROUNDUP

- In order to pass this exam it is vital that you acquire a thorough understanding of the **principles of double entry bookkeeping** outlined in this chapter and developed in Chapters 3 and 4.

- A **business** may be defined in various ways. Its purpose is to make a **profit** for its owner(s).

- **Profit** is the excess of income over expenditure.

- A business **owns assets** and **owes liabilities**.

- **Assets** are items belonging to a business and used in the running of the business. They may be **non-current** (such as machinery or office premises), or **current** (such as inventory, receivables and cash).

- **Liabilities** are sums of money owed by a business to outsiders such as a bank or a supplier.

- For accounting purposes it is important to keep business assets and liabilities **separate** from the personal assets and liabilities of the proprietor(s).

- **Assets = Capital + Liabilities** is the accounting equation.

- **P = I + D − C** is the business equation.

  Where

  P = Profit earned in current period
  I = Increase/decrease in net assets in current period
  D = Drawings in current period
  C = Capital introduced in current period

- Double entry bookkeeping requires that every transaction has two accounting entries, a **debit** and a **credit**.

QUICK QUIZ

1 What is a business's prime objective?

2 Define profit.

3 What is an asset?

4 What is a liability?

5 How does the accounting view of the relationship between a business and its owner differ from the strictly legal view?

6 State the basic accounting equation.

7 What is capital?

8 What are drawings? Where do they fit in the accounting equation?

9 What does the business equation attempt to show?

10 What is the main difference between a cash and a credit transaction?

11 What is an account payable? What is an account receivable?

12 Define double entry bookkeeping.

ANSWERS TO QUICK QUIZ

1 A business's prime objective is earning a profit.

2 Profit is the excess of income over expenditure.

3 An asset is something valuable which a business owns or has the use of.

4 A liability is something which is owed to someone else.

5 In accounting a business is always treated as a separate entity from its owners, even though in law there is not always a distinction (in the cases of a sole trader and a partnership).

6 Assets = Capital + Liabilities.

7 Capital is the investment of funds with the intention of earning a profit.

8 Drawings are the amounts of money taken out of a business by its owner. In the accounting equation drawings are a reduction of capital.

9 The business equation describes the relationship between a business's increase in net assets in a period, the profit earned, drawings taken and capital introduced.

10 The main difference between a cash and a credit transaction is simply a matter of time – cash changes hands immediately in a cash transaction, whereas in a credit one it changes hands some time after the initial sale/purchase takes place.

11 An account payable is a balance for goods purchased by the business for which it owes money. An account receivable is a balance for goods sold by the business for which it is owed money.

12 Double entry bookkeeping is a system of accounting which reflects the fact that every financial transaction gives rise to two equal accounting entries, a debit and a credit.

Now try ...

Attempt the questions below from the **Practice Question Bank**

Number	Level	Marks	Time
Q1	Examination	2	2.4 mins
Q2	Examination	2	2.4 mins
Q3	Examination	2	2.4 mins
Q4	Examination	2	2.4 mins
Q5	Examination	2	2.4 mins
Q6	Examination	2	2.4 mins
Q7	Examination	2	2.4 mins

CHAPTER

02

The **statement of financial position** and the **statement of profit or loss** are the two basic primary statements used by sole traders to present their financial information.

The statement of financial position shows assets, liabilities and capital at the period end date.

The statement of profit or loss shows how the profit or loss of a period has been made.

Statement of financial position and statement of profit or loss

Study Guide	Intellectual level
B The principles and process of basic bookkeeping	
1 The elements of the financial statements	
(c) Describe the components of a set of final accounts for a sole trader	K
D Recording transactions and events	
4 Tangible non-current assets and depreciation	
(a) Define non-current assets	K
(b) Recognise the difference between current and non-current assets	K
(c) Explain the difference between asset and expense items	K
(d) Classify expenditure as asset expenditure or expenses charged to profit or loss	S
(e) Explain the impact of misclassification of asset expenditure as expenses and vice versa on the statement of profit or loss and the statement of financial position	K
G The trial balance and the extended trial balance	
2 Preparation of the final accounts including incomplete records	
(b) Explain the format and purpose of the statement of profit or loss and statement of financial position for a sole trader	K

1   Introduction to financial statements

The statement of financial position and the statement of profit or loss are the basic accounting statements of any business, including sole traders. In Chapter 1 you were introduced to the idea of the accounting and business equations. If you understand these, you should have little difficulty in getting to grips with the **statement of financial position** and **statement of profit or loss**. These are two primary statements described in an accounting standard for companies (IAS 1 *Presentation of Financial Statements*) issued by the International Accounting Standards Board (IASB). However, as stated above, sole traders also use these two basic statements.

The statement of financial position layout shows assets, liabilities and capital in the same way as the accounting equation. Sole traders generally have a choice over whether they:

(a)   Aggregate different items under key headings on the statement of financial position and the statement of profit or loss, and include extra detail in supporting notes **or**

(b)   Include more or all of the detail on the basic statements themselves.

We focus on the general headings under which assets, liabilities, income and expenses are grouped, but as we progress through examples you will see that, for sole traders, further sub headings or detail are sometimes included on the face of the basic statements.

Technical Performance Objective 9 requires you to demonstrate that you are competent in preparing the final accounts of unincorporated entities, such as sole traders and partnerships. The knowledge you gain in this chapter will help you to demonstrate your competence in this area.

2 Statement of financial position

A **statement of financial position** shows the financial position of a business at a given moment in time. A distinction is made between **non-current liabilities** and **current liabilities,** and between **non-current assets** and **current assets**.

A statement of financial position is a statement of the assets, liabilities and capital of a business at a given moment in time. It is drawn up 'as at' a particular date. Typically, the statement is prepared to show the assets, liabilities and capital as at the **end** of the accounting period to which the financial statements relate.

A **statement of financial position** is therefore very similar to the **accounting equation**.

Assets = Capital introduced + Retained profit + Liabilities

In fact, there are only two differences between a statement of financial position and the accounting equation, which are as follows:

(a)   The manner or **format** in which the assets and liabilities are presented.
(b)   The extra **detail** which is usually contained in a statement of financial position.

A statement of financial position is divided into two halves, usually showing **capital and liabilities** in one half and **assets** in the other.

NAME OF BUSINESS
STATEMENT OF FINANCIAL POSITION AS AT (DATE)

	$
Assets	X
Capital	X
Liabilities	X
	X

The total value in one half of the statement will equal the total value in the other half. You should readily understand this from the **accounting equation**.

For many businesses, the way in which assets and liabilities are categorised and presented is a matter of choice, and you may come across different formats. The format that follows should help you see how a typical statement of financial position is compiled.

BUSINESS NAME
STATEMENT OF FINANCIAL POSITION AS AT 31 DECEMBER 20X8

	$	$
Non-current assets		
Land and buildings	X	
Plant and machinery	X	
Fixtures and fittings	X̲	
		X
Current assets		
Inventories	X	
Trade and other receivables	X	
Cash at bank and in hand	X̲	
		X̲
		X̲
Capital		
Proprietor's capital	X	
Retained profits (including previous and current year profits)	X̲	
		X
Non-current liabilities		
Loan		X
Current liabilities		
Trade and other payables	X	
Bank overdraft	X̲	
		X̲
		X̲

'As at' has been picked out in bold type in these illustrative examples in order to draw your attention to the fact that the statement of financial position represents the financial position at a specific point in time.

3 Non-current assets

Non-current assets are those acquired for long-term use within the business.

Assets in the statement of financial position are divided into **non-current** and **current** assets.

A **non-current asset** is an asset acquired for use within the business (rather than for selling to a customer), with a view to earning income or making profits from its use, either directly or indirectly, over more than one accounting period.

Examples are as follows. These are only ideas; you may well be able to think of other assets for both.

Industry	Example of non-current asset
Manufacturing	A production machine, because it makes goods which are then sold.
Service	Equipment used by employees giving service to customers, such as testing machines and ramps in a garage, and furniture in a hotel.

To be classed as a non-current asset in the statement of financial position of a business, an item must satisfy two further conditions:

(a) It must be **used by the business**. For example, the proprietor's own house would not normally appear on the business statement of financial position.

(b) The asset must have a **'life' in use of more than one year** (strictly, more than one 'accounting period', which might be more or less than one year).

4 Current assets

Current assets are expected to be converted into cash within one year.

Current assets are:

- Items owned by the business with the intention of turning them into cash within one year (inventories of goods, and receivables).

- Cash, including money in the bank, owned by the business.

- Assets are 'current' in the sense that they are continually flowing through the business.

QUESTION

Asset

The type of asset held by of a business depends on the nature of its trading activities. Try to imagine what the main assets might be in the accounts of:

(a)   A steel manufacturing company
(b)   A bank

ANSWER

(a)   A **steel manufacturing company** would have a high proportion of its asset values locked up in non-current assets (factory premises, heavy machinery). It might also hold large inventories of raw materials and finished goods, and the value of receivables might be significant too.

(b)   A **bank's** main asset is its receivables, namely the people to whom it lends money by way of loan or overdraft. Curiously enough, cash holdings may be much smaller than receivables balances, because banks aim to **use** cash (ie lend it or invest it) rather than merely sitting on it. In the case of a bank with a large number of branches, land and buildings will also be a significant item, but still not as great as receivables.

4.1 Example: turning inventory and receivables into cash within one year

Let us suppose that a trader, Jackson Boxer, runs a business selling farm and other machinery, and has a showroom with machines for sale. We will also suppose that he obtains the machines from a dealer, and pays for them cash on delivery (COD).

(a)   If he sells a machine in a **cash sale**, the 'goods' are immediately converted back into cash (hopefully more cash than he paid for them, making a profit). This cash might then be used to buy more machinery for re-sale.

(b)   If he sells a machine in a **credit sale**, expecting payment in 30 days time, the machine will be given to the customer who then becomes an **account receivable** of the business. Eventually, the customer will pay what he owes, and Jackson Boxer will receive cash. The cash might then be used to buy more machines for sale.

The machines, receivables and cash are all current assets. Why?

(a)   The machines (**goods**) held for re-sale are current assets, because Jackson Boxer intends to sell them within one year, in the normal course of trade.

(b)   The **account receivable** is a current asset, as he is expected to pay what he owes in 30 days.

(c)   **Cash** is a current asset.

The transactions described above could be shown as a **cash cycle**.

Cash is used to buy goods which are sold. Sales on credit create receivables, but eventually cash is earned from the sales. Some, perhaps most, of the cash will then be used to replenish inventories.

QUESTION   Current or non-current

Which of the following assets falls into the 'non-current' category and which should be treated as 'current'?

Asset	Business	Current or non-current
Van	Delivery firm	
Cement mixer	Builder	
Car	Car trader	

ANSWER

Asset	Business	Current or non-current
Van	Delivery firm	Non-current
Cement mixer	Builder	Non-current
Car	Car trader	Current

5 Liabilities

Current liabilities are debts which are payable within one year.

In the case of liabilities, we also draw a distinction between:

- **Current** liabilities
- **Non-current** liabilities

5.1 Current liabilities

Current liabilities are accounts payable of the business that must be paid within a fairly short period of time (by convention, within one year).

Examples of current liabilities include **loans** repayable in one year, **bank overdrafts**, **trade payables** and **income tax due**.

Some may argue that a **bank overdraft** is not a current liability, because a business is usually able to negotiate an overdraft facility for a long period of time. If an overdraft thus becomes a more permanent source of borrowing, it is really a long-term liability. However, you should normally expect to account for an overdraft as a current liability, since banks usually reserve the right to have repayment on demand, even if this rarely happens in practice.

QUESTION

Classification

Try to classify the following items as non-current assets , current assets or current liabilities.

(a)   A PC used in the accounts department of a retail store
(b)   A PC on sale in an office equipment shop
(c)   Wages due to be paid to staff at the end of the week
(d)   A van for sale in a motor dealer's showroom
(e)   A delivery van used in a grocer's business
(f)   An amount owing to a bank for a loan for the acquisition of a van, to be repaid over nine months

ANSWER

(a)   Non-current asset
(b)   Current asset
(c)   Current liability
(d)   Current asset
(e)   Non-current asset
(f)   Current liability

Note that the same item can be categorised differently in different businesses.

5.2 Non-current liabilities

Non-current liabilities are debts which are not payable within the 'short term' and so any liability which is not current must be non-current. Just as 'current' by convention means one year or less, 'non-current' means more than one year.

Examples of non-current liabilities are bank or venture capital fund loans **repayable after more than one year**. Where a loan is being repaid over a period longer than one year, the amount outstanding will be split. The amount due within one year will be shown under 'current liabilities' and the balance will be shown under 'non-current liabilities'.

5.3 Capital

The make-up of the 'capital' section of the statement of financial position will vary, depending on the legal nature of the business. It will include **amounts invested** by the owner(s) in the business, plus **profits earned and retained** by the business. This is the business's capital account.

QUESTION

Carlo

Reproduced below is an example of a statement of financial position of a sole trader, Carlo.

CARLO
STATEMENT OF FINANCIAL POSITION AS AT 31 DECEMBER 20X0

	$	$
Non-current assets		
Land and buildings		57,000
Plant and machinery		32,500
Fixtures and fittings		6,000
		95,500
Current assets		
Inventories	8,300	
Trade and other receivables	5,600	
Cash	1,800	
		15,700
Total assets		111,200

	$	$
Capital		
Capital account		40,000
Profit for the year		75,200
Drawings		(10,000)
		105,200
Current liabilities		
Trade and other payables	3,900	
Bank overdraft	2,100	
		6,000
		111,200

Required

Using the figures shown above, check that the accounting equation holds good in the form: Assets = Capital + Liabilities.

ANSWER

Assets	=	Capital	+	Liabilities
$111,200	=	$105,200	+	$6,000

6 Statement of profit or loss

A **statement of profit or loss** shows in detail how the profit or loss of a period has been made.

The **statement of profit or loss** matches the **revenue** earned in a period with the **costs** incurred in earning it. It is usual to distinguish between a **gross profit** (sales revenue less the cost of goods sold) and a **net profit** (being the gross profit less the expenses of selling, distribution, administration etc). If costs exceed revenue the business has made a **loss**.

Any organisation needs income or revenue) from one or more sources. A **business** will **sell** its **goods or services** to **customers** in exchange for **cash**.

The income generated will be used to finance the activities of the business which incur **costs**: purchasing ready-made goods for onward sale, purchasing equipment, paying expenses such as staff salaries, stationery, lighting and heating, rent and so on.

Revenue less **costs** result in a **profit or loss**. Periodically the organisation will prepare a **statement of profit or loss.**

6.1 The statement of profit or loss

Many businesses try to distinguish between a **gross profit** earned on trading, and a **net profit**. They therefore prepare the **statement of profit or loss** in two parts.

In the first part of the statement revenue from selling goods and services is compared with direct costs of acquiring, producing or supplying the goods sold to arrive at a **gross profit figure**.

From this, deductions are made in the second half of the statement in respect of indirect costs (overheads) to arrive at a **net profit figure**.

As with the statement of financial position earlier in this chapter, it may help you to focus on the content of the statement of profit or loss if you have an example in front of you. The specimen below is based on a format prescribed for limited liability companies; as usual, other entities have greater flexibility in presentation.

The statement of profit or loss normally covers a one year accounting period but this is not always the case; other accounting periods are permissible in certain circumstances.

BUSINESS NAME
STATEMENT OF PROFIT OR LOSS FOR THE YEAR ENDED 31 DECEMBER 20X8

	$	$
Revenue		X
Cost of sales		(X)
Gross profit		X
Salaries	X	
Delivery costs	X	
Marketing costs	X	
Rent expense	X	
		(X)
Profit for the year		X

'For the year ended' has been picked out in bold type in this example in order to draw your attention to the fact that the statement of profit or loss represents financial performance over a period of time.

The list of expenses above is not exhaustive. An explanation of the nature of costs which are included in both cost of sales and expenses is provided below and will be developed through the chapter.

The **statement of profit or loss** shows both the gross profit and the net profit for the accounting period.

Gross profit is the difference between:

- The value of revenue (sales)
- The purchase cost of the goods sold

Net profit is the difference between:

- Gross profit
- All other expenses incurred in running the business

From your study of management accounting, you may already be familiar with the term 'overheads', which is often used in financial accounting to describe the expenses which are deducted from gross profit. It is sometimes useful to collate overheads into a number of categories in the statement of profit and loss. The most common categories are: selling costs, distribution costs and administration expenses, which typically include the following:

Overhead expenses	Include
Selling	• Salaries of a sales management and sales staff • Salaries and commissions of sales staff • Travelling and entertainment expenses of sales staff • Marketing costs (eg advertising and sales promotion expenses) • Discounts allowed to customers for early payment of their debts
Distribution	The costs of getting goods to customers, such as the costs of running and maintaining delivery vans
Administration	The expenses of providing management and administration for the business, for example, rent (and local taxes), insurance, telephone, postage, stationery

QUESTION

Admin

Suggest three items which might be included in administration expenses.

ANSWER

You could have thought of some of the following.

- Salaries of management and office staff
- Rent and local taxes of offices

- Insurance
- Telephone and postage
- Printing and stationery
- Heating and lighting of offices

6.2 Example: statement of profit or loss

On 1 October 20X8, Rita Blake started trading as a snack vendor, selling hot and cold food from a van which she parks in a local lay-by on a main road.

(a)   She borrowed $3,200 from her bank, and the interest cost of the loan was $40 per month.

(b)   She rented the van at a cost of $1,500 for 3 months. Running expenses for the van averaged $450 per month.

(c)   She hired a part-time helper at a cost of $150 per month.

(d)   Her main business was to sell food to customers who stop their cars by her van, but she also did some special catering arrangements for business customers, supplying food for office parties. Sales to these customers were usually on credit.

(e)   For the three months to 31 December 20X8, her total sales were:

(i)   Cash sales $10,300
(ii)   Credit sales $2,000 (all paid by 31 December 20X8)

(f)   She purchased food from a local food wholesaler, Best Stores Ever. The cost of purchases in the three months to 31 December 20X8 was $7,300, and at 31 December she had sold all of it. She still owed $1,000 to Best Stores Ever for unpaid purchases on credit.

(g)   She used her own home for her office work. Telephone and postage expenses for the three months to 31 December were $220.

(h)   During the period she paid herself $330 per month.

We need to prepare a statement of profit or loss for the three months 1 October – 31 December 20X8.

Solution

RITA BLAKE STATEMENT OF PROFIT OR LOSS FOR THE THREE MONTHS ENDED 31 DECEMBER 20X8

	$	$
Revenue $(10,300 + 2,000) (e)		12,300
Cost of sales (f)		(7,300)
Gross profit		5,000
Expenses		
Wages (c)	450	
Van rental (b)	1,500	
Van expenses (b)	1,350	
Telephone and postage (g)	220	
Interest charges (a)	120	
		(3,640)
Net profit earned in the period		1,360

Note the following points.

1   The **net profit** is the profit for the period, and it is transferred to the proprietor's capital account in the statement of financial position.

2   **Drawings** are withdrawals of profit and not expenses. They must not be included in the statement of profit or loss. In this example, the payments that Rita Blake makes to herself ($990) are drawings. **These are shown as a reduction in the capital account figure on the face of the statement of financial position**.

3   The cost of sales is $7,300, even though $1,000 of the costs have not yet been paid for and Best Stores Ever is still a payable (creditor) for $1,000 in the statement of financial position.

QUESTION

Rita Blake

Having arrived at a net profit figure, see if you can draw up a statement of financial position for Rita Blake. Don't panic – fill in the figures below.

Step 1

	$
Cash	
Borrowed from bank 1 October 20X8	
(a) Interest charges	
(b) Van hire	
Van running expenses	
(c) Part-time helper	
(d) Cash sales	
Credit sales	
(e) Purchase of food	
(f) Telephone and postage	
(g) Drawings	
Balance in hand at 31 December 20X8	_____

Step 2

Accounting equation at 1 October 20X8

Assets	$	=	Capital	$	+	Liabilities	$
Cash	_____			0		Bank loan	_____

Accounting equation at 31 December 20X8

Assets	$	=	Capital	$	+	Liabilities	$
Cash			Profit			Bank loan	
	_____		Drawings	_____		BSE Ltd	_____

Step 3

Business equation (to check profit figure)

$$P = I + D - C$$

$$P = \$ + \$ - \$0$$

Step 4   RITA BLAKE

STATEMENT OF FINANCIAL POSITION AS AT 31 DECEMBER 20X8

	$	$
Current assets		
Cash		_____
Capital		
Proprietor's opening capital		0
Net profit for period		1,360
Drawings		_____
Current liabilities		
Trade payables		
Bank loan	_____	
		_____

ANSWER

If you succeeded in filling in all the figures then you should be very pleased with yourself indeed! If you struggled, work through this answer **very** carefully to see where you went wrong.

Step 1

Cash		$
Borrowed from bank 1 October 20X8		3,200
(a)	Interest charges (3 × $40)	(120)
(b)	Van hire	(1,500)
	Van running expenses (3 × $450)	(1,350)
(c)	Part-time helper (3 × $150)	(450)
(d)	Cash sales	10,300
	Credit sales (all paid)	2,000
(e)	Purchase of food	(6,300)
(f)	Telephone and postage	(220)
(g)	Drawings (3 × $330)	(990)
	Balance in hand at 31 December 20X8	4,570

Step 2

Accounting equation at 1 October 20X8

Assets	$	= Capital	$	+ Liabilities	$
Cash	3,200		0	Bank loan	3,200

Accounting equation at 31 December 20X8

Assets	$	= Capital	$	+ Liabilities	$
Cash	4,570	Profit	1,360	Bank loan	3,200
		Drawings	(990)	Best Stores Ever	1,000
	4,570		370		4,200

Step 3

Business equation (to check retained profit figure)

$P = I + D - C$

$P = \$370^* + \$990 - \$0$

$\quad = \$1,360$

* Increase in net assets = Net assets at 31 December less net assets at 1 October

$\qquad\qquad \$(4{,}570 - 4{,}200) - \$(3{,}200 - 3{,}200)$

$\qquad\qquad = \$370$

Step 4

RITA BLAKE
STATEMENT OF FINANCIAL POSITION AS AT 31 DECEMBER 20X8

	$	$
Current assets		
Cash		4,570
Capital		
Proprietor's opening capital		0
Net profit for period		1,360
Drawings		(990)
		370
Current liabilities		
Trade payables	1,000	
Bank loan	3,200	
		4,200
		4,570

7 What goes where?

An important distinction is made between **asset** and **expense** items. If these are not identified correctly, then the resulting **profit figure** will be wrong and misleading.

You have seen how the statement of profit or loss and statement of financial position are developed, and how they are linked via the accounting equation. What you may still be concerned about is how we distinguish between items which appear in the **calculation of profit**, and those which belong on the **statement of financial position**.

Consider the following examples.

(a)   Suppose that a business sells goods worth $50,000 (for cash) during one month, and during the same month borrows $20,000 from a bank. Its total receipts for the month are therefore $70,000.

(b)   Suppose that a business spends $25,000 buying some land, and receives $2,500 rent from the tenant farmer in the year.

How would these amounts be accounted for in the statement of profit or loss and/or statement of financial position?

The answer is as follows.

(a)   (i)   The $50,000 of sales appear as **revenue** in the **statement of profit or loss** and as an **asset** (cash) in the **statement of financial position**.

        (ii)   The $20,000 borrowed will not be shown in the statement of profit or loss, but will be shown as an **asset** (cash) and a **liability** (loan) of $20,000 in the **statement of financial position**.

(b)   (i)   The cost of the land will not be an expense in the statement of profit or loss. It will appear as a **non-current asset** in the **statement of financial position**. Paying out the cash will decrease an **asset** (cash) in the **statement of financial position**.

        (ii)   The rent of $2,500 will appear as **income** of the business in the **statement of profit or loss,** and as an **asset** (cash) in the **statement of financial position**.

So how do we make these decisions? To try to make them we must now turn our attention to the distinction between **asset** and **expense** items.

7.1 Asset expenditure and expenses charged to profit or loss

Asset expenditure is expenditure which results in the acquisition of non-current assets, or an improvement in their earning capacity.

–   Asset expenditure on non-current assets results in the appearance of a non-current asset in the **statement of financial position** of the business.

        Asset expenditure is **not** charged as an expense in the **statement of profit or loss**.

The cost of a non-current asset includes its **purchase price** as well as what are called **directly attributable costs** such as initial delivery costs, installation costs and professional fees eg for architects and engineers.

Asset expenditure is also sometimes referred to as **capital expenditure**.

Expenses charged to profit or loss is expenditure which is incurred:

–   For the purpose of the trade of the business, including expenditure classified as selling and distribution expenses, administration expenses and finance charges.

–   To maintain the **existing** earning capacity of non-current assets, eg repairs to non-current assets.

Expenses charged to profit or loss are shown in the statement of profit or loss of **a specific period**, provided that they relate to the trading activity and sales of that particular period. If they carry over into the next period, the expenses would appear as a **current asset** in the statement of financial position.

Expenses charged to profit or loss are sometimes referred to as **revenue expenditure**.

7.2 Example: expenses charged to profit or loss

If a bathroom business buys 10 sinks for $4,000 ($400 each) and sells 8 of them during an accounting period, it will have two sinks left at the end of the period. The full $4,000 is an **expense charged to profit or loss** but only (8 × $400) = $3,200 is a cost of goods sold during the period. The remaining $800 (cost of two sinks) will be included in the inventory of goods held – as a **current asset** valued at $800.

7.3 Why is the distinction between asset and expense items important?

Since **asset expenditure** and **expenses charged to profit and loss** are accounted for in different ways (in the **statement of financial position** and **statement of profit or loss** respectively), the correct and consistent calculation of profit for any accounting period depends on the correct and consistent classification of items as asset or expense. Failure to classify items correctly will lead to the production of misleading profit figures.

For instance, a business spends $500 on a computer and $500 on maintenance. The computer is asset expenditure which should be shown as an asset in the statement of financial position, maintenance is an expense which should be deducted from profit in the statement of profit or loss. If the computer is incorrectly classified as an expense charged to profit or loss, it will appear as an expense and profit will be understated by $500. If the maintenance expense is treated as asset expenditure, it will be incorrectly shown as an asset in the statement of financial position and profit will be overstated by $500. Since retained profit is carried forward in the statement of financial position, the error will also have an impact in subsequent years.

> ### EXAM FOCUS POINT
>
> Questions on the distinction between asset expenditure and expenses charged to profit or loss could easily come up in the exam, so make sure you attempt the next two activities.

EXAMPLES

Say a sole trader purchased an asset, which should be fully depreciated over 5 years, for $10,000 and mistakenly classed it as an expense charged to profit or loss. The profit would be understated in Year 1 by $8,000 (purchase price of $10,000 incorrectly included and depreciation of $2,000 not charged), but overstated in Years 2 to 5 by $2,000 because there would not be any depreciation charge in those years. Assets would be understated until the end of Year 5.

Say an administrative expense of $1,000 was mistakenly classified as asset expenditure and depreciated over 5 years. The profit would then be overstated in Year 1 by $800 and understated in Years 2 to 5 by $200 as a result of the incorrect depreciation charge. Assets would be overstated until the end of Year 5.

Note. Depreciation on non-current assets is covered fully in Chapter 9.

QUESTION

Assets and expenses I

Complete the missing words to ensure you fully understand the difference between asset and expense items.

Expenses charged to profit or loss result from the purchase of goods and services that will either:

(a)   Be .... fully in the accounting period in which they are .... , and so be a cost or expense in the statement of profit or loss; or

(b)   Result in a .... asset as at the end of the accounting period (because the goods or services have not yet been consumed or made use of).

BPP
LEARNING MEDIA

Asset expenditure results in the purchase or improvement of .... assets, which are assets that will provide benefits to the business in more than .... accounting period, and which are not acquired with a view to being resold in the normal course of trade. The cost of purchased non-current assets is not charged to statement of profit or loss of the period in which the purchase occurs.

ANSWER

The missing words are: used; purchased; current; non-current; one.

QUESTION

Assets and expenses II

State whether each of the following items should be classified as asset expenditure, expenses charged to profit or loss or income for the purpose of preparing the statement of profit or loss and the statement of financial position of the business.

(a)   Purchase of leasehold premises

(b)   Solicitors' fees in connection with the purchase of leasehold premises

(c)   Costs of adding extra storage capacity to a mainframe computer used by the business

(d)   Computer repair and maintenance costs

(e)   Profit on the sale of an office building

(f)   Revenue from sales by credit card

(g)   Cost of new machinery

(h)   Customs duty charged on the machinery when imported into the country

(i)   'Carriage' costs of transporting the new machinery to the premises of the business purchasing the machinery

(j)   Cost of installing the new machinery in the premises of the business

(k)   Wages of the machine operators

ANSWER

(a)   Asset expenditure

(b)   The legal fees associated with the purchase of a property may be added to the purchase price and classified as asset expenditure

(c)   Asset expenditure (enhancing an existing non-current asset)

(d)   Expenses charged to profit or loss

(e)   Income (net of any costs relating to the sale)

(f)   Income

(g)   Asset expenditure

(h)   If customs duties are borne by the purchaser of the non-current asset, they may be added to the cost of the machinery and classified as asset expenditure

(i)   Similarly, if carriage costs are paid for by the purchaser of the non-current asset, they may be included in the cost of the non-current asset and classified as asset expenditure

(j)   Installation costs of a non-current asset are also added to the non-current asset's cost and classified as asset expenditure

(k)   Expenses charged to profit or loss

CHAPTER ROUNDUP

↪ A **statement of financial position** shows the financial position of a business at a given moment in time. A distinction is made between **non-current liabilities** and **current liabilities,** and between **non-current assets** and **current assets**.

↪ **Non-current assets** are those acquired for long-term use within the business.

↪ **Current assets** are expected to be converted into cash within one year.

↪ **Current liabilities** are debts which are payable within one year.

↪ A **statement of profit or loss** shows in detail how the profit or loss of a period has been made.

↪ An important distinction is made between **asset expenditure** and **expenses charged to profit or loss** items. If these are not identified correctly, then the resulting **profit figure** will be wrong and misleading.

QUICK QUIZ

1   What is a statement of financial position?

2   How long does a business keep a non-current asset?

3   What are current liabilities?

4   Is a bank overdraft a current liability?

5   What is a statement of profit or loss?

6   Distinguish between asset expenditure and expenses charged to profit or loss.

1   A statement of financial position is a listing of asset and liability balances on a certain date. It gives a 'snapshot' of the net worth of the company at a single point in time.

2   At least one accounting period and usually several.

3   Amounts owed which must be paid soon, usually within one year.

4   Yes, usually, because it is repayable on demand (in theory at least).

5   A statement of profit or loss matches revenue with the costs incurred in earning it.

6   Asset expenditure results in a non-current asset appearing on the statement of financial position. Expenses charged to profit or loss is trading expenditure or expenditure in maintaining non-current assets, which appears in the statement of profit or loss.

Now try ...

Attempt the questions below from the **Practice Question Bank**

Number	Level	Marks	Time
Q8	Examination	2	2.4 mins
Q9	Examination	2	2.4 mins
Q10	Examination	2	2.4 mins
Q11	Examination	2	2.4 mins
Q12	Examination	2	2.4 mins

CHAPTER

03

This chapter not only looks at how a business records its transactions, but also describes the accounting records generated as a result of that recording process and how each is used.

Recording and summarising transactions

TOPIC LIST	SYLLABUS REFERENCE
1 Importance of maintaining financial records	A2(a), A2(b)
2 Recording business transactions: an overview	B2(a)
3 Recording sales	D1(a), D1(b)
4 Recording purchases	D1(a), D1(b)
5 The cash received and cash payments day books	B2(a), D2(a)
6 Cash registers and cash received sheets (remittance lists)	C2(a), D2(a)
7 The general ledger	C2(c)
8 Discounts, rebates and allowances	D1(c)
9 Posting cash receipts to the general ledger	D2(a)

Study Guide   Intellectual level

A   Generally accepted accounting principles and concepts

2   Maintaining financial records

(a)   Explain the importance of maintaining financial records for   K
      internal and external use

(b)   Describe the type of accounting records that a business should   K
      maintain and the main uses of each

B   The principles and process of basic bookkeeping

**2   Books of prime entry and the flow of accounting information
      in the production of financial statements**

(a)   Explain the purpose and use of books of prime entry and ledger   K
      accounts

C   The preparation of journals and ledger accounts

2   Preparation of ledger accounts

(a)   Explain the purpose and use of ledger accounts   K

(c)   Balance the ledger accounts carrying down and bringing down   S
      balances as appropriate

D   Recording transactions and events

1   Sales and purchases

(a)   Record sale and purchase transactions in ledger accounts   S

(b)   Record sales and purchase returns   S

(c)   Account for trade and settlement discounts.   S

2   Cash and bank

(a)   Record cash and bank transactions in ledger accounts   S

1   Importance of maintaining financial records

It is very important that businesses keep financial records for both **internal** and **external** use.

The objective of general purpose financial reporting is to provide financial information about the reporting entity that is useful to existing and potential investors, lenders and other creditors in making decisions relating to providing resources to the entity.

(Conceptual Framework, para.1.2)

Accounting records will consist of:

- Source documents, these are the source of the data in the accounting records, eg sales invoices, credit notes, purchase invoices (see section 2.1).

- Books of prime entry, form the record of all the data transactions sent and received by the business, eg sales invoices (source record) are recorded in the sales day book (book of prime entry). See section 2.2 for more examples.

- Ledger accounts, these are the summaries of source documents, eg the receivable and payables ledgers. This covered in more detail in Chapter 4. These are summarised in a trial balance.

- Financial statements, these are often referred to as 'final accounts'. The ledger accounts are closed off to form a trial balance (see Chapter 4) and the balances are transferred to the financial statements eg the statement of profit or loss and the statement of financial position (see Chapter 10).

In the sections that follow, you will see how the information on numerous source documents is summarised using the books of prime entry and ledger accounts. These ledger accounts can then be used as a basis for constructing financial statements, a process we look at in later chapters. These records may be kept manually, but the majority of businesses will use computers to keep these records.

But why is it so important to keep financial records?

One of many reasons is that businesses **may** be required by law to keep accounting records. Another important reason is to allow income tax and sales tax returns to be submitted. This will be easier if the returns are based on good accounting records which summarise the relevant information. Also, even though it may not be required by law, it would be hard for a business to function if it did not keep accounting records.

Detailed records are used on a day to day basis by the management of the company. They are used internally for **control purposes**. For example, receivables and payables ledgers keep a record of how much is owed to or owed by other businesses. The proprietor or their staff can review these ledgers regularly and make sure they pay suppliers on time, and that customers pay on time. Where there are disputes, source documents can be referred to as they contain the most detail about a transaction.

As we look at source documents, books of prime entry and ledger accounts in the sections that follow, we look at how each is used **internally** and why it is important.

In practice, financial information prepared using the accounting records (such as the financial statements) are used by those both **internal and external** to the business.

(a)   **Managers of the business** (people appointed by the entity's owners to supervise the day to day activities of the business) use information about the business's financial situation as it is currently and as it is expected to be in the future to manage the business efficiently and to take effective control and planning decisions.

(b)   **Owners of the business** use the financial information to assess how effectively management is performing its stewardship function. They will want to know how profitably management is running the business's operations and how much profit they can afford to withdraw from the business for their own use.

(c)   **Suppliers** may use the financial statements to assess the business's ability to pay its debts while **customers** can assess whether or not the business is a secure source of supply.

(d)   **Providers of finance to the business** may include a bank which permits the company to operate an overdraft, or provides longer-term finance by granting a loan. The business will need to provide financial information to the bank demonstrating that the company is able to keep up with interest payments, and eventually to repay the amounts advanced.

(e)   **The tax authorities** require financial statements supporting stated business profits in order to assess the tax payable by the enterprise.

(f)   **Employees of the company** will look at information about the business's financial situation, because their future careers and the size of their wages and salaries depend on it.

EXAM FOCUS POINT

In the exam covering January to June 2014, a question gave two statements as being possible reasons for a business entity to maintain accounting records in double entry format. Statement 1 was that it is a legal requirement, and statement 2 was that it assists managers in exercising control. The examining team report pointed out that there is no legal requirement for unincorporated entities (sole traders and partnerships) to maintain any accounting records at all, let alone double entry records. Indeed, many small entities will simply maintain daybooks. While this is not best practice, it is common and therefore the statement 1 was incorrect. Statement 2 was a correct answer.

2 Recording business transactions: an overview

> Business transactions are initially recorded on **source documents**. The most important are **invoices** and **credit notes**. Records of the details on these documents are made in **books of prime entry**.

2.1 Source documents

Source documents are the source of all the information recorded by a business.

Here are some source documents with which you should be familiar already:

- Invoices
- Credit notes
- Petty cash vouchers
- Cheques received
- Cheque stubs (for cheques paid out)
- Wages, salary and employee tax records

You should be familiar with all of these documents from your earlier studies.

Remember the definitions of the two most important documents.

An **invoice** is a demand for payment.

A **credit note** is used by a seller to cancel part or all of a previously issued invoice(s).

2.2 Recording source documents

During the course of its business, a company sends out and receives **many** source documents. The details on these source documents need to be recorded, otherwise the business might forget to ask for some money, or forget to pay some, or even accidentally pay something twice. In other words, it needs to **keep records of source documents** – of transactions – so that it can keep tabs on what is going on.

Such records are made in books of prime entry, sometimes called the books of original entry.

Books of prime entry form the record of all the documented transactions sent and received by the company. They are as follows.

Book(s) of prime entry	Documents/transactions recorded	Summarised and posted to
Sales day book	Sales invoices	Receivables control account
Sales returns day book	Credit notes sent	Receivables control account
Purchase day book	Purchase invoices	Payables control account
Purchase returns day book	Credit notes received	Payables control account
Cash received day book	Cash received	General ledger/receivables ledger
Cash payments day book	Cheques, standing orders, direct debits	General ledger/payables ledger
Petty cash book	Notes and coins paid and received	General ledger
Journal	Adjustments	General ledger

QUESTION

Books of prime entry

State which books of prime entry the following transactions would be entered into.

(a)   Your business pays J Sunderland (a supplier) $6,200
(b)   You send Hall & Co (a customer) an invoice for $1,320
(c)   You receive an invoice from J Sunderland for $1,750
(d)   You pay Hall & Co $1,000
(e)   Sarti (a customer) returns goods to the value of $100
(f)   You return goods to Elphick & Co to the value of $2,400
(g)   Sarti pays you $760

ANSWER

(a)   Cash payments day book
(b)   Sales day book
(c)   Purchase day book
(d)   Cash payments day book
(e)   Sales returns day book
(f)   Purchase returns day book
(g)   Cash received day book

2.3 Summarising source documents

Because of the volume of source documents, and the fact that they come from and are sent to a very large number of suppliers and customers, it is vital that the information in them is **summarised.** This is done in two ways.

Need for summary	Ledger used
Summaries need to be kept of all the transactions undertaken with an **individual** supplier or customer – invoices, credit notes, cash – so that a net amount due or owed can be calculated.	Receivables ledger Payables ledger
Summaries need to be kept of **all** the transactions undertaken with all suppliers and customers, so a total for receivables and a total for payables can be calculated.	**General ledger** (a) Receivables control account (b) Payables control account

Note. You may also see the general ledger described as a 'nominal ledger': your exam will use the term 'general ledger'.

2.4 Posting to the ledgers

Now we will look at how financial information moves around the system. The diagram that follows shows how items are **posted** to (**entered in**) the ledgers, ultimately to arrive at the financial statements. Don't worry that some of the terms are unfamiliar currently – you will be able to trace through what is going on when you have completed this and the next chapter.

Note. The following diagram shows cheques received and paid being recorded in a 'cash book'. This is a commonly used term in businesses that record both payments and receipts in a single book. However, as we will see in Section 5 of this chapter and the remainder of the chapter, many businesses maintain two separate books – one for cheques issued (and other payments) and one for cheques received (and other receipts). These are collectively known as cash day books.

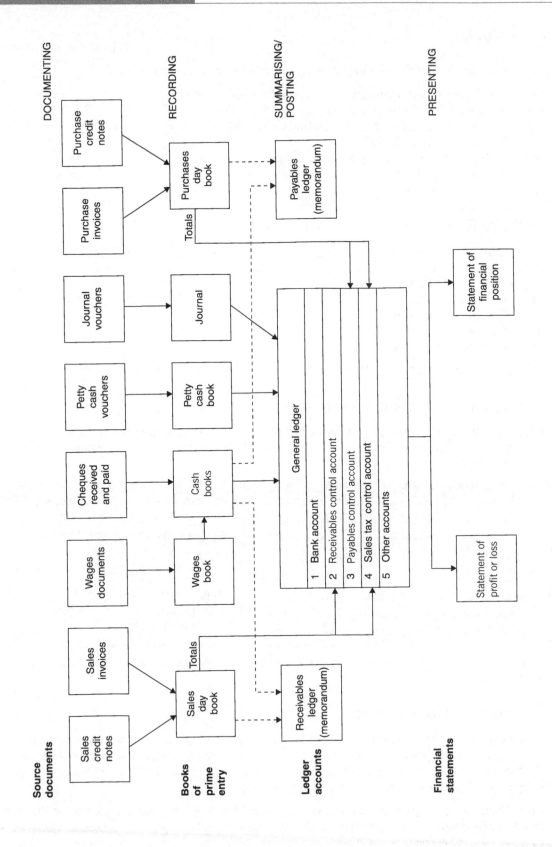

3 Recording sales

By now you will be familiar with the books of prime entry for recording sales – the sales day book and the sales returns day book.

Invoices are entered in the sales day book and credit notes in the sales returns day book. The invoices and credit notes are then posted to the customer account, with a corresponding credit/debit to the sales account in the statement of profit or loss. The double entry for sales is covered in more detail in Section 2 of Chapter 4.

However it is likely that in practice you have never encountered these books of prime entry. Even very small businesses now record and summarise their transactions using an accounting package. In fact, the package probably produces the sales invoice. A hard copy is printed and sent to the customer and the program holds the invoice in a file, which we can think of as the equivalent of the sales day book. The most widely used packages will produce a report called a **day book listing**.

The invoice can then be posted to the ledgers, literally with one click. This can be done as each invoice is produced, or they can all be held on file and posted at the end of the month. If the package does not produce the invoices, they can be keyed into the system and posted.

All customers will have an account in the receivables ledger. This account will be updated by the posting of invoices and credit notes and also by the posting of cash etc received from the customer. At the end of the month, the system will produce a statement which can be sent to the customer. This will detail movements on their account during the month and notify them of the balance due on their account.

One of the important checks to be done every month is the reconciliation of the receivables ledger to the receivables control account. The receivables control account is an account shown in the statement of financial position and it should exactly reflect the receivables ledger, which does not appear in the accounts. This reconciliation is explained more fully in later chapters and it is important to understand it, as it is very popular in examinations. However, it is worth noting that, in a computerised system, discrepancies do not often arise between the receivables ledger and the receivables control account.

4 Recording purchases

The points made about the sales day book are also applicable to the purchase day book. Businesses which run a computerised payables ledger will simply key invoices into the system as they arrive, or as they are authorised for payment. They will key in for each invoice the due date for payment.

The system will produce as required a day book listing of all the invoices input that day. The invoices will be posted to the supplier account, with the debit entry going to the relevant statement of profit or loss or statement of financial position account. The double entry for purchases is covered in more detail in Section 2 of Chapter 4.

When payments arc due to be made, the system will produce a listing of all invoices due for payment. Some systems will actually print the cheques and remittance advices, which is where a computerised payables ledger system really becomes useful. Increasingly, the computerised ledgers are being linked to the business's online banking, which allows for electronic bank transfers, such as BACS, to be processed to pay the outstanding amounts directly to the supplier's bank account. Then the system will post the payments to the supplier accounts.

When the supplier statement arrives at the end of the month, it can be checked against the balance on the supplier account.

Reconciling the payables control account to the payables ledger is an important monthly routine, which is made very easy in a computerised system. It is explained more fully in Chapter 4.

5 The cash received and cash payments day books

Most businesses maintain separate receipts and payments day books for cash. The **cash received day book** and **cash payments day book** are books of prime entry, used to keep a cumulative record of money received and money paid out by the business via its bank account.

Money received on the business premises may be notes, coins and cheques which are subsequently banked. There are also receipts and payments made by bank transfer, standing order, direct debit, and, in the case of bank interest and charges, directly by the bank.

The **cash received day book** is used to record **receipts of cash** including **notes, coins, cheques, electronic bank transfers and till receipts (including daily summaries from debit card payment machines)**.

The **cash payments day book** is used to **record all forms of bank payments**. These payments include **cheques, standing orders, electronic bank transfers (for example BACS, CHAPS)** and **direct debits**. The best way to see how these day books work is to follow through an example.

Note that in this example we are continuing to ignore sales tax, which we will consider at the end of this chapter. Note also that, while manual sales day books and purchase day books may now be uncommon, many businesses, even those with quite sophisticated computer systems, still maintain manual cash received and cash payments day books.

5.1 Example: Cash received and cash payments day books

At the beginning of 10 January, Peter Jeffries had $2,100 in the bank. During 10 January 20X8, he had the following receipts and payments.

(a)   Cash sale: receipt of $220
(b)   Payment from credit customer Khan: $3,100 (S/L ref. 07)
(c)   Payment from credit customer Likert: $1,480 (R/L ref. 12)
(d)   Payment from credit customer Lee: $2,400 (S/L ref. 10)
(e)   Cash sale: receipt of $190
(f)   Cash received for sale of machine: $370
(g)   Payment to supplier Price: $1,250 (P/L ref. 27)
(h)   Payment to supplier Burn: $2,420 (P/L ref. 16)
(i)   Payment of telephone bill: $235
(j)   Payment of gas bill: $640
(k)   Payment of $3,400 to Fawcett for new plant and machinery

If you look through these transactions, you will see that six of them are receipts and five of them are payments.

Solution

The cash received day book and the cash payments day book for Peter Jeffries would be as shown on the next page. Do not worry too much about the details at the moment – we will follow them through later on in this Text.

- Receipts are listed in the **cash received** day book (receipts are debits as they result in an increase of an asset).

- Payments are listed in the **cash payments** day book (payments are credits as they decrease an asset).

- Both of these day books have columns for these details.

    –   Date
    –   Narrative
    –   Reference
    –   Total

- Each day book has a number of **columns for further analysis** – receipts from customers, cash sales and other receipts; payments to suppliers, expenses and non-current assets for payments.

PETER JEFFRIES – CASH RECEIVED DAY BOOK

RECEIPTS

Date 20X8	Narrative	Ref.	Total $	Receipts from customers $	Cash sales $	Other $
	(a) Cash sale		220		220	
	(b) Customer pays: Khan	SL07	3,100	3,100		
	(c) Customer pays: Likert	SL12	1,480	1,480		
	(d) Customer pays: Lee	SL10	2,400	2,400		
	(e) Cash sale		190		190	
	(f) Non-current asset sale		370			370
			7,760	6,980	410	370

PETER JEFFRIES – CHEQUES ISSUED DAY BOOK

PAYMENTS

Date 20X8	Narrative	Ref.	Total $	Payments to suppliers $	Expenses $	Non-current assets $
10 Jan	(g) Supplier paid: Rice	PL27	1,250	1,250		
	(h) Supplier paid: Burn	PL16	2,420	2,420		
	(i) Telephone expense		235		235	
	(j) Gas expense		640		640	
	(k) Plant & machinery purchase		3,400			3,400
			7,945	3,670	875	3,400

5.2 Balancing the bank ledger account

At the beginning of the day there is a debit **opening balance** of $2,100. During the day, the total receipts and payments were as follows.

	$
Opening balance	2,100
Receipts	7,760
	9,860
Payments	(7,945)
Closing balance	1,915

The **closing balance** of $1,915 represents the excess of receipts over payments. It means that Peter Jeffries still has cash available at the end of the day, so he 'carries it down' at the end of 10 January and 'brings it down' at the beginning of 11 January as a debit balance on the ledger account. Accountants generally use the terminology 'balance brought down' or 'balance b/d' and 'balance carried down' or 'balance c/d' instead of 'opening balance' and 'closing balance'.

Balance b/d	Balance brought down	Opening balance
Balance c/d	Balance carried down	Closing balance

In this example we used separate day books – a cash receipts day book and a cash payments day book. As mentioned before, some organisations use a single book called the **cash book**, which has both a receipts and a payments section.

5.3 Bank statements

Weekly or monthly, a business will receive a **bank statement**. Bank statements should be used to check that the amount shown as a balance in the bank ledger account agrees with the amount on the bank statement, and that no cash has 'gone missing'.

5.4 Petty cash book

Most businesses keep a small amount of cash on the premises to make occasional **small payments in cash** – eg to pay the milkman, to buy a few postage stamps, to pay the office cleaner, or to pay for some bus or taxi fares. This is often called the **cash float**; it can also be the resting place for occasional small receipts, such as cash paid by a visitor to make a phone call, or to take some photocopies.

The **petty cash book** is the book of prime entry which keeps a cumulative record of the small amounts of cash received into and paid out of the cash float.

There are usually more payments than receipts, and petty cash must be 'topped-up' from time to time with cash from the business bank account.

6 Cash registers and cash received sheets (remittance lists)

We have looked at how the cash day books work, but these are not always the first place that receipts are recorded. In bigger entities, other methods for recording cash receipts and payments are commonplace.

- Cash registers
- Cash received sheets or remittance lists see section 6.3 of this chapter

Cash registers in some form have been in use for a long time in retail shops. They used to be mechanically operated, but today most are computerised. The more sophisticated and larger stores will have cash registers which are all connected to a central computer. The cash registers will update the computer automatically as a sale takes place, and each cash register can be updated for price changes.

6.1 Recording cash received by the register

The total of daily sales recorded by the cash register will be used in the following ways.

(a) To **check the amount of money** in the cash register at the end of the day against the summary (commonly known as an 'end of day' report). If there are any discrepancies they are investigated. Most modern tills have automated links between the debit card machines and the cash register; this speeds up the process of ensuring the end of day summaries balance.

(b) To **record receipts in the cash received day book**

The entry in the cash received day book will be the total amount of cash received. This will be analysed into sales and sales tax, to facilitate **posting to the general ledger**.

6.2 Security and controls

We have seen how accurate a cash register can be and how well it can **control receipts**; but the cash register will only act as an effective control if it is used properly.

(a) **Access keys** should be given to the appropriate members of staff and they should be kept in a safe and secure place. A spare set should be kept by the person in authority.

(b) Staff should be **trained in the use of the cash register** and their work should be observed for a period.

(c) The maximum possible amount of **preset information** should be programmed into the cash register. This saves cashier time and reduces the risk of fraud.

(d) **Periodic information** produced by the cash register such as average sales proceeds per customer, average sales value of the items sold and sales by clerk or operator should be analysed carefully by the manager or owner, with perhaps a brief weekly or monthly report being written. All variations should be investigated.

6.3 Cash received sheets (remittance lists)

Businesses which do not have a cash register still need to record money received from sales they have made. Very small shops or businesses will probably just write down on a piece of paper the money received as they sell something. (Note that 'cash' here means cash, cheques, cards or any other form of receipt.) This is a basic **cash received sheet.**

Acorn Antiques

Sales Takings 22 July 20X7

	$
Two Victorian chairs: cheque	45.00
One Victorian table: cheque	155.00
Two Watercolours: cheque	100.00
Bookshelves: cash	40.00
One Edwardian chair: cheque	55.00
Pair Chinese vases: credit card	360.00
Two sidetables: credit card	180.00
Total for day	$935.00

Larger non-retail companies may have **pre-printed cash received sheets** or **remittance lists** on which they record receipts as they arrive through the post.

| CASH RECEIVED SHEET 7141 (b) | | JOE'S BUILDING SUPPLIES | |
| DATE 10/4/X7 | | (a) | |
NAME		**ACCOUNT**	**AMOUNT**
P Jones and Son	1	00437	169.00
S Car Co	2	01562	62.70
Tax refund	3	00002	55.00
Moblem	4	02137	3,233.99
Lobells	5	05148	244.91
Cannery Whiff	6	02420	9,553.72
Lymping	7	09370	62.20
Yorker	8	09682	322.41
Mowley	9	01433	43.30
Regalia	10	03997	978.50
Herod Sons	11	05763	71.40
Forman Co	12	07211	4,288.52
Thatchers	13	04520	610.00
Eggary Co	14	08871	4,823.50
Redwood Sons	15	08759	420.68
TOTAL		10000 (c)	24,939.83 (d)

(a) **Account number.** This is the ledger account number of the customer in the **sales ledger**. When the details from the cash received sheet are entered into the accounting system, this code number will tell the system (whether it is manual or computerised) which customer has paid off all or part of their debt. For non-sales ledger receipts, the code of the account in the general ledger is substituted. In this case 00002 is the code for the tax authorities refunding sales tax.

(b) **Cash received sheet number.** Preprinted cash received sheets may be sequentially numbered. This is a control which helps to make sure that all receipts have been recorded, a check can be carried out to make sure all cash received sheets are present.

(c) **Bank account number (10000).** This is the ledger account number of the cash account in the general ledger.

(d) **Total receipts.** The money received is summarised here so only the totals need to be recorded in the cash received day book.

7 The general ledger

Most accounts are contained in the **general ledger** (or nominal ledger).

The rules of double entry state that every financial transaction gives rise to two accounting entries – a debit and a credit.

The general ledger is the accounting record which summarises the financial affairs of a business. It contains details of assets, liabilities and capital, income and expenditure and so profit and loss. It consists of a large number of different **ledger accounts**, each account having its own purpose or 'name' and an identity or code. Another name for the general ledger is the **nominal ledger**.

Each ledger account represents a specific item of income, expense, asset, liability or capital. Entries are made in the account to record how the value of the item has been affected by transactions. Therefore the purpose of a ledger account is to summarise how transactions change the value of a specific item of

income, expense, asset, liability or capital. As we shall see in Chapter 4, this process leads to a single value for each item, which is included first in the trial balance, and is then reported in the final accounts. Transactions are **posted** to accounts in the general ledger from the books of prime entry.

Posting means to enter transactions in ledger accounts in the general ledger from books of prime entry. Often this is done in total (ie all sales invoices in the sales day book for a day are added up and the total is posted to the receivables control account) but individual transactions are also posted (eg non-current assets).

Examples of ledger accounts in the general ledger include the following

Ledger account	Non-current asset	Current asset	Current liability	Non-current liability	Capital	Expense	Income
Plant and machinery at cost	✓						
Motor vehicles at cost	✓						
Proprietor's capital					✓		
Inventories: raw materials		✓					
Inventories: finished goods		✓					
Total receivables		✓					
Total payables			✓				
Wages and salaries						✓	
Rent and local taxes						✓	
Advertising expenses						✓	
Bank charges						✓	
Motor expenses						✓	
Telephone expenses						✓	
Revenue							✓
Bank		✓					
Bank overdraft			✓				
Bank loan				✓			

7.1 The format of a ledger account

If a ledger account were to be kept in an actual book rather than as a computer record, its **format** might be as follows.

ADVERTISING EXPENSES

Date 20X8	Narrative	Ref.	DEBIT $	Date	Narrative	Ref.	CREDIT $
15 Jan	WBSC Agency for quarter to 31 Dec 20X7	PL 97	4,000				

Only one entry in the account is shown here, because the example is introduced simply to illustrate the general format of a ledger account.

There are two sides to the account, and an account heading on top, and so it is convenient to think in terms of 'T' accounts:

(a)   On top of the account is its name
(b)   There is a left hand side, or **debit** side
(c)   There is a right hand side, or **credit** side

NAME OF ACCOUNT

DEBIT SIDE	$	CREDIT SIDE	$

The 'T' account format for ledger accounts is probably the most widely used but other formats are acceptable.

7.2 Carrying/bringing forward balances

Sometimes it may be necessary to square or balance off an account and carry forward a balance. This may be necessary at the end of a period or for more basic reasons, when you have come to the foot of a page.

PAYABLES CONTROL ACCOUNT

Date 20X8	Narrative	Ref.	$	Date 20X8	Narrative	Ref.	$
3 Oct	Bank	CB4	60,500	1 Oct	Balance	b/f	142,750
30 Nov	Bank	CB7	72,250	31 Oct	Purchases	PDB24	72,250
31 Dec	Bank	CB10	52,250	30 Nov	Purchases	PDB32	61,420
31 Dec	Balance	c/f	176,000	31 Dec	Purchases	PDB38	84,580
			361,000				361,000

The process is as follows:

(a)   Add up debit side and credit side as they stand in the ledger account.

(b)   Establish whether debits or credits are greater. If debits are greater, we have a debit balance to be carried forward. If credits are greater, we have a credit balance to be carried forward.

(c)   Slot in debit balance on credit side to square or balance the totals of debits and credits. Where there is a credit balance, insert balancing figure on debit side to make the total debits agree with the total credits.

(d)   Add up both columns and fill in totals. Rule off the totals accordingly. One line above and double line below is the usual convention for indicating the total.

(e)   Bring forward the balance on the appropriate side in the new period or the next page; excess of debits to debit side and excess of credits onto the credit side.

(f)   Remember you 'carry' from one period or page and 'bring' to another period or page. Also you can use 'carry forward' or 'carry down' a balance. Similarly a balance may be 'brought forward' or 'brought down' into a new period or onto a new page.

We will go on to use the cash received and cash payments day books to demonstrate double-entry, in the next chapter. First of all however, we need to go over two important areas, which you may already be familiar with:

(a)   Discounts, rebates and allowances
(b)   Sales tax or value added tax

These will be important in the next chapter and later on in this Text.

8   Discounts, rebates and allowances

There are two kinds of discount.

–   **Trade discount**: a reduction in the cost of goods, often for bulk purchases or special offers.

–   **Settlement or prompt payment discount**: a reduction in the amount payable to the supplier, usually as a result of prompt payment within a set timescale. Also referred to as a cash discount.

A **trade discount** is a reduction in the price of goods below the amount at which those goods would normally be sold to other customers of the supplier.

8.1 Types of discount

There are two types of discount.

Type of discount	Description	Timing	Status
Trade discount	A reduction in the **cost of goods** owing to the nature of the trading transaction. It usually results from buying goods in bulk. For example: (a) A customer might be quoted a price of $1 per unit for a particular item, but a lower price of, say, 95 cents per unit if the item is bought in quantities of, say, 100 units or more at a time (b) An important customer or a regular customer might be offered a discount on all the goods they buy, regardless of the size of each individual order, because the total volume of their purchases over time is so large Customers who receive trade discounts are often other business customers, but not always.	Given on supplier's invoice	Permanent
Settlement (sometimes called prompt payment or cash) discount	A reduction in the **amount payable** to the supplier, in return for immediate or very early payment in cash, rather than purchase on credit. For example, a supplier might charge $1,000 for goods, but offer a cash discount of, say, 10% if the goods are paid for immediately in cash, 5% if they are paid for within 7 days of the invoice date but payment anyway within 30 days. In this case the invoice would show '10% 0 days, 5% 7 days, net 30 days', indicating these terms. The invoice will usually have already accounted for the settlement discount if the supplier believes that the customer will take up the offer (from historical knowledge). **Adjustments are only required if the discount, which was assumed to be taken, was later not taken up (late payment)**	Given for immediate or very prompt payment	Withdrawn if payment not received within time period expected

The distinction between trade and settlement discounts is important as they may require different accounting treatment.

8.2 Example: Discounts

Trent Marcus has three major suppliers.

(a) Parker is in the same business as Trent and offers 5% trade discount.

(b) Scott offers a trade discount of 6% on amounts **in excess of** $200 (ie the trade discount does not apply to the first $200).

(c) Alan offers a 10% settlement discount for all items paid for within 30 days of purchase.

In January 20X8, Trent makes purchases of goods worth the following amounts before discounts have been deducted.

(a) From Parker: $600
(b) From Scott: $850
(c) From Alan: $920 to be paid on 14.1.X8 for goods purchased on 3.1.X8

Calculate how much Trent has received as discounts in January. How much were trade and settlement discounts?

Solution

		$	
From Parker	$600 × 5%	30	Trade
From Scott	($850 – $200) × 6%	39	Trade
From Alan	$920 × 10%	92	Settlement
		161	

8.3 Accounting for trade discounts

A **trade discount** is a reduction in the amount of money **demanded** from a customer.

If a trade discount is **received** by a business for goods purchased from a supplier, the **amount of money demanded from the business** by the supplier will be **net** of discount (ie it will be the normal sales value less the discount). In other words, the trade discount **does not appear** in the accounting records of either party.

Similarly, if a trade discount is **allowed** by a business for goods sold to a customer, the amount of money demanded by the business will be after deduction of the discount.

8.4 Accounting for settlement discounts

A **settlement or prompt payment discount** is an **optional** reduction in the amount of money **payable** by a customer.

8.4.1 Settlement or prompt payment discounts received

Taking advantage of a settlement discount is a matter of **financing policy**, not of **trading policy**. This is because the discount is **optional**.

8.5 Example: optional settlement discounts received

Suppose that Sacker buys goods from Hashes Co, on the understanding that Sacker will be allowed a period of credit before having to pay for the goods. The terms of the transaction might be as follows.

Date of sale: 1 November 20X8

Credit period allowed: 30 days

Invoice price of the goods (the invoice will be issued at this price when the goods are delivered): $5,000

Settlement discount offered: 3% for immediate payment

Sacker has the choice between:

(a)   Holding on to the $5,000 for 30 days and then paying the full amount.
(b)   Paying $5,000 less 3% (a total of $4,850) now.

This is a financing decision about whether it is worthwhile for Sacker to save $150 by paying its debts sooner, or whether it can employ its cash more usefully for 30 days, and pay the debt at the latest acceptable moment.

Assume that if Sacker pays now, its bank account would go overdrawn for a month. The bank would charge an overdraft fee of $70 together with interest of 2.0% per month (also charged on the overdraft fee). Sacker currently has $500 in the bank (and has an agreed overdraft facility). Assuming no other transactions, what should Sacker do? Work it out before looking at the solution.

Solution

If Sacker pays now, the bank account will be as follows.

	$
Funds	500.00
Less: payment	(4,850.00)
overdraft fee	(70.00)
Overdraft	(4,420.00)

Interest (2.0% × $4,420) added at end of the month	88.40

Whereas the discount is worth $150, bank charges and interest of $70 + $88.40 = $158.40 will be incurred. In this case the amount of the discount is worth **less** than the bank charges by $8.40. Sacker should therefore **not** take advantage of the discount offered by Hashes. The situation may not always be as straightforward as this because of other transactions.

8.5.1 Settlement discounts allowed

The same principle is applied in accounting for settlement (or prompt payment) discounts given (allowed) to customers. Goods are sold at a trade price, and the offer of a cash discount on that price is a matter of financing policy for the selling business and not a matter of trading policy. The business will make an assessment based upon previous transactions (has the customer regularly taken up the settlement discount?), and will decide whether to account for this discount at the **time of the transaction** being recorded in the accounts. If the customer has rarely or never taken up the settlement discount, then the full value of the invoice will be recorded.

Not all sales will be recorded net of the settlement discount. Only those where historical data suggests that these discounts will be taken up by the customer. If the customer fails to take advantage of the discount, then an adjustment to revenue is made when the customer pays at a later date. This accounting treatment is consistent with IFRS 15 *Revenue from Contracts with Customers*. We look at how discounts are accounted for in later chapters.

Allowing settlement discounts to customers, as opposed to receiving discounts from suppliers, is subject to similar business and financing considerations.

- It may be worth your while to **receive an amount of cash now**, as you can earn more in **interest** on it than you would lose by offering the discount.

- If you are in a **precarious financial position**, your bank manager might be happier to see the money now rather than later (and you might save money on overdraft interest and bank charges).

- You may be concerned that the **customer's own financial position** is insecure. Accepting cash now, rather than more later, means that at least the money is securely yours.

QUESTION

Champer

Champer purchases goods with a list price of $30,000. The supplier offers a 10% trade discount, and a 2.5% settlement discount for payment within 10 days.

Required

(a) Calculate the amount Champer will have to pay if it delays longer than 10 days before paying.
(b) Calculate the amount the company will pay if it pays within 10 days.

Note. Ignore sales tax.

ANSWER

	$
List price	30,000
Less 10% trade discount	(3,000)
	27,000
Less 2.5% settlement discount $27,000 × 2.5%	(675)
	26,325

(a)   If Champer pays after 10 days it will receive only the trade discount. The company will therefore pay $27,000.

(b)   If payment is made within 10 days, the company will be able to take advantage of the settlement discount and pay only $26,325.

Note. The settlement discount is calculated as a percentage of the list price **net of trade discount**.

Businesses may be offered other kinds of 'discounts' as incentives, to encourage them to buy in bulk or even just to stop them buying goods from other businesses. **Rebates** and **allowances** do not affect the cash function to a great extent and they are only mentioned briefly here.

(a)   An example of a **rebate** is where the gas company will lower its overall tariff for customers who use over a certain number of units per year. The rebate will be given in the form of either:

(i)   A reduction in the bills for the following year.

(ii)   A cheque or electronic payment for the calculated rebate amount.

(b)   An example of an **allowance** is where, if a certain number of units are ordered at one time, then a few extra units are given free of charge. For instance, if a record shop orders 50 compact discs, then another 5 may be sent **free of charge.**

EXAM FOCUS POINT

For more information on calculating settlement (prompt payment) discounts, there is a useful technical article available on the ACCA website which was published in November 2016. It explains the background to the changes relating to IFRS 15 and the level of understanding required for this exam.

EXAM FOCUS POINT

In the September 2018 – August 2019 Examiner's report, there was a question addressing the types of discounts on purchases. Discounts can sometimes cause confusion as following the introduction of IFRS 15 Revenue from contracts from customers, the discounts on purchases are treated differently from those on sales.

When looking at discounts on purchases, the trade discount is guaranteed, and therefore must be deducted before recording the transaction in the accounts. Any settlement discount is not taken into account until we know if we are going to qualify for the discount by making the payment within the allotted time period. Any settlement discount received would be treated as a discount received and shown as other income.

9 Posting cash receipts to the general ledger

It is only when we post the receipts recorded in the cash received day book to the cash (or bank) account in the general ledger that we can be said to have accounted for cash receipts.

Book of prime entry	P	Ledger account
Cash received day book	O	Cash (or bank) account
(Records individual cash receipts)	S	(Summarises cash receipts)
	T →	
	I	
	N	
	G	

Provided all the procedures have been followed correctly in preparing the cash received day book, posting it to the general ledger should be straightforward.

Step 1	**Add up** all the columns of the cash received day book.
Step 2	Check that the **totals of the analysis columns** (excluding the discount allowed memorandum column) add up to the total cash received column.
Step 3	**Identify general ledger accounts** which require posting by marking against amount shown in the cash received day book.
Step 4	Draw up a **posting summary** and post the general ledger.

CHAPTER ROUNDUP

↳ It is very important that businesses keep financial records for both **internal** and **external** use.

↳ Business transactions are initially recorded on **source documents**. The most important are **invoices** and **credit notes**. Records of the details on these documents are made in **books of prime entry**.

↳ Most accounts are contained in the **general ledger** (or nominal ledger).

↳ The rules of double entry state that every financial transaction gives rise to two accounting entries – a debit and a credit.

↳ There are two kinds of discount.

- **Trade discount**: a reduction in the cost of goods often for bulk purchases or special offers

- **Settlement (or prompt payment) discount**: a reduction in the amount payable to the supplier usually as a result of prompt payment within a set timescale. Also referred to as a cash discount.

QUICK QUIZ

1 What are books of prime entry?

2 What is recorded in the sales day book?

3 What is a trade discount?

4 What is a settlement discount?

5 Why might you offer a settlement discount to customers?

1 The books of prime entry record all the documented transactions undertaken by the company.

2 The sales day book records the list of invoices sent out to customers each day.

3 A reduction in the amount of money demanded from a customer.

4 An optional reduction in the amount of money payable by a customer.

5 To save or gain interest; the business or the customer is in a difficult financial situation.

Attempt the questions below from the **Practice Question Bank**

Number	Level	Marks	Time
Q13	Examination	2	2.4 mins
Q14	Examination	2	2.4 mins
Q15	Examination	2	2.4 mins
Q16	Examination	2	2.4 mins
Q17	Examination	2	2.4 mins

04

Posting transactions, balancing accounts and the trial balance

Double entry bookkeeping was introduced in Chapter 1 and we start this chapter by covering this very important principle in more detail before looking at how the information contained in the day books is summarised in **ledger accounts**.

Double entry bookkeeping is used to post the day book totals to the appropriate ledger accounts. Transactions not accounted for in the day books can be recorded using **journals**.

The ledger account balances at the end of the period can be collated in a **trial balance** which can be used as a tool to identify certain **errors**.

This chapter also introduces some records which are not part of the double entry system. These include the **receivables ledger** used to keep track of amounts due from individual customers and the **payables ledger** which lists amounts owed to individual suppliers. The total for these lists of balances can be compared with the balance on the related **control** accounts.

Sales tax is a tax levied on the sale of goods and services and we also look at this in this chapter as well as how computerised systems can help to record it.

TOPIC LIST	

Study Guide	Intellectual level
A **Generally accepted accounting principles and concepts**	
1 **The key accounting principles and characteristics**	
(a) Explain the principles of accounting.	K
(iv) Double entry	
B **The principles and process of basic bookkeeping**	
2 **The books of prime entry and flow of accounting information in the production of financial statements**	
(b) Identify reasons for closing off accounts and producing a trial balance	K
C **The preparation of journals and ledger accounts**	
1 **Preparation of journals from the books of prime entry**	
(b) Prepare journals to record transactions in an appropriate format	S
2 **Preparation of ledger accounts**	
(b) Post journals and other entries into the appropriate ledger account	S
D **Recording transactions and events**	
1 **Sales and purchases**	
(d) Identify sources of information on sales tax and explain the relationship between the entity and the relevant government agency	K
(e) Explain the general principles of the operation of a sales tax including:	K
(i) Requirements for registration	
(ii) Main information to be included on business documentation	
(iii) Types of taxable supplies and their classification for sales tax	
(iv) Accounting and payment of sales tax	
(v) Penalties for late returns or late payment of sales tax	
(f) Explain the different methods of accounting and reporting for sales tax	K
(g) Identify and obtain sales tax data from the accounting system	S
(h) Calculate sales tax on inputs and outputs	S
(i) Record the consequent accounting entries and calculate the sales tax due to/from the business	S
(j) Compute the main components of a sales tax return	S
(k) Communicate effectively with the relevant tax authority about sales tax matters including potential adjustments, errors or omissions	S

(l)   Calculate the cash flow impact on the business of the payment of sales tax and the potential impact on the business of any changes in legislation for sales tax   S

E   **Preparing a trial balance and errors**

1   **Trial balance**

(a)   Explain the purpose of the trial balance   K

(b)   Distinguish between errors which will be detected by extracting a trial balance and those which will not   S

(d)   Identify the limitations of the trial balance   K

(e)   Prepare the initial trial balance   S

F   **Reconciliations**

1   **Control account reconciliations**

(a)   Explain the purpose of reconciliation of the receivables and payables control accounts   K

1   Double entry bookkeeping

The rules of double entry state that every financial transaction gives rise to **two accounting entries**, one a **debit**, the other a **credit**. It is vital that you understand this principle.

A **debit** is one of the following.

- An increase in an asset
- An increase in an expense
- A decrease in a liability

A **credit** is one of the following.

- An increase in a liability
- An increase in income
- A decrease in an asset

In Chapter 1 we saw that double entry bookkeeping allowed us to keep the accounting equation always in balance, because **every financial transaction gives rise to two accounting entries, one a debit and the other a credit**.

DEBIT To own/have ↓	CREDIT To owe ↓
AN ASSET INCREASES eg new office furniture	AN ASSET DECREASES eg pay out cash
CAPITAL/ A LIABILITY DECREASES eg pay a supplier	CAPITAL/A LIABILITY INCREASES eg buy goods on credit
INCOME DECREASES eg cancel a sale	INCOME INCREASES eg make a sale
AN EXPENSE INCREASES eg incur advertising costs	AN EXPENSE DECREASES eg cancel a purchase
Left hand side	**Right hand side**

1.1 Cash transactions: double entry

Students coming to the subject for the first time often have difficulty in knowing where to begin. A good starting point is the **cash received day book** and the **cash payments day book** (from now on, when referring to these collectively, we shall refer to them as the cash day books). These are simply the books of prime entry for the general ledger bank account in which receipts and payments of cash are recorded.

Remember that these cash day books are books of prime entry while the **bank account** is the ledger account in the general ledger. It is the bank account which is part of the double entry system. **(Do not confuse this with the actual account at the bank.)**

Book of prime entry		Ledger account in general ledger
Cash received day book	Summary posted to	Bank account

EXAM FOCUS POINT

From your previous studies you may have encountered the term 'cash book' which is a single day book used to record both cash payments and cash receipts, and some businesses have an integrated cash book which means that it is both a book of prime entry and a ledger account.

However, this is not normal practice, except in the smallest companies, so it is extremely unlikely that you will be required to use this approach in the exam.

Therefore, you can assume that exam questions are based on the assumption that two separate day books are maintained (one to record cash received and one to record payments) and that these day books are posted to the bank ledger account in the general ledger. If the question is based on a different approach, this will be stated.

The rule to remember about the bank account is as follows.

(a)   A **payment** is a **credit entry** in the bank account. Here the **asset** (cash at bank) **is decreasing**. Money may be paid out, for example, to pay an expense (such as rates) or to purchase an asset (such as a machine). The **matching debit entry** is therefore made in the appropriate **expense** account or **asset** account.

(b)   A **receipt** is a **debit entry** in the bank account. Here the **asset** (cash at bank) **is increasing**. Money might be received, for example, by a retailer who makes a cash sale. The **matching credit entry** would then be made in the **revenue** account.

Cash transactions	DEBIT	CREDIT
Sell goods for cash	Bank	Revenue
Buy goods for cash	Purchases	Bank

Note. We refer here to 'cash' but this also includes cheques. Where a business is concerned, most payments will be made by cheque, direct debit or by electronic transfer.

1.2 Example: Double entry for cash transactions

In the cash day books of a business, the following transactions have been recorded.

(a)   A cash sale (ie a receipt) of $40
(b)   Payment of an electricity bill totalling $270
(c)   Buying some goods for cash at $150
(d)   Paying cash of $320 for an office desk

How would these four transactions be posted to the ledger accounts? For that matter, which ledger accounts should they be posted to? Don't forget that each transaction will be posted twice, in accordance with the rule of double entry.

Solution

(a)   The two sides of the transaction are:

(i)   Cash is received (**debit** entry in the bank account)

(ii)   Sales increase by $40 (**credit** entry in the revenue account)

BANK ACCOUNT

	$		$
Revenue a/c	40		

REVENUE ACCOUNT

	$		$
		Bank a/c	40

(Note that the entry in the bank account is cross-referenced to the revenue account and *vice versa*. This enables a person looking at one of the accounts to trace where the other half of the double entry can be found.)

(b)   The two sides of the transaction are:

(i)   Cash is paid (**credit** entry in the bank account)

(ii)   Electricity expense increases by $270 (**debit** entry in the electricity account)

BANK ACCOUNT

	$		$
		Electricity a/c	270

ELECTRICITY ACCOUNT

	$		$
Bank a/c	270		

(c)   The two sides of the transaction are:

(i)   Cash is paid (**credit** entry in the bank account)

(ii)   Purchases increase by $150 (**debit** entry in the purchases account)

BANK ACCOUNT

	$		$
		Purchases a/c	150

PURCHASES ACCOUNT

	$		$
Bank a/c	150		

(d)   The two sides of the transaction are:

(i)   Cash is paid (**credit** entry in the bank account)

(ii)   Assets (in this case, office furniture) increase by $320 (**debit** entry in office furniture account)

BANK ACCOUNT

	$		$
		Office furniture a/c (desk)	320

OFFICE FURNITURE (ASSET) ACCOUNT

	$		$
Bank a/c	320		

If all four of these transactions related to the same business, the **summary bank account** of that business would end up looking as follows.

BANK ACCOUNT

	$		$
Revenue a/c	40	Electricity a/c	270
		Purchases a/c	150
		Office furniture a/c	320

QUESTION

Cash day books

In the cash day books of a business, the following transactions have been recorded on 7 December 20X8.

(a) Received $37 for a cash sale
(b) Paid a rent bill of $6,000
(c) Paid $1,250 cash for some goods
(d) Paid $4,500 cash for some office shelves

Required

Draw the appropriate ledger ('T') accounts and show how these four transactions would be posted to them.

ANSWER

(a) The two sides of the transaction are:

(i) Cash is received (**debit** bank account)
(ii) Sales increase by $37 (**credit** revenue account)

BANK ACCOUNT

		$		$
07.12.X8	Revenue a/c	37		

REVENUE ACCOUNT

			$
	07.12.X1	Bank a/c	37

(b) The two sides of the transaction are:

(i) Cash is paid (**credit** bank account)
(ii) Rent expense increases by $6,000 (**debit** rent account)

BANK ACCOUNT

	$			$
		07.12.X8	Rent a/c	6,000

RENT ACCOUNT

		$		$
07.12.X8	Cash a/c	6,000		

(c) The two sides of the transaction are:

(i) Cash is paid (**credit** bank account)
(ii) Purchases increase by $1,250 (**debit** purchases account)

BANK ACCOUNT

	$			$
		07.12.X8	Purchases a/c	1,250

PURCHASES ACCOUNT

		$		$
07.12.X8	Bank a/c	1,250		

(d) The two sides of the transaction are:

(i) Cash is paid (**credit** bank account)
(ii) Assets (in this case, office furniture) increase by $4,500 (**debit** office furniture account)

BANK ACCOUNT

	$			$
		07.12.X8	Office furniture a/c	4,500

OFFICE FURNITURE (ASSET) ACCOUNT

		$		$
07.12.X8	Bank a/c	4,500		

Tutorial note. If all four of these transactions related to the same business, the bank account of that business would end up looking as follows.

BANK ACCOUNT

		$			$
07.12.X8	Revenue a/c	37	07.12.X8	Rent a/c	6,800
				Purchases a/c	1,250
				Office furniture a/c	4,500

1.3 Credit transactions: double entry

Not all transactions are settled immediately in cash. A business might purchase goods from its suppliers on **credit terms**, so that the suppliers would be **creditors** (accounts payable) of the business until settlement was made in cash. Equally, the business might grant credit terms to its customers who would then be **debtors** (accounts receivable) of the business. Clearly no entries can be made in the cash day books when a credit transaction occurs, because initially no cash has been received or paid. Where then can the details of the transactions be entered?

The solution to this problem is to use **ledger accounts for accounts receivable and accounts payable,** often referred to as receivables and payables.

Credit transactions	DEBIT	CREDIT
Sell goods on credit terms	Receivables	Revenue
Receive cash from customer	Bank	Receivables
Net effect = cash transaction	Bank	Revenue
Buy goods on credit terms	Purchases	Payables
Pay cash to creditor	Payables	Bank
Net effect = cash transaction	Purchases	Bank

The net effect in the ledger accounts is the same as for a cash transaction – the only difference is that there has been a time delay during which the receivables/payables accounts have been used.

You will see in the following example that, although a business has many customers, within the general ledger credit transactions from all customers are usually included in one account for receivables rather than keeping a separate general ledger account for each customer (although separate general ledger accounts may be kept if the business has only a few customers). The same is true for suppliers whose transactions usually all end up in one payables account in the general ledger.

The receivables and payables accounts collating all customer and supplier transactions are known as 'control' accounts (receivables control account and payables control account) and these are covered in detail later in this Text. A separate record of what each customer owes and what is owed to each supplier is usually kept outside of the general ledger and we look at this in Section 3.

Throughout the Text we adopt an approach where separate records (ledgers) known as personal accounts are kept for the purposes of keeping track of amounts owed from individual customers (or owed to individual suppliers). In the exam it can be assumed that separate personal ledgers are maintained unless another approach is referred to in the question.

1.4 Example: Credit transactions

Recorded in the sales day book and the purchase day book on 1 April 20X9 are the following transactions.

(a)   The business sells goods on credit to a customer Mr Ahmed for $3,200.

(b)   The business buys goods on credit from a supplier Blip for $2,000.

How and where are these transactions posted in the ledger accounts?

Solution

(a)

RECEIVABLES ACCOUNT

	$		$
1 Apr X9 Revenue a/c	3,200		

REVENUE ACCOUNT

	$		$
		1 Apr X9 Receivables account (Mr Ahmed)	3,200

(b)

PAYABLES ACCOUNT

	$		$
		1 Apr X9 Purchases a/c	2,000

PURCHASES ACCOUNT

	$		$
1 Apr X9 Payables a/c (Blip)	2,000		

1.5 Example continued: When cash is paid to suppliers or by customers

Suppose that, in the example above, the business paid $2,000 to Blip one month after the goods were acquired. The two sides of this new transaction are:

(a)   Cash is paid (**credit** entry in the bank account)

(b)   The amount owing to suppliers is reduced (**debit** entry in the payables account)

BANK ACCOUNT

	$		$
		1 May X9 Payables a/c (Blip)	2,000

PAYABLES ACCOUNT

	$		$
1 May X9 Bank a/c	2,000		

If we now bring together the two parts of this example, the original purchase of goods on credit and the eventual settlement in cash, we find that the accounts appear as follows.

BANK ACCOUNT

	$		$
		1 May X9 Payables a/c	2,000

PURCHASES ACCOUNT

	$		$
1 Apr X9 Payables a/c	2,000		

PAYABLES ACCOUNT

	$		$
1 May X9 Bank a/c	2,000	1 Apr X9 Purchases a/c	2,000

Over time the **two entries in the payables account cancel each other out**, indicating that no money is owing to suppliers any more. We are left with a credit entry of $2,000 in the cash account and a debit entry of $2,000 in the purchases account. These are exactly the entries which would have been made to record a **cash** purchase of $2,000. This is what we would expect: after the business has paid off its suppliers it is in exactly the position of a business which has made cash purchases of $2,000, and the accounting records reflect this similarity.

Similar reasoning applies when a **customer pays their account**. In the example above when Mr Ahmed pays his debt of $3,200 on 1 May 20X9 the two sides of the transaction are:

(a)   Cash is received (debit entry in the bank account)

(b)   The amount owed by customers is reduced (credit entry in the receivables account)

BANK ACCOUNT

	$		$
1 May X9 Receivables a/c (Mr Ahmed)	3,200		

RECEIVABLES ACCOUNT

	$			$
		1 May X9	Bank a/c	3,200

The accounts recording this sale to, and payment by, Mr Ahmed now appear as follows.

BANK ACCOUNT

	$		$
1 May X9 Receivables a/c	3,200		

REVENUE ACCOUNT

	$			$
		1 Apr X9	Receivables a/c	3,200

RECEIVABLES ACCOUNT

	$			$
1 Apr X9 Revenue a/c	3,200	1 May X9	Bank a/c	3,200

Again, over time the **two entries in the receivables account cancel each other out**, while the entries in the bank account and revenue account reflect the same position as if the sale had been made for cash. Receivables and payables exist in the period between the sale/purchase and the receipt/payment of money.

QUESTION

Debit and credit

Identify the debit and credit entries in the following transactions.

(a)   Bought a machine on credit from Angelo, cost $6,400
(b)   Bought goods on credit from Barnfield, cost $2,100
(c)   Sold goods on credit to Carla, value $750
(d)   Paid Daris (a supplier) $250
(e)   Collected $300 from Elsa, a customer
(f)   Paid wages of $5,000
(g)   Received rent bill of $1,000 from landlord Graham
(h)   Paid rent of $1,000 to landlord Graham
(i)   Paid an insurance premium of $150

ANSWER

(a)	DEBIT	Machine account (non-current asset)	$6,400	
	CREDIT	Payables (Angelo)		$6,400
(b)	DEBIT	Purchases account	$2,100	
	CREDIT	Payables (Barnfield)		$2,100
(c)	DEBIT	Receivables (Carla)	$750	
	CREDIT	Revenue		$750
(d)	DEBIT	Payables (Daris)	$250	
	CREDIT	Bank		$250
(e)	DEBIT	Bank	$300	
	CREDIT	Receivables (Elsa)		$300
(f)	DEBIT	Wages expense	$5,000	
	CREDIT	Bank		$5,000
(g)	DEBIT	Rent expense	$1,000	
	CREDIT	Payables (Graham)		$1,000
(h)	DEBIT	Payables (Graham)	$1,000	
	CREDIT	Bank		$1,000
(i)	DEBIT	Insurance expense	$150	
	CREDIT	Bank		$150

QUESTION

Transaction identification

Your business, which is not registered for sales tax, has the following transactions.

(a) The sale of goods on credit
(b) Credit notes to credit customers upon the return of faulty goods
(c) Daily cash takings paid into the bank

Required

For each transaction identify clearly:

(a) The original document(s)
(b) The book of prime entry for the transaction
(c) The way in which the data will be incorporated into the double entry system

ANSWER

		Original document	Book of prime entry	Accounts in general ledger to be posted to	
				DEBIT	*CREDIT*
(a)	Sale of goods on credit	Sales invoice	Sales day book	Receivables	Revenue
(b)	Allowances to credit customers	Credit note	Sales returns day book	Sales/Returns inward	Receivables
(c)	Daily cash takings	Till rolls and/or sales invoices and receipts, bank paying-in book	Cash receipts day book	Cash	Revenue

Tutorial note. All these transactions would be incorporated into the double entry system by means of periodic postings from the books of prime entry to the general ledger.

EXAM FOCUS POINT

The Examiner's report for September 2019 – August 2020 states that the easiest working for a question testing a candidate's understanding of double entry bookkeeping to a series of bank transactions would be to use a ledger account. It is important to note that if there is an overdraft at the start of the year it would be recorded as a credit balance. The bank account would be increased (debited) during the year by both the cash sales banked and the interest received and reduced (credited) by the overdraft interest and payments made.

2 Posting from the day books

> The accounts in the general ledger are **impersonal accounts**. There are also **personal accounts** for customers and suppliers and these are contained in the **receivables ledger** and **payables ledger**.

2.1 Sales day book to receivables account

Here are four transactions entered into the sales day book.

SALES DAY BOOK

Date	Invoice	Customer	Receivables ledger ref	Total amount invoiced	Boot sales	Shoe sales
20X8				$	$	$
Sept 10	540	Socco Shops	RL 22	207.45	159.09	48.36
	541	Richards	RL 31	42.77	42.77	
	542	Sandy & Co	RL 04	113.82		113.82
	543	Bits and Pieces Co	RL 42	2,409.00	1,861.00	547.20
				2,773.04	2,063.66	709.38

How do we post these transactions to the general ledger, and which accounts do we use in the general ledger?

We would post the total of the total amount invoiced column to the debit side of the receivables account (often called the **receivables control account**, whichever term is used, the word 'trade' is sometimes included) in the general ledger. The credit entries would be to the different sales accounts, in this case, boot sales and shoe sales.

RECEIVABLES CONTROL ACCOUNT

	$		$
Boot and shoe sales	2,773.04		

BOOT SALES

	$		$
		Receivables	2,063.66

SHOE SALES

	$		$
		Receivables	709.38

That is why the analysis of sales is kept. Exactly the same reasoning lies behind the analyses kept in other books of prime entry.

So how do we know how much we are owed by individual customers? The answer is that we keep two sets of accounts running in parallel – the **receivables control account** in the general ledger and the memorandum **receivables ledger** (individual debtor accounts). **Only the receivables control account is actually part of the double-entry system,** but **individual** debtors' transactions are posted to the receivables ledger from the sales day book.

2.2 Purchases day book to payables account

Here are four transactions entered into the purchase day book.

PURCHASE DAY BOOK

Date 20X8	Supplier (2)	Payables ledger ref (1)	Total amount Invoiced $	Purchases (3) $	Expenses $
Sept 15	R Dysan	PL 14	177.50	177.50	
	Peters and Co	PL 07	221.08	221.08	
	NW Power	PL 23	49.00		49.00
	Regally	PL 19	380.41	380.41	
			827.99	778.99	49.00

This time we will post the total of the total amount invoiced column to the credit side of the payables account (or **payables control account**, whichever term is used, the word 'trade' is sometimes included) in the general ledger. The debit entries are to the different expense accounts, in this case purchases and electricity.

PAYABLES CONTROL ACCOUNT

	$		$
		Purchases and electricity	827.99

PURCHASES

	$		$
Payables	778.99		

ELECTRICITY

	$		$
Payables	49.00		

Again, we keep a separate record of how much we owe individual suppliers by keeping two sets of accounts running in parallel – the **payables control account** in the general ledger, part of the double-entry system, and the memorandum **payables ledger** (individual suppliers' accounts). Individual suppliers' transactions are entered in their payables ledger account from the purchase day book.

Section summary

Credit transactions	DR		CR	
	Memorandum	General ledger*	General ledger*	Memorandum
Sell goods to Bits & Pieces Co	Receivables ledger: Bits & Pieces	Receivables control a/c	Revenue	–
Receive cash from Bits & Pieces Co	–	Bank a/c	Receivables control a/c	Receivables ledger: Bits & Pieces
Buy goods from R Dysan	–	Purchases	Payables control a/c	Payables ledger: R Dysan Ltd
Pay cash to R Dysan	Payables ledger: R Dysan	Payables control a/c	Bank a/c	–

*Individual transactions included in **totals** posted from books of prime entry.

In the next three sections of this chapter we shall look at the receivables and payables ledgers, and the total accounts, in more detail.

3 The receivables ledger

3.1 Impersonal accounts and personal accounts

Accounts in the general ledger (ledger accounts) relate to types of income, expense, asset, liability – rent, sales, receivables, payables etc – rather than to the person to whom the money is paid or from whom it is received. They are therefore called **impersonal accounts**. However, there is also a need for **personal accounts**, most commonly for customers and suppliers, and these are contained in the receivables ledger and payables ledger.

Personal accounts include details of transactions which have already been summarised in ledger accounts (eg sales invoices are recorded in revenue and receivables, payments to payables in the cash and payables accounts). **The personal accounts do not therefore form part of the double entry system**, as otherwise transactions would be recorded twice over (ie two debits and two credits for each transaction). They are **memorandum** accounts only.

3.2 Personal accounts in the receivables ledger

The receivables ledger consists of a number of personal **customer** accounts. They are separate accounts for each individual customer, and they enable a business to keep a continuous record of how much a customer owes the business at any time. The receivables ledger is often also known as the debtors ledger or sales ledger.

The **sales day book** provides a chronological record of invoices sent out by a business to credit customers. For many businesses, this might involve very large numbers of invoices per day or per week. The same customer might appear in several different places in the sales day book, for purchases they have made on credit at different times. So at any point in time, a customer may owe money on several unpaid invoices.

In addition to keeping a chronological record of invoices, a business should also keep a record of how much money each individual credit customer owes, and what this total debt consists of. The need for a **personal account for each customer** is therefore a practical one.

(a) A customer might **telephone**, and ask how much they currently owe. Staff must be able to tell them.

(b) It is a common practice to send out **statements** to credit customers at the end of each month, showing how much they still owe, and itemising new invoices sent out and payments received during the month.

(c) The managers of the business will want to keep a check on the **credit position** of an individual customer, and to ensure that no customer is exceeding their credit limit by purchasing more goods.

(d) Most important is the need to **match payments received against debts owed**. If a customer makes a payment, the business must be able to set off the payment against the customer's debt and establish how much they still owe on balance.

Receivables ledger accounts are written up as follows.

(a) When individual entries are made in the **sales day book** (invoices sent out), they are subsequently also made in the **debit side** of the relevant customer account in the receivables ledger.

(b) Similarly, when individual entries are made in the **cash receipts day book** (payments received), or in the sales returns day book, they are also made in the **credit side** of the relevant customer account.

Each customer account is given a reference or code number, and it is that reference which is the 'receivables ledger ref' in the **sales day book** and the cash day book. Amounts are **entered** from the sales day book and the cash day book into the receivables ledger.

Here is an example of how a receivables ledger account is laid out.

	BITS & PIECES			A/c no: RL 42
		$		$
10.9.X8 Balance b/d		670.50		
10.9.X8 Sales: SDB 253				
(invoice no 543)		2,409.00	10.9. X8 Balance c/d	3,079.50
		3,079.50		3,079.50
11.9.X8 Balance b/d		3,079.50		

The debit side of this personal account, then, shows amounts owed by Bits & Pieces. When Bits & Pieces pays some of the money it owes it will be recorded in the cash day book (receipts) and this receipt will subsequently be posted individually to the **credit** side of the personal account, the **credit** side of the receivables account (as part of a total) and the **debit** side of the bank account (as part of a total). For example, if Bits & Pieces paid $670.50 on 10.9.X8, it would appear as follows.

	BITS & PIECES			A/c no: RL 42
		$		$
10.9. X8 Balance b/d		670.50	10.9. X8 Bank	670.50
10.9. X8 Sales: SDB 253				
(invoice no 543)		2,409.00	10.9. X8 Balance c/d	2,409.50
		3,079.50		3,079.50
11.9. X8 Balance b/d		2,409.50		

The opening balance owed by Bits & Pieces on 11.9.X8 is now $2,409.50 instead of $3,079.50, because of the receipt of $670.50 which came in on 10.9.X8.

4 The payables ledger

The payables ledger, like the receivables ledger, consists of a number of **personal supplier accounts**. These are separate accounts for each individual supplier, and they enable a business to keep a continuous record of how much it owes each supplier at any time. The payables ledger is often known as the **bought ledger, creditors ledger or purchase ledger**.

After transactions are recorded in the purchase day book, cash payments day book, or purchase returns day book – ie after entries are made in the books of prime entry – they are also entered in the relevant supplier account in the payables ledger. The **double entry posting,** however, is to the **payables account** and the **cash account**.

Here is an example of how a payables ledger personal account is laid out.

	R. DYSAN			A/c no: PL 14
		$		$
			15.9. X8 Balance b/d	320.00
15.9. X8 Balance c/d		497.50	15.9. X8 Purchases: PDB 258	177.50
		497.50		497.50
			16 9. X8 Balance b/d	497.50

The credit side of this personal account, then, shows amounts owing to R. Dysan. If the business paid R. Dysan some money, it would be entered into the cash payments day book (payments) and subsequently be entered individually into the **debit** side of the personal account, and posted to the **debit** side of the payables account (as part of a total) and the **credit** side of the bank account (as part of a total). For example, if the business paid R. Dysan $150 on 15 September 20X8, it would appear as follows.

R DYSON			A/c no: PL 31	
	$			$
15.9. X8 Bank	150.00	15.9. X8 Balance b/d		320.00
15.9. X8 Balance c/d	347.50	15.9. X8 Purchases: PDB 258		177.50
	497.50			497.50
		16.9. X8 Balance b/d		347.50

The opening balance owed to R. Dysan on 16.9.X8 is now $347.50 instead of $497.50 because of the $150 payment made on 15.9.X8.

5 Control accounts

A **control account** is an account in the general ledger in which a record is kept of the total value of a number of similar but individual items.

– A **receivables control account** (or receivables account) records all transactions involving all customers in total.

– A **payables control account** (or payables account) records transactions involving all suppliers in total.

So far we have talked about the receivables and the payables control accounts being part of the double entry system in the general ledger, and effectively duplicating the entries to the receivables ledger and payables ledger respectively. So why do we need them? The answer is that they act as **control accounts.**

A control account is an account in the **general ledger** in which a record is kept of the **total** value of a number of similar but individual items. Control accounts are used chiefly for receivables and payables. **They should agree with the total of the individual balances** and act as a check to ensure that all transactions have been recorded correctly in the individual ledger accounts.

The receivables control account is a control account in which records are kept of transactions involving all customers **in total**. It is posted with **totals** from the **sales day book** and the **cash receipts day book**. The balance on the receivables control account at any time will be the total amount due to the business at that time from its customers, and will agree with the total of the receivables ledger accounts.

The payables control account is an account in which records are kept of transactions involving all suppliers **in total**, being posted with **totals** from the **purchase day book** and the **cash payments day book**. The balance on the payables control account at any time will be the total amount owed by the business at that time to its suppliers, and will agree with the total of the payables ledger accounts.

Note that it is the **control account balances** which will appear in the **final accounts** of the business; the receivables ledger and payables ledger act as memoranda for the list of individual account balances.

Although control accounts are used mainly in accounting for receivables and payables, they can also be kept for other items, such as inventories of goods, **wages and salaries** and **sales tax**. The same principles apply to all the other control accounts in the general ledger.

Section summary

Control accounts	Posted from	With	Agrees with	Part of general ledger double entry?
Receivables	Sales day book Sales returns day book Cash receipts day book	Totals	Receivables ledger balances in total	✓
Payables	Purchase day book Purchase returns day book Cash payments day book	Totals	Payable ledger balances in total	✓

Memorandum accounts	Posted from	With	Agrees with	Part of general ledger double entry?
Receivables ledger	As for control a/c	Individual transactions	Receivables a/c	×
Payables ledger	As for control a/c	Individual transactions	Payables a/c	×

QUESTION

Janet Andrew

Janet Andrew runs her own business as a sole trader. She needs an integrated manual system of accounting and has divided up the various accounts to form Cash Day Books, a Receivables Ledger, a Payables Ledger (all of which are part of the double entry) and a General Ledger. The following transactions have taken place.

(a) John Phillips, the landlord, is paid $2,300 rent by cheque. The liability had not previously been accounted for.

(b) $475 of goods are sold to R Sobers on credit.

(c) A credit note for $105 is issued to M Felix for goods returned.

(d) $3,175 of goods are purchased for resale from Rachet on credit.

(e) Equipment costing $15,000 is purchased by the business by cheque.

(f) An invoice for $75 is received being the installation charge for the equipment. A cheque is issued for this amount.

(g) The $3,175 owing to Rachet is paid by electronic bank transfer.

Required

For each transaction identify clearly:

(a) The name of the account to be debited.
(b) The ledger in which the account to be debited would be located.
(c) The name of the account to be credited.
(d) The ledger in which the account to be credited would be located.

ANSWER

	Account to be debited	*Ledger*	*Account to be credited*	*Ledger*
(a)	Rent	General	Bank	General
(b)	R Sobers	Receivables	Revenue	General
(c)	Returns inwards	General	M Felix	Receivables
(d)	Purchases	General	Rachet	Payables
(e)	Non-current assets	General	Bank	General
(f)	Non-current assets	General	Bank	General
(g)	Rachet	Payables	Bank	General

QUESTION

General ledger

(a) Name **five** accounts which may be found in the general ledger.

(b) Explain what **control accounts** are and what they are used for.

ANSWER

(a) Any five of the following.

- Plant and machinery
- Motor vehicles
- Inventory – raw materials
- Inventory – finished goods
- Receivables
- Payables
- Wages and salaries
- Rent
- Advertising expenses
- Bank charges
- Motor expenses
- Telephone expenses
- Revenue
- Total cash or bank overdraft

(b) A control account is an account in which a record is kept of the total value of a number of similar but individual items. They are used to **check** that the sum of the individual balances in receivables and payables ledgers is correct.

It is the control account balance which will appear in the final accounts of the business; the receivables ledger and payables ledger act as **memoranda**.

6 Sales tax

Sales tax rules can be quite complex but the main points to remember are:

– **Output tax** is charged on sales
– **Input tax** is incurred on purchases
– **Sales invoices** must show sales tax

Technical Performance Objective 10 is about demonstrating you are competent in preparing and completing sales tax/VAT returns. The knowledge you gain in this chapter will help you to demonstrate your competence in this area.

You may already be familiar with sales tax or VAT (Value Added Tax) as it is known in the UK, or the equivalent term applicable in your country. We will start with looking at how sales tax operates in general.

Many business transactions involve sales tax, and most invoices show any sales tax charged separately.

Sales tax is a tax levied on the sale of goods and services. Most of the work of collecting the tax falls on businesses, which hand the tax they collect over to the tax authorities.

Output tax Sales tax charged on goods and services sold by a business (that is, the business 'output').

Input tax Sales tax paid on goods and services bought in by a business.

6.1 Calculating sales tax

If a product has a **net price** of, say $120 and sales tax at 20% is to be added, then it is just a question of working out 20% of $120.

Sales tax $= \$120 \times 20/100$
$= \$24$

The **gross price** of the product is therefore $120 + $24 = $144. **It is always true that gross price = net price + sales tax.**

	$
Purchaser pays gross price	144
Tax authorities take sales tax	(24)
Seller keeps net price	120

If you are given the gross price of a product (say, $282), then you can work out the sales tax at 20% which it includes by multiplying by 20/120.

$$\$282 \times 20/120 = \$47$$

Therefore the net price must be $282 – $47 = $235.

EXAM FOCUS POINT

In the examples above we used a sales tax rate of 20%. This is for illustrative purposes only. Sales tax rates go up and down over time and vary from country to country. In the exam you will be given the rate to be used which could differ from question to question, so be sure to pay careful attention to this. In the questions and examples that follow we use different rates.

QUESTION   Sales tax

The gross price of Product A is $690 and the net price of Product B is $480. Sales tax is charged at 20%. What is the sales tax charged on each product?

ANSWER

(a)   Sales tax for product A = 20/120 × $690 = $115. (So net price was $690 – $115 = $575.)

(b)   Sales tax for product B = 20/100 × $480 = $96. (So gross price was $480 + $96 = $576.)

6.2 Input and output sales tax

Usually sales tax charged on sales (output tax) exceeds sales tax suffered on purchases (input tax). The excess is paid over to the tax authorities. If output tax is less than input tax in a period, the tax authorities will refund the difference to the business. In other words, if a business pays out more in sales tax than it receives from customers it will be paid back the difference.

Output tax received	Input tax paid	Total	Treatment
$1,000	$(900)	$100 received	Pay to tax authorities
$900	$(1,000)	$(100) paid	Refund from tax authorities

6.3 Example: Input and output tax

A company sells goods for $127,350 including sales tax at 20% in a quarter (three months of a year). It buys goods for $101,290 including sales tax. What amount will it pay to or receive from the tax authorities for the quarter (round to the nearest $)?

Solution

The **output tax** will be:

	$
$127,350 \times \dfrac{20}{120} =$	21,225

The **input tax** will be:

$101,290 \times \dfrac{20}{120} =$	(16,882)

The tax **payable** is the output

tax less the input tax = 4,343

Now that you know about double entry and the books of prime entry, it is appropriate to outline how sales tax is accounted for. The principles will be similar for most countries, although the rates will be different.

6.4 Statement of profit or loss

A business does not keep the output sales tax it charges – it pays it back to the tax authorities. It therefore follows that its **records of sales should not include sales tax.**

6.5 Example: accounting for output sales tax

If a business sells goods for $600 + $120 sales tax, ie for $720 gross price, the revenue account should only record the $600 excluding sales tax. The accounting entries for the sale would be as follows (the sales tax rate used in this example is 20%):

DEBIT	Bank **or** trade receivables	$720	
CREDIT	Revenue		$600
CREDIT	Sales tax account (output sales tax)		$120

Similarly, the business does not want to show input sales tax paid on purchases as a cost of the business – it must reclaim it from the tax authorities. However, the cost of purchases in the statement of profit or loss may or may not include the 'input' sales tax paid, depending on whether or not the input sales tax is recoverable.

(a)   If input sales tax is **recoverable**, the cost of purchases should exclude the tax. For example, if a business purchases goods on credit for $400 + recoverable sales tax $80, the transaction would be recorded as follows.

DEBIT	Purchases	$400	
DEBIT	Sales tax account (input sales tax)	$80	
CREDIT	Trade payables		$480

(b)   If the input sales tax is **not recoverable**, the cost of purchases must include the tax, because it is the business itself which must bear the cost of the tax.

DEBIT	Purchases	$480	
CREDIT	Trade payables		$480

6.6 When is sales tax accounted for?

Sales tax is accounted for when it first arises – when recording credit purchases/sales in credit transactions, and when recording cash received or paid in cash transactions.

6.6.1 Sales tax in credit transactions

When a business makes a credit sale the total amount invoiced, including sales tax, will be recorded in the **sales day book**. The analysis columns will then separate the sales tax from the sales income of the business as follows.

			Sales tax
Date	Total	Revenue	(20%)
	$	$	$
Johnson & Co	2,400	2,000	400

When a business is invoiced by a supplier the total amount payable, including sales tax, will be recorded in the **purchase day book**. The analysis columns will then separate the recoverable input sales tax from the purchase cost to the business as follows.

Date	Total	Purchase cost	Sales tax
	$	$	$
Mayhew (Merchants)	576	480	96

When customers pay what they owe, or suppliers are paid, there is no need then to show the sales tax in an analysis column of the relevant cash day book, because input and output sales tax were recorded when the sale or purchase was made, not when the debt is settled.

6.6.2 Sales tax in credit transactions: cash flow implications

Before we move on to look at cash transactions, we will just pause to consider the important cash flow implications for businesses of paying sales tax based on credit transactions.

It is the customers of a business who actually pay the output tax. The business just collects it on the authority's behalf from its customers. However it could be that the business needs to offer its customers a long period of credit (or its customers are just slow payers!). If this is the case and prompt payment of sales tax is made to the tax authority, the business will have to advance a large sum of money it has not yet collected and will need to ensure it has appropriate funds to do so.

The effect will be reduced to some degree if suppliers also offer the business a long period of credit meaning the input tax is recovered before it needs to be paid to suppliers (via payment of their invoices). However if the company also has to pay its suppliers promptly, the problem will be even worse and more cash will need to be found in the short term.

We look at cash flow implications again later in the chapter when we consider some of the alternative sales tax schemes set up by the UK tax authority to help small businesses with managing cash flows.

6.6.3 Sales tax in cash transactions

Sales tax charged on **cash sales** or sales tax paid on **cash purchases will be analysed in a separate column of the relevant cash day book**. This is because output sales tax, having just arisen from the cash sale, must be credited to the sales tax account. Similarly, input sales tax paid on cash purchases, having just arisen, must be debited to the sales tax account.

For example, the cash day books for Peter Jeffries which we saw in Section 5 of Chapter 3 would be written up as shown on the following page if items (a), (e) and new item (l) were cash transactions involving sales tax. In this example, we are using a sales tax rate of 20%.

PETER JEFFRIES – CASH RECEIVED DAY BOOK

RECEIPTS

Date 20X1	Narrative	Folio	Total $	Output sales tax on cash sales $	Receipts from customers $	Cash sales $	Other $
	(a) Cash sale		220	36.67		183.33	
	(b) Debtor pays: Khan	SL07	3,100		3,100		
	(c) Debtor pays: Likert	SL12	1,480		1,480		
	(d) Debtor pays: Lee	SL10	2,400		2,400		
	(e) Cash sale		190	31.67		158.33	
	(f) Non-current asset sale		370				370
			7,760	68.34	6,980	341.66	370

PETER JEFFRIES – CASH PAYMENTS DAY BOOK

PAYMENTS

Date 20X1	Narrative	Folio	Total $	Input sales on cash purchases $	Payments to suppliers $	Exps $	Non-current assets $
10 Jan	(g) Creditor paid: Price	PL27	1,250.00		1,250		
	(h) Creditor paid: Burn	PL16	2,420.00		2,420		
	(i) Telephone expense		235.00			235.00	
	(j) Gas expense		640.00			640.00	
	(k) Plant & machinery purchase		3,400.00				3,400
	(l) Cash purchase: Stationery		149.75	24.96		124.79	
			8,094.75	24.96	3,670	999.79	3,400

6.7 The sales tax account

The sales tax paid to or recovered from the authorities is the **balance on the sales tax account**. This is a control account to which these items are posted.

* The total input sales tax in the purchases day book (**debit**)
* The total output sales tax in the sales day book (**credit**)
* Sales tax on cash sales (**credit**)
* Sales tax on cash purchases (**debit**)

For example, if Peter Jeffries is invoiced for input sales tax of $175 on his credit purchases and charges sales tax of $450 on his credit sales on 10 January 20X8, his sales tax account would be as follows.

SALES TAX ACCOUNT

	$		$
Purchase day book (input sales tax)	175.00	Sales day book (output sales tax invoiced)	450.00
Bank (input sales tax on cash purchases)	24.96	Bank (output sales tax on cash sales)	68.34
Balance c/d (owed to tax authorities)	318.38		
	518.34		518.34

Payments to or refunds from the tax authorities do not coincide with the end of the accounting period of a business, and so at the reporting date there will be a balance on the sales tax account. If this balance is for an amount **payable**, the outstanding liability for sales tax will appear as a **current liability**. Occasionally, a business will be **owed money** back by the tax authorities, and in such a situation, the sales tax refund owed by the tax authorities would be a **current asset**.

EXAM FOCUS POINT

Unless you are told otherwise in the exam, you should assume the following postings will be made for sales tax transactions. We use a sales tax rate of 20% in this example but you could be given a different rate in the exam.

Credit transactions	DR		CR	
	Memorandum	*General ledger*	*General ledger*	*Memorandum*
Sell goods on credit	Receivables ledger 120.00	Receivables control account 120.00	Revenue 100.00 Sales tax 20.00	–
Receive cash in settlement	–	Bank 120.00	Receivables control account 120.00	Receivables ledger 120.00
Buy goods on credit	–	Purchases 100.00 Sales tax 20.00	Payables control account 120.00	Payables ledger 120.00
Pay cash in settlement	Payables ledger 120.00	Payables control account 120.00	Bank 120.00	–
Cash transactions				
Sell goods for cash	–	Bank 120.00	Revenue 100.00 Sales tax 20.00	–
Buy goods for cash	–	Purchases 100.00 Sales tax 20.00	Bank 120.00	–

6.8 Example: the UK Sales Tax system

Having looked in general at the way in which sales tax is calculated and accounted for, we will use the UK sales tax, VAT, to illustrate some other aspects of sales tax systems that businesses must consider. This includes registration for sales tax, different types of taxable supplies, and penalties arising for late payment of sales tax or late filing of returns.

6.8.1 Overview of the UK system

The VAT system in the UK is administered by HM Revenue & Customs (HMRC).

Businesses registered for VAT in the UK are allocated a registration number which must be included on invoices and other business documents.

A business registered for VAT in the UK must charge its customers VAT on all of its taxable supplies or sales normally at the standard rate. This is the output tax we referred to earlier when talking about sales tax in general. The VAT that the business pays when buying from suppliers or paying expenses can be recovered back from HMRC. This is the Input tax.

Under the standard system of VAT in the UK, the business completes a VAT return every three months showing the output and input VAT. The business effectively acts as an agent for HMRC. The excess of output VAT over input VAT must be paid to HMRC with the VAT return. However, if the input VAT exceeds the output VAT then a refund is due from HMRC. It VAT is owed, the VAT return and payment of the VAT owed are usually due one month after the end of the VAT period.

Regardless of the country which is operating the sales tax system, if sales tax returns or payments are late, there is likely to be interest, surcharges or penalties arising.

In the UK, there is a surcharge system. If a business does not submit a VAT return and pay over any VAT due on the return within the stated period, HMRC warns the business that if the business defaults in respect of an accounting period within the next 12 months then a default surcharge will be issued.

The surcharge is based on a percentage of the VAT that is unpaid ranging between 2% and 15% (HMRC, 2018). If the business does not send in a VAT return then the amount of VAT owed will be assessed and the surcharge will be based upon this assessment. HMRC (and indeed other sales tax authorities) may also charge interest on unpaid VAT (sales tax).

6.8.2 Sources of information

HMRC issues advice notes and guidance online via its website and also issues a 'VAT Guide', which provides a business with all the information it needs about accounting for, recording and paying over VAT.

Tax authorities in all countries operating a sales tax system will have similar procedures for keeping businesses up to date on how they should be accounting for sales tax.

6.8.3 Registration

Registration rules vary from country to country but, in the UK, if the **taxable sales** of a business exceed a certain amount for a year then a business **must** register for VAT.

If a business's level of taxable sales is below the annual registration limit it is still possible for the business to register for VAT on a **voluntary basis**. A business might do this to recover input tax, especially if a business makes zero-rated supplies (we look at the different types of taxable supplies and their rates below) then it may be advantageous to register for VAT.

This is because zero-rated supplies have an output VAT rate of 0%. Therefore nothing has to be charged on its sales. At the same time it can still reclaim any input VAT on its purchases and expense which results in the business being in a net cash repayment position.

Some businesses may want to register for VAT to enhance the image of the business. However the disadvantages include:

(a)   The administrative burden of preparing regular VAT returns
(b)   The potential for incurring penalties
(c)   Loss of business from non-registered customers if prices increase by output tax

6.8.4 Types of supply

Supplies of goods or services fall into one of three categories:

(a)   **Outside the scope of VAT**. Supplies outside the scope of VAT have no effect for VAT. These include paying wages or dividends.

(b)   **Exempt supplies**. These are supplies on which no VAT is charged at all, at any rate. Examples include some postal services, education, healthcare, insurance and betting/gambling. A supplier selling only exempt supplies cannot register for VAT and so cannot reclaim the input VAT on any of their purchases and expenses. For example, an insurance company cannot reclaim the VAT on its expenses as its supplies (selling insurance) are exempt. So the cost to the insurance company of its purchases and expenses is the VAT inclusive amount.

(c)   **Taxable supplies**. The supplies not falling into the two categories above are taxable supplies. There are currently three rates of VAT in the UK.

  (i)   **Standard rate**. Standard rates have varied for this since VAT was introduced, but in recent years the rates most commonly used have been 17.5% and 20% of the value of most goods and services. At the time of writing this text, the UK standard rate is 20%. If the standard rate is set at 20%, this means if you sell a standard rated item which is worth £100 you must also charge £20 in tax, so that the total paid by your customer will be £120. (Note that the prices you pay in shops generally **include** VAT.)

  (ii)   **Zero-rate**. This is 0% and applies to most food (other than restaurant and hot take-away meals), books, newspapers, most young children's clothing, sales of new houses and exports. Zero-rated supplies are often essential items which, if they were taxed, would be an additional burden to the less well-off.

  (iii)   **Reduced rate**. This is set at 5% and applies to the installation of certain energy saving materials and to fuel and power used in the home and by charities.

EXAM FOCUS POINT

Please note that the rates for the UK used above are just one example of rates of sales tax within a particular country at a particular point in time. Rates vary over time and other countries have different rates of sales tax – for example sales tax is charged by all members of the European Union, but different rates are applied by different members. As we pointed out before, any questions involving VAT/Sales Tax in your exam will include the appropriate rates – you are not required to memorise tax rates.

Now is a good time to emphasise the difference between exempt supplies and zero-rated supplies. If a supplier sells exempt supplies then that supplier **cannot reclaim the input VAT on purchases** and expenses. However a business which sells zero-rated supplies charges output VAT at 0% on its sales is allowed to VAT register and so can reclaim any input VAT on its purchases.

6.8.5 Information to be included on VAT invoices

If a business is registered for VAT in the UK and it sends out an invoice to another VAT– registered business then it must send a VAT invoice within 30 days of the supply as shown on the following page:

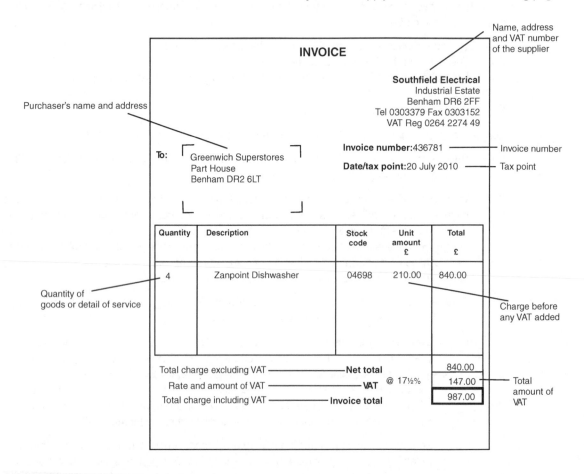

6.8.6 Special schemes for small businesses

Some countries have special schemes which make sales tax accounting easier for small businesses which fall under specified taxable sales limits. Three such schemes in the UK are as follows.

(a)   **Annual accounting scheme**. This scheme is helpful to small businesses as it cuts down the administrative burden of VAT by allowing the business to submit one VAT return every 12 months. The taxable sales limits are regularly reviewed and are based on VAT exclusive sales.

The VAT return is due within two months of the end of the year. Under this scheme the business makes nine (usually) equal monthly direct debit payments of 1/10 of the estimated of the amount of VAT liability for the year. If the business has been trading for a period of time, the estimate will usually be the liability of the previous 12 months. The first payment is due at the end of the fourth month. The balancing payment will be sent with the VAT return, within two months after the year end.

(b)   **Cash accounting scheme**. Provided a business has a clean record with HMRC, it may be able to apply to use this scheme. All VAT returns and payments must be up to date. Again, the taxable sales limits are based on VAT exclusive sales.

The scheme allows the accounting for VAT to be based upon the date of receipt or payment of money rather than on the invoice date.

This is useful for a business which gives its customers a long period of credit but has to pay its suppliers promptly as under the cash accounting scheme output VAT will be paid to HMRC later as cash is received later from customers, but input VAT is reclaimed at the same time/earlier as suppliers are paid early.

However it is not suitable for a business which receives a long period of credit from its suppliers but receives payment promptly from its customers as, under the cash accounting scheme, output tax will be paid to HMRC at the same time/earlier as cash is received early from customers, but input tax is reclaimed later as suppliers are paid later.

The scheme also gives automatic relief from irrecoverable debts since no output VAT is payable to HMRC if the customer does not pay.

VAT return and payment dates are as for the standard scheme (quarterly returns), unless the business is also in the annual accounting scheme.

(c)   **Flat rate scheme**. This scheme allows some businesses to account for VAT by applying a **flat rate percentage** to the business's total business supplies for a period, the result being the VAT owed to HMRC. The taxable sales limits are a lot lower than for the annual accounting scheme and the cash accounting scheme. The limits for joining the scheme are based on VAT exclusive sales, but the point at which a business must leave the scheme depends on the level of VAT inclusive sales.

The main advantages of this scheme are:

(i)   It simplifies the administration considerably, as VAT does not have to be accounted for on each individual sales and purchase invoice

(ii)   There is frequently less VAT payable to HMRC than under the normal rules

There are different flat rates set by HMRC for different trade sectors. This percentage is applied to the **VAT inclusive** turnover of the business. However note **that there is no deduction for input VAT**. Therefore the rate applied is **lower** than the standard rate of VAT.

VAT returns and payments are made as for the standard scheme.

6.9 Errors on sales tax returns

Sometimes businesses make errors when recording sales tax, when they extract sales tax information from the accounting system, or when they enter information on the sales tax return. This may mean that they have over or under paid sales tax to the authorities. It is important that the tax authorities are notified as soon as such errors are picked up.

If errors are not deemed to be large, tax authorities may allow adjustment for them to be made on the next sales tax return. For example a 'small' understatement of output tax on a previous return can be shown as an increase in the output tax on the current return, and similarly a 'small' overstatement of input tax on a previous return can be shown as a decrease in the input tax on the current return.

QUESTION

Sales tax error

A business slightly overstated input tax on the sales tax return in a prior period and has just picked up the error. What effect will this have on the current sales tax payable to the tax authorities?

ANSWER

An increase in the sales tax payable via the current return. There was too much input tax deducted on the previous return, so the input tax on the current return needs to be reduced, resulting in an increase in the amount of sales tax due.

If a larger error is made (over a limit set by the tax authorities), or the tax authority involved does not allow adjustment via a future return, the relevant department of the tax authority must be informed of the error as soon as possible, in writing (using any specific form provided by the authority if there is one).

Interest may be charged on unpaid sales tax and there may well be a penalty. The penalty may be a percentage of the unpaid tax or additional reclaim. The level of any penalty (or percentage charge) is likely to depend on the type of error made and the **nature** of it. If it appears that reasonable care was taken in preparing the incorrect return(s), then the authorities may reduce the penalty. Additionally disclosure of the error will usually reduce the level of any penalty.

6.10 Changes in rates of sales tax

A change in the standard rate of sales tax has both a financial and operational impact on a business.

A change in the sales tax rate will mean that from a certain date a different amount of sales tax must be charged on certain supplies. Of course, when the standard rate changes it will be applicable to both inputs and outputs.

Let's consider the effect of a **sales tax rate increase**, say from 20% to 22%.

First of all we can re-visit the **cash flow implications** we talked about earlier in Section 6.6.2. If prices to customers stay the same, these cash flow implications are magnified by the use of a higher rate. More cash needs to be advanced to the tax authority in advance of collection from customers. A decrease in the rate will have the opposite effect.

Where a business has a **computerised accounting system or tills** this can give rise to problems. The systems will be set to calculate sales tax at a set percentage for certain supplies. In these circumstances it is usual for the company that developed the software package to give instructions as to how the sales tax rate can be changed on the system. Of course, this applies whether the rate change is an increase or decrease.

If a manual system is in use the trader simply needs to ensure that they are careful about applying the correct tax rate for a particular supply.

The business also needs to consider the **effect on customers**. If the customers are registered for sales tax then they should also be aware of changes in legislation.

However, where customers are not registered, for example in a retail business (where the customer is the general public), notice should be given to customers about changes in rates. In a retail environment this would usually be via notices displayed around the store. A change in rate could impact on the charge to the customer.

An item costing a customer $1,200 (inclusive of sales tax) before would now cost $1,220 if the trader intends to have the same sales tax exclusive charge. An alternative is for the trader to keep the same sales tax inclusive price so that there is no impact on their customers, but this will reduce the business's profits. Note that this means a rate decrease could favour the trader here if customers do not demand a decrease in price when there is a reduction in the sales tax rate.

EXAM FOCUS POINT

The September 2018 – August 2019 Examiner's report explained that with all sales tax questions, the most important thing is to recognise if the figures are inclusive or exclusive of sales tax and what the sales tax rate is.

The specific question in the report clearly stated that the figures were exclusive of sales tax at 15%. The question asked what the input tax amount was on the transactions.

Input tax is the tax on expenditures (with output tax being the tax on income), so candidates needed to calculate the sales tax at 15% on any purchases, costs and acquisitions of assets.

7 The journal

A **journal** keeps a record of unusual movements between accounts. The format of a journal is:

		$	$
DEBIT	Account to be debited	X	
CREDIT	Account to be credited		X

Narrative to explain the transaction

You should remember that one of the books of prime entry is the journal.

The journal keeps a record of unusual movement between accounts. It is used to record any double entries made which do not arise from the other books of prime entry.

Whatever type of transaction is being recorded, the **format of a journal entry** is:

Date		Folio		
			$	$
DEBIT	Account to be debited		X	
CREDIT	Account to be credited			X
Narrative to explain the transaction				

(Remember: in due course, the ledger accounts will be written up to include the transactions listed in the journal.)

A narrative explanation **must** accompany each journal entry. It is required for audit and control, to indicate the purpose and authority of every transaction which is not first recorded in a book of prime entry.

7.1 Example: Journal entries

The following is a summary of the transactions of the Manon Beauty Salon of which David Blake is the sole proprietor.

1 October	Put in cash of $5,000 as capital
	Purchased brushes, combs and scissors for cash of $185
	Purchased hair driers from Juno Ltd on credit for $240
30 October	Paid three months rent to 31 December of $500
	Collected and paid in to the bank takings of $1,000
31 October	Gave Mrs Sweet a perm and manicure on credit for $100

Show the transactions by means of journal entries.

Solution

JOURNAL

			$	$
1 October	DEBIT	Bank	5,000	
	CREDIT	David Blake: capital account		5,000
		Initial capital introduced		
1 October	DEBIT	Brushes, combs and scissors account	185	
	CREDIT	Bank		185
		The purchase for cash of brushes etc as non-current assets		
1 October	DEBIT	Hair dryer account	240	
	CREDIT	Sundry payables account *		240
		The purchase on credit of hair driers as non-current assets		
30 October	DEBIT	Rent account	500	
	CREDIT	Bank		500
		The payment of rent to 31 December		
30 October	DEBIT	Bank	1,000	
	CREDIT	Revenue		1,000
		Cash takings		
31 October	DEBIT	Receivables account	100	
	CREDIT	Revenue		100
		The provision of a hair-do and manicure on credit		

*Note. Balances due for the supply of non-current assets are included amongst **sundry payables**, as distinct from creditors who have supplied goods for resale, who are **trade payables**. It is quite common to have separate 'payables' accounts, one for trade payables and another for sundry other payables.

7.2 The correction of errors

The journal is most commonly used to record **corrections to errors that have been made** in writing up the general ledger accounts. Errors corrected by the journal **must be capable of correction by means of a double entry** in the ledger accounts. In other words, the error must not have caused total debits and total credits to be unequal. (When errors are made which break the rules of double entry, a suspense account must first be created; this is explained in Chapter 6.)

7.3 Journal vouchers

Journal entries might be logged, not in a single 'book' or journal, but on a separate slip of paper, called a journal voucher.

A **journal voucher** is used to record the equivalent of one entry in the journal.

The use of journal vouchers is fairly widespread because of:

(a)   The **repetitive nature** of certain journal entries (vouchers can be pre-printed to standardise the narrative of such entries, and to save time in writing them out).

(b)   A voucher is able to hold **more information** than a conventional journal record.

8 The trial balance

Balances on ledger accounts can be collected in a **trial balance**. The debit and credit balances should be **equal**.

We have already seen that, via the technique of double entry bookkeeping the dual aspect of accounting transactions is reflected in the accounts using debits and credits. It follows that if each transaction involves equal debit and credit entries, the total of all debits will equal the total of all credits.

Although there is no foolproof method for making sure that all entries have been posted to the correct ledger account, a technique which shows up the more obvious mistakes is to prepare a **trial balance**.

A trial balance is a list of ledger account balances shown in debit and credit columns. It is sometimes known as the list of balances and it is used as a basis for preparing the final accounts. Its purpose is to **highlight certain errors** that may have occurred in the double entry accounting system.

The trial balance also serves other purposes as follows.

(a)   To provide summary values for certain key information (eg the totals of trade receivables and payables)

(b)   To speed up the process of preparing the final accounts (through the provision of summary values and confirmation that certain errors have not occurred)

The trial balance can be viewed as the point at which recording transactions (bookkeeping) ends and preparing the final accounts (accounting) commences. It is important to note that, although the trial balance is useful for discovering some errors, there are certain types of error that will not be detected when a trial balance is prepared. We look at errors detected and not detected by a trial balance in Sections 8.5 and 8.6. We will start by looking at how the ledger accounts are collected and balanced, and then how the balances on these accounts are listed in the trial balance.

8.1 Collecting together the ledger accounts

Before you draw up a trial balance, you must have a **collection of ledger accounts**. This involves balancing each account by adding up all the debits and the credits in each account separately and deducting the smaller total from the larger total. The difference is the balance. If the total of the debits in the account is larger than the total credits then the balance on the account is a debit balance.
If the total of the credits in the account is larger than the total debits then the balance on the account is a credit balance.

These are the ledger accounts of James McHugh, a sole trader.

BANK

	$		$
Capital: James McHugh	10,000	Rent	4,200
Bank loan	3,000	Shop fittings	3,600
Revenue	14,000	Payables control account	7,000
Receivables control account	3,300	Bank loan interest	130
		Incidental expenses	2,200
		Drawings	1,800
			18,930
		Balancing figure: the amount of cash left over after payments have been made	11,370
	30,300		30,300

CAPITAL (JAMES McHUGH)

	$		$
		Bank	10,000

BANK LOAN

	$		$
		Bank	3,000

PURCHASES

	$		$
Payables control account	7,000		

PAYABLES CONTROL ACCOUNT

	$		$
Bank	7,000	Purchases	7,000

RENT

	$		$
Bank	4,200		

SHOP FITTINGS

	$		$
Bank	3,600		

REVENUE

	$		$
		Cash	14,000
		Receivables control account	3,300
			17,300

RECEIVABLES CONTROL ACCOUNT

	$		$
Revenue	3,300	Cash	3,300

BANK LOAN INTEREST

	$		$
Bank	130		

OTHER EXPENSES

	$		$
Bank	2,200		

DRAWINGS ACCOUNT

	$		$
Bank	1,800		

The first step is to **'balance' each account**.

8.2 Balancing ledger accounts

At the end of an accounting period, a balance is struck on each account in turn. This means that all the **debits** on the account are totalled and so are all the **credits**.

- If the total debits exceed the total credits there is said to be a debit balance on the account.
- If the total credits exceed the total debits then the account has a credit balance.

Action		Eg James McHugh's Bank a/c
Step 1	Calculate a total for both sides of each ledger account	DEBIT $30,300, CREDIT $18,930
Step 2	Deduct the lower total from the higher total	$(30,300 – 18,930) = $11,370
Step 3	Insert the result of Step 2 as the balance c/d on the side of the account with the lower total	Here it will go on the credit side, because the total credits on the account are less than the total debits

Action		Eg James McHugh's Bank a/c
Step 4	Check that the totals on both sides of the account are now the same	DEBIT $30,300, CREDIT $(18,930 + 11,370) = $30,300
Step 5	Insert the amount of the balance c/d as the new balance b/d on the other side of the account. The new balance b/d is the balance on the account	The balance b/d on the account is $11,370 DEBIT

In our simple example, there is very little balancing to do.

(a)   Both the trade payables account and the receivables account balance off to zero.
(b)   The bank account has a debit balance (the new balance b/d) of $11,370 (see above).
(c)   The total on the revenue account is $17,300, which is a credit balance.

Otherwise, the accounts have only one entry each, so there is no totalling to do to arrive at the balance on each account.

8.3 Collecting the balances on the ledger accounts

If the basic principle of double entry has been correctly applied throughout the period it will be found that the **credit balances equal the debit balances** in total. This can be illustrated by collecting together the balances on James McHugh's accounts.

	DEBIT $	CREDIT $
Bank	11,370	
Capital		10,000
Bank loan		3,000
Purchases	7,000	
Trade payables	–	–
Rent	4,200	
Shop fittings	3,600	
Revenue		17,300
Receivables	–	–
Bank loan interest	130	
Other expenses	2,200	
Drawings	1,800	
	30,300	30,300

It does not matter in what order the various accounts are listed in the **trial balance**, because it is not a document that a business **has** to prepare. It is just a method used to test the accuracy of the double entry bookkeeping methods.

8.4 What if the trial balance shows unequal debit and credit balances?

If the two columns of the trial balance are not equal, there must be an **error in recording of transactions in the accounts** or an error in balancing the individual accounts.

8.5 Possible errors not revealed in the trial balance

EXAM FOCUS POINT

This topic in one that is likely to be regularly examined.

A trial balance, however, will **not** disclose the following types of errors.

(a)   The **complete omission** of a transaction, because neither a debit nor a credit is made (an error of omission). For example, if an invoice for purchases worth $200 was mislaid before it was recorded, the books would still balance. Both purchases and creditors would be understated by $200.

(b)   The posting of a debit or credit to the correct side of the ledger, but to a **wrong account** (sometimes called **errors of commission**). For example, if the invoice referred to above was entered as a credit to the account of a different supplier and the debit either correctly to purchases or incorrectly to an expense account, the books would be incorrect, but they would still balance.

(c)   **Compensating errors** (eg debit error of $100 is exactly cancelled by credit $100 error elsewhere) These are unconnected errors which by coincidence cancel out.

(d)   **Error of principle** (eg cash received from customers being debited to the receivables account and credited to bank instead of the other way round). Another example of an error of principle is where a purchase of, say, $200 has been credited to revenue and debited to receivables instead of debited to purchases and credited to payables.

(e)   **Posting incorrect amounts**. An example of this type of error would be when an invoice is misread and instead of the correct amount of say $600, $800 is posted as both a debit and credit. The trial balance would still balance.

(f)   **Error of original entry**. This arises where the original entry has been wrongly recorded in the day book.

(g)   **Error of reversal**. In this case debit and credit entries have been reversed.

8.6 Possible errors which will be revealed by the trial balance

Those errors which **will** be revealed by the trial balance are:

(a)   Error of partial omission (error of single entry). In this case either the debit or the credit entry will be missing.

(b)   Error of transposition, eg $209 posted as $290. This will be detected where the error is made on **one** entry. If the transposition error is made in both debit and credit postings, this will not be picked up by the trial balance.

(c)   Both entries posted to either debit or credit.

(d)   The wrong amount on **one** entry.

Summary

Type of error	Detected by trial balance	Notes
Complete omission	No	Whole transaction missing
Partial omission	Yes	One side of transaction missing
Commission	No	Posting to wrong account
Principle	No	Posting to wrong category of account
Compensating	No	Errors cancel each other out
Original entry	No	Wrong amount posted to both sides
Transposition	Yes	Detected if error made on one entry only (not detected if error is made in both debit and credit postings)
Reversal	No	Debit and credit entries reversed
Reversal – one side	Yes	Gives two debits or two credits
Original entry – one side	Yes	**One** entry has wrong amount

8.7 Usefulness and limitations of the trial balance

We have seen how a trial balance can be extracted from a set of T accounts. Later in the text we shall see how to derive a statement of profit or loss and statement of financial position from the trial balance. The usefulness of the trial balance as a method of deriving the financial statements is that it brings out clearly the relationship between the statement of profit and loss and statement of financial position.

The main limitation of the trial balance is that it only shows that the total debits equal the total credits and that the arithmetic is correct. There are a number of errors as explained above which will not be revealed by a balanced TB.

8.8 Example: Trial balance

As at the end of 29 November 20X8, your business Light & Mighty has the following balances on its ledger accounts.

Account	Balance
	$
Bank loan	15,000
Bank	13,080
Capital	11,000
Rates	2,000
Trade payables	14,370
Purchases	16,200
Revenue	18,900
Sundry payables	2,310
Receivables	13,800
Bank loan interest	1,000
Other expenses	12,500
Vehicles	3,000

During 30 November the business made the following transactions.

(a)   Bought materials for $1,400, half for cash and half on credit
(b)   Made $1,610 sales, $1,050 of which were for credit
(c)   Paid wages to shop assistants of $300

You are required to draw up a trial balance showing the balances as at the end of 30 November 20X8.

Solution

Step 1   Put the opening balances into a trial balance, ie decide which are debit and which are credit balances.

Account	DEBIT	CREDIT
	$	$
Bank loan		15,000
Bank	13,080	
Capital		11,000
Rates	2,000	
Trade payables		14,370
Purchases	16,200	
Revenue		18,900
Sundry payables		2,310
Receivables	13,800	
Bank loan interest	1,000	
Other expenses	12,500	
Vehicles	3,000	
	61,580	61,580

Step 2   Take account of the effects of the three transactions which took place on 30 November 20X8.

			$	$
(a)	DEBIT	Purchases	1,400	
	CREDIT	Bank		700
		Payables control account		700
(b)	DEBIT	Bank	560	
		Receivables control account	1,050	
	CREDIT	Revenue		1,610
(c)	DEBIT	Other expenses	300	
	CREDIT	Bank		300

Step 3   Amend the trial balance for these entries.

LIGHT & MIGHTY: TRIAL BALANCE AT 30 NOVEMBER 20X8

	12/11/20X8 DEBIT	12/11/20X8 CREDIT		Transactions DEBIT	Transactions CREDIT		30/11/20X8 DEBIT	30/11/20X8 CREDIT
Bank loan		15,000						15,000
Bank	13,080		(b)	560	700	(a)	12,640	
					300	(c)		
Capital		11,000						11,000
Rates	2,000						2,000	
Trade payables		14,370			700	(a)		15,070
Purchases	16,200		(a)	1,400			17,600	
Revenue		18,900			1,610	(b)		20,510
Sundry payables		2,310						2,310
Receivables	13,800		(b)	1,050			14,850	
Bank loan interest	1,000						1,000	
Other expenses	12,500		(c)	300			12,800	
Vehicles	3,000						3,000	
	61,580	61,580		3,310	3,310		63,890	63,890

QUESTION

Bailey Hughes

Bailey Hughes started trading as a wholesale bookseller on 1 June 20X8 with a capital of $10,000 with which he opened a bank account for his business.

During June the following transactions took place.

June	1	Bought warehouse shelving for cash from Warehouse Fitters Ltd for $3,500
	2	Purchased books on credit from Ransome House for $820
	4	Sold books on credit to Waterhouses for $1,200
	9	Purchased books on credit from Big, White for $450
	11	Sold books on credit to Books & Co for $740
	13	Paid cash sales of $310 from the warehouse shop intact into the bank
	16	Received cheque from Waterhouses in settlement of their account
	17	Purchased books on credit from RUP for $1,000
	18	Sold books on credit to R S Jones for $500
	19	Sent cheque to Ransome House in settlement of their account
	20	Paid rent of $300 by cheque
	21	Paid delivery expenses of $75 by cheque
	24	Received $350 from Books & Co on account
	30	Drew cheques for personal expenses of $270 and assistant's wages $400
	30	Settled the account of Big, White

Required

(a)   Record the foregoing in appropriate books of original entry.
(b)   Post the entries to the ledger accounts.
(c)   Balance the ledger accounts where necessary.
(d)   Extract a list of balances at 30 June 20X8.

Tutorial note. You are not required to complete any entries in personal accounts.

ANSWER

(a)   The relevant books of prime entry are the cash received day book, the cash payments day book, the sales day book and the purchase day book.

CASH RECEIVED DAY BOOK (RECEIPTS)

Date	Narrative	Total $	Capital $	Revenue $	Receivables $
June 1	Capital	10,000	10,000		
June 13	Revenue	310		310	
June 16	Waterhouses	1,200			1,200
June 24	Books & Co	350			350
		11,860	10,000	310	1,550

CASH PAYMENTS DAY BOOK (PAYMENTS)

Date June	Narrative	Total $	Fixtures and fittings $	Payables $	Rent $	Delivery expenses $	Drawings $	Wages $
1	Warehouse Fittings	3,500	3,500					
19	Ransome House	820		820				
20	Rent	300			300			
21	Delivery expenses	75				75		
30	Drawings	270					270	
30	Wages	400						400
31	Big, White	450		450				
		5,815	3,500	1,270	300	75	270	400

SALES DAY BOOK

Date	Customer	Amount $
June 4	Waterhouses	1,200
June 11	Books & Co	740
June 18	R S Jones	500
		2,440

PURCHASE DAY BOOK

Date	Supplier	Amount $
June 2	Ransome House	820
June 9	Big, White	450
June 17	RUP	1,000
		2,270

(b) and (c)

The relevant ledger accounts are for bank, revenue, purchases, payables, receivables, capital, fixtures and fittings, rent, delivery expenses, drawings and wages.

BPP
LEARNING MEDIA

BANK ACCOUNT

	$		$
June receipts	11,860	June payments	5,815
		Balance c/d	6,045
	11,860		11,860

REVENUE ACCOUNT

	$		$
		Bank	310
Balance c/d	2,750	Receivables control account	2,440
	2,750		2,750

PURCHASES ACCOUNT

	$		$
Payables control account	2,270	Balance c/d	2,270

RECEIVABLES CONTROL ACCOUNT

	$		$
Revenue	2,440	Bank	1,550
		Balance c/d	890
	2,440		2,440

PAYABLES CONTROL ACCOUNT

	$		$
Bank	1,270	Purchases	2,270
	1,000	Balance c/d	
	2,270		2,270

CAPITAL ACCOUNT

	$		$
Balance c/d	10,000	Bank	10,000

FIXTURES AND FITTINGS ACCOUNT

	$		$
Bank	3,500	Balance c/d	3,500

RENT ACCOUNT

	$		$
Bank	300	Balance c/d	300

DELIVERY EXPENSES ACCOUNT

	$		$
Bank	75	Balance c/d	75

DRAWINGS ACCOUNT

	$		$
Bank	270	Balance c/d	270

WAGES ACCOUNT

	$		$
Bank	400	Balance c/d	400

(d)   TRIAL BALANCE AS AT 30 JUNE 20X8

Account	DEBIT $	CREDIT $
Bank	6,045	
Revenue		2,750
Purchases	2,270	
Receivables	890	
Payables		1,000
Capital		10,000
Fixtures and fittings	3,500	
Rent	300	
Delivery expenses	75	
Drawings	270	
Wages	400	
	13,750	13,750

9 Computerised systems

> **Computerised accounting systems** perform the same tasks as manual accounting systems, but they can cope with greater volumes of transactions and process them at a faster rate.

We have looked at the way an accounting system is organised in the last few chapters. It is important to realise that all of the books of prime entry and the ledgers may be either **hand-written books** or **computer records.** Most businesses now use computers, ranging in size from one **PC** used by a one-man business to large networked **computer systems used** by multi-national companies.

All computer activity can be divided into three processes.

Areas	Activity
Input	Entering data from original documents
Processing	Entering up books and ledgers and generally sorting the input information
Output	Producing any report desired by the managers of the business, including financial statements

9.1 Batch processing and control totals

Batch processing is where similar transactions are gathered into batches, and then each batch is sorted and processed by the computer.

Rather than inputting individual invoices into a computer for processing, which would be time consuming and expensive, invoices can be gathered into a **batch** and **input and processed all together**. Batches can vary in size, depending on the type and volume of transactions and on any limit imposed by the system on batch sizes. This type of processing is less time consuming than **transaction processing,** where transactions are processed individually as they arise.

Control totals are used to make sure that there have been no errors when the batch is input. A control total is used to make sure that the total value of transactions input is the same as that previously calculated.

As an example, say a batch of 30 sales invoices has a manually calculated total value of $42,378.47. When the batch is input, the computer adds up the total value of the invoices input and produces a total of $42,378.47. The control totals agree and therefore no further action is required.

Should the control total **not agree** then checks would have to be carried out until the difference was found. It might be the case that an invoice had accidentally not been entered or the manual total had been incorrectly calculated.

A batch of customers' cheques could be entered together into the cash receipts day book and the total value of cheques to suppliers written that day would be entered in the cash payments day book.

9.2 Extracting sales tax from computerised accounting systems

In Section 6 we looked at how sales tax is recorded and accounted for so that businesses are able to compile the information needed to fill in their sales tax returns.

In computerised systems, one of the normal outputs that can be generated is a sales tax report. As long as invoices are entered correctly (for example with the correct date) and entered with the right sales tax details, then at the end of the sales tax period the details to be included on the return can be reported at the click of a button.

CHAPTER ROUNDUP

↳ The rules of double entry state that every financial transaction gives rise to **two accounting entries**, one a **debit**, the other a **credit**. It is vital that you understand this principle.

A **debit** is one of the following.

– An increase in an asset
– An increase in an expense
– A decrease in a liability

A **credit** is one of the following.

– An increase in a liability
– An increase in income
– A decrease in an asset

↳ The accounts in the general ledger are **impersonal accounts**. There are also **personal accounts** for customers and suppliers and these are contained in the **receivables ledger** and **payables ledger**.

↳ A **control account** is an account in the general ledger in which a record is kept of the total value of a number of similar but individual items.

– A **receivables control account** records all transactions involving all customers in total.
– A **payables control account** records transactions involving all suppliers in total.

↳ Sales tax rules can be quite complex but main points to remember are:

– **Output tax** is charged on sales
– **Input tax** is incurred on purchases
– **Sales invoices** must show sales tax

↳ A **journal** keeps a record of unusual movements between accounts. The format of a journal is:

		$	$
DEBIT	Account to be debited	X	
CREDIT	Account to be credited		X

Narrative to explain the transaction

↳ Balances on ledger accounts can be collected in a **trial balance**. The debit and credit balances should be **equal**.

↳ **Computerised accounting systems** perform the same tasks as manual accounting systems, but they can cope with greater volumes of transactions and process them at a faster rate.

1   Does a debit entry on an asset account increase or decrease the asset?

2   What is the double entry when goods are sold for cash?

3   What is the double entry when goods are purchased on credit?

4   Personal accounts form part of the double entry system. True or false?

5   How do control accounts act as a check?

6   What is the double entry for goods sold on credit which are subject to a 20% sales tax and whose price excluding sales tax is $100?

7   Why must a journal include a narrative explanation?

8   A journal can be used to correct errors which cause the total debits and credits to be unequal. True or false?

9   What is another name for a trial balance?

10 If the total debits in an account exceed the total credits, will there be a debit or credit balance on the account?

11 What types of error will not be discovered by drawing up a trial balance?

12 What are the advantages of batch processing?

1   It increases the asset balance.

2   *DEBIT* Cash; *CREDIT* Revenue.

3   *DEBIT* Purchases; *CREDIT* Payables control account.

4   False. They are memoranda accounts only.

5   Control accounts should agree with the total of the individual balances of receivables or payables to show all transactions have been recorded correctly.

6   *DEBIT* Receivables control account $120; *CREDIT* Revenue $100; *CREDIT* sales tax $20.

7   The narrative is required for audit and control, to show the purpose and authority of the transaction.

8   False. The error must be capable of correction by double entry.

9   The trial balance is also sometimes called the 'list of account balances'.

10 There will be a debit balance on the account.

11 Those not detected include the following: complete omission; posted to wrong account; compensating errors; errors of principle.

12 Batch processing is faster than transaction processing and checks on input can be made using control totals.

Now try ...

Attempt the questions below from the **Practice Question Bank**

Number	Level	Marks	Time
Q18	Examination	2	2.4 mins
Q19	Examination	2	2.4 mins
Q20	Examination	2	2.4 mins
Q21	Examination	2	2.4 mins
Q22	Examination	2	2.4 mins
Q23	Examination	2	2.4 mins

part

B

Advanced accounting procedures

CHAPTER

05

In this chapter we look at the **basic accounting principles and characteristics** to be applied when deciding on the appropriate accounting treatment for specific items.

Accounting principles and characteristics

Study Guide

Intellectual level

A **Generally accepted accounting principles and concepts**

1 **The key accounting principles and characteristics**

(a) Explain the principles of accounting.   K

    (i) Going concern

    (ii) Accruals

    (iii) Consistency

    (iv) Double entry

    (v) Business entity concept

    (vi) Materiality

    (vii) Historical cost

    (viii) Prudence

(b) Explain the accounting qualitative characteristics relating to   K

    (i) Relevance

    (ii) Faithful representation

    (iii) Comparability

    (iv) Verifiability

    (v) Timeliness

    (vi) Understandability

3 **The regulatory framework**

(a) Describe the main requirements of accounting standards in   K
relation to syllabus area D

---

1   Introduction: basic accounting principles and characteristics

In preparing financial information, certain fundamental principles and characteristics are adopted as a framework.

EXAM FOCUS POINT

The definitions given in this chapter as key terms are very **important**. You will almost certainly be tested on some of them in the exam.

In this chapter of the Interactive Text, we look at **why** certain items are treated in specific ways and, where there is a choice of treatment, **how to decide** which treatment to use.

To some extent at least, the decision is made for you by one or both of two authorities.

(a) **Local legal regulation.** Virtually all countries have legislation governing the form and content of company financial statements. In this exam you will **not** be examined on these legal requirements.

(b) **Accounting standards.** Many countries follow **accounting standards** (either their own, or International Standards) which supplement the legal requirements. The International Standards set by the International Accounting Standards Board (IASB) have been adopted by many countries.

The International Standards issued by the IASB mentioned above are known collectively as **International Financial Reporting Standards (IFRSs)**, although some of the standards are individually named as **International Accounting Standards (IASs)**. IFRSs and IASs are developed through an **international due process** that involves accountants, financial analysts and other users of financial statements, the business community, stock exchanges, regulatory and legal authorities, academics and other interested individuals and organisations from around the world. Accounting standards are obligatory for incorporated entities, but their use is also recommended for unincorporated entities and therefore are examinable in the FA2 exam. The IFRSs and IASs that are examinable at FA2 level are:

IAS 1   *Presentation of Financial Statements*
IAS 2   *Inventories*
IAS 16   *Property, Plant and Equipment*
IAS 37   *Provisions, Contingent Liabilities and Contingent Assets*
IFRS 15   *Revenue from Contracts with Customers*

In addition, the *Conceptual Framework* is also examinable.

EXAM FOCUS POINT

You are not expected to have a detailed knowledge of accounting standards but you must know the key issues which apply to your syllabus – for instance, the requirement that inventory should be valued at lower of cost and net realisable value (NRV). You should refer to the list of examinable documents published on the ACCA website.

We look at the relevant points of these standards when we cover the related topics (for example we will refer to IAS 16 we when cover non-current assets in Chapter 9). For the remainder of this Chapter we focus on the basic accounting principles and the qualitative characteristics of financial information. Many of these are covered in the IASB *Conceptual Framework for Financial Reporting* an examinable document for FA2. It is not another accounting standard like those listed above. Instead it sets out the principles and characteristics that underlie the preparation and presentation of financial statements for external users.

When there is no specific legal regulation or accounting standard which covers an item in the accounts, you must make decisions on its accounting treatment by applying **basic accounting principles and characteristics** (such as those set out in the framework). These underpin and are embodied in the law and accounting standards.

1.1 What are basic accounting principles and characteristics?

Accounting practice has developed gradually over a long period of time. Many of its procedures are operated automatically by accounting personnel and these procedures in common use imply the **acceptance of certain principles and characteristics**. These principles and characteristics are not necessarily obvious, nor are they the only possible ones which could be used to build up an accounting framework, but they are the principles and characteristics which our current system has ended up being based upon.

Basic accounting principles and characteristics are the broad assumptions which underlie the periodic financial accounts of business entities.

Here are some important principles and characteristics, which are mentioned specifically in the Study Guide and which we will cover.

- **Going concern assumption**
- **Accruals basis of accounting**
- **Historical cost**

- **Consistency**
- **Materiality**
- **Prudence**

There are also some other principles and characteristics of which you should be aware and which will be mentioned occasionally throughout this Interactive Text.

The **business entity concept**: a business, for accounting purposes, is a separate entity from its owners or managers (we looked at this in Chapter 1).

Double entry bookkeeping (introduced in Chapter 1 and covered in detail in Chapter 4) is the system of accounting which reflects the fact that:

- Every financial transaction affects the entity in two ways and gives rise to two accounting entries, one a debit and the other a credit

- The total value of debit entries is therefore always equal at any time to the total value of credit entries

The **money measurement principle**: accounts only deal with items to which a monetary value can be attributed

The **separate valuation principle**: each component part of an asset or liability on the statement of financial position must be valued separately

2 The going concern assumption

> **Going concern**: the business is expected to stay 'in business' for the foreseeable future.

Going concern. Financial statements are normally prepared on the assumption that the reporting entity is a going concern, and will continue in operation for the foreseeable future. Hence it is assumed that the entity has neither the intention nor the necessity of liquidation nor the need to cease trading.

(*Conceptual Framework*, para.3.9)

The main significance of the going concern assumption is that the assets of the business should not be valued at their 'break-up' value, which is the amount that they would sell for if they were sold off piecemeal and the business were thus broken up.

2.1 Example: going concern assumption

Suppose that Emma buys a T-shirt printing machine for $60,000. The asset is expected to last for six years, and it is normal to write off the cost of the asset to the statement of profit or loss over this time (as we will see in Chapter 9). In this case a depreciation cost of $10,000 per annum will be charged.

Using the going concern assumption, it is assumed that the business will continue its operations and so the asset will live out its full six years in use. A depreciation charge of $10,000 will be made each year, and the value of the asset in the statement of financial position will be its cost less the accumulated amount of depreciation charged to date. After 1 year, the carrying amount of the asset will be $(60,000 − 10,000) = $50,000, after 2 years it would be $40,000, after 3 years $30,000 etc, until it has been written down to a value of zero after 6 years.

Now suppose that this asset has no other operational use outside the business, and in a forced sale it would only sell for scrap. After one year of operation, its scrap value might be, say, $8,000. What would the carrying amount be after one year?

BPP
LEARNING MEDIA

The carrying amount of the asset, applying the going concern assumption, would be $50,000 after one year, but its immediate sell-off value only $8,000. It might be argued that the asset is overvalued at $50,000 and that it should be written down to its break-up value (ie in the statement of financial position it should be shown at $8,000 and the rest of its cost should be treated as an expense). However, provided that the going concern assumption is valid, so that the asset will continue to be used and will not be sold, it is appropriate accounting practice to value the asset at its carrying amount.

3 The accruals basis of accounting

Accruals: revenues and costs should be matched in the same time period.

Accrual accounting: The effects of transactions and other events and circumstances on a reporting entity's economic resources and claims are recognised in the period in which they occur, even if the resulting cash receipts and payments occur in a different period.

(*Conceptual Framework*, para.1.17)

The accruals basis requires that the impacts of transactions and other events are recognised when they occur, and not as cash is received or paid. Transactions should be recorded in the accounting records and reported in the period to which they relate. Expenses are recognised in the statement of profit or loss on the basis of a direct association between costs incurred and the earning of specific items from income. The expenditure incurred in earning the profit for an accounting period is matched to that profit; for this reason the accruals basis is sometimes referred to as the 'matching' concept.

3.1 Example: Accruals basis

Zandra Shah has a business importing and selling toy model ponies. In October 20X2, she makes the following purchases and sales.

Purchases

Invoice date	Number	Invoiced cost $	Invoice paid
7.10. X2	30	300	1.11.X2

Sales

Invoice date	Number	Invoice value $	Invoice paid
8.10.X2	6	90	1.11.X2
12.10.X2	9	135	1.11.X2
23.10.X2	15	225	1.12.X2

What is Zandra's statement of profit or loss for October on both a cash basis and an accruals basis?

Solution

	$
Cash basis	
Sales	–
Purchases	–
Profit/loss	–
Accruals basis	
Sales $(90 + 135 + 225)	450
Purchases	(300)
Profit	150

If, furthermore, Zandra had only sold 25 ponies, it would have been wrong to charge her statement of profit or loss with the cost of 30 ponies, as she still has five ponies in inventory. If she intends to sell them in November she is likely to make a profit on the sale. Therefore, only the purchase cost of 25 ponies ($250) should be matched with her sales revenue, leaving her with a profit of $125.

Her statement of financial position would therefore look like this.

	$
Assets	
Inventory (at cost, ie 5 × $10)	50
Receivables (25 × $15)	375
	425
Capital and liabilities	
Proprietor's capital (profit for the period)	125
Liabilities: Payables	300
	425

Obviously, the accruals basis gives a truer picture than the cash basis. Zandra has no cash to show for her efforts until November but her customers are legally bound to pay her and she is legally bound to pay for her purchases.

Her statement of financial position as at 31 October 20X2 would therefore show her assets and liabilities as follows.

	$
Assets	
Receivables $(90 + 135 + 225)	450
Capital and liabilities	
Proprietors capital	150
Liabilities: Payables	300
Net assets	450

If, however, Zandra had decided to give up selling ponies, then the **going concern assumption** would no longer apply and the value of the five ponies in the statement of financial position would be a 'break-up' valuation rather than cost, ie the amount that would be obtained by selling them following break-up or liquidation of the business.

Similarly, if the five unsold ponies were now unlikely to be sold at more than their cost of $10 each (say, because of damage or a fall in demand) then they should be recorded on the statement of financial position at their **net realisable value** (ie the likely eventual sales price less any expenses incurred to make them saleable, eg paint) rather than cost.

In this example, the concepts of going concern and accruals are **linked**. Because the business is assumed to be a going concern it is possible to carry forward the cost of the unsold ponies as a charge against profits of the next period.

The accruals concept means that revenue and profits are dealt with in the statement of profit or loss of the period in which they occur, along with associated costs and expenses. This is done by including the costs incurred in earning these revenues and profits in the same accounting period. Businesses must take credit for sales and purchases when made, rather than when paid for, and they must also carry unsold inventory forward in the statement of financial position to future period that will get the benefit rather than deduct its cost from profit for the period.

4 Consistency

> **Consistency**: requires that similar items should be accorded similar accounting treatment.

Accounting is not an exact science. There are many areas in which **judgement** must be used to calculate or estimate the money values of items appearing in accounts. Over the years certain procedures and principles have come to be recognised as good accounting practice, but within these limits there are often various acceptable methods of accounting for similar items.

Although the *Conceptual Framework* doesn't specifically have a qualitative accounting characteristic of consistency, it recognises the importance of consistency by its inclusion within the scope of the enhancing qualitative characteristic of comparability.

Consistency refers to the use of the same methods for the same items, either from period to period within a reporting entity or in a single period across entities. Comparability is the goal; consistency helps to achieve that goal.

(Conceptual Framework, para.2.26)

In preparing accounts consistency should be observed in two respects.

(a)   **Similar items** within a single set of accounts should be given similar accounting treatment.

(b)   The same treatment should be applied **from one period to another** in accounting for similar items. This allows valid comparisons to be made from one period to the next.

To understand the importance of the consistency principle, consider how **meaningless** asset values would be to a reader of a set of accounts if the basis on which they were decided changed completely from one year to the next – one year purchased cost, the next replacement cost (the cost of buying a new one), the next fair value.

Consistency is linked with the idea of **comparability** – users of accounts must be able to compare financial performance and position over a period of time.

5   Materiality

Materiality: in some cases, attention to detail can obscure the 'big picture'.

Materiality: Information is material if omitting it or misstating it could influence decisions that the primary users of general purpose financial statements make on the basis of those reports, which provide financial information about a specific reporting entity.

(Conceptual Framework, para.2.11)

An error which is too trivial to affect a user's understanding of the accounting statements is referred to as **immaterial**.

Determining whether or not an item is material is a very **subjective exercise**. There is no absolute measure of materiality. It is common to apply a convenient rule of thumb (eg to define material items as those with a value greater than 5% of the net profit in the accounts).

Some items disclosed in accounts are regarded as particularly sensitive and even a very small misstatement of such an item would be seen as a material error.

Therefore, an item may be considered material based on either its **value** or **nature** within the financial statements. In assessing whether or not an item is material, it is not only the amount of the item which needs to be considered. The **context** is also important.

(a)   If a statement of financial position shows non-current assets of $2 million and inventories of $30,000, an error of $20,000 in the depreciation calculations might not be regarded as material, whereas an error of $20,000 in the inventory valuation probably would be.

(b)   If a business has a bank loan of $50,000 and a $55,000 balance on bank deposit account, it might well be regarded as a material misstatement if these two amounts were displayed on the statement of financial position netted off as 'cash at bank $5,000'. In other words, incorrect presentation may amount to material misstatement even if there is no monetary error.

The concept of materiality links in with the qualitative characteristic of relevance, whereby the users of the financial statements will need to be aware of all the relevant information, which may be of a material nature in terms of monetary value (large new assets purchased for example), or relevant to the user in their understanding of the results (maybe director remuneration or new share capital issued). This is covered in more detail, later in the chapter.

QUESTION

You work for a large organisation and you are preparing two accounting documents:

(a)   A statement for a customer, listing invoices and receipts, and detailing the amounts owed

(b)   A report sent to the senior management of a division, who want a brief comparative summary of how well the firm is doing in the UK and in France

How would considerations of **materiality** influence your preparation of each document?

ANSWER

Materiality as an accounting concept does have strict limitations. It refers primarily to financial reporting, but has no bearing at all on detailed procedural matters such as bank reconciliations or statements of account sent to customers.

Consequently, the statement sent to the customer, described in option (a), must be accurate to the last cent, however large it is. After all, if you receive a bill from a company for $147.50, you do not 'round it up' to $150 when you pay. Nor will the company billing you be prepared to 'round it down' to $145. A customer pays an agreed price for an agreed product or service. Paying more is effectively giving money away, and if you are going to do that, there might be worthier beneficiaries of your generosity. Paying less exposes your supplier to an unfair loss.

On the other hand, if you are preparing a performance report comparing how well the company is doing in the UK and France, entirely different considerations apply.

There is little point in being accurate to the last cent (and inconsistencies might occur from the choice of currency rate used). This is because senior management are interested in the broad picture, and they are looking to identify comparisons between the overall performance of each division.

Assume that UK profits were $1,233,750.57 and profits in France were $1,373,370.75. Results have been converted into $ for ease of comparison.

France	UK
$	$
1,373,370.75	1,233,750.57
or	or
$'000	$'000
1,373	1,234

The rounded figures are much easier to understand, and so the relative performance is easier to compare. Considerations of materiality would allow you to ignore the rounding differences, because they are so small and the information is used for comparative purposes only.

EXAM FOCUS POINT

Materiality is an important principle in financial accounting. Items in the financial statements can be misstated, but are only misleading if they are materially misstated.

6 Historical cost accounting

Accounting concepts are part of the theoretical framework on which accounting practice is based. It is worth looking at one further general point: the problem of attributing **monetary values** to the items which appear in accounts.

A basic principle of accounting (some writers include it in the list of fundamental accounting concepts) is that transactions are normally stated in accounts at their historical amount.

Using historical cost has a number of implications.

Transactions are stated at their **value when they occurred**. This means, for example, that the cost of goods sold is not suddenly increased at the end of the year.

Assets are stated at their **historical cost**. In other words, the value of an asset in a statement of financial position is based on the price that was paid for it.

An important advantage of recording items at their historical cost is that there is usually **objective**, documentary evidence to prove the purchase price of an asset, or amounts paid as expenses.

In general, accountants prefer to deal with objective costs, rather than with estimated values. This is because valuations tend to be subjective and to vary according to what the valuation is for. There are some **problems** with the principle of historical cost.

(a) The wearing out of assets over time
(b) The increase in market value of property
(c) Inflation

There may be other problems you can think of.

6.1 Example: problems with historical cost

Suppose that a partnership buys a machine to use in its business. The machine has an expected useful life of four years. At the end of two years the company is preparing a statement of financial position and has to decide what monetary amount to attribute to the asset. Numerous possibilities might be considered.

* The original cost (historical cost) of the machine
* Half of the historical cost, on the ground that half of its useful life has expired
* The amount the machine might fetch on the second-hand market
* The amount it would cost to replace the machine with an identical machine
* The amount it would cost to replace the machine with a more modern machine incorporating the technological advances of the previous two years
* The machine's economic value, ie the amount of the profits it is expected to generate for the company during its remaining life

All of these valuations have something to recommend them, but the great advantage of the first two is that they are based on a figure (the machine's historical cost) which is **objectively verifiable**.

6.2 Fair presentation

The fundamental requirement for a set of accounts is that they provide users with an accurate picture of the profit and financial position of the entity – a **fair presentation**. This is what accounting standards are seeking to achieve. The principle of **fair presentation of financial information** is included in the accounting rules of the EU. This overriding requirement must be borne in mind when any conflict arises between accounting standards.

7 | Qualitative characteristics of financial information

Qualitative characteristics of financial information are those **characteristics that make them more meaningful** to anyone using them. The two most important of these (the *Conceptual Framework* refers to them as being 'fundamental') are:

- – **Relevance**
- – **Faithful representation**

The following characteristics enhance the usefulness of financial information:

- – **Comparability**
- – **Verifiability**
- – **Timeliness**
- – **Understandability**

In Section 1 we talked about concepts, principles and standards that help businesses decide how to present items in their accounts. Even having applied general principles and the guidance in accounting standards, businesses still need to take a step back and consider the qualitative characteristics of the financial information that has been prepared.

This involves looking at the financial information and considering its **qualitative characteristics**.

Qualitative characteristics of financial information are those **characteristics that make the information more meaningful** to anyone using them. Although there are a number of qualitative characteristics of financial information, two are generally accepted to be the most important (the *Conceptual Framework* refers to them as being 'fundamental'):

- Relevance
- Faithful representation

The following characteristics enhance the usefulness of financial information:

- Comparability
- Verifiability
- Timeliness
- Understandability

7.1 Relevance

Relevance: Relevant information is capable of making a difference in the decisions made by users. Financial information is capable of making a difference in decisions if it has **predictive value**, **confirmatory value** or both.

(Conceptual Framework: para.2.6–2.7)

Financial information is used to make decisions and therefore it is important that the information is relevant to those decisions.

Relevant information possesses either predictive or confirmatory value or both. Predictive values are capable of predicting and influencing future decisions. Confirmatory values are used to check, confirm or even correct prior predictions. For example, a business with a best-selling mobile phone decides to launch a new version in the next quarter, they base their sales on the existing model (predictive). However, sales are weaker than expected, so the budget is revised for the rest of the year (confirmatory).

7.2 Faithful representation

To be a **faithful representation** information must be **complete, neutral** and **free from error**.

To be **complete** the information must include all information necessary for a user to understand the phenomenon being depicted, including all necessary descriptions and explanations.

To be **neutral** the information 'must be without bias in the selection or presentation of financial information' (*Conceptual Framework*, para.2.15). This means that information must not be manipulated in any way in order to influence the decisions of users.

Free from error means there are no errors or omissions and no errors made in the process by which the financial information was produced. It does not mean that no inaccuracies can arise, particularly where estimates have to be made.

7.2.1 Prudence

Prudence is the exercise of caution when making judgements under conditions of uncertainty

(*Conceptual Framework,* para.2.16)

Prudence helps to support the enhancing qualitative characteristic of neutrality; in essence, making sure that the assets and liabilities are not overstated or understated in the financial statements. For example, if the financial statements have a provision for a legal claim made against the entity, it is important that this is recorded at the correct value: How has the estimated provision been calculated? How likely is the claim? Is there a risk of understating (or overstating) the expected claim?

7.3 Comparability

Comparability is the qualitative characteristic that enables users to identify and understand similarities in, and differences among, items. (*Conceptual Framework*: para.2.25)

Therefore, it requires more than one item to be subject to this characteristic, for example, two periods of financial results or comparing companies within the same industry. In order to be able to do this in a meaningful manner, the bases of the preparation of the financial statements should have some degree of consistency.

Consistency, as we have seen in section 4, is related to comparability, **but it is not the same**. It refers to the use of the same methods for the same items (ie consistency of treatment) either from period to period within a reporting entity or in a single period across entities (*Conceptual Framework*, para.2.26)

The **disclosure of accounting policies** is particularly important here. Users must be able to distinguish between different accounting policies in order to be able to make a valid comparison of similar items in the accounts of different entities.

When an entity **changes an accounting policy**, the change is applied retrospectively so that the results from one period to the next can still be usefully compared.

Comparability is **not the same as uniformity**. Entities should change accounting policies if previously used accounting policies become inappropriate or are superseded by new accounting standards.

Corresponding information for preceding periods should be shown to enable comparison over time. The way in which financial information is presented should make it possible for users to compare the results of a business with its own prior years and with the results of other businesses.

7.4 Verifiability

Verifiability helps assure users that information faithfully represents the economic phenomena it purports to represent. Verifiability means that different knowledgeable and independent observers could reach consensus, although not necessarily complete agreement, that a particular depiction is a faithful representation.

(*Conceptual Framework*: para.2.30)

Information that can be independently verified is generally more useful for decision-making than information that cannot. Verifiability means that a number of users with the same information would be likely to reach the same conclusion.

7.3 Timeliness

Timeliness means having information available to decision-makers in time to be capable of influencing their decisions. Generally, the older information is the less useful it is.

(Conceptual Framework: para.2.33)

Information may become less useful if there is a delay in reporting it. There is a **balance between timeliness and the provision of reliable information**.

If information is reported on a timely basis when not all aspects of the transaction are known, it may not be complete or free from error.

Conversely, if every detail of a transaction is known, it may be too late to publish the information because it has become irrelevant. The overriding consideration is how best to satisfy the economic decision-making needs of the users.

7.4 Understandability

Understandability: Classifying, characterising and presenting information clearly and concisely makes it understandable.   *(Conceptual Framework*: para.2.34)

Financial reports are prepared for users who have a **reasonable knowledge of business and economic activities** and who review and analyse the information diligently (*Conceptual Framework,* para.2.36). Some phenomena are inherently complex, such as financial instruments and cannot be made easy to understand. Information should not be excluded simply because it may be difficult to understand.

Financial information needs to be capable of being understood by users having a reasonable knowledge of business and economic activities and accounting.

In summary, understandability ensures that a financial statement user with a certain level of accounting and business knowledge can gain information on the performance and financial position of the business.

8 Summary of key terms

We have covered a lot of accounting principles and related key terms during the course of the chapter, so we will end it with a recap of those terms. The table below collates the key terms, principles and characteristics covered during the chapter.

Key term	Description
Key accounting principles and characteristics	The broad assumptions which underlie the periodic financial statements of business entities.
Business entity concept	A business, for accounting purposes, is a separate entity from its owners or managers.
Double entry bookkeeping	The system of accounting which reflects the fact that: – Every financial transaction affects the entity in two ways and gives rise to two accounting entries, one a debit and the other a credit – The total value of debit entries is therefore always equal at any time to the total value of credit entries

Key term	Description
Money measurement principle	Accounting records only deal with items to which a monetary value can be attributed.
Separate valuation principle	Each component part of an asset or liability on the statement of financial position must be valued separately.
Going concern assumption	Financial statements are normally prepared on the assumption that the reporting entity is a going concern, and will continue in operation for the foreseeable future. Hence it is assumed that the entity has neither the intention nor the necessity of liquidation nor the need to cease trading. *(Conceptual Framework, para.3.9)*
Accruals basis of accounting	The effects of transactions and other events and circumstances on a reporting entity's economic resources and claims are recognised in the period in which they occur, even if the resulting cash receipts and payments occur in a different period. *(Conceptual Framework, para.1.17)*
Consistency	Consistency refers to the use of the same methods for the same items, either from period to period within a reporting entity or in a single period across entities. Comparability is the goal; consistency helps to achieve that goal. *(Conceptual Framework, para.2.26)*
Materiality	Information is material if omitting it or misstating it could influence decisions that the primary users of general purpose financial statements make on the basis of those reports, which provide financial information about a specific reporting entity. *(Conceptual Framework, para.2.11)*
Historical cost accounting	Transactions are stated at their value when they occurred. This means, for example, that the cost of goods sold is not suddenly increased at the end of the year. Assets are stated at their historical cost. In other words, the value of an asset in a statement of financial position is based on the price that was paid for it.
Qualitative characteristics	Qualitative characteristics of financial information are those characteristics that make them more meaningful to anyone using them. The two most important of these are: – Relevance – Faithful representation The following characteristics enhance the usefulness of financial information: – Comparability – Verifiability – Timeliness – Understandability
Relevance	Relevant information is capable of making a difference in the decisions made by users. Financial information is capable of making a difference in decisions if it has **predictive value**, **confirmatory value** or both. *(Conceptual Framework: para.2.6-2.7)*
Prudence	Prudence is the exercise of caution when making judgements under conditions of uncertainty. *(Conceptual Framework, para.2.16)*

Key term	Description
Faithful representation	To be a faithful representation information must be **complete, neutral** and **free from error**.
Comparability	Comparability is the qualitative characteristic that enables users to identify and understand similarities in, and differences among, items. *(Conceptual Framework*: para.2.25)
Verifiability	Verifiability helps assure users that information faithfully represents the economic phenomena it purports to represent. Verifiability means that different knowledgeable and independent observers could reach consensus, although not necessarily complete agreement, that a particular depiction is a faithful representation. *(Conceptual Framework*: para.2.30
Timeliness	Timeliness means having information available to decision-makers in time to be capable of influencing their decisions. Generally, the older information is the less useful it is. *(Conceptual Framework*: para.2.33)
Understandability	Classifying, characterising and presenting information clearly and concisely makes it understandable. *(Conceptual Framework*: para.2.34)

EXAM FOCUS POINT

There is a useful technical article available on the ACCA called 'A matter of principle' which outlines the key points of each principle at the FA2 level.

CHAPTER ROUNDUP

↳ In preparing financial information, certain fundamental principles and characteristics are adopted as a framework.

↳ **Going concern**: the business is expected to stay 'in business'.

↳ **Accruals**: revenues and costs should be matched in the same time period.

↳ **Consistency**: like items should be treated in a like way.

↳ **Materiality**: in some cases, attention to detail can obscure the 'big picture'.

↳ Qualitative characteristics of financial statements information are those **characteristics that make them more meaningful** to anyone using them. The two most important of these (the Conceptual Framework refers to them as being 'fundamental') are:

– **Relevance**
– **Faithful representation**

The following characteristics enhance the usefulness of financial information:

– **Comparability**
– **Verifiability**
– **Timeliness**
– **Understandability**

QUICK QUIZ

1 Where is most guidance given on how items should be treated in the accounts?

2 When can a profit be considered to be realised?

3 When will the assets of a business be valued on a break up basis?

4 Whether an item is material or not in a set of accounts is entirely objective. True or false?

5 Mention briefly some problems with the historical cost convention.

6 Which of the following is not one of the six main qualitative characteristics of financial statements?

A   Reliability
B   Faithful representation
C   Credibility
D   Comparability

1   International accounting standards and local company law.

2   When it is in the form of cash or another asset with a certain cash value.

3   When the going concern assumption no longer applies.

4   False. Deciding whether an item is material or not is always a subjective exercise.

5   The wearing out of assets over time; increase in the value of property; inflation.

6   C   The answer is credibility. The other qualitative characteristics not listed are verifiability, timeliness and understandability.

Now try ...

Attempt the questions below from the **Practice Question Bank**

Number	Level	Marks	Time
Q24	Examination	2	2.4 mins
Q25	Examination	2	2.4 mins

CHAPTER

06

Control accounts and the correction of errors

We introduced control accounts in Chapter 4. In this chapter we cover control accounts in more detail. A control account is an account which keeps a **total record for a collective item** (eg receivables) which in reality consists of many individual items (eg individual trade receivable).

The individual entries in day books are entered one by one in the appropriate personal accounts contained in the **receivables ledger** and **payables ledger**.

A reconciliation of the control account with the total of the personal accounts on the ledger will help to highlight **errors**, some of these errors can be put right using **journal entries** but some errors will require a **suspense account** to be opened temporarily.

We also cover bank reconciliations in this chapter. A **bank reconciliation** is a comparison of a bank statement with the bank account in the general ledger.

Study Guide	Intellectual level
D **Recording transactions and events**	
6 **Receivables, payables and provisions**	
(h) Account for contras between trade receivables and payables	S
E **Preparing a trial balance and errors**	
1 **Trial balance**	
(c) Calculate and explain the impact of errors on the statement of profit or loss and the statement of financial position	S
2 **Correction of errors**	
(a) Explain the purpose of, and reasons for, creating a suspense account	K
(b) Identify different types of bookkeeping error including those that result in suspense accounts	K
(c) Identify and explain the action required to correct errors including clearing any suspense accounts	K
(d) Prepare correcting journal entries	S
(e) Record correcting entries in the ledgers	S
(f) Demonstrate how the final accounts are affected by the correction of errors	S
F **Reconciliations**	
1 **Control account reconciliations**	
(a) Explain the purpose of reconciliation of the receivables and payables ledger control accounts	K
(b) Identify errors in the ledger control accounts and list of balances	S
(c) Make correcting entries in the ledger control accounts	S
(d) Prepare a reconciliation between the list of balances and the corrected ledger control accounts	S
(e) Identify the control account balance to be reported in the final accounts	K
(f) Prepare a reconciliation between a supplier's statement and the supplier's account in the payables ledger	K
2 **Bank reconciliation**	
(a) Explain the purpose of reconciliation between the bank ledger account and the corresponding bank statement	K
(b) Identify errors and omissions in the bank ledger account and bank statement	K
(c) Identify timing differences	K
(d) Make the correcting entries in the bank ledger account	S
(e) Prepare the reconciliation between the bank statement balance and the corrected bank ledger account	S

1 Introduction: control accounts revisited

The two most important **control accounts** are those for **receivables** and **payables**. They are part of the double entry system.

So far in this text we have assumed that the bookkeeping and double entry (and subsequent preparation of financial accounts) has been carried out by a business without any mistakes. This is not likely to be the case in real life: even the bookkeeper of a very small business with hardly any accounting entries to make will be prone to **human error**.

For example, if a debit is written as $123 and the corresponding credit as $321, then the books of the business are immediately out of balance by $198.

Once an error has been detected, it has to be corrected. In addition, a business is likely to have late adjustments to make to the figures in its accounts (eg depreciation; allowance for receivables). A business needs to have some method available for making these corrections or adjustments.

In this chapter we explain how errors can be detected, what kinds of error might exist, and how to post corrections and adjustments.

1.1 What are control accounts?

We looked at control accounts briefly in Chapter 4. Let us review and expand upon what we know about Them.

A control account is an account in the general ledger in which a record is kept of the total value of a number of similar but individual items. Control accounts are used chiefly for trade receivables and payables.

A receivables control account is an account in which records are kept of transactions involving all receivables in total. The balance on the receivables control account at any time will be the total amount due to the business at that time from its customers.

A payables control account is an account in which records are kept of transactions involving all payables in total, and the balance on this account at any time will be the total amount owed by the business at that time to its suppliers.

Although control accounts are used mainly in accounting for receivables and payables, they can also be kept for other items, such as inventories, wages and salaries. The first important idea to remember, however, is that a control account is an account which keeps a **total record for a collective item** (eg receivables) which in reality consists of many individual items (eg individual trade receivable).

A control account is an **(impersonal) ledger account** which will appear in the general (nominal) ledger. Before we look at the reasons for having control accounts, we will first look at how they are made up.

1.2 Control accounts and personal accounts

The personal accounts of individual customers of the business are kept in the **receivables ledger**, and the amount owed by each customer will be a balance on their personal account. The amount owed by all the customers together (ie all the trade account receivables) will be a balance on the **receivables control account**.

At any time the balance on the receivables control account should be **equal** to the sum of the individual balances on the personal accounts in the receivables ledger.

EXAM FOCUS POINT

An exam question may present you with a scenario in which the list of balances on the personal accounts does not agree to the control account total, along with details of the necessary correcting entries to be made.

For example, a business has three trade receivable: A Arnold owes $80, B Bagshaw owes $310 and C Cloning owes $200. The debit balances on the various accounts would be:

Receivables ledger (personal accounts)

	$
A Arnold	80
B Bagshaw	310
C Cloning	200
General ledger: receivables control account	590

What has happened here is that the three entries of $80, $310 and $200 were first entered into the sales day book. They were also recorded in the three personal accounts of Arnold, Bagshaw and Cloning in the receivables ledger – but remember that this is not part of the double entry system.

Later, the **total** of $590 is posted from the sales day book into the receivables (control) account. It is fairly obvious that if you add up all the debit figures on the personal accounts, they also should total $590.

2 The operation of control accounts

Day books (cash day books, sales day book and purchases day book) are totalled periodically (say once a month) and the appropriate totals are posted to the **control accounts**. The individual entries in day books will have been entered one by one in the appropriate personal accounts contained in the receivables ledger and payables ledger. These **personal accounts** are not part of the double entry system.

You might still be uncertain **why we need to have control accounts** at all. Before turning our attention to this question, it will be useful first of all to see how transactions involving receivables are accounted for by means of an illustrative example. Reference numbers are shown in the accounts to illustrate the cross-referencing that is needed, and in the example reference numbers beginning:

(a) SDB, refer to a page in the sales day book
(b) RL, refer to a particular account in the receivables ledger
(c) GL, refer to a particular account in the general ledger
(d) CRDB, refer to a page in the cash received day book
(e) CIDB, refer to a page in the cash payments day book

2.1 Example: accounting for receivables

At 1 July 20X2, the Outer Business Company had no trade receivable. During July, the following transactions affecting credit sales and customers occurred.

(a) July 3: Invoiced A Arnold for the sale on credit of hardware goods: $100, he is offered a settlement discount of 10% if he pays within 7 days.

(b) July 11: Invoiced B Bagshaw for the sale on credit of electrical goods: $150

(c) July 15: Invoiced C Cloning for the sale on credit of hardware goods: $250

(d) July 10: Received payment from A Arnold of $90, in settlement of his debt in full, having taken a permitted settlement discount of $10 for payment within 7 days

(e) July 18: Received a payment of $72 from B Bagshaw in part settlement of $80 of his debt

BPP LEARNING MEDIA

(f)   July 28:   Received a payment of $120 from C Cloning, who was unable to claim any discount

Ledger account numbers are as follows:

RL 4   Personal account: A Arnold
RL 9   Personal account: B Bagshaw
RL 13   Personal account: C Cloning
GL 6   Receivables control account
GL 21   Sales: hardware
GL 22   Sales: electrical
GL 1   Bank control account

Required

Write up all the accounts listed above for the transactions which took placed in July.

Solution

The accounting entries, suitably dated, would be as follows.

			SALES DAY BOOK		SDB 35
Date	*Name*	*Ref.*	*Total*	*Hardware*	*Electrical*
20X2			$	$	$
July 3	A Arnold	RL 4 Dr	90.00	90.00	
11	B Bagshaw	RL 9 Dr	150.00		150.00
15	C Cloning	RL13 Dr	250.00	250.00	
			490.00	340.00	150.00
			NL 6 Dr	NL 21 Cr	NL 22 Cr

Notes

Under the revised rules for revenue recognition in IFRS 15, there have been changes to how settlement discounts may be treated. The business will make an assessment on past transactions with the customer who has been offered the settlement discount. If they have regularly taken up the discount in the past, then the sale will be recorded net of the discount in the revenue account at the time of the sale.

If the customer rarely takes up the settlement discount, then the sale will be recorded without the discount.

In all cases, if the customer's payment differs then the adjustment will be made at the point of payment. Therefore, if the customer later does not take advantage of the discount, the additional $10 of revenue will be entered (DR Cash, CR Revenue)

The personal accounts in the receivables ledger are debited on the day the invoices are sent out. The double entry in the ledger accounts might be made at the end of each day, week or month; here it is made at the end of the month, by posting from the sales day book, in effect, as follows.

			$	$
DEBIT	NL 6	Receivables control account	490	
CREDIT	NL 21	Sales: hardware		340
	NL 22	Sales: electrical		150

CASH RECEIVED DAY BOOK
EXTRACT – JULY 20X2

CRDB 23

			Total	*Accounts receivable*
Date	*Narrative*	*Ref.*	$	$
20X2				
July 10	A Arnold	RL 4 Cr	90.00	90.00
18	B Bagshaw	RL 9 Cr	72.00	80.00
28	C Cloning	RL13 Cr	120.00	120.00
			282.00	290.00
			NL 1 Dr	NL 6 Cr

The personal accounts in the receivables ledger are memorandum accounts, because they are not a part of the double entry system.

MEMORANDUM RECEIVABLES LEDGER
A ARNOLD

A/c no: RL 4

Date 20X2	Narrative	Ref.	$	Date 20X2	Narrative	Ref.	$
July 3	Revenue	SDB 35	90.00	July 10	Bank	CRDB 23	90.00
			100.00				100.00

B BAGSHAW

A/c no: RL 9

Date 20X2	Narrative	Ref.	$	Date 20X2	Narrative	Ref.	$
July 11	Revenue	SDB 35	150.00	July 18	Bank	CRDB 23	72.00
				July 31	Balance	c/d	78.00
			150.00				150.00
Aug 1	Balance	b/d	78.00				

C CLONING

A/c no: RL 13

Date 20X2	Narrative	Ref.	$	Date 20X2	Narrative	Ref.	$
July 15	Revenue	SDB 35	250.00	July 28	Bank	CRDB 23	120.00
				July 31	Balance	c/d	130.00
			250.00				250.00
Aug 1	Balance	b/d	130.00				

In the general ledger, the accounting entries can be made from the books of prime entry to the ledger accounts, in this example at the end of the month.

GENERAL LEDGER (EXTRACT)
RECEIVABLES (RECEIVABLES CONTROL ACCOUNT)

A/c no: NL 6

Date 20X2	Narrative	Ref.	$	Date 20X2	Narrative	Ref.	$
July 31	Revenue	SDB 35	490.00	July 31	Bank		
						CRDB 23	282.00
				July 31	Balance	c/d	208.00
			490.00				490.00
Aug 1	Balance	b/d	208.00				

Note. At 31 July the closing balance on the receivables control account ($208) is the same as the total of the individual balances on the personal accounts in the receivables ledger ($0 + $78 + $130). This is an **important check** which should be done every month. If the balance on the control account does **not** equal the sum of the individual balances, an **error** has been made.

BANK CONTROL ACCOUNT

A/c no: NL 1

Date 20X2	Narrative	Ref.	$	Date	Narrative	Ref.	$
July 31	Cash received	CRDB 23	282.00				

SALES: HARDWARE

A/c no: NL 21

Date	Narrative	Ref.	$	Date 20X2	Narrative	Ref.	$
				July 31	Receivables	SDB 35	340.00

SALES: ELECTRICAL

A/c no: NL 22

Date	Narrative	Folio	$	Date 20X2	Narrative	Folio	$
				July 31	Receivables	SDB 35	150.00

If we took the balance on the accounts shown in this example as at 31 July 20X2 the trial balance (insofar as it is appropriate to call these limited extracts by this name) would be as follows.

TRIAL BALANCE

	DEBIT	CREDIT
	$	$
Bank (all receipts)	282	
Receivables	208	
Sales: hardware		340
Sales: electrical		150
	490	490

The trial balance is shown here to emphasise the point that a trial balance includes the balances on control accounts, but excludes the balances on the personal accounts in the receivables ledger and payables ledger.

2.2 Accounting for payables

If you were able to follow the example above dealing with the receivables control account, you should have no difficulty in dealing with similar examples relating to purchases/payables. If necessary refer back to revise the entries made in the purchase day book and payables ledger personal accounts.

2.3 Entries in control accounts

The following are typical control account entries. Reference 'Jnl' indicates that the transaction is first lodged in the journal before posting to the control account and other accounts indicated. References SRDB and PRDB are to sales returns and purchase returns day books. Have a look at these *ad hoc* examples.

RECEIVABLES CONTROL ACCOUNT

	Ref.	$		Ref.	$
Opening debit balances	b/d	7,000	Opening credit balances		
Sales	SDB	53,640	(if any)	b/d	200
Dishonoured bills or	Jnl	1,000	Cash received	CRDB	52,250
cheques			Returns inwards from		
Cash paid to clear credit			customers	SRDB	800
balances	CIDB	110	Irrecoverable debts	Jnl	300
			Closing debit balances	c/d	8,200
					61,750
Debit balances b/d		8,200			

Notes

(a)   Opening credit balances are unusual in the receivables control account. They represent customers to whom the business owes money, probably as a result of the over-payment of debts or for advance payments of debts for which no invoices have yet been sent.

(b)   No breakdown is provided here of the debit and credit balance brought down. In practice, these would be supported by a schedule extracted from the receivables ledger.

(c)   Don't worry too much about irrecoverable debts here: we will look at them in detail in the next chapter. You only need to know that the double entry to record an irrecoverable debt written off is:

DEBIT   Receivables expense
CREDIT   Receivables control account

PAYABLES CONTROL ACCOUNT

	Ref.	$		Ref.	$
Opening debit balances (if any)	b/d	70	Opening credit balances	b/d	8,300
Cash paid	CIDB	29,840	Purchases and other expenses	PDB	31,000
Discounts received	CIDB	30	Cash received clearing debit balances	CRDB	20
Returns outwards to suppliers	PRDB	60	Closing debit balances (if any)	c/d	80
Closing credit balances	c/d	9,400			
		39,400			39,400
Debit balances	b/d	80	Credit balances	b/d	9,400

Note. Opening debit balances in the payables control account would represent suppliers who owe the business money, perhaps because debts have been overpaid or because debts have been prepaid before the supplier has sent an invoice. Again, details of these at the beginning and end of the year would be obtained from the trade payables.

Posting from the journal to the memorandum receivables or trade payables and to the general ledger may be effected as in the following example, where C Cloning has returned goods with a sales value of $50.

Journal entry	Ref.	DEBIT $	CREDIT $
Sales	NL 21	50	
To receivables control account	NL 6		50
To C Cloning (memorandum)	RL 13	–	50

Return of electrical goods inwards

(This entry is not part of the example control account given above)

Another control account entry you may come across which is not included in the example control accounts above is a **contra.**

If two businesses owe money to each other they might agree to set one amount off against the other. This type of transaction is known as a contra.

Consider a business X that owes supplier Y $1,000 in respect of a purchase invoice for services provided. However X also delivered some goods to Y along with a sales invoice for $750. This means Y is both a customer and a supplier of X.

The entries made in X's books in the control accounts (and memorandum ledgers) to date will reflect $1,000 owed to Y and $750 due from Y.

X may want to simply show that overall Y is owed $250 and will agree with Y that the two amounts can be set off. If this is the case a **contra** entry will be made in X's books:

DEBIT   Trade payables control account $750
CREDIT   Receivables control account $750

Y will make the opposite entries and both businesses will update the memorandum ledgers.

Have a go at the next question which includes a contra with the receivables control account.

QUESTION   Payables control

A payables control account contains the following entries:

	$
Bank	79,500
Credit purchases	83,200
Discounts received	3,750
Contra with receivables control account (to offset an amount due from a customer)	4,000
Balance c/f at 31 December 20X8	12,920

There are no other entries in the account. What was the opening balance brought forward at 1 January 20X8?

ANSWER

	$	$
Accounts payable at 1 January (balancing figure)		16,970
Purchases in year		83,200
		100,170
Less: Cash paid to suppliers in year	79,500	
Discounts received	3,750	
Contra with receivables control	4,000	
		(87,250)
Amounts still unpaid at 31 December		12,920

QUESTION

Receivables control

The total of the balances in a company's receivables ledger is $800 more than the debit balance on its receivables control account. Which one of the following errors could by itself account for the discrepancy?

A   The sales day book has been undercast by $800

B   Trade discounts totalling $800 have been omitted from the general ledger

C   One receivables ledger account with a credit balance of $800 has been treated as a debit balance

D   The cash received day book has been undercast by $800

ANSWER

A   The total of sales invoices in the day book is debited to the control account. If the total is understated by $800, the debits in the control account will also be understated by $800. Options B and D would have the opposite effect: credit entries in the control account would be understated. Option C would lead to a discrepancy of 2 × $800 = $1,600.

It may help you to see how the receivables ledger and receivables (control) account are used set out in **flowchart form.**

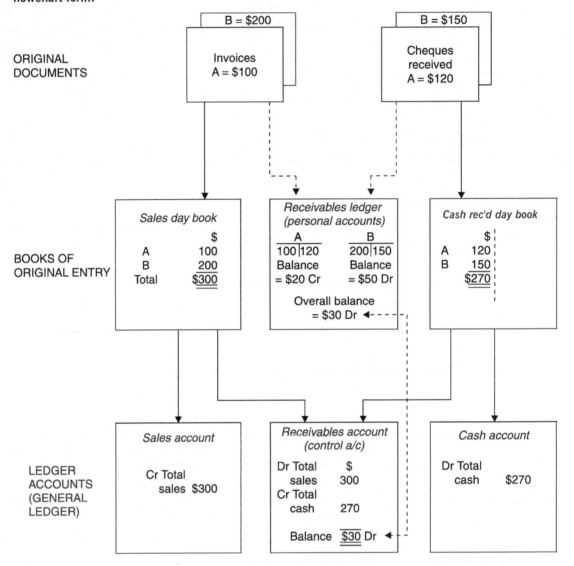

EXAM FOCUS POINT

Remember these important points

- The receivables ledger is not part of the double entry system (it is not used to post the ledger accounts).

- Nevertheless, the total balance on the receivables ledger (ie all the personal account balances added up) should equal the balance on the receivables control account.

QUESTION   Exports Co

On examining the books of Exports Co, you ascertain that on 1 October 20X8 the receivables ledger balances were $8,024 debit and $57 credit, and the trade payables balances on the same date $6,235 credit and $105 debit.

For the year ended 30 September 20X9 the following particulars are available.

	$
Revenue	63,728
Purchases	39,974
Cash from trade receivable	55,212
Cash to trade payable	37,307
Discount received	1,475
Returns inwards	3,330
Returns outwards	535
Irrecoverable debts written off	326
Cash received in respect of debit balances in trade payables	105
Amount due from customer as shown by receivables ledger, offset against amount	
due to the same firm as shown by trade payables (settlement by contra)	434
Cash received in respect of debt previously written off as irrecoverable	94
Allowances to customers on goods damaged in transit	212

On 30 September 20X9 there were no credit balances in the receivables ledger except those outstanding on 1 October 20X8, and no debit balances in the trade payables. You are required to write up the following accounts recording the above transactions bringing down the balances as on 30 September 20X9:

(a) Receivables control account
(b) Payables control account

ANSWER

(a)

RECEIVABLES CONTROL ACCOUNT

20X8		$	20X8		$
Oct 1	Balances b/f	8,024	Oct 1	Balances b/f	57
20X9			20X9		
Sept 30	Sales	63,728	Sept 30	Cash received from credit	
				customers	55,212
	Balances c/f	57			
				Returns	3,330
				Irrecoverable debts	
				written off	326
				Transfer payables	
				control account (contra)	434
				Allowances on goods	
				damaged	212
				Balances c/f	12,238
		71,809			71,809

(b)

PAYABLES CONTROL ACCOUNT

20X8		$	20X8		$
Oct 1	Balances b/f	105	Oct 1	Balances b/f	6,235
20X9			20X9		
Sept 30	Cash paid to credit		Sept 30	Purchases	39,974
	suppliers	37,307		Cash	105
	Discount received	1,475			
	Returns outwards	535			
	Transfer receivables				
	control account				
	(contra)	434			
	Balances c/f	6,458			
		46,314			46,314

Note. The double entry in respect of cash received for the irrecoverable debt previously written off is:

DEBIT	Cash	$94	
CREDIT	Receivables expense		$94

3 The purpose of control accounts

At suitable intervals the balances on personal accounts are extracted from the ledgers, listed and totalled. The total of the outstanding balances can then be **reconciled** to the balance on the appropriate **control account** and any errors located and corrected.

3.1 Reasons for having control accounts

The main reasons for having control accounts are as follows.

3.1.1 Accuracy check

They provide a **check on the accuracy** of entries made in the personal accounts in the sales ledger and purchase ledger. It is very easy to make a **mistake in posting entries**, because there might be hundreds of entries to make. **Figures** might get **transposed**. Some entries might be **omitted altogether**, so that an invoice or a payment transaction does not appear in a personal account as it should. It is possible to identify the fact that errors have been made by comparing:

(i)   The total balance on the receivables control account with the total of individual balances on the personal accounts in the sales ledger.

(ii)   The total balance on the payables control account with the total of individual balances on the personal accounts in the purchase ledger.

3.1.2 Discovering errors

The control accounts could also assist in the **location of errors**, where postings to the control accounts are made daily or weekly, or even monthly. If a clerk fails to record an invoice or a payment in a personal account, or makes a transposition error, it would be a formidable task to locate the error or errors at the end of a year, say, given the hundreds or thousands of transactions during the year. By using the control account, a comparison with the individual balances in the sales or purchase ledger can be made for every week or day of the month, and the error found much more quickly than if control accounts did not exist.

Where there is a separation of clerical (bookkeeping) duties, the control account provides an **internal check**. The person posting entries to the control accounts will act as a check on a different person whose job it is to post entries to the sales and purchase ledger accounts.

3.1.3 Provides a total balance

To provide receivables and payables balances more quickly for producing a trial balance or statement of financial position. A single balance on a control account is obviously **extracted more simply and quickly** than many individual balances in the sales or purchase ledger. This means also that the number of accounts in the **double entry bookkeeping** system can be kept down to a **manageable size**, since the personal accounts are memorandum accounts only and the control accounts instead provide the accounts required for a double entry system.

However, particularly in **computerised systems**, it may be feasible to use receivables and trade payables **without** the **need for operating separate control accounts**. In such a system, the sales or purchase ledger printouts produced by the computer constitute the list of individual balances as well as providing a total balance which represents the control account balance.

3.2 Reconciling control accounts with receivables and payables ledgers

The control accounts should be **balanced regularly** (at least monthly), and the balance on the control account agreed with the schedule of the individual receivables' or payables' balances extracted from the sales or bought ledgers respectively.

It is one of the sad facts of an accountant's life that more often than not the balance on the control account does not agree with the schedule of balances extracted, for one or more of the following reasons.

3.2.1 Possible reasons for disagreement between control account balance and total of the list of balances

Circumstance/error	Explanation and action needed
An **incorrect amount** may be **posted** to the control account because of a **miscast** of the total in the **book of original entry** (ie adding up incorrectly the total value of invoices or payments).	The general ledger debit and credit postings will balance, but the control account balance will not agree with the sum of individual balances extracted from the (memorandum) receivables ledger or trade payables. A journal entry must then be made in the general ledger to correct the control account and the corresponding sales or expense account (or bank account).
A **transposition error** may occur in posting an individual's balance from the book of prime entry to the memorandum ledger, eg the sale to C Cloning of $250 might be posted to his account as $520.	This means that the sum of balances extracted from the memorandum ledger must be corrected. No accounting entry would be required to do this, except to alter the figure in C Cloning's account, which will decrease the total of the list of balances by $270 (which is $520 less $250 – the difference between the amount recorded and what should have been recorded).
The **list of balances** extracted from the memorandum ledger may be **incorrectly extracted or miscast**.	To fix this would involve simply correcting the total of the balances, since they are maintained outside of the general ledger. As well as being miscast, a customer/supplier balance may be omitted. The amount relating to the missing account will need to be added back in to arrive at the corrected total for the list of balances.
Credit notes entered as invoices or invoices entered as credit notes in the control account (but correctly entered in the personal accounts).	This will result in the amount of the invoice/credit note being entered on the wrong side of the control account. Therefore to correct this via a journal will mean posting an entry which is **double** the amount of the original entry. For example, suppose a credit note issued to a customer for $500 was treated as an invoice when recording it in the control account (or was listed as such in the day books). This means an entry of DR Receivables control $500 CR Sales $500 was made. There should have been a CR of $500 to Receivables control, so in order to both reverse the original entry and record the proper entry the journal to correct this will be CR Receivables control $1,000, DR Sales $500, DR Sales returns $500.
Credit note entered as an invoice or invoice entered as a credit note in the personal accounts (but correctly entered in the control account).	Here, no entries are needed in the control accounts, but the adjustment to the individual personal account (and therefore total of the list of balances) in the receivables ledger will again be twice that of the invoice/credit note.

Circumstance/error	Explanation and action needed
Invoices posted to the wrong side in the control account (only).	The correcting journal to the control account will involve an entry to the control account twice the value of the original entry, to account for the fact the original entry must be reversed **and** the amount needs to be recorded on the correct side.
Credit balances treated as Debit balances in the list of balances (eg personal account debit balance treated as a credit balance).	Assuming this is treated correctly in the control account, the list of balances total will need to be adjusted by twice the amount of the incorrectly treated balance. For example a debit balance of $20 on a customer's personal account treated as a credit balance would mean the list of balances would be $40 too low.
Contra entries made in the personal accounts, but not in the control accounts.	Contra entries are made where a receivables balance is offset against a payables balance (as the customer and supplier are the same individual or business entity). If this entry is made in the personal accounts but not the control accounts, the total of the list of personal account balances will be lower than the control account. The contra entry of DR payables, CR receivables will be needed to bring the control account up to date. (Note that if the contra has been reflected in the control account, but not the personal accounts, the personal accounts will need adjusting instead).
Discounts entered in the personal ledgers not recorded in the control account (or vice-versa).	A journal is needed to correct the control account to reduce its balance by the amount of the discount, with the other side of the journal entry being posted to discounts allowed/received. (If the discount is recorded in the control account but not the personal account, the adjustment is needed in the personal account which will adjust the list of balances total.)

Note that there are other possible reasons for disagreement and the list above is not exhaustive. You need to understand the purpose of and theory behind the control account reconciliation so you are able to apply your knowledge to different situations arising in exam questions.

It is important that you realise that the reconciliation is a means of confirming the accuracy of the corrected control account balance. It is always the corrected control account balance that is reported in the statement of financial position.

3.3 Example: agreeing control account balances with the underlying ledgers

Reconciling the control account balance with the sum of the balances extracted from the (memorandum) receivables ledger or trade payables should be done in two stages.

(a)   Correct the total of the balances extracted from the memorandum ledger. (The errors must be located first of course.)

	$	$
Receivables ledger total		
Original total extracted		15,320
Add difference arising from transposition error ($95 written as $59)		36
		15,356
Less		
Credit balance of $60 extracted as a debit balance ($60 × 2)	120	
Overcast of list of balances	90	
		(210)
		15,146

Note. In practice it is likely that the individual items in the list of balances would be amended accordingly and a revised total arrived at. However, in an exam, this would not leave a trail for the examining team to see what you have done.

(b) Bring down the balance before adjustments on the control account, and adjust or post the account with correcting entries.

RECEIVABLES CONTROL ACCOUNT

	$		$
Balance before adjustments	15,091	Petty cash: posting omitted	10
		Returns inwards: individual posting omitted from control Account	35
		Balance c/d (now in agreement	
Undercast of total invoices issued		with the corrected total of	
in sales day book	100	individual balances in (a))	15,146
	15,191		15,191
Balance b/d	15,146		

QUESTION
April Showers

April Showers sells goods on credit to most of its customers. In order to control its receivables collection system, the company maintains a receivables control account. In preparing the accounts for the year to 30 October 20X3 the accountant discovers that the total of all the personal accounts in the receivables ledger amounts to $12,802, whereas the balance on the receivables control account is $12,550.

Upon investigating the matter, the following errors were discovered.

(a) Sales for the week ending 27 March 20X3 amounting to $850 had been omitted from the control account.
(b) A customer's account balance of $300 had not been included in the list of balances.
(c) Cash received of $750 had been entered in a personal account as $570.
(d) Faulty goods returned totalling $100 had not been entered in the control account.
(e) A personal account balance had been undercast by $200.
(f) A contra item of $400 with the trade payables had not been entered in the control account.
(g) An irrecoverable debt of $500 had not been entered in the control account.
(h) Cash received of $250 had been debited to a personal account.
(i) Discounts received of $50 had been debited to Bell's receivables ledger account.
(j) Returns inwards valued at $200 had not been included in the control account.
(k) Cash received of $80 had been credited to a personal account as $8.
(l) A cheque for $300 received from a customer had been dishonoured by the bank, but no adjustment had been made in the control account.

Required

(a) Prepare a corrected trade receivables control account, bringing down the amended balance as at 1 November 20X3.
(b) Prepare a statement showing the adjustments that are necessary to the list of personal account balances so that it reconciles with the amended receivables control account balance.

ANSWER

(a)   TRADE RECEIVABLES CONTROL ACCOUNT

	$		$
Uncorrected balance b/f	12,550	Faulty goods returned (d)	100
Sales omitted (a)	850	Contra entry omitted (f)	400
Bank: cheque dishonoured (l)	300	Irrecoverable debt omitted (g)	500
		Returns inwards omitted (j)	200
		Amended balance c/d	12,500
	13,700		13,700
Balance b/d	12,500		

Note. Items (b), (c), (e), (h), (i) and (l) are matters affecting the personal accounts of customers. They have no effect on the control account.

(b)   STATEMENT OF ADJUSTMENTS TO LIST OF PERSONAL ACCOUNT BALANCES

	$	$
Original total of list of balances		12,802
Add: debit balance omitted (b)	300	
debit balance understated (e)	200	
		500
		13,302
Less: transposition error (c): understatement of cash received	180	
cash debited instead of credited (2 × $250) (h)	500	
discounts received wrongly debited to Bell (i)	50	
understatement of cash received (l)	72	
		(802)
		12,500

QUESTION

Haldane Co

The balance on the accounts payable control account of Haldane Co as at 31 December 20X6 was $110,000.

A review of the individual accounts payable revealed the following:

	$
Total on list of credit balances in the accounts payable ledger	106,280

List of debit balances in accounts payable ledger:	$
Glen Co's account	630
Hewson Co's account	3,000
	3,630

1   The debit balance on Glen Co's account was caused by a transposition error when posting a payment as $1,928 instead of $1,298.

2   The purchase day book has been added incorrectly overstating the total by $600.

3   Purchases of $3,800 had not been posted to Hewson's personal account in the trade payables.

4   Goods returned of $1,340 had been posted to the personal supplier accounts concerned but not to the control account.

5   An irrecoverable debt of $980 written off Jim Birch's account in the receivables ledger had been incorrectly posted to the payables control account instead of the receivables control account.

Required

(a)   Make the necessary corrections to the payables control account.

(b)   Make the necessary corrections to the trade payables, ensuring that the revised control account balance agrees with the adjusted list of balances in the trade payables.

(c)   Give the correct balance to be reported in the statement of financial position, and state where it will appear.

ANSWER

(a)

	$
Balance per trade payables control account	110,000
Less:overstatement of purchase day book totals	(600)
Less:goods returned not posted to control a/c	(1,340)
Less:irrecoverable debt written off, incorrectly posted in the trade payables	
control account	(980)
	107,080

(b)   Adjustments to the list of balances in the trade payables

	DEBIT $	CREDIT $
Total credit balances in the trade payables		106,280
Trade debit balances in the trade payables	(3,630)	
Adjust for transposition error in Glenn Co's account	630	
Adjust for invoice of $3,800 not posted in Hewson Co's personal account	3,800	
		800
		107,080

(c)   The balance to be reported is $107,800 under 'current liabilities'.

EXAM FOCUS POINT

In the September 2019 – August 2020 Examiner's Report, candidates were given a receivables control account with several errors and asked to enter the closing receivables control account balance.

This was an example of a number entry objective test question and therefore candidates are required to type the number in to the relevant gap.

This style of question tests the preparation of a ledger account containing errors. Candidates must have a thorough understanding of the way in which receivables control accounts (and payables control accounts) are prepared. It is important to note that not all entries in the ledger account given in the exam were incorrect.

In the exam, candidates can use the highlighter tool to select entries that are incorrect before calculating the answer.

Technical Performance Objective 7 requires you to be able to open a suspense account to record any imbalance and also to identify and correct errors to close the suspense account through journal entries. The knowledge you gain in this chapter will help you to demonstrate your competence in this area.

4 Types of error in accounting

It is not really possible to draw up a complete list of all the errors which might be made by bookkeepers and accountants. Even if you tried, it is more than likely that as soon as you finished, someone would commit a completely new error that you had never even dreamed of! However, it is possible to describe **five types of error** which cover most of the errors which might occur. They are as follows.

–   Errors of **transposition** – one or both entries
–   Errors of **omission** – complete or partial
–   Errors of **principle**
–   Errors of **commission** – misposting, reversal, original entry
–   **Compensating errors**

Once an error has been detected, it needs to be put right.

(a)   If the correction **involves a double entry** in the ledger accounts, then it is done by using a **journal entry** in the journal.

(b)   When the error **breaks the rule of double entry**, then it is corrected by the use of a **suspense account** as well as a journal entry.

(c)   Certain errors when corrected will affect profit calculations whereas others may affect only the statement of financial position and some may affect both.

In this section we will:

(a)   Look at the five common types of error (which were introduced in Chapter 4)
(b)   Review journal entries (which we briefly looked at earlier in this text)
(c)   Define a **suspense account**, and describe how it is used

4.1 Errors of transposition

An **error of transposition** is when two digits in an amount are accidentally recorded the wrong way round.

For example, suppose that a sale is recorded in the sales account as $6,843, but it has been incorrectly recorded in the receivables account as $6,483. The error is the transposition of the 4 and the 8. The consequence is that total debits will not be equal to total credits. You can often detect a transposition error by checking whether the difference between debits and credits can be divided exactly by 9. For example, $6,843 – $6,483 = $360; $360 ÷ 9 = 40.

In this case, the error will not affect the statement of profit or loss. Correction of the error will only involve adjusting the total receivables' account. As the error breaks the rule of double entry it is corrected by the use of a suspense account (Section 6).

4.2 Errors of omission

An **error of omission** means failing to record a transaction at all **(complete omission)**, or making a debit or credit entry, but not the corresponding double entry **(error of partial omission)**.

Here is an example.

(a)   If a business receives an invoice from a supplier for $250, the transaction might be omitted from the books entirely. As a result, both the total debits and the total credits of the business will be out by $250. The correction of such an error will affect both the statement of profit or loss and the statement of financial position, as both purchases and payables are understated.

The correcting journal would be as follows:

		$	$
DEBIT	Purchases	250	
CREDIT	Payables		250

Being correction of omission of purchase invoice.

(b)   If a business receives an invoice from a supplier for $300, the payables control account might be credited, but the debit entry in the purchases account might be omitted. In this case, the total credits would not equal total debits (because total debits are $300 less than they ought to be).

This is an error of **partial omission** or **single entry**. Such an error would affect the statement of profit or loss as the purchases account has not been debited. As this error breaks the rule of double entry, it is corrected by the use of a suspense account.

4.3 Errors of principle

An **error of principle** involves making a double entry in the belief that the transaction is being entered in the correct accounts, but subsequently finding out that the accounting entry breaks the 'rules' of an accounting principle or concept.

A typical example of such an error is to treat certain revenue expenditure incorrectly as capital expenditure.

(a) For example, repairs to a machine costing $150 should be treated as revenue expenditure, and debited to a repairs account. If, instead, the repair costs are added to the cost of the non-current asset (capital expenditure) an error of principle would have occurred. As a result, although total debits still equal total credits, the repairs account is $150 less than it should be and the cost of the non-current asset is $150 greater than it should be.

(b) Similarly, suppose that the proprietor of the business sometimes takes cash out of the till for their personal use and during a certain year these withdrawals on account of profit amount to $280. The bookkeeper states that they have reduced cash sales by $280 so that the relevant cash day book could be made to balance. This would be an error of principle, and the result of it would be that the withdrawal account is understated by $280, and so is the total value of sales in the sales account.

4.4 Errors of commission

Errors of commission are where the bookkeeper makes a mistake in carrying out their task of recording transactions in the accounts.

Here are two common types of errors of commission.

(a) **Putting a debit entry or a credit entry in the wrong account**. For example, if telephone expenses of $540 are debited to the electricity expenses account, an error of commission would have occurred. The result is that although total debits and total credits balance, telephone expenses are understated by $540 and electricity expenses are overstated by the same amount.

(b) **Errors of casting (adding up).** Suppose for example that the total daily credit sales in the sales day book of a business should add up to $28,425, but are incorrectly added up as $28,825. The total sales in the sales day book are then used to credit total sales and debit receivables in the general ledger accounts, so that total debits and total credits are still equal, although incorrect.

4.5 Compensating errors

Compensating errors are errors which are, coincidentally, equal and opposite to one another.

For example, two transposition errors of $540 might occur in extracting ledger balances, one on each side of the double entry. In the administration expenses account, $2,282 might be written instead of $2,822, while in the sundry income account, $8,391 might be written instead of $8,931. Both the debits and the credits would be $540 too low, and the mistake would not be apparent when the list of account balances is cast. Consequently, compensating errors hide the fact that there are errors in the list of account balances.

Two types of compensating error are:

- **Error of reversal**. In this case debit and credit entries have been reversed.
- **Error of transposition**. This is where numbers in the amount are transposed, eg 54 becomes 45. If the incorrect amount is posted on both sides, this will not be detected.

4.6 Errors of original entry

An error of original entry means that the transaction was incorrectly recorded in a day book, leading to incorrect ledger postings.

For instance, cash received of $3,500 is entered in the cash received day book as $3,000. This amount is then debited to the bank account and credited to the receivables account in the ledger. As both the debit and credit entries are incorrect, this will not show up in the trial balance.

4.7 Errors of reversal

An **error of reversal** occurs when the debit and credit postings are reversed.

This will not cause an imbalance if **both** entries are reversed. For instance, a posting which should have been Debit Bank; Credit Sales is posted as Debit Sales; Credit Bank. The trial balance will still balance.

4.8 Casting errors

These occur when amounts have been incorrectly totalled in a day book or within a ledger account.

4.9 Correcting errors

The effect of correcting any entry needs to be carefully considered. If draft accounts have been prepared before the error has been corrected the correction will revise the balance(s) on the affected account(s). Thus the final accounts will be affected by the correction. Whether it is the statement of profit or loss or the statement of financial position that is affected, will depend on whether the account records income, expense asset, liability or capital.

5 | The correction of errors: journal entries

Errors which leave total debits and total credits on the ledger accounts in balance can be corrected by using **journal entries**. Otherwise, a suspense account has to be opened.

5.1 Journal entries

Some errors can be corrected by journal entries. To remind you, the format of a journal entry is:

Date	DEBIT	CREDIT
	$	$
Account to be debited	X	
Account to be credited		X
(Narrative to explain the transaction)		

The journal requires a debit and an equal credit entry for each 'transaction', ie for each correction. This means that if total debits equal total credits before a journal entry is made then they will still be equal after the journal entry is made. This would be the case if, for example, the original error was a debit wrongly posted as a credit or vice versa.

Similarly, if total debits and total credits are unequal before a journal entry is made, then they will still be unequal (by the same amount) after it is made.

For example, suppose a bookkeeper accidentally posts a bill for $40 to the local taxes account instead of to the electricity account. A list of account balances is drawn up, and total debits are $40,000 and total credits are $40,000. A journal entry is made to correct the misposting error as follows.

1.7.20X7

DEBIT	Electricity account	$40	
CREDIT	Local taxes account		$40

To correct a misposting of $40 from the rates account to electricity account

After the journal has been posted, total debits will still be $40,000 and total credits will be $40,000. Total debits and totals credits are still equal.

Now suppose that, because of some error which has not yet been detected, total debits were originally $40,000 but total credits were $39,900. If the same journal correcting the $40 is put through, total debits will remain $40,000 and total credits will remain $39,900. Total debits were different by $100 **before** the journal, and they are still different by $100 **after** the journal.

This means that journals can only be used to correct errors which require both a credit and (an equal) debit adjustment.

5.2 Example: journal entries

Listed below are five errors which were used as examples earlier in this chapter. Write out the journal entries which would correct these errors.

(a)   A business receives an invoice for $250 from a supplier which was omitted from the books entirely.

(b)   Repairs worth $150 were incorrectly debited to the non-current asset (machinery) account instead of the repairs account.

(c)   The bookkeeper of a business reduces cash sales by $280 because they were not sure what the $280 represented. In fact, it was a withdrawal on account of profit.

(d)   Telephone expenses of $540 are incorrectly debited to the electricity account.

(e)   A page in the sales day book has been added up to $28,425 instead of $28,825.

Solution

(a)   DEBIT   Purchases $250
        CREDIT   Trade payables $250

        A transaction previously omitted

(b)   DEBIT   Repairs account $150
        CREDIT   Non-current asset (machinery) a/c $150

        The correction of an error of principle: Repairs costs incorrectly added to non-current asset costs

(c)   DEBIT   Drawings $280
        CREDIT   Revenue $280

        An error of principle, in which sales were reduced to compensate for cash withdrawals not accounted for

(d)   DEBIT   Telephone expenses $540
        CREDIT   Electricity expenses $540

        Correction of an error of commission: telephone expenses wrongly charged to the electricity account

(e)   DEBIT   Trade receivable $400
        CREDIT   Revenue $400

        The correction of a casting error in the sales day book
        ($28,825 – $28,425 = $400)

5.3 Use of journal entries in examinations

In the examination you may be asked to select the correct answer from a selection of 'journalised' transactions (ie transactions set out in the form of a journal entry). This is just one way the examining team can find out whether you know your debits and credits. For example:

Transaction: A business sells $1,300 of goods on credit.

Correct journalised transaction:

            DEBIT   Trade receivables $1,300
            CREDIT   Revenue $1,300

            Goods to the value of $1,300 sold on credit

No error has occurred here, just a normal credit sale of $1,300 but by asking you to identify the correct journal entries of this, the examining team can test that you understand the double-entry bookkeeping involved.

5.4 Effect of errors on statement of profit or loss and statement of financial position

As you have seen, some types of error will cause an imbalance in the trial balance. The bookkeeper will then know that an error has been made and will look for it and correct it. However, errors of principle, omission or commission, or compensating errors may not be immediately detected. In this case, the trial balance will balance but the statement of profit or loss, or the statement of financial position may be incorrect. You may be asked in the exam to consider how errors, and the correction of errors, affect the statement of profit or loss and statement of financial position.

To take some of the examples from 5.2 above:

(a)   If the $250 supplier invoice has been entirely excluded, the trial balance will balance. However, the payables will be understated by $250 and the profit in the statement of profit or loss will be overstated. When this error is corrected profit will go down by $250 and proprietor's capital will be reduced by the same amount. This will be balanced by the increase of $250 in payables, so the statement of financial position totals will not change.

(b)   The $150 incorrectly debited to non-current assets will have overstated non-current assets in the statement of financial position and overstated profit by the same amount. When this error is corrected the assets will go down by $150 and the capital will be reduced by the same amount.

(c)   The failure to account for cash drawings will have a reduced profit and capital by $280 and overstated capital by the same amount (drawings are deducted from capital in the statement of financial position). Correcting this error will increase sales and profit in the statement of profit or loss and leave capital unchanged as the $280 extra profit credited to capital will be offset by the $280 drawings.

Remember: the net profit is credited to capital, so everything ends up in the statement of financial position in the end.

6   The correction of errors: suspense accounts

Suspense accounts, as well as being used to correct some errors, are also opened when it is not known immediately where to post an amount. When the mystery is solved, the suspense account is closed and the amount correctly posted using a journal entry.

A suspense account is an account showing a balance equal to the difference in a trial balance.

A suspense account is a **temporary** account which can be opened for a number of reasons. The most common reasons are as follows.

(a)   A trial balance is drawn up which does not balance (ie total debits do not equal total credits).

(b)   The bookkeeper of a business knows where to post the credit side of a transaction, but does not know where to post the debit (or vice versa). For example, a cash payment might be made and must obviously be credited to cash. But the bookkeeper may not know what the payment is for, and so will not know which account to debit.

In both these cases, a temporary suspense account is opened up until the problem is sorted out. The next few paragraphs explain exactly how this works.

6.1 Use of suspense account: when the trial balance does not balance

When an error has occurred which results in an imbalance between total debits and total credits in the ledger accounts, the first step is to open a suspense account. For example, suppose an accountant draws up a trial balance and finds that, for some reason they cannot immediately discover, total debits exceed total credits by $162.

They know that there is an error somewhere, but for the time being they open a suspense account and enters a credit of $162 in it. This serves two purposes.

(a)   Because the suspense account now exists, the accountant will not forget that there is an error (of $162) to be sorted out.

(b)   Now that there is a credit of $162 in the suspense account, the list of account balances.

When the cause of the $162 discrepancy is tracked down, it is corrected by means of a journal entry. For example, suppose it turned out that the accountant had accidentally failed to make a credit of $162 to purchases. The journal entry would be:

DEBIT	Suspense a/c	$162	
CREDIT	Purchases		$162

To close off suspense a/c and correct error

The correction of this error will affect the statement of profit or loss as purchases had originally been overstated by $162. Whenever an error occurs which results in total debits not being equal to total credits, the first step an accountant makes is to open up a suspense account. Three more examples are given below.

6.2 Example: transposition error

The bookkeeper of Mixem Gladly Co made a transposition error when entering an amount for sales in the sales account. Instead of entering the correct amount of $37,453.60 they entered $37,543.60, transposing the 4 and 5. The trade receivable were posted correctly, and so when total debits and credits on the ledger accounts were compared, it was found that credits exceeded debits by $(37,543.60 − 37,453.60) = $90.

The initial step is to equalise the total debits and credits by posting a one sided debit entry of $90 to a suspense account.

When the cause of the error is discovered, the double entry to correct it should be logged in the journal as:

DEBIT	Revenue	$90	
CREDIT	Suspense a/c		$90

To close off suspense a/c and correct transposition error

The correction of this error will affect the statement of profit or loss as sales have been overstated by the transposition error.

6.3 Example: error of omission

When Guttersnipe Builders paid the monthly salary cheques to its office staff, the payment of $5,250 was correctly entered in the cash account, but the bookkeeper omitted to debit the office salaries account. As a consequence, the total debit and credit balances on the ledger accounts were not equal, and credits exceeded debits by $5,250.

The initial step in correcting the situation is to debit $5,250 to a suspense account, to equalise the total debits and total credits.

When the cause of the error is discovered, the double entry to correct it should be logged in the journal as:

DEBIT	Office salaries account	$5,250	
CREDIT	Suspense a/c		$5,250

To close off suspense account and correct error of omission

The correcting entry will affect the statement of profit or loss as expenses have been understated by the omission of office salaries.

6.4 Example: error of commission

A bookkeeper might make a mistake by entering what should be a debit entry as a credit, or vice versa. For example, suppose that a credit customer pays $460 of the $660 they owe to Ashdown Tree Felling Contractors, but Ashdown's bookkeeper has debited $460 on the receivables account in the nominal ledger by mistake instead of crediting the payment received.

The total debit balances in Ashdown's ledger accounts would now exceed the total credits by 2 × $460 = $920. The initial step in correcting the error would be to make a credit entry of $920 in a suspense account. When the cause of the error is discovered, it should be corrected as follows.

DEBIT	Suspense a/c	$920
CREDIT	Trade receivable	$920

To close off suspense account and correct error of commission

The correction of this error will not affect the statement of profit or loss. It will affect the statement of financial position as receivables are overstated by $920.

In the receivables control account in the general ledger, the correction would appear therefore as follows.

TRADE RECEIVABLES CONTROL ACCOUNT

	$		$
Balance b/f	660	Suspense a/c: error corrected	920
Payment incorrectly debited	460	Balance c/f	200
	1,120		1,120

6.5 Use of suspense account: not knowing where to post a transaction

Another use of suspense accounts occurs when a bookkeeper does not know in which account to post one side of a transaction. Until the mystery is sorted out, the credit entry can be recorded in a suspense account. A typical example is when the business receives cash through the post from a source which cannot be determined. The double entry in the accounts would be a debit in the bank ledger account, and a credit to a suspense account.

Similarly, when the bookkeeper knows in which account to make one entry, but for some reason does not know where to make the corresponding entry, this can be posted to a suspense account. A very common example is to credit proceeds on disposal of a non-current asset to the suspense account instead of working out the profit or loss on disposal.

6.6 Example: not knowing where to post a transaction

Windfall Garments received a cheque in the post for $620. The name on the cheque is R J Beasley, but Windfall Garments have no idea who this person is, nor why they should be sending $620. The bookkeeper decides to open a suspense account, so that the double entry for the transaction is:

DEBIT	Cash	$620
CREDIT	Suspense a/c	$620

Eventually, it transpires that the cheque was in payment for a debt owed by the Haute Couture Corner Shop and paid out of the proprietor's personal bank account. The suspense account can now be cleared, as follows.

DEBIT	Suspense a/c	$620
CREDIT	Trade receivable	$620

QUESTION
Suspense account

You are assisting the accountant of Ranchurch Ltd in preparing the accounts for the year ended 31 December 20X0. You draw up a trial balance and you notice that the credit side is greater than the debit side by $5,607.82. You enter this difference in a suspense account.

On investigation, the following errors and omissions are found to have occurred.

(a)   An invoice for $1,327.40 for general insurance has been posted to cash but not to the ledger account.

(b)   A customer went into liquidation just before the year end, owing Ranchurch $428.52. The amount was taken off trade receivables but the corresponding entry to expense the irrecoverable debt has not been made.

(c)   A cheque paid for purchases has been posted to the purchases account as $5,296.38, when the cheque was made out for $5,926.38.

(d)   A van was purchased during the year for $1,610.95, but this amount was credited to the motor vehicles account.

Required

(a)   Show the journal required to clear the suspense account.
(b)   Show the suspense account in ledger account form.

ANSWER

(a)   *Journal*

		$	$
DEBIT	Insurance	1,327.40	
	Receivables expense	428.52	
	Purchases ($5,926.38 – $5,296.38)	630.00	
	Motor vehicles ($1,610.95 × 2)	3,221.90	
CREDIT	Suspense account		5,607.82

(b)   *In ledger account form*

SUSPENSE ACCOUNT

	$		$
Balance b/f	5,607.82	Insurance	1,327.40
		Receivables expense	428.52
		Purchases	630.00
Payment incorrectly debited		Motor vehicles	3,221.90
	5,607.82		5,607.82

6.7 Suspense accounts might contain several items

If more than one error or unidentifiable posting to a ledger account arises during an accounting period, they will all be merged together in the same suspense account. Indeed, until the causes of the errors are discovered, the bookkeepers are unlikely to know exactly how many errors there are. An examination question might give you a balance on a suspense account, together with enough information to make the necessary corrections, leaving a nil balance on the suspense account and correct balances on various other accounts. In practice, of course, finding these errors is far from easy!

6.8 Suspense accounts are temporary

It must be stressed that a **suspense account can only be temporary**. Postings to a suspense account are only made when the bookkeeper doesn't know yet what to do, or when an error has occurred. Mysteries must be solved, and errors must be corrected.

Under no circumstances should there still be a suspense account when it comes to preparing the statement of financial position of a business. The suspense account must be cleared and all the correcting entries made before the final accounts are drawn up.

EXAM FOCUS POINT

The clearance of a suspense account is an important accounting technique.

In practice, there should be proper controls in force over the use of a suspense account.

(a)   Regular analysis of contents of the suspense account

(b)   Ageing of items in the account with some targets set eg items should be cleared out within three months, though sometimes this might not be possible

(c)   Review of analysis by an independent person

(d)   Retention of any available supporting documentation, perhaps in a separate file, to provide the basis for further clarification

QUESTION   Suspense account

At the year end of T Down & Co, an imbalance in the list of account balances was revealed which resulted in the creation of a suspense account with a credit balance of $1,040.

Investigations revealed the following errors.

(i)   A sale of goods on credit for $1,000 had been omitted from the sales account.

(ii)   Delivery and installation costs of $240 on a new item of plant had been recorded as a revenue expense.

(iii) Settlement discount of $150 on paying a supplier, JW, had been taken, even though the payment was made outside the time limit.

(iv)   Inventory of stationery at the end of the period of $240 had been ignored.

(v)   A purchase of raw materials of $350 had been recorded in the purchases account as $850.

(vi)   The purchase returns day book included a sales credit note for $230 which had been entered correctly in the account of the receivable concerned, but included with purchase returns in the general ledger.

Required

(a)   Prepare journal entries to correct **each** of the above errors. Narratives are **not** required.

(b)   Open a suspense account and show the corrections to be made.

(c)   Prior to the discovery of the errors, T Down & Co's gross profit for the year was calculated at $35,750 and the net profit for the year at $18,500. Calculate the revised gross and net profit figures after the correction of the errors.

ANSWER

(a)

			DEBIT $	CREDIT $
(i)	DEBIT	Suspense a/c	1,000	
	CREDIT	Revenue		1,000
(ii)	DEBIT	Plant	240	
	CREDIT	Delivery cost		240
(iii)	DEBIT	Settlement discount received	150	
	CREDIT	JW a/c		150
(iv)	DEBIT	Inventory of stationery	240	
	CREDIT	Stationery expense		240
(v)	DEBIT	Suspense a/c	500	
	CREDIT	Purchases		500
(vi)	DEBIT	Purchase returns	230	
	DEBIT	Sales returns	230*	
	CREDIT	Suspense a/c		460

(b) SUSPENSE A/C

	$		$
(i) Revenue	1,000	End of year balance	1,040
(v) Purchases	500	(vi) Purchase returns/sales returns	460
	1,500		1,500

(c)

	$
Gross profit originally reported	35,750
Sales omitted	1,000
Plant costs wrongly allocated *	240
Incorrect recording of purchases	500
Sales credit note wrongly allocated	(460)
Adjusted gross profit	37,030

	$
Net profit originally reported	18,500
Adjustments to gross profit $(37,030 – 35,750)	1,280
Cash discount incorrectly taken	(150)
Stationery inventory	240
Adjusted net profit	19,870

* **Note.** It has been assumed that the delivery and installation costs on plant have been included in purchases.

7 Bank reconciliations

Bank reconciliations identify and explain differences between the bank statement and the bank ledger account.

A **bank reconciliation** is a comparison of a bank statement with the bank account in the general ledger. Differences between the balance on the bank statement and the balance in the ledger account will be errors or timing differences, and they should be identified and satisfactorily explained.

EXAM FOCUS POINT

Like control accounts, this is a likely topic for the exam. It is important that the mechanics of a bank reconciliation are fully understood, and that any missing information is identified.

7.1 The bank statement

It is a common practice for a business to issue a **monthly statement** to each **credit customer**, itemising:

(a) The **balance** they owed on their account at the **beginning** of the month.
(b) **New debts** incurred by the customer during the month.
(c) **Payments** made by them during the month.
(d) The **balance** they owe on their account at the **end** of the month.

In the same way, a bank statement is sent by a bank to its short-term customers (receivable) and suppliers (payables) – ie customers with bank overdrafts and customers with money in their account – itemising the opening balance on the account, receipts into the account and payments from the account during the period, and the balance at the end of the period.

Remember that if a customer has money in their account, the bank owes them that money. The customer is therefore a **creditor** (payable) of the bank (hence the phrase 'to be in credit'). So, if a business has $8,000 cash in the bank, it will have a debit balance in its own bank ledger account, but the bank statement, if it reconciles exactly with the ledger account, will state that there is a credit balance of $8,000. (**The bank's records are a 'mirror image' of the customer's own records, with debits and credits reversed**.)

7.2 Why is a bank reconciliation necessary?

A bank reconciliation is needed to identify and account for the differences between the general ledger bank account and the bank statement. By reconciling the figures in the ledger account with those in the bank statement we can ensure that both the books and the ledger account are accurate.

Cause of difference	Comments
Error	Errors in calculation, or recording income and payments, are more likely to have been made by you than by the bank, but it is conceivable that the bank has made a mistake too. If the error has not been made by the bank, appropriate entries must be made in the general ledger to correct the ledger balance.
Bank charges or bank interest	The bank might deduct charges for interest on an overdraft or for its services, which you are not informed about until you receive the bank statement. As the business had either incurred a cost or earned the interest, but has not recorded it, these are effectively errors. The general ledger must be updated to correct the omission.
Timing differences	There might be some cheques that you have received and paid into the bank, but which have not yet been '**cleared**' and added to your account (**outstanding lodgements**). So although your own records show that some cash has been added to your account, it has not yet been acknowledged by the bank – although it will be in a very short time when the cheque is eventually cleared.
	Similarly, you might have made some payments by cheque, and reduced the balance in your bank ledger account accordingly, but the person who receives the cheque might not bank it for a while (**unpresented or 'outstanding' cheques**). Even when it is banked, it takes a day or two for the banks to process it and for the money to be deducted from your account.
	Timing differences, such as unpresented cheques or outstanding lodgements, will be included in the reconciliation statement, as they explain the difference between the balance on the bank statement and the corrected ledger balance.

There is a range of terminology used for money paid into the bank eg lodgements or amounts lodged, bankings, paying-in, receipts, or even deposits. Your exam will normally use 'lodgement' or 'lodged'.

Outstanding or uncleared receipts or lodgements usually occur because of what is known as bank float time. For example, you pay your salary cheque in on the 31 December 20X2, but the actual credit only hits your account on say 5 January 20X3.

7.3 What to look for when doing a bank reconciliation

The ledger account and bank statement will rarely agree at a given date. If you are doing a bank reconciliation, you have to identify the following items.

Items on bank statement not in the ledger account

- Payments made to or from the bank account by **standing order**, which have not yet been entered in the ledger account.

- **Dividends received** (on investments held by the business), paid direct into the bank account but not yet entered in the ledger account.

- **Bank interest and bank charges**, not yet entered in the ledger account.

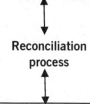

Reconciliation process

Items in the corrected ledger account not on the bank statement:

- Cheques drawn (ie paid) by the business and credited in the ledger account, which have not yet been presented to the bank, or 'cleared', and so do not yet appear on the bank statement (**unpresented or outstanding cheques**).

- Cheques received, paid into the bank and debited in the ledger account, but which have not been cleared and entered in the account by the bank, and so do not appear on the bank statement (**outstanding lodgements**).

7.4 Outline of a bank reconciliation statement

In preparing a bank reconciliation, the following procedure is normally followed:

Step 1	Start with the balance shown on the bank statement
Step 2	Adjust the general ledger account (Bank) for items that appear in the bank statement and are not in the ledger account. These may include: • Bank charges and interest • Direct transfers (bank giros) • Direct debits or standing orders For items such as bank charges and direct transfers it may be the case that the business had not yet received notification and therefore had not incorporated these items in the relevant day book. Other regular payments such as direct debits and standing orders should normally be incorporated in the relevant day book but may have been omitted in error.

Step 3	Adjust the bank statement balance for items entered in the ledger account which have not yet reached the bank. These would be:
	• Lodgements of cash and cheques not yet credited
	• Cheques issued not yet presented

Step 4	Reconcile between the adjusted bank statement balance and the corrected ledger balance.
	The correct balance to be reported in the financial accounts is the corrected ledger balance.

EXAM FOCUS POINT

A bank reconciliation reconciles the bank statement balance with the general ledger 'Bank' account balance (the bank ledger account).

Please note that you may need to correct the bank ledger account for errors in the cash day books (the cash received day book and the cash payments day book) because totals from these are recorded in the bank ledger account. Adjusting for these is part of step 2 of the preceding outline of the bank reconciliation process.

7.5 Common errors and adjustments encountered when performing bank reconciliations

Below we look at some examples (errors, circumstances and reasons for adjustments) that you may encounter when performing a bank reconciliation, and the action to be taken in each case.

Circumstance/error	Action needed
Bank charges and interest on the bank statement not recorded in the general ledger (or cash day books)	This is a transaction occurring in the period not recorded, so the bank ledger account needs adjusting. The bank ledger account balance will decrease for charges and interest payable, and increase for interest received.
Timing differences such as cheques that have not yet cleared and outstanding lodgements	Cheques would have been recorded in the cash day books when written and receipts posted when received. They are correctly reflected in the general ledger so **no action is needed** in the general ledger unless an error has been highlighted in relation to the amount entered. Instead the bank statement balance is adjusted during the reconciliation (as per step 3 in section 7.4).
A cheque to a supplier has been cancelled but the cancellation has not been recorded	The bank ledger account (control account) balance will be too low since the payment will have been recorded initially when the cheque was written (as CREDIT Bank, DEBIT Payables) but no entry has been made to reflect the cancellation. The bank account balance in the general ledger will need to be adjusted and the payables account will need to be increased – so overall DEBIT Bank CREDIT Payables to correct the general ledger.

Circumstance/error	Action needed
A dishonoured cheque from a customer not recorded	This is referring to a cheque received by a customer originally recorded as a receipt (therefore DEBIT Bank, CREDIT Receivables, increasing the bank ledger account balance) but then subsequently found to be dishonoured (the customer's bank will not honour the cheque due to insufficient funds). The fact the cheque was dishonoured will be reflected in the bank statement but not in the general ledger accounts so an entry is needed to reduce the bank ledger account balance and increase receivables (to show the amount is still outstanding) ie CREDIT Bank, DEBIT Receivables.
A transfer to/from the owner's personal bank account to the business bank account not recorded in the bank ledger account	The bank account (Cash book) needs to be adjusted for this. It will be reflected on the bank statement and is a transaction that should have been recorded. A transfer from the business account will be drawings and will decrease the bank ledger account balance; a transfer in will increase the bank ledger account balance.
Cash withdrawn by the owner not recorded	The treatment is the same as for the transfer from the business account above, since this is essentially drawings.
A transposition error occurs while entering a cheque in the cash day book (eg $89 entered as $98)	Using the example of a cheque for $89 entered as $98 – this will cause the bank balance on the general ledger account to be $9 (= $98 – $89) lower than it should be since the payment posted (CREDIT Bank) is too high by $9. The adjustment to put this right must therefore increase the bank balance on the bank ledger account by that amount ($9).
Standing orders/direct debits not recorded	These have gone through the bank and will appear on the bank statement. The bank ledger account needs to reflect these so the balance on the bank ledger account needs to be reduced via journal (CREDIT Bank, DEBIT appropriate Expense account).
Addition error leading to understatement or overstatement of cash payments recorded in the general ledger	One example of this sort of error is where the payments side of the bank ledger account is 'overcast' or 'undercast'. If this is overcast (payments are overstated) by, say $100, this means payments are $100 too high and the balance on the ledger account is therefore $100 too low. The adjustment to put this right will therefore increase the bank ledger account balance by $100. An undercast of the payment side will have the opposite effect. Note that the overcast or undercast could also happen in the cash day books.
Addition error leading to understatement or overstatement of cash banked recorded in the general ledger	In contrast to the example above, if the receipts side of the bank ledger account is overcast, receipts will be too high and the ledger account balance also too high. The adjustment to correct this will decrease the balance on the bank ledger account.

Note that there are other possible examples and the list in the table above is not exhaustive. You need to understand the purpose of and theory behind the bank reconciliation so you are able to apply your knowledge to different situations arising in exam questions.

7.6 Example: bank reconciliation

At 30 September 20X6, the balance on the bank ledger account of Wordsworth Co was $805.15 debit. A bank statement on 30 September 20X6 showed Wordsworth Co to be in credit by $1,112.30.

On investigation of the difference between the two sums, it was established that:

(a)   The cash receipts day book total recorded in the ledger account had been undercast by $90.00.
(b)   Cheques paid in not yet credited by the bank amounted to $208.20.
(c)   Cheques drawn not yet presented to the bank amounted to $425.35.

Required

(a)   Show the correction to the bank ledger account.

(b)   Prepare a statement reconciling the balance per bank statement to the balance per the ledger account.

Solution

		$
(a)	Establishment of correct ledger account balance:	
	Ledger account balance brought forward	805.15
	Add	
	Correction of undercast	90.00
	Corrected ledger account balance	895.15

		$	$
(b)	Bank reconciliation statement:		
	Balance per bank statement		1,112.30
	Add		
	Cheques paid in, recorded in the ledger account, but not yet credited to the account by the bank	208.20	
	Less		
	Cheques paid by the company but not yet presented to the company's bank for settlement	(425.35)	
			(217.15)
	Balance per ledger account		895.15

QUESTION
Bank reconciliation

On 31 January 20X8 a business's bank ledger account showed a credit balance of $150 which did not agree with the bank statement balance. In performing the reconciliation the following points come to light.

	$
Not recorded in the relevant cash day books	
Bank charges	36
Transfer from deposit account to current account	500
Not recorded on the bank statement	
Unpresented cheques	116
Outstanding lodgements	630

It was also discovered that the bank had debited the business account with a cheque for $400 in error. What was the original balance on the bank statement?

ANSWER

BANK ACCOUNT

	$		$
Transfer from deposit a/c	500	Balance b/d	150
		Charges	36
		Balance c/d	314
	500		500

	$
Revised balance per bank ledger account	314
Add unpresented cheques	116
Less outstanding lodgements	(630)
Less error by bank	(400)
Balance per bank statement	(600)

Note that on the bank statement the account is overdrawn

QUESTION

Bank balance

A business's bank statement shows $715 direct debits and $353 investment income not recorded in the bank ledger account. The bank statement does not show a customer's cheque for $875 entered in the ledger account on the last day of the accounting period. If the bank ledger account shows a credit balance of $610 what balance appears on the bank statement?

ANSWER

	$	$
Balance per ledger		(610)
Items on statement, not in ledger		
Direct debits	(715)	
Investment income	353	
		(362)
Corrected balance per ledger		(972)
Item in ledger not on statement:		
Customer's cheque		(875)
Balance per bank statement		(1,847)

The corrected ledger balance ($(972)) will be reported in the final accounts.

7.7 Example: more complicated bank reconciliation

On 30 June 20X6, Lahl's bank ledger account showed that he had an overdraft of $300 on his current account at the bank. A bank statement as at the end of June 20X6 showed that Lahl was in credit with the bank by $65.

On checking the ledger account with the bank statement you find the following.

(a) Cheques drawn, amounting to $500, had been entered in the ledger account but had not been presented.

(b) Cheques received, amounting to $400, had been entered in the ledger account, but had not been credited by the bank.

(c) On instructions from Lahl the bank had transferred interest received on his deposit account amounting to $60 to his current account, recording the transfer on 5 July 20X6. This amount had been credited in the ledger account as on 30 June 20X6.

(d) Bank charges of $35 shown in the bank statement had not been entered in the ledger account.

(e) The payments side of the ledger account had been undercast by $10.

(f) Dividends received amounting to $200 had been paid direct to the bank and not entered in the ledger account.

(g) A cheque for $50 drawn on deposit account had been shown in the ledger account as drawn on current account.

(h) A cheque issued to Zhong for $25 was replaced when out of date. It was entered again in the ledger account, no other entry being made. Both cheques were included in the total of unpresented cheques shown above.

Required

(a) Indicate the appropriate adjustments to the ledger account.
(b) Prepare a statement reconciling the amended balance with that shown in the bank statement.

Solution

(a)   The errors to correct are given in notes (c) (e) (f) (g) and (h) of the problem. Bank charges (note (d)) also call for an adjustment.

		Adjustments in ledger account*	
		DEBIT (ie add to balance at bank)	CREDIT (ie deduct from balance at bank)
		$	$
Item			
(c)	Ledger account incorrectly **credited** with interest on 30 June It should have been **debited** with the receipt	60	
(c)	Debit account (current a/c) with transfer of interest from deposit a/c (note 1)	60	
(d)	Bank charges		35
(e)	Undercast on payments (credit) side of account		10
(f)	Dividends received should be debited to the account	200	
(g)	Cheque drawn on deposit account, not current account Add cash back to current account	50	
(h)	Cheque paid to Zhong is out of date and so cancelled Bank ledger account should now be debited, since previous credit entry is no longer valid (note 2)	25	
		395	45

*Please note that additions/deductions will be the other way around if the balance at bank is initially overdrawn. That is because a debit will result in a reduction of the overdraft and a credit will result in an increase of the overdraft.

	$	$
Ledger account: balance on current account as at 30 June 20X6		(300)
Adjustments and corrections:		
Debit entries (adding to cash)	395	
Credit entries (reducing cash balance)	(45)	
Net adjustments		350
Corrected balance in the ledger account		50

Notes

1   Item (c) is rather complicated. The instruction to transfer interest from the deposit to the current account was presumably given to the bank on or before 30 June 20X6. The correct entry is to debit the current account (and credit the deposit account). The correction in the ledger should be to debit the current account with $2 \times \$60 = \$120$ – ie to cancel out the incorrect credit entry and then to make the correct debit entry. The bank does not record the transfer until 5 July, and so it does not appear in the bank statement.

2   Item (h). Two cheques have been paid to Zhong, but one is now cancelled. Since the ledger account is credited whenever a cheque is paid, it should be debited whenever a cheque is cancelled. The amount of cheques paid but not yet presented should be reduced by the amount of the cancelled cheque.

(b)   BANK RECONCILIATION STATEMENT AT 30 JUNE 20X6

	$	$
Balance per bank statement		65
Add: outstanding lodgements		
(ie cheques paid in but not yet credited)	400	
deposit interest not yet credited	60	
		460
		525
Less: unpresented cheques	500	
less cheque to Zhong cancelled	(25)	
		(475)
Balance per corrected ledger account		50

Tutorial note. You might be interested to see the adjustments to the ledger account in part (a) of the problem presented in ledger account format, as follows (corrections would be made via the journal).

BANK

20X6		$	20X6		$
Jun 30	Bank interest – reversal of incorrect entry	60	Jun 30	Balance brought down	300
	Bank interest account	60		Bank charges	35
	Dividends paid direct to bank	200		Correction of undercast	10
	Cheque drawn on deposit account written back	50		Balance carried down	50
	Cheque issued to Zhong Cancelled	25			
		395			395

In preparing a bank reconciliation it is good practice to begin with the balance shown by the **bank statement** and end with the balance shown by the ledger account. It is this corrected balance which will appear in the statement of financial position as 'cash at bank' or overdraft.

QUESTION

Sanderson

From the information that follows relating to Sanderson you are required:

(a) To correct the bank ledger account of Sanderson as at 31 October 20X2

(b) To prepare a statement reconciling the correct balance in the bank account (as shown in (a) above) with the balance at 31 October 20X2 that is shown on the bank statement from Z Bank plc

BANK ACCOUNT

20X2 October		$	20X2 October		$
1	Balance b/d	274	1	Wages	3,146
8	Q Manufacturing	3,443	1	Petty Cash	55
8	R Cement	1,146	8	Wages	3,106
11	S	638	8	Petty Cash	39
11	T & Sons	512	15	Wages	3,029
11	U & Co	4,174	15	Petty Cash	78
15	V plc	1,426	22	A & Sons	929
15	W Electrical	887	22	B	134
22	X and Associates	1,202	22	C & Company	77
26	Y	2,875	22	D & E	263
26	Z	982	22	F	1,782
29	ABC	1,003	22	G Associates	230
29	DEE	722	22	Wages	3,217
29	GHI	2,461	22	Petty Cash	91
31	Balance c/d	14	25	H & Partners	26
			26	J	868
			26	K	107
			26	L, M & N	666
			28	O	112
			29	Wages	3,191
			29	Petty Cash	52
			29	P	561
		21,759			21,759

BANK – STATEMENT OF ACCOUNT WITH SANDERSON

20X2 October		Payments $	Receipts $		Balance $
1					1,135
1	cheque	55			
1	cheque	3,146			
1	cheque	421		O/D	2,487
2	cheque	73			
2	cheque	155		O/D	2,715
6	cheque	212		O/D	2,927
8	sundry credit		4,589		
8	cheque	3,106			
8	cheque	39		O/D	1,483
11	sundry credit		5,324		3,841
15	sundry credit		2,313		
15	cheque	78			
15	cheque	3,029			3,047
22	sundry credit		1,202		
22	cheque	3,217			
22	cheque	91			941
25	cheque	1,782			
26	cheque	929			
26	sundry credit		3,857		
26	cheque	230			1,723
27	cheque	263			
27	cheque	77			1,383
29	sundry credit		4,186		
29	cheque	52			
29	cheque	3,191			
29	cheque	26			
29	dividends on investments		2,728		
29	cheque	666			4,362
31	bank charges	936			3,426

ANSWER

(a)
BANK ACCOUNT

		$			$
31 Oct	Dividends received	2,728	31 Oct	Unadjusted balance b/d (overdraft)	14
			31 Oct	Bank charges	936
			31 Oct	Adjusted balance c/d	1,778
		2,728			2,728

(b) BANK RECONCILIATION STATEMENT
AT 31 OCTOBER 20X2

	$
Balance as per bank statement	3,426
Unpresented cheques	(1,648)
Outstanding lodgements	0
Balance as per corrected ledger account	1,778

Workings (entries in the cash received day book and the cash payments day book will have been posted to the ledger account)

1	Payments shown on bank statement but not in day book* $(421 + 73 + 155 + 212) * Presumably recorded in day book before 1 October 20X2 but not yet presented for payment as at 30 September 20X2	$861
2	Payments in the day book and on the bank statement $(3,146 + 55 + 3,106 + 39 + 78 + 3,029 + 3,217 + 91 + 1,782 + 134 + 929 + 230 + 263 + 77 + 52 + 3,191 + 26 + 666)	$20,111
3	Payments in the day book but not on the bank statement = Total payments in day book $21,759 minus $20,111 =	$1,648

		$
Alternatively	J	868
	K	107
	O	112
	P	561
		1,648

4	Bank charges, not in the day book	$936
5	Receipts recorded by bank statement but not in day book: dividends on investments	$2,728
6	Receipts in the day book and also bank statement (8 Oct $4,589; 11 Oct $5,324; 15 Oct $2,313; 22 Oct $1,202; 26 Oct $3,857; 29 Oct $4,186)	$21,471
7	Receipts recorded in day book but not bank statement	None

8 Other controls over business operations

The use of control accounts and the (correct) use of suspense accounts are two of several ways in which businesses monitor the accurate operation of the accounting system. You should already be aware of these procedures individually, but we will mention them again briefly. All these procedures must be carried out with **sufficient frequency and regularity.**

8.1 Petty cash count/reconciliation

Petty cash should be reconciled regularly and any **discrepancies cleared or authorised** for write off. This will usually take place when the imprest is topped up. An organisation should also do independent spot checks on petty cash which are unannounced, as a check on the honesty of the petty cashier.

8.2 Reconciliation of payables ledger accounts to supplier statements

Reconciliation of any part of a business's records to a **third party's records** is always a useful check on the accuracy of the accounting system. As with a bank reconciliation, this is a way of checking that your own records are correct **and** those of the supplier (or bank).

8.2.1 Supplier statements

A supplier will usually send a monthly statement showing invoices issued, credit notes, payments received and discounts given. It is **vitally important** that these statements are compared to the supplier's personal account in the trade payables. Any discrepancies need to be identified and any errors corrected.

A statement of account is reproduced below.

STATEMENT OF ACCOUNT

**Pickett (Handling Equipment) Co
Unit 7, Western Industrial Estate
Dunford   DN2 7RJ**

Tel: (01990) 72101   Fax: (01990) 72980   VAT Reg No 982 7213 49

Accounts Department
Finstar Co
67 Laker Avenue
Dunford DN4 5PS

Date: 31 May 20X1

A/c No: F023

Date	Details	Debit $ c	Credit $ c	Balance $ c
30/4/X1	Balance brought forward from previous statement			492 22
3/5/X1	Invoice no. 34207	129 40✓		621 62
4/5/X1	Invoice no. 34242	22 72✓		644 34
5/5/X1	Payment received - thank you		412 17✓	232 17
17/5/X1	Invoice no. 34327	394 95✓		627 12
18/5/X1	Credit note no. 00192		64 40✓	562 72
21/5/X1	Invoice no. 34392	392 78		955 50
28/5/X1	Credit note no. 00199		107 64✓	847 86

Amount now due	$	847 86

Terms: 30 days net, 1% discount for payment in 7 days. E & OE

Registered office: 4 Arkwright Road, London E16 4PQ Registered in England No 2182417

The statement is received on 1 June 20X1 and is passed to Linda Kelly who is the purchase ledger clerk at Finstar Co. Linda obtains a printout of the transactions with Pickett (Handling Equipment) Co from Finstar's purchase ledger system. (The reason why Linda has made ticks on the statement and on the printout which follows will be explained below.)

FINSTAR CO		**PURCHASE LEDGER**
ACCOUNT NAME:	PICKETT (HANDLING EQUIPMENT) CO	
ACCOUNT REF:	PO42	
DATE OF REPORT:	1 JUNE 20X1	

Date	Transaction	(DEBIT)/CREDIT $
16.03.X1	Invoice 33004	350.70
20.03.X1	Invoice 33060	61.47
06.04.X1	Invoice 34114	80.05
03.05.X1	Invoice 34207	129.40 ✓
04.05.X1	Payment	(412.17) ✓
06.05.X1	Invoice 34242	22.72 ✓
19.05.X1	Invoice 34327	394.95 ✓
19.05.X1	Credit note 00192	(64.40) ✓
28.05.X1	Payment	(117.77)
30.05.X1	Credit note 00199	(107.64) ✓
	Balance	337.31

The purchase ledger of Finstar shows a balance due to Pickett of $337.31, while Pickett's statement shows a balance due of $847.86.

8.2.2 Supplier statement reconciliations

Linda wants to be sure that her purchase ledger record for Pickett is correct and so she prepares a **supplier statement reconciliation**.

These are the steps to follow.

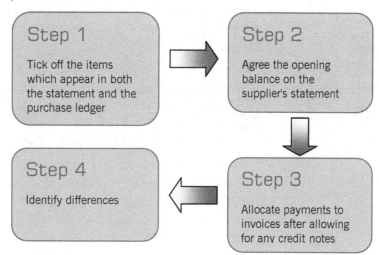

Step 1

Tick off the items which appear in both the statement and the purchase ledger

Step 2

Agree the opening balance on the supplier's statement

Step 4

Identify differences

Step 3

Allocate payments to invoices after allowing for any credit notes

8.2.3 Example: Supplier reconciliation

Linda applies the above steps to Pickett's statement.

Step 1	The common items have been ticked off on the statement and purchase ledger above.

Step 2   The balance brought forward at 30.4.X1 consists of three invoices.

	$
33004	350.70
33060	61.47
34114	80.05
	492.22

Step 3   Invoices 33004 and 33060 were paid on 4 May and 34114 was part of the payment on 28 May.

Step 4   Pickett's statement does not show the payment of $117.77 made on 28 May. However this is reasonable, as the cheque was probably still in the post. The statement also shows an invoice 34392 dated 21 May, which is not in the purchase ledger. This is surprising. Finstar needs to check if the invoice has been received (using the purchase day book), if so has it been posted to the wrong account? If it has not been received, Linda will need to contact Pickett and ask for a duplicate.

SUPPLIER STATEMENT RECONCILIATION

ACCOUNT: PICKETT (HANDLING EQUIPMENT) CO (PO42)

	$
Balance per supplier's statement	847.86
Less: Payment (28 May) not on statement	(117.77)
Invoice (supplier no 34392) on statement, not on purchase ledger	(392.78)
Balance per purchase ledger	337.31

8.2.4 The reasons for reconciling items

Reconciling items may occur as a result of the following items.

Reconciling item	Effect	Status
Payments in transit	A payment will go in the purchase ledger when the cheque is issued or when a bank transfer instruction is made. There will be delay (postal, processing) before this payment is entered in the records of the supplier. Any statement of account received by post will also be out of date by the length of time taken to deliver it.	Timing difference
Omitted invoices and credit notes	Invoices or credit notes may appear in the ledger of one business but not in that of the other due to error or omission. However, the most common reason will be a timing difference in recording the items in the different ledgers.	Error or omission or timing difference
Other errors	Addition errors can occur, particularly if a statement of account is prepared manually. Invoice, credit note or payment amounts can be misposted. Regular reconciliation of supplier statements will minimise the possibility of missing such errors.	Error

8.3 Clearance of wages and other control accounts

All other types of control accounts should be checked regularly and **cleared** of all items which are not valid. There should be no 'unknowns' left in a control account balance.

8.4 Sales tax reconciliation

The same principle applies here, and the need for regular checks on the VAT or sales tax accounts is all the greater because the tax authorities may impose **severe penalties** for errors made.

8.5 Reconciliation of non-current assets to the register

Non-current assets should be checked by sight, not only to check that they actually exist, but to make sure that they have not been **stolen or damaged**. Checks should also be made from the register to the physical assets to ensure that 'ghost' assets are not kept on the register. We will look at this in more detail in Chapter 9.

8.6 Internal audit

Organisations of any size will often have an internal audit department. Internal auditors will, as part of their work, **check controls and procedures** (including those above). They will also carry out other any other work required to ensure the accounting system is operating properly and accurately.

CHAPTER ROUNDUP

↳ The two most important **control accounts** are those for **receivables and payables**. They are part of the double entry system.

↳ Day books (cash day books, sales day book and purchases day book) are totalled periodically (say once a month) and the appropriate totals are posted to the **control accounts**. The individual entries in day books will have been entered one by one in the appropriate personal accounts contained in the receivables ledger and trade payables. These **personal accounts** are not part of the double entry system.

↳ At suitable intervals the balances on personal accounts are extracted from the ledgers, listed and totalled. The total of the outstanding balances can then be **reconciled** to the balance on the appropriate **control account** and any errors located and corrected.

↳ It is not really possible to draw up a complete list of all the errors which might be made by bookkeepers and accountants. Even if you tried, it is more than likely that as soon as you finished, someone would commit a completely new error that you had never even dreamed of! However, it is possible to describe **five types of errors** which cover most of the errors which might occur. They are as follows:

- – Errors of **transposition** – one or both entries
- – Errors of **omission** – complete or partial
- – Errors of **principle**
- – Errors of **commission** – misposting, reversal, original entry
- – **Compensating errors**

↳ Errors which leave total debits and total credits on the ledger accounts in balance can be corrected by using **journal entries**. Otherwise, a suspense account has to be opened.

↳ **Suspense accounts**, as well as being used to correct some errors, are also opened when it is not known immediately where to post an amount. When the mystery is solved, the suspense account is closed and the amount correctly posted using a journal entry.

↳ Bank reconciliations identify and explain differences between the bank statement and the bank ledger account.

QUICK QUIZ

1 What is a control account?

2 Is a write off of irrecoverable debts a debit or a credit in the receivables control account?

3 What are the main reasons for having control accounts?

4 List four errors that will cause the control account not to agree with the list of balances?

5 What are the five main types of error which might occur in accounting?

6 What are the two common errors of commission?

7 What is a suspense account?

8 Suspense accounts are temporary. True or false?

9 What kind of checks should be made on petty cash?

10 What is a bank reconciliation?

ANSWERS TO QUICK QUIZ

1   A control account is an account in the general ledger in which a record is kept of the total value of a number of similar but individual items

2   A credit: it reduces the debit balance on the control account.

3   (a)   A check on the accuracy of the personal ledger
    (b)   Assist in the location of errors
    (c)   An internal check
    (d)   Provides a total balance for the trial balance

4   (a)   Miscasting (adding up) of the book of prime entry
    (b)   A transposition error in posting to the memorandum ledger
    (c)   A transaction missed out of the control account or in the memorandum account
    (d)   The balances are incorrectly extracted from the memorandum ledger, or miscast

    Note. Only four were needed but other possible errors are listed within the chapter.

5   Errors of transposition, omission, principle, commission and compensating errors.

6   (a)   Putting a debit entry or a credit entry in the wrong account
    (b)   Errors of casting (adding up)

7   A suspense account is an account showing a balance equal to the difference in a trial balance.

8   True. Suspense accounts must be cleared before the final accounts are drawn up.

9   Petty cash should be reconciled regularly, and spot counts should also be carried out.

10 A comparison of a bank statement with the bank account in the general ledger.

Now try ...

Attempt the questions below from the **Practice Question Bank**

Number	Level	Marks	Time
Q26	Examination	2	2.4 mins
Q27	Examination	2	2.4 mins
Q28	Examination	2	2.4 mins
Q29	Examination	2	2.4 mins
Q30	Examination	2	2.4 mins
Q31	Examination	2	2.4 mins
Q32	Examination	2	2.4 mins
Q33	Examination	2	2.4 mins
Q34	Examination	2	2.4 mins
Q35	Examination	2	2.4 mins
Q36	Examination	2	2.4 mins

07

A business needs to allocate revenue and expenses to the period covered by the financial statements. **Accruals** and **prepayments** play an important role in helping the business to do this and we cover these in the first part of this chapter.

Irrecoverable debts are also covered here. Some trade receivables may need to be written off if they are known to be irrecoverable debts.

Additionally, an **allowance for receivables** may be created based on a general estimate of the percentage of debts which are not expected to be repaid.

Accruals and prepayments, receivables and irrecoverable debts

TOPIC LIST	SYLLABUS REFERENCE
1 What are accruals and prepayments?	D5(a), D5(d), D5(e)
2 Accruals: ledger accounts and examples	D5(b), D5(d), D5(e)
3 Prepayments: ledger accounts and examples	D5(b), D5(d) to (f)
4 Receivables and trade receivables	D6(a)
5 Irrecoverable debts	D6(b) to (g)
6 Current assets and liabilities	D2(b), D6(a), F2(f)
7 Provisions	D6(i), D6(j), D6(l)
8 Non-current liabilities	D6(i), D6(l)

Study Guide	**Intellectual level**
D **Recording transactions and events**	
2 **Cash and bank**	
(b) Report cash and bank balances in the final accounts	S
5 **Accruals and prepayments**	
(a) Apply the matching concept to accruals and prepayments	S
(b) Identify and calculate the adjustments needed for accruals and prepayments when preparing financial statements	S
(d) Prepare the journal entries and ledger entries for the creation of an accrual or prepayment	S
(e) Identify the impact on profit, net assets and capital of accruals and prepayments	K
(f) Report accruals and prepayments in the final accounts	S
6 **Receivables, payables and provisions**	
(a) Explain and identify examples of receivables and payables	K
(b) Prepare the bookkeeping entries to write off an irrecoverable debt	S
(c) Record an irrecoverable debt recovered	S
(d) Identify the impact of irrecoverable debts on the statement of profit or loss and on the statement of financial position	S
(e) Calculate the movement in the allowance for receivables and the closing balance	S
(f) Prepare the bookkeeping entries to create and adjust an allowance for receivables	S
(g) Illustrate how to include movements in the allowance for receivables in the statement of profit or loss and how the closing balance of the allowance should be reported in the statement of financial position	S
(i) Explain the nature of provisions and liabilities	K
(j) Distinguish between a provision and liability	S
(l) Report provisions and liabilities in the final accounts	S
F **Reconciliations**	
2 **Bank reconciliation**	
(f) Identify the bank balance to be reported in the final accounts	K

Technical Performance Objective 7 requires you to be able to establish necessary accounting adjustments under the accruals concept and process necessary adjustments. The knowledge you gain in this chapter will help you to demonstrate your competence in this area.

1 What are accruals and prepayments?

Accrued expenses are expenses which relate to (ie have been incurred during) an accounting period but have not yet been paid. They are **a charge against the profit** for the period and they are shown in the statement of financial position as at the end of the period as a **current liability**.

Prepayments are expenses which have already been paid but relate to a future accounting period. They are not **charged against the profit** of the current period, and they are shown in the statement of financial position at the end of the period as a **current asset**.

1.1 Nature and purpose of accruals and prepayments

When a business prepares periodic financial statements it has to address the problem of allocating revenue and expense to the period covered by the statements. The simplest way of reporting the results of an accounting period is to present the cash received and cash paid as equivalent to the business's income and expenditure. Very small entities may use such statements known as receipts and payments accounts as their main accounting statements.

Receipts and payments statements are not adequate as the main financial statements for a number of reasons.

- Goods and services are normally bought and sold on credit where payment is made or received at a later date then the delivery of the goods or provision of the service. The important event for the business is the date of the purchase or the sale and not the receipt or payment of the cash.
- Assets acquired are expected to benefit the business over a number of accounting periods. To show the payment for the asset as an expense for the period in which it was made would be misleading. The payment should be matched to the future benefits that the business expects to receive from use of the asset.
- Items such as gas and electricity may be obtained on credit or paid in arrears. It would be misleading for the business to receive the benefit without recording the obligation to pay for it.

In all the above cases, there is a problem as the amounts **do not relate wholly to the period in which they were recorded**. Businesses need to focus on goods and services sold during the accounting period and goods and services consumed in the same period relating to those sales.

When income and expenditure is recorded, it is usually because an invoice has been received or an invoice has been issued, and the expense or income must therefore be recognised. The same applies when purchases or sales are made for cash. At the end of the accounting period, however, it may be that some bills have not been received, although it is known that the expense has been incurred. The liability will therefore not be recorded until the following period. Similarly, an invoice may have been received and paid during the year, but it may cover part of the following year.

As we saw earlier, the **accruals concept** states that income and expenditure should be matched to each other and recognised as they are earned or incurred, not when money is received or paid.

Accruals, or accrued expenses, are expenses charged against profits which relate to (ie have been incurred during) a particular accounting period, even though they have not yet been paid.

Prepayments are payments which have been made in one accounting period, but should not be wholly or partly charged against profit until a later period, because they relate to that later period.

Here are two very simple examples to demonstrate the principles of accruals and prepayments.

1.2 Example: Accrual

Cleverley started in business as a paper plate and cup manufacturer on 1 January 20X6, making up accounts to 31 December 20X6. The electricity bills received were as follows.

	$
30 April 20X6	5,279.47
31 July 20X6	4,663.80
31 October 20X6	4,117.28
31 January 20X7	6,491.52

What should the electricity charge be for the year ended 31 December 20X6?

Solution

The total of the three invoices received during 20X6 was $14,060.55, but this is not the full charge for the year: the November and December electricity charge was not invoiced until the end of January. To show the correct charge for the year, it is necessary to **accrue** the charge for November and December based on the bill received in January 20X7. The charge for 20X6 will be:

	$
Paid in year	14,060.55
Accrual (2/3 × $6,491.52)	4,327.68
	18,388.23

The **double entry** for the accrual will be:

DEBIT	Electricity account (statement of profit or loss)	$4,327.68	
CREDIT	Accruals (statement of financial position)		$4,327.68

1.3 Example: Prepayment

Hillyard opened for business on 1 January 20X6 in a new shop which was on a 20 year lease. The rent is payable quarterly in advance and amounts to $20,000 per year. The payments were made on what are know as the 'quarter-days' (except for the first payment) as follows.

	$
1 January 20X6	5,000.00
25 March 20X6	5,000.00
24 June 20X6	5,000.00
29 September 20X6	5,000.00
25 December 20X6	5,000.00

What will the rental charge be for the year ended 31 December 20X6?

Solution

The total amount paid in the year is $25,000. The yearly rental, however, is only $20,000. The last payment was almost entirely a prepayment (give or take a few days) as it is **payment in advance** for the first three months of 20X7. The charge for 20X6 is therefore:

	$
Paid in year	25,000.00
Prepayment	(5,000.00)
	20,000.00

The **double entry** for this prepayment is:

DEBIT	Prepayment (statement of financial position)	$5,000.00	
CREDIT	Rent account (statement of profit or loss)		$5,000.00

You can see from the double entry shown for both these examples that the other side of the entry is taken to the **statement of financial position**.

- **Prepayments** are included in **receivables** in current assets. Prepayments are assets in the sense that they represent the money that has been paid out in advance of the expense being incurred.

- **Accruals** are included in **payables** in current liabilities as they represent liabilities which have been incurred but not yet invoiced.

QUESTION

Accrual

An electricity accrual of $375 was treated as a prepayment in preparing a company's statement of profit or loss.

What was the resulting effect on the profit of the company?

ANSWER

By classifying a liability as an asset the company has improved its profit figure. The amount of $375 has been treated as an increase in profit, instead of a $375 deduction from profit. The net effect is to overstate profit by $750.

QUESTION

Rent

At 31 December 20X1 the accounts of a company show accrued rent payable of $250. During 20X2 the company pays rent bills totalling $1,275, including one bill for $375 in respect of the quarter ending 31 January 20X3.

What is the statement of profit or loss charge for rent payable for the year ended 31 December 20X2?

ANSWER

The statement of profit or loss charge for the year is $900, as the ledger account shows.

RENT PAYABLE

20X2		$	20X2		$
31 Dec	Bank: paid in year	1,275	1 Jan	Balance b/f	250
			31 Dec	Balance c/f	
				(prepaid: 1/3× $375)	125
				Statement of P/L	900
		1,275			1,275

EXAM FOCUS POINT

In the exam you could be given information on the period covered by an expense invoice along with details of when the invoice was recorded and paid. You could then be asked for the appropriate accrual or prepayment needed to match the expense with the period to which it relates.

2 Accruals: ledger accounts and examples

Now we look at the preparation of ledger account entries for accruals. Carrying on from the example and solution in 1.2 above, the electricity account would appear as follows.

ELECTRICITY ACCOUNT

20X6		$	20X6		$
30.4	Cash	5,279.47	31.12	Statement of P/L	18,388.23
31.7	Cash	4,663.80			
31.10	Cash	4,117.28			
31.12	Balance c/d (accrual)	4,327.68			
		18,388.23			18,388.23
20X7			20X7		
			1.1	Balance b/d(accrual reversed)	4,327.68

You should be able to see from this that, as with all accruals and prepayments, the double entry will be **reversed** in the following period. At the beginning of each new accounting period the bookkeeper will **reverse** all accruals and prepayments from the previous period.

Instead of recording the accrual directly as a item on the statement of financial position, an accrual ledger account can be set up. The accrual account for this example would be as follows:

ACCRUAL ACCOUNT

20X6		$	20X6		$
31.12	Balance c/d	4,327.68	31.12	Electricity account	4,327.68
		4,327.68			4,327.68
20X7			20X7		
1.1	Electricity account (accrual reversed)	4,327.68	1.1	Balance b/d	4,327.68

Here are some further examples and activities for you to attempt in order to practice calculating the correct expense to be shown in the statement of profit or loss and the accrual to be shown in the statement of financial position.

2.1 Example: accruals

Horace Goodrunning, trading as Goodrunning Motor Spares, ends his financial year on 28 February each year. His telephone was installed on 1 April 20X6 and he receives his telephone account quarterly at the end of each quarter. He pays it promptly as soon as it is received. On the basis of the following data, you are required to calculate the telephone expense to be charged to the statement of profit or loss for the year ended 28 February 20X7.

Goodrunning Motor Spares – telephone expense for the three months ended:

	$
30.6.20X6	23.50
30.9.20X6	27.20
31.12.20X6	33.40
31.3.20X7	36.00

Solution

The telephone expenses for the year ended 28 February 20X7 are as follows.

	$
1 March – 31 March 20X6 (no telephone)	0.00
1 April – 30 June 20X6	23.50
1 July – 30 September 20X6	27.20
1 October – 31 December 20X6	33.40
1 January – 28 February 20X7 (two months)	24.00
	108.10

The charge for the period 1 January – 28 February 20X7 is two-thirds of the quarterly charge received on 31 March. As at 28 February 20X7, no telephone bill has been received for the quarter, because it is not due for another month. However, it would be inappropriate to ignore the telephone expenses for January and February, and so an accrued charge of $24 should be made, being two-thirds of the quarter's bill of $36.

The accrued charge will also appear in the statement of financial position of the business as at 28 February 20X7, as a current liability.

QUESTION
Ratsnuffer

Ratsnuffer is a business dealing in pest control. Its owner, Roy Dent, employs a team of eight who were paid $12,000 per annum each in the year to 31 December 20X1. At the start of 20X2 he raised salaries by 10% to $13,200 per annum each.

On 1 July 20X2, he hired a trainee at a salary of $8,400 per annum.

He pays his work force on the first working day of every month, one month in arrears, so that his employees receive their salary for January on the first working day in February, etc.

Required

(a)   Calculate the cost of salaries which would be charged in the statement of profit or loss of Ratsnuffer for the year ended 31 December 20X2.

(b)   Calculate the amount actually paid in salaries during the year (ie the amount of cash received by the work force).

(c)   State the amount of accrued charges for salaries which would appear in the statement of financial position of Ratsnuffer as at 31 December 20X2.

ANSWER

(a)   *Salaries cost in the statement of profit or loss*

	$
Cost of 8 employees for a full year at $13,200 each	105,600
Cost of trainee for a half year	4,200
	109,800

(b)   *Salaries actually paid in 20X2*

	$
December 20X1 salaries paid in January (8 employees × $1,000 per month)	8,000
Salaries of 8 employees for January – November 20X2 paid in February – December (8 employees × $1,100 per month × 11 months)	96,800
Salaries of trainee (for July – November paid in August - December 20X2: 5 months × $700 per month)	3,500
Salaries actually paid	108,300

(c)   *Accrued salary costs as at 31 December 20X2*
(ie costs charged in the statement of profit or loss, but not yet paid)

	$
8 employees × 1 month × $1,100 per month	8,800
1 trainee × 1 month × $700 per month	700
	9,500

Summary

	$
Accrued wages costs as at 31 December 20X1	8,000
Add salaries cost for 20X2 (statement of profit or loss)	109,800
	117,800
Less salaries paid	(108,300)
Equals accrued wages costs as at 31 December 20X2	9,500

2.2 Further example: accruals

Suppose that Willie Walker opens a shop on 1 May 20X6 to sell hiking and camping equipment. The rent of the shop is $12,000 per annum, payable quarterly in arrears (with the first payment on 31 July 20X6). Willie decides that his accounting period should end on 31 December each year.

Solution

The rent account as at 31 December 20X6 will record only two rental payments (on 31 July and 31 October) and there will be two months' accrued rental expenses for November and December 20X6, ($2,000) since the next rental payment is not due until 31 January 20X7.

The charge to the statement of profit or loss for the period to 31 December 20X6 will be for 8 months' rent (May–December inclusive) and so it follows that the total rental cost should be $8,000.

So far, the rent account appears as follows.

RENT ACCOUNT

		$			$
20X6			*20X6*		
31 July	Cash	3,000			
31 Oct	Cash	3,000	31 Dec	Statement of P/L	8,000

To complete the picture, the accruals of $2,000 have to be put in to bring the account balance up to the full charge for the year.

RENT ACCOUNT

		$			$
20X6			20X6		
31 July	Cash *	3,000			
31 Oct	Cash *	3,000			
31 Dec	Balance c/d (accruals)	2,000	31 Dec	Statement of P/L	8,000
		8,000			8,000
			20X7		
			1 Jan	Balance b/d (accrual reversed)	2,000

* The corresponding credit entry would be cash if rent is paid without the need for an invoice – eg with payment by standing order or direct debit at the bank. If there is always an invoice where rent becomes payable, the double entry would be:

DEBIT	Rent account	$2,000	
CREDIT	Payables		$2,000

Then when the rent is paid, the ledger entries would be:

DEBIT	Payables	$2,000	
CREDIT	Cash		$2,000

The rent account for the **next** year to 31 December 20X7, assuming no increase in rent in that year, would be as follows.

RENT ACCOUNT

		$			$
20X7			20X7		
31 Jan	Cash	3,000	1 Jan	Balance b/d (accrual reversed)	2,000
30 Apr	Cash	3,000			
31 Jul	Cash	3,000			
31 Oct	Cash	3,000			
31 Dec	Balance c/d (accruals)	2,000	31 Dec	Statement of P/L	12,000
		14,000			14,000
			20X8		
			1 Jan	Balance b/d (accrual reversed)	2,000

Here, you will see that for a full year, a full 12 months' rental charges are taken as an expense to the statement of profit or loss.

3 Prepayments: ledger accounts and examples

As with accruals, you must be able to show the ledger accounting entries for prepayments. Looking back to the example and solution in Section 1.3 of this chapter, the ledger account for rent would appear as follows.

RENT ACCOUNT

		$			$
20X6			20X6		
1.1	Cash	5,000.00	31.12	Statement of P/L	20,000.00
25.3	Cash	5,000.00	31.12	Balance c/d	
24.6	Cash	5,000.00		(prepayment)	5,000.00
29.9	Cash	5,000.00			
25.12	Cash	5,000.00			
		25,000.00			25,000.00
20X7					
1.1	Balance b/d (prepayment reversed)	5,000.00			

Again, you can see that the double entry for the prepayment will be **reversed** in the next period.

If a prepayment ledger account was prepared it would be as follows:

PREPAYMENT ACCOUNT

20X6		$	20X6		$
31.12	Rent account	5,000.00	31.12	Balance c/d	5,000.00
		5,000.00			5,000.00
20X7			20X7		
1.1	Balance b/d	5,000.00	1.1	Rent account (prepayment reversed)	5,000.00

Try the following examples and activities so that you understand prepayments.

3.1 Example: prepayments

The Square Wheels Garage pays fire insurance annually in advance on 1 June each year. The firm's financial year end is 28 February. From the following record of insurance payments you are required to calculate the charge to the statement of profit or loss for the financial year to 28 February 20X7.

	Insurance paid $
1.6.20X5	600
1.6.20X6	700

Solution

Insurance cost for:

		$
(a)	The 3 months, 1 March – 31 May 20X6 (3/12 × $600)	150
(b)	The 9 months, 1 June 20X16 – 28 February 20X7 (9/12 × $700)	525
	Insurance cost for the year, charged to the statement of profit or loss	675

At 28 February 20X7 there is a prepayment for fire insurance, covering the period 1 March – 31 May 20X7. This insurance premium was paid on 1 June 20X6, but only nine months worth of the full annual cost is chargeable to the accounting period ended 28 February 20X7. The prepayment of (3/12 × $700) $175 as at 28 February 20X7 will appear as a current asset in the statement of financial position of the Square Wheels Garage as at that date.

In the same way, there was a prepayment of (3/12 × $600) $150 one year earlier as at 28 February 20X6.

Summary	$
Prepaid insurance premiums as at 28 February 20X6	150
Add insurance premiums paid 1 June 20X6	700
	850
Less insurance costs charged to the statement of profit or loss for the year ended 28 February 20X7	(675)
Equals prepaid insurance premiums as at 28 February 20X7	175

QUESTION

Barley Print Shop

The Barley Print Shop rents a photocopying machine from a supplier for which it makes a quarterly payment as follows:

(a)   Three months rental in advance
(b)   A further charge of 2 cents per copy made during the quarter just ended

The rental agreement began on 1 August 20X1 and the first six quarterly bills were as follows.

Bills dated and received	Rental	Costs of copies taken	Total
	$	$	$
1 August 20X1	2,100	0	2,100
1 November 20X1	2,100	1,500	3,600
1 February 20X2	2,100	1,400	3,500
1 May 20X2	2,100	1,800	3,900
1 August 20X2	2,700	1,650	4,350
1 November 20X2	2,700	1,950	4,650

The bills are paid promptly, as soon as they are received.

(a) Calculate the charge for photocopying expenses for the year to 31 August 20X1 and the amount of prepayments and/or accrued charges as at that date.

(b) Calculate the charge for photocopying expenses for the following year to 31 August 20X2, and the amount of prepayments and/or accrued charges as at that date.

ANSWER

(a) *Year to 31 August 20X1*

	$
One months' rental (1/3 × $2,100) *	700
Accrued copying charges (1/3 × $1,500) **	500
Photocopying expense (statement of profit or loss)	1,200

*   From the quarterly bill dated 1 August 20X1
**   From the quarterly bill dated 1 November 20X1

There is a prepayment for 2 months' rental ($1,400) as at 31 August 20X1.

(b) *Year to 31 August 20X2*

	$	$
Rental from 1 September 20X1 – 31 July 20X2 (11 months at		
$2,100 per quarter or $700 per month)		7,700
Rental from 1 August – 31 August 20X2 (1/3 × $2,700)		900
Rental charge for the year		8,600
Copying charges:		
1 September – 31 October 20X1 (2/3 × $1,500)	1,000	
1 November 20X1 – 31 January 20X2	1,400	
1 February – 30 April 20X2	1,800	
1 May – 31 July 20X2	1,650	
Accrued charges for August 20X2 (1/3 × $1,950)	650	
		6,500
Total photocopying expenses (statement of profit or loss)		15,100

There is a prepayment for 2 months' rental ($1,800) as at 31 August 20X2.

Summary of year 1 September 20X1 – 31 August 20X2

	Rental charges	Copying costs
	$	$
Prepayments as at 31.8.20X1	1,400	
Accrued charges as at 31.8.20X1		(500)
Bills received during the year		
1 November 20X1	2,100	1,500
1 February 20X2	2,100	1,400
1 May 20X2	2,100	1,800
1 August 20X2	2,700	1,650
Prepayment as at 31.8.20X2	(1,800)	
Accrued charges as at 31.8.20X2		650
Charge to the statement of profit or loss for the year	8,600	6,500

	Rental charges $	Copying costs $
Statement of financial position items as at 31 August 20X2		
Prepaid rental (current asset)	1,800	
Accrued copying charges (current liability)		650

3.2 Further example: prepayments

Suppose that Terry Trunk commences business as a landscape gardener on 1 September 20X6. He immediately decides to join his local trade association, the Confederation of Luton Gardeners, for which the annual membership subscription is $180, payable annually in advance. He paid this amount on 1 September. Terry decides that his account period should end on 30 June each year.

Solution

In the first period to 30 June 20X7 (10 months), a full year's membership will have been paid, but only ten twelfths of the subscription should be charged to the period (ie 10/12 × $180 = $150). There is a prepayment of two months of membership subscription – ie 2/12 × $180 = $30.

It is therefore necessary to recognise the prepayment in the ledger account for subscriptions. This is done in much the same way as accounting for accruals.

CREDIT	Subscriptions account with prepayment		$30
DEBIT	Prepayment (statement of financial position)	$30	

The remaining expenses in the subscriptions account should then be taken to the statement of profit or loss. At the beginning of the following financial year the prepayment will be reversed and the subscriptions account will be debited with $30, now posted to the correct financial year.

SUBSCRIPTIONS ACCOUNT

20X6/X7		$	20X6/X7		$
1 Sept	Cash	180	30 Jun	Statement of P/L	150
			30 Jun	Balance c/d (prepayment)	30
		180			180
20X7/X8					
1 Jul	Balance b/d	30			

The subscription account for the next year, assuming no increase in the annual charge and that Terry Trunk remains a member of the association, will be:

SUBSCRIPTIONS ACCOUNT

20X6/X7		$	20X6/X7		$
1 Jul	Balance b/d (prepayment reversed)	30	30 Jun	Statement of P/L	180
1 Sep	Cash	180	30 Jun	Balance c/d (prepayment)	30
		210			210
20X7/X8					
1 Jul	Balance b/d (prepayment reversed)	30			

Again, we see here for a full accounting year, the charge to the statement of profit or loss is for a full year's subscriptions.

4 Receivables and trade receivables

Receivables can be broken down into **trade receivables** and **non-trade receivables**.

In Chapter 1 we defined an **account receivable** and distinguished between what a receivable is in general and what a trade receivable is. We can simplify that distinction here.

A **receivable** is a balance owing to the business.

A **trade receivable** is a balance arising in the course of normal trading operations, when a customer buys goods without paying cash for them straight away and who therefore owes money to the business.

A trade receivable is therefore a specific type of receivable, and in most businesses trade receivables will comprise the bulk of total receivables shown in the accounts.

What, then, are **non-trade receivables**? These may arise from many different types of transaction, depending on the type of business, for example there may be loans to employees for season travel tickets.

5 Irrecoverable debts

Some trade receivables may need to be written off as **irrecoverable debts**. Additionally, an **allowance for receivables** may be created. Rather than affecting individual customer balances, an allowance for receivables recognises the fact that ordinarily a certain proportion of all debts may not be collected.

For some debts on the ledger, there may be little or no prospect of the business being paid, usually for one of the following reasons.

- The customer has gone **bankrupt.**

- The customer is **out of business.**

- **Dishonesty** may be involved.

- Customers in another country might be prevented from paying by the unexpected introduction of **foreign exchange control** restrictions by their country's government during the credit period.

For one reason or another, therefore, a business might decide to give up expecting payment and to **write the debt off.**

An **irrecoverable debt** is a specific debt which is not expected to be repaid.

5.1 Irrecoverable debts written off: ledger accounting entries

For irrecoverable debts written off, there is a **irrecoverable debt expense account** in the general ledger. The double-entry bookkeeping is fairly straightforward. When it is decided that a particular debt will not be paid, the customer is no longer called an outstanding receivable, and becomes an irrecoverable debt. We therefore:

DEBIT   Irrecoverable debt expense
CREDIT   Total receivables account

A write off of any irrecoverable debt will need the authorisation of a senior official in the organisation.

5.2 Example: Irrecoverable debts written off

At 1 October 20X6 a business had total outstanding debts of $8,600. During the year to 30 September 20X7:

(a)   Credit revenue amounted to $44,000

(b)   Payments from various receivables amounted to $49,000

(c)   Two debts, for $180 and $420 (both including sales tax) were declared irrecoverable. These are to be written off.

We need to prepare the receivables control account and the irrecoverable debt expense account for the year.

Solution

RECEIVABLES ACCOUNT

Date	Details	$	Date	Details	$
1.10.X6	Balance b/d	8,600		Cash	49,000
	Sales for the year	44,000	30.9.X7	Irrecoverable debts	180
			30.9.X7	Irrecoverable debts	420
			30.9.X7	Balance c/d	3,000
		52,600			52,600
	Balance b/d	3,000			

IRRECOVERABLE DEBT EXPENSE

Date	Details	$	Date	Details	$
30.9.X7	Receivables	180	30.9.X7	Balance	600
30.9.X7	Receivables	420			
		600			600

In the receivables ledger, personal accounts of the customers whose debts are irrecoverable will be **taken off the ledger**. The business should then take steps to ensure that it does not sell goods to those customers again.

5.3 Irrecoverable debts and sales tax

The extent to which a business can claim relief for sales tax on irrecoverable debts varies from country to country. If relief is available, the entries will be, assuming a debt of $100 with sales tax at 20%.

DEBIT	Sales tax account	20.00	
	Irrecoverable debt expense	100.00	
CREDIT	Total receivables		120.00

5.4 Example: Irrecoverable debts and sales tax

If both the debts written off above **were inclusive of sales tax** (assuming a rate of 20% for this example), the accounts would look as follows:

RECEIVABLES ACCOUNT – no change

IRRECOVERABLE DEBT EXPENSE

Date	Details	$	Date	Details	$
30.9.X7	Receivables	150.00	30.9.X7	Balance	500.00
30.9.X7	Receivables	350.00			
		500.00			500.00

SALES TAX ACCOUNT (part)

Date	Details	$	Date	Details	$
30.9.X7	Receivables	30.00			
30.9.X7	Receivables	70.00			

5.5 Irrecoverable debts written off and subsequently paid

If an irrecoverable debt is unexpectedly paid after it has been written off, then the accounting treatment depends on when the payment is made.

(a)   If the payment is received **before** the end of the period in which the debt was written off, simply reverse the entry for the write off.

DEBIT   Receivables control account
CREDIT   Irrecoverable debt expense

and then record the receipt in the normal way.

(b)   If the payment is received **after** the end of the period in which the debt was written off, then it is treated as sundry income in the statement of profit or loss.

DEBIT   Bank account
CREDIT   Sundry income – irrecoverable debts recovered

5.6 An allowance for receivables

An allowance for receivables is rather different from an irrecoverable debt written off. A business might determine that 2% of customers' balances are unlikely to be collected. It would then be considered prudent to make a **receivables allowance of 2% of total receivables.** It may be that no particular customers are regarded as suspect and so it is not possible to write off any individual customer balances as irrecoverable debts.

An allowance for receivables is a best estimate of the percentage of debts which are not expected to be repaid.

As far as the ledger accounting is concerned, the procedure is then to leave the total receivables account completely untouched, but to **open up an allowance account** by the following entries:

DEBIT   Irrecoverable debt expense
CREDIT   Allowance for receivables

When preparing a statement of financial position, the credit balance on the allowance account is deducted from the trade receivables balance.

In **subsequent years**, adjustments may be needed to the amount of the allowance. The procedure to be followed then is as follows.

Step 1	Calculate the new allowance required.

Step 2	Compare it with the existing balance on the allowance account (ie the balance b/f from the previous accounting period).

Step 3	Calculate the increase or decrease required.

(a)   If a **higher** allowance is required now (either because the total of receivables has increased, or because the percentage of total receivables which may not pay has increased, or both):

DEBIT   Irrecoverable debt expense
CREDIT   Allowance for receivables

with the amount of the increase.

(b)   If a **lower** allowance is needed now than before (either because the total of receivables has decreased, or because the percentage of total receivables which may not pay has decreased, or both):

DEBIT   Allowance for receivables
CREDIT   Irrecoverable debt expense

with the amount of the decrease.

5.7 Example: allowance for receivables

Andrew Carter has total receivables balances outstanding at 31 December 20X6 of $28,000. He believes that about 1% of these balances will not be paid and wishes to make an appropriate allowance. Before now, he has not made any allowance for receivables at all.

On 31 December 20X7 his receivables balances amount to $40,000. His experience during the year has convinced him that an allowance of 5% should be made.

What accounting entries should Andrew make on 31 December 20X6 and 31 December 20X7, and what figures for receivables will appear in his statement of financial position as at those dates?

Solution

At 31 December 20X6

Allowance required = 1% × $28,000
                    = $280

Andrew will make the following entries.

DEBIT	Irrecoverable debt expense	$280	
CREDIT	Allowance for receivables		$280

The receivables will appear as follows under current assets.

	$
Trade receivables ledger balances	28,000
Less allowance for receivables	(280)
	27,720

At 31 December 20X7

Following the procedure described above, Andrew will calculate as follows.

	$
Allowance required now (5% × $40,000)	2,000
Existing allowance	(280)
Additional allowance required	1,720

DEBIT	Irrecoverable debt expense	$1,720	
CREDIT	Allowance for receivables		$1,720

The allowance account will by now appear as follows.

ALLOWANCE FOR RECEIVABLES

Date	Details	$	Date	Details	$
20X6			20X6		
31 Dec	Balance c/d	280	31 Dec	Irrecoverable debt expense account	280
			20X7		
			1 Jan	Balance b/d	280
20X7			31 Dec	Irrecoverable debt expense account	1,720
31 Dec	Balance c/d	2,000			2,000
		2,000			
			20X8		
			1 Jan	Balance b/d	2,000

For the statement of financial position, receivables will be valued as follows.

	$
Trade receivables	40,000
Less allowance for receivables	(2,000)
	38,000

5.7.1 Receivables allowance and sales tax

The **allowance for receivables has no effect whatsoever on sales tax**.

QUESTION

Real Coffee and Tea Shop

Simon Fawcett owns and runs the Real Coffee and Tea Shop. He began trading on 1 January 20X1, selling coffee, tea and related products to customers, most of whom make use of a credit facility that Simon offers. (Customers are allowed to purchase up to $50 of goods on credit but must repay a certain proportion of their outstanding debt every month.)

This credit system gives rise to a large number of irrecoverable debts, and the figures for receivables, irrecoverable debts and receivables' allowances for the first three years of trading for Simon Fawcett are as follows.

Year to 31 December 20X1
Irrecoverable debts written off during the year	$2,000
Balances owed by customers as at 31 December 20X1	$10,000
Allowance for receivables	2½% of outstanding receivables

Year to 31 December 20X2
Irrecoverable debts written off during the year	$2,500
Balances owed by customers as at 31 December 20X2	$13,000
Allowance for receivables	2½% of outstanding receivables

Year to 31 December 20X3
Irrecoverable debts written off during the year	$2,750
Balances owed by customers as at 31 December 20X3	$7,500
Allowance for receivables	3% of outstanding receivables

Required

For each of these three years, prepare the irrecoverable debt expense account and allowance for receivables account. State the value of receivables appearing in the statement of financial position as at 31 December.

ANSWER

IRRECOVERABLE DEBT EXPENSE

		$			$
20X0	Receivables control a/c	2,000	20X0	Statement of P/L	2,250
	Allowance for receivables a/c	250			
		2,250			2,250
20X1	Receivables control a/c	2,500	20X1	Statement of P/L	2,575
	Allowance for receivables	75			
		2,575			2,575
20X2	Receivables control a/c	2,750	20X2	Allowance for receivables a/c	100
				Statement of P/L	2,650
		2,750			2,750

ALLOWANCE FOR RECEIVABLES

		$			$
			20X0	Irrecoverable debt expense a/c ($10,000 × 2½%)	250
20X0	Balance c/d	250			
20X1	Balance c/d ($13,000 × 2½%)	325	20X1	Balance b/d	250
				Irrecoverable debt expense a/c ($13,000 × 2½% less 250)	75
		325			325
20X2	Irrecoverable debt expense a/c ($7,500 × 3% less $325)	100	20X2	Balance b/d	325
	Balance c/d ($7,500 × 3%)	225			
		325			325

The allowance required at the end of 20X3 is lower than that required in 20X2. The reduction in allowance will be credited to the irrecoverable debt expense account.

STATEMENT OF FINANCIAL POSITION EXTRACTS AS AT 31 DECEMBER

	20X1 $	20X2 $	20X3 $
Receivables	10,000	13,000	7,500
Less allowance	(250)	(325)	(225)
	9,750	12,675	7,275

EXAM FOCUS POINT

In the June 2015 report, the examining team highlighted irrecoverable debts as an area where candidates often experience difficulties. The correct approach is based on several key points:

An irrecoverable debt is 'written off' by a credit entry in the receivable account and a debit entry in the irrecoverable debt expense account. (In other words, the receivables balance is reduced and the charge against profit is increased.)

The movement in the receivables allowance is the difference between the existing allowance (which will be the balance at the date of the last statement of financial position) and the allowance which is now required (calculated on the basis given in the question).

An increase in the allowance will give rise to a charge against profit, and a decrease in the allowance will lead to a credit in the statement of profit or loss.

The total irrecoverable debt expense is thus either: the value of any irrecoverable balances written off plus the increase in the allowance

OR

the value of any irrecoverable balances written off less the decrease in the allowance.

Remember to read the question carefully!

6 Current assets and liabilities

Prepayments and receivables (both trade and non-trade) are part of the **current assets** of a business. Similarly, trade and non-trade payables and accruals represent a significant proportion of **current liabilities**. Do you remember the definitions of current assets and liabilities from Chapter 2?

Current assets are:

- Items owned by the business with the intention of turning them into cash within one year (inventories of goods, and receivables)

- Cash, including money in the bank, owned by the business

Assets are 'current' in the sense that they are continually flowing through the business.

Current liabilities are debts of the business that must be paid within a fairly short period of time (by convention, within one year).

We now look at **all the current assets and liabilities**.

	$'000	$'000
Non-current assets		500
Current assets		
Inventories	20	
Trade receivables (net of allowance for receivables)	37	
Non-trade receivables	11	
Prepayments	6	
Cash at bank and in hand	4	
		78
		578
Equity		
Proprietor's capital b/f		327
Profit for the year		181
Less drawings		(40)
		468
Non-current liabilities		55
Current liabilities		
Trade payables	25	
Non-trade payables	16	
Accruals	12	
Bank overdraft	2	
		55
		578

Receivables, accruals and prepayments have all been discussed in this and other chapters. There are a few further comments to make.

6.1 Cash at bank and in hand/overdraft

A business may show **both a cash current asset and a bank overdraft** at the same time. The current asset will be petty cash in hand or a debit balance in the general ledger which is separate from the overdrawn account (for example, the business may have a separate bank account for buying foreign currency to pay for goods bought from abroad).

From your earlier studies you should be very clear that a bank account balance appearing in the accounts is **not** the balance shown on the bank statement, but rather the reconciled balance on the bank account in the general ledger. A bank overdraft is usually classed as a current liability because it is repayable on demand, in theory at least.

6.2 Trade/non-trade payables

Trade payables shown in the statement of financial position, as you should already know, will represent the reconciled balance on the payables control account. We defined payables and trade payables in Chapter 1.

Non-trade payables will consist of items such as amounts owed to tax authorities for sales taxes and so on.

6.3 Inventories

Inventories represent a significant amount in the statements of financial position of most businesses. The value shown for inventories also has a significant impact on the statement of profit or loss through the value of cost of sales. We will examine inventories in detail in the next chapter.

7 Provisions

A provision is an amount set aside out of profits to 'provide' for a situation which is **expected** to arise.

'A provision is a liability of uncertain timing or amount.

A liability is a present obligation of the entity arising from past events, the settlement of which is expected to result in an outflow from the entity of resources embodying economic benefits'

(IAS 37, para.10)

So, a provision differs from other liabilities (for example accruals) because of the **uncertainty** or **estimation** involved. A provision is an obligation to pay someone at some point in the future, but which lacks the certainty needed in order to describe it is a liability.

Provisions are often contrasted with accruals. With an accrual you usually know (or can be virtually certain) of the timing of the expected payment and amount to be paid. For example, if you know you get a quarterly electricity charge and how much that charge will be, if the invoice is not received you can make an accurate accrual (look back at Sections 1 and 2 if you need to refresh your memory on accruals). With a provision you may not know exactly how much you will need to pay, or when you will need to pay. In fact sometimes there may still be a chance that nothing will need be paid but if it is more likely than not an amount will be due because of something that happened in the past, a provision should be made. Where a provision is required, the value which is applied is the **best estimate**.

An example of a situation where a provision would be appropriate would be where an entity knows at the year end that a legal dispute in which it is involved is likely to be resolved in favour of the other party, and that it will have substantial damages to pay. In this situation it will include in its accounts a provision for the best estimate of the costs involved. For instance, if you had a business and a customer claimed to have sustained damage using one of your products and your solicitor advised that they could be awarded $2,000, you would include a provision for $2,000 as the solicitor will have the knowledge to provide the best estimate.

A provision of this nature will appear under current liabilities with the corresponding entry under 'legal expenses' in the statement of profit or loss.

The solicitor's advice would be regarded as the 'best estimate' as they are able to make a judgement based on professional knowledge and competence. In any situation where a provision is required, the 'best estimate' will be provided by whoever is best placed to exercise an informed and unbiased opinion.

8 Non-current liabilities

We have already defined current liabilities as being due within one year. Those current liabilities which usually appear on statements of financial position are:

- Trade payables
- Amounts due to the authorities for sales tax
- Amounts due to the tax office for payroll taxes
- Company tax payable
- Loans repayable within one year
- Amounts due on hire purchase agreements, payable within one year

Amounts due after more than one year are classified as **non-current liabilities.** For instance, if the business had taken out a loan on which no repayments were due for the first year, the loan would appear on the statement of financial position under non-current liabilities. However, the following year, the amount repayable over the next 12 months would be re-classified under **current liabilities**, leaving the balance in non-current liabilities. The same procedure is adopted for hire purchase agreements. The amount of capital repayable over the next 12 months appears under current liabilities and the balance remains under non-current liabilities.

If it is expected that settlement of a provision will not take place within 12 months of the date of the statement of financial position, it will be reported as a non-current liability.

EXAM FOCUS POINT

In the December 2015 report, the examining team highlighted that students did not have a full understanding of the definition of assets and liabilities. Ensure that you understand the fundamental definitions and carefully read the question to focus on what is being asked.

BPP
LEARNING MEDIA

CHAPTER ROUNDUP

↳ **Accrued expenses** are expenses which relate to (ie have been incurred during) an accounting period but have not yet been paid. They are a **charge against the profit** for the period and they are shown in the statement of financial position as at the end of the period as a **current liability**.

↳ **Prepayments** are expenses which have already been paid but relate to a future accounting period. They are not **charged against the profit** of the current period, and they are shown in the statement of financial position at the end of the period as a **current asset**.

↳ **Receivables** can be broken down into **trade receivables** and **non-trade receivables**.

↳ Some trade receivables may need to be written off as **irrecoverable debts**. Additionally, an **allowance for receivables** may be created. Rather than affecting individual customer balances, an allowance for receivables recognises the fact that ordinarily a certain proportion of all debts may not be collected.

QUICK QUIZ

1 If a business has paid rent of $1,000 for the year to 31 March 20X7, what is the prepayment in the accounts for the year to 31 December 20X6?

2 Define an accrual.

3 What happens to the double entry made for accruals and prepayments in the following period?

4 What is a trade receivable?

5 What is the double entry to write off an irrecoverable debt?

6 What is the double entry for an irrecoverable debt subsequently received after the period end?

7 Why might a business have both cash as a current asset and an overdraft as a current liability?

8 What will be included in non-trade payables?

ANSWERS TO QUICK QUIZ

1 $3/12 \times \$1{,}000 = \$250$

2 An accrual is an expense which is charged against the profits of a particular period, even though it has not yet been paid off, because it was incurred in that period.

3 The entries are reversed.

4 A trade receivable is a customer who buys goods without paying cash for them straight away and who therefore owes money to the business.

5 DEBIT   Irrecoverable debts expense
  CREDIT   Receivables account

6 DEBIT   Cash
  CREDIT   Irrecoverable debts recovered

7 A business may have a petty cash balance and a bank overdraft, or two separate accounts, one in credit and one overdrawn.

8 Amounts owed to tax authorities for income and sales taxes, amounts owed for non-current assets and so on.

Now try ...

Attempt the questions below from the **Practice Question Bank**

Number	Level	Marks	Time
Q37	Examination	2	2.4 mins
Q38	Examination	2	2.4 mins
Q39	Examination	2	2.4 mins
Q40	Examination	2	2.4 mins
Q41	Examination	2	2.4 mins

08

Inventory is an important area of the accounts as it directly affects **gross profit** and it also has an impact on the **current assets** in the statement of financial position.

Inventory valuation rules are embodied in IAS 2 *Inventories.* Inventory should be valued at the lower of **cost** and **net realisable value (NRV)**.

Cost of goods sold and the treatment of inventories

TOPIC LIST	SYLLABUS REFERENCE
1 Cost of goods sold	D3(a)
2 Accounting for opening and closing inventories	D3(b), D3(i)
3 Inventory counting and inventory accruals	D3(f)
4 Valuing inventories	D3(d)
5 Determining the purchase cost	D3(c), D3(e), D3(g)
6 Inventory valuations and profit	D3(c), D3(h)

189

D   Recording transactions and events

3   Inventory

(a) Recognise the need for adjustments for inventory in preparing financial statements   K

(b) Record opening and closing inventory   S

(c) Identify and apply the alternative methods of valuing inventory   K

(d) Explain and apply the IASB requirements for valuing inventories   S

(e) Recognise which costs should be included in valuing inventories   K

(f) Explain the use of continuous and period end inventory records   K

(g) Calculate the value of closing inventory using FIFO (first in, first out) and AVCO (average cost) – both periodic weighted average and continuous weighted average   S

(h) Identify the impact of inventory valuation methods on profit, assets and capital including: S

    (i)   Periodic weighted average

    (ii)   Continuous weighted average

    (iii) FIFO

(i) Report inventory in the final accounts   S

1   Cost of goods sold

The **cost of goods sold** is calculated by applying the formula:

	$
Opening inventory value	X
Add cost of purchases (net of returns)	X
Less closing inventory value	(X)
Equals cost of goods sold	X

There is an important area we need to examine which has a direct bearing on the preparation of accounts: **inventories**. The valuation of inventories is important as it directly affects **gross profit**, as we will see in Section 4 of this chapter. It also has an impact on the **current assets** in the statement of financial position. Inventory valuation rules are embodied in IAS 2 *Inventories*.

1.1 What is inventory?

International Accounting Standard 2 *Inventories* defines inventories as 'assets held for sale in the ordinary course of business' *(IAS 2, para.6)*.

In some countries 'inventory' is referred to as 'stock'.

When we looked at the statement of profit or loss in Chapter 2, we defined **profit** as the value of sales less the cost of sales and expenses.

This definition might seem simple enough, but it is not always clear how much the cost of sales or expenses are. A variety of difficulties can arise in measuring them and this chapter describes some of these problems and their solutions.

1.2 Unsold goods in inventory at the end of an accounting period

Goods might be unsold at the end of an accounting period and so still be held in inventory at the end of the period. The purchase cost of these goods should *not* be included therefore in the cost of sales of the period.

1.3 Example: Closing inventory

James Terry, trading as the Raincoat Store, ends his financial year on 30 June each year. On 1 July 20X6 he had no goods in inventory. During the year to 30 June 20X7 he purchased 6,000 raincoats costing $36,000 from raincoat wholesalers and suppliers. He resold the raincoats for $10 each, and sales for the year amounted to $45,000 (4,500 raincoats). At 30 June there were 1,500 unsold raincoats left in inventory, valued at $6 each.

What was James Terry's gross profit for the year?

Solution

James Terry purchased 6,000 raincoats, but only sold 4,500. Purchase costs of $36,000 and sales of $45,000 do not represent the same quantity of goods.

The gross profit for the year should be calculated by 'matching' the sales value of the 4,500 raincoats sold with the cost of those 4,500 raincoats. The cost of sales in this example is therefore the cost of purchases minus the cost of goods in inventory at the year end.

	$	$
Sales (4,500 units)		45,000
Purchases (6,000 units)	36,000	
Less closing inventory (1,500 units @ $6)	(9,000)	
Cost of sales (4,500 units)		(27,000)
Gross profit		18,000

1.4 Example continued

We shall continue the example of the Raincoat Store into its next accounting year, 1 June 20X7 to 30 June 20X8. Suppose that during the course of this year, James Terry purchased 8,000 raincoats at a total cost of $55,500. During the year he sold 8,500 raincoats for $95,000. At 30 June 20X8 he had 1,000 raincoats left in inventory, which had cost $7,000.

What was his gross profit for the year?

Solution

In this accounting year, he purchased 8,000 raincoats to add to the 1,500 he already had in inventory at the start of the year. He sold 8,500, leaving 1,000 raincoats in inventory at the year end. Once again, gross profit should be calculated by matching the value of 8,500 units of sales with the cost of those 8,500 units.

The cost of sales is the value of the 1,500 raincoats in inventory at the beginning of the year, plus the cost of the 8,000 raincoats purchased, less the value of the 1,000 raincoats in inventory at the year end.

	$	$
Sales (8,500 units)		95,000
Opening inventory (1,500 units) *	9,000	
Add purchases (8,000 units)	55,500	
	64,500	
Less closing inventory (1,000 units)	(7,000)	
Cost of sales (8,500 units)		(57,500)
Gross profit		37,500

*Taken from the closing inventory value of the previous accounting year, see Paragraph 1.3.

1.5 The cost of goods sold

The cost of goods sold is found by applying the following formula.

FORMULA TO LEARN

	$
Opening inventory value	X
Add cost of purchases	X
	X
Less closing inventory value	(X)
Equals cost of goods sold	X

In other words, to **match 'sales' and the 'cost of goods sold'**, it is necessary to adjust the cost of goods purchased to allow for increases or reduction in inventory levels during the period.

1.6 Example: Cost of goods sold

On 1 January 20X6, Freddie's Health Food Store had goods in inventory valued at $10,000. During 20X6 its proprietor, who ran the shop, purchased supplies costing $70,000. Sales turnover for the year to 31 December 20X6 amounted to $120,000. The cost of goods in inventory at 31 December 20X6 was $22,000.

Calculate the gross profit for the year.

Solution

FREDDIE'S HEALTH FOOD STORE
STATEMENT OF PROFIT OR LOSS FOR THE YEAR ENDED 31 DECEMBER 20X6

	$	$
Revenue		120,000
Opening inventory	10,000	
Add purchases	70,000	
	80,000	
Less closing inventory	(22,500)	
Cost of goods sold		(57,500)
Gross profit		62,500

1.7 Carriage inwards and carriage outwards

Carriage refers to the cost of transporting purchased goods from the supplier to the premises of the business which has bought them. Someone has to pay for these delivery costs: sometimes the supplier pays, and sometimes the purchaser pays.

When the purchaser pays, the cost to the purchaser is **carriage inwards**.

When the supplier pays, the cost to the supplier is known as **carriage outwards**.

BPP
LEARNING MEDIA

The cost of **carriage inwards** is added to the cost of purchases in the statement of profit or loss and therefore enters into the calculation of gross profit.

The cost of **carriage outwards** is a selling and distribution expense in the statement of profit or loss. It is therefore a cost which is **deducted from** gross profit in order to calculate net profit.

1.8 Example: Carriage inwards and carriage outwards

Janice Young, trading as Sven Interiors, imports and resells Scandinavian furniture. She must pay for the costs of delivering the furniture from her supplier in Sweden to her shop in Wales. She resells the furniture to other traders throughout the country, paying the costs of carriage for the consignments from her business premises to her customers.

On 1 July 20X6, she had furniture in inventory valued at $35,000. During the year to 30 June 20X7 she purchased more furniture at a cost of $180,000. Carriage inwards amounted to $5,000. Sales for the year were $330,000. Other expenses of the business amounted to $72,000 excluding carriage outwards which cost $7,200. Janice Young took drawings of $36,000 from the business during the course of the year. The value of the goods in inventory at the year end was $44,200.

Required

Prepare the statement of profit or loss of Sven Interiors for the year ended 30 June 20X7.

Solution

SVEN INTERIORS
STATEMENT OF PROFIT OR LOSS
FOR THE YEAR ENDED 30 JUNE 20X7

	$	$
Revenue		330,000
Opening inventory	35,000	
Purchases	180,000	
Carriage inwards	5,000	
	220,000	
Less closing inventory	(44,200)	
Cost of goods sold		(175,800)
Gross profit		154,200
Carriage outwards	7,200	
Other expenses	72,000	
		(79,200)
Net profit (transferred to Janice Young's capital account)		75,000

QUESTION

Dearden

The following amounts appear in the books of Dearden at the end of the financial year.

	$
Opening inventory	5,700
Closing inventory	8,540
Carriage outwards	6,220
Purchases	75,280
Returns inwards	5,540
Carriage inwards	3,680

Required

Calculate the figure for cost of sales for the statement of profit or loss.

ANSWER

Returns inwards are a reduction in sales and do not affect cost of sales. Carriage outwards is a distribution expense in the statement of profit or loss and is therefore irrelevant here.

Cost of sales	$
Opening inventory	5,700
Purchases	75,280
Carriage inwards	3,680
	84,660
Closing inventory	(8,540)
Cost of sales	76,120

1.9 Goods written off or written down

A trader might be **unable to sell** all the goods that they purchase, because a number of things might happen to the goods before they can be sold.

- Goods might be **lost or stolen.**
- Goods might be **damaged**, and so become worthless. Such damaged goods might be thrown away.
- Goods might become **obsolete or out of fashion**. These might have to be thrown away, or possibly sold off at a very low price in a clearance sale.

When goods are lost, stolen or thrown away as worthless, the business will **make a loss** on those goods because their 'sales value' will be nil.

Similarly, when goods lose value because they have become obsolete or out of fashion, the business will make a loss if their clearance sales value is less than their cost. For example, if goods which originally cost $1,000 are now obsolete and could only be sold for $400, the business would suffer a loss of $600.

If, at the end of an accounting period, a business still has goods in inventory which are either worthless or worth less than their original cost, the value of the inventories should be **written down** to:

(a) **Nothing** if they are worthless
(b) Their **net realisable value** if this is less than their original cost

This means that the loss will be reported as soon as the loss is foreseen, even if the goods have not yet been thrown away or sold off at a cheap price.

Net realisable value of inventory is the estimated selling price less any costs still to be incurred in getting the inventory ready to sell and selling it.

The costs of inventory written off or written down should not usually cause any problems in calculating the gross profit of a business, because the cost of goods sold will include the cost of inventories written off or written down, as the following example shows.

1.10 Example: inventories written off and written down

Sarah Hughes, trading as Serina Fashions, ends her financial year on 31 December. At 1 January 20X6 she had goods in inventory valued at $21,500. During the year to 31 December 20X6, she purchased goods costing $73,000. Fashion goods which cost $4,300 were still held in inventory at 31 December 20X6, and Sarah Hughes believes that these could only now be sold at a sale price of $800. The goods still held in inventory at 31 December 20X6 (including the fashion goods) had an original purchase cost of $18,700. Sales for the year were $132,500.

Calculate the gross profit of Serina Fashions for the year ended 31 December 20X6.

Solution

The initial calculation of closing inventory values is as follows.

INVENTORY COUNT

	At cost $	Revalued amount $	Amount written down $
Fashion goods	4,300	800	3,500
Other goods	14,400	14,400	–
	18,700	15,200	3,500

SERINA FASHIONS
STATEMENT OF PROFIT OR LOSS FOR THE YEAR ENDED 31 DECEMBER 20X6

	$	$
Revenue		132,500
Value of opening inventory	21,500	
Purchases	73,000	
	94,500	
Less closing inventory	(15,200)	
Cost of goods sold		(79,300)
Gross profit		53,200

You should see that the write off of $3,500 is **automatic** because the closing inventory deducted from cost of sales is $3,500 less than it would have been if valued at cost; cost of sales is therefore $3,500 higher than it would have been without the write down of inventory.

QUESTION

Jackson

Jackson's draft statement of financial position includes an inventory figure of $28,850. On further investigation the following facts are discovered.

(a) One inventory sheet has been over-added by $212 and another under-added by $74.
(b) Goods included at their cost of $460 had deteriorated. They could still be sold at their normal selling price ($800) once repair work costing $270 was complete.
(c) Goods costing $430 sent to customers on a sale or return basis had been included in inventory at their selling price of $665.

Required

Calculate the revised inventory figure.

ANSWER

		$
Draft inventory figure		28,850
(a)	Overstatement due to wrong addition $(212 – 74)	(138)
(b)	No change (note 1)	
(c)	Reduction to cost $(665 – 430) (note 2)	(235)
		28,477

Notes

1 A comparison of cost and net realisable value shows that cost is still lower:

$460 < $(800 – 270)

and therefore no adjustment is required.

2 It is correct to include such items in inventory, to avoid anticipating profit, but at cost value. Using the selling price means that the profit element has been included.

2 Accounting for opening and closing inventories

The value of **closing inventory** is accounted for in the general ledger by debiting the inventory account and crediting the statement of profit or loss. The inventory account will therefore always have a debit balance at the end of a period, and this balance will be shown in the statement of financial position as a **current asset** for inventories.

Opening inventories brought forward in the inventory account are transferred to the statement of profit or loss, so the closing balance on the inventory account is the closing inventory value carried forward.

We have now seen that in order to calculate gross profit it is necessary to work out the cost of goods sold, and in order to calculate the cost of goods sold it is necessary to have values for the **opening inventory** (inventory in hand at the beginning of the accounting period) and **closing inventory** (inventory in hand at the end of the accounting period). In other words, the trading part of a statement of profit or loss includes the following.

FORMULA TO LEARN

	$
Opening inventory	X
Plus purchases	X
Less closing inventory	(X)
Equals cost of goods sold	X

However, just writing down this formula hides three problems.

(a) How do you manage to get a precise **count of inventory** in hand at any one time?

(b) Even once it has been counted, how do you **value the inventory**?

(c) Assuming the inventory is given a value, how does the **double entry bookkeeping** for inventory work?

Let us look at (c) first.

2.1 Ledger accounting for inventories

Purchases are introduced to the statement of profit or loss by means of the double entry:

DEBIT	Statement of profit or loss	$X	
CREDIT	Purchases account		$X

But what about opening and closing inventories? How are their values accounted for in the double entry bookkeeping system? The answer is that an **inventory account** must be kept. This inventory account is only ever used at the end of an accounting period, when the business counts up and values the inventory in hand, in a counting of inventory (sometimes known as a stocktake).

(a) When an inventory count is made, the business will have a value for its closing inventory, and the double entry is:

DEBIT	Inventory account (closing inventory value)	$X	
CREDIT	Statement of profit or loss		$X

However, rather than show the closing inventory as a 'plus' value in the statement of profit or loss (say by adding it to sales) it is usual to show it as a 'minus' figure in arriving at cost of sales. This is illustrated above. The debit balance on inventory account represents an asset, which will be shown as part of current assets in the statement of financial position.

(b) Closing inventory at the end of one period becomes opening inventory at the start of the next period. The inventory account remains unchanged until the end of the next period, when the value of opening inventory is taken to the statement of profit or loss.

DEBIT	Statement of profit or loss	$X	
CREDIT	Inventory account (value of opening inventory)		$X

2.2 Example: Ledger accounting for inventory

A business is established with capital of $4,000 and this amount is paid into a business bank account by the proprietor. During the first year's trading, the following transactions occurred.

	$
Purchases of goods for resale, on credit	8,200
Payments to trade suppliers	7,100
Sales, all on credit	8,000
Payments from customers	6,000
Non-current assets purchased for cash	2,900
Other expenses, all paid in cash	1,600

The bank has provided an overdraft facility of up to $6,000. All 'other expenses' relate to the current year.

Closing inventories of goods are valued at $3,500. (Because this is the first year of the business, there are no opening inventories.)

Prepare the ledger accounts and a statement of profit or loss for the year. Ignore depreciation and drawings.

Solution

BANK

	$		$
Capital	4,000	Trade payables	7,100
Receivables	6,000	Non-current assets	2,900
Balance c/d	1,600	Other expenses	1,600
	11,600		11,600
		Balance b/d	1,600

CAPITAL

	$		$
Balance c/d	5,700	Bank	4,000
		Statement of profit or loss	1,700
	5,700		5,700
		Balance b/d	5,700

TRADE PAYABLES

	$		$
Bank	7,100	Purchases	8,200
Balance c/d	1,100		
	8,200		8,200
		Balance b/d	1,100

PURCHASES ACCOUNT

	$		$
Trade payables	8,200	Statement of profit or loss	8,200

NON-CURRENT ASSETS

	$		$
Bank	2,900	Balance c/d	2,900
Balance b/d	2,900		

REVENUE

	$		$
Statement of profit or loss	8,000	Receivables	8,000

RECEIVABLES

	$		$
Revenue	8,000	Bank	6,000
		Balance c/d	2,000
	8,000		8,000
Balance b/d	2,000		

OTHER EXPENSES

	$		$
Bank	1,600	Statement of profit or loss	1,600

STATEMENT OF PROFIT OR LOSS

	$		$
Purchases account	8,200	Revenue	8,000
Gross profit c/d	3,300	Closing inventory (inventory account)	3,500
	11,500		11,500
Other expenses	1,600	Gross profit b/d	3,300
Net profit (transferred to capital account)	1,700		
	3,300		3,300

The statement of profit or loss is shown here in 'horizontal' (debit and credit) styles to emphasise the double entry aspect.

Alternatively, closing inventory could be shown as a minus value on the debit side of the trading account, instead of a credit entry, giving purchases $8,200 less closing inventory $3,500 equals cost of goods sold $4,700.

INVENTORY ACCOUNT

	$		$
Statement of P/L (closing inventory)	3,500		

This will be the opening inventory of the new period.

Make sure you can see what has happened here. The balance on the inventory account was $3,500, which appears in the statement of financial position as a current asset. As it happens, the $3,500 closing inventory was the only entry in the inventory account: there was no figure for opening inventory.

If there had been, it would have been eliminated by transferring it as a **debit balance** to the statement of profit or loss:

CREDIT   Inventory account (with value of opening inventory)
DEBIT   Statement of profit or loss (with value of opening inventory)

The debit in the statement of profit or loss would then have increased the cost of sales, ie opening inventory is added to purchases in calculating cost of sales. Again, this is illustrated above.

EXAM FOCUS POINT

It is very important that you understand the entries that are made for opening and closing inventory, and how changes in inventory levels affect the profit for the year.

So if we can establish the value of inventories on hand, the above paragraphs and example show us how to account for that value. That takes care of one of the problems noted in the introduction of this section. But now another of those problems becomes apparent: how do we establish the value of inventories on hand? The first step must be to establish **how much inventory** is held.

Note that inventories sent to customers on a **sale or return basis** should be **included** in closing inventory if the customer still has not sold them at the year end. This means that no accounting entries should be made until the inventory is sold by the customer.

3 Inventory counting and inventory accruals

An **inventory ledger account** is kept which is only ever used at the end of an accounting period, when the business counts up and values inventory in hand. The quantity of inventory held at the year end is established by means of a physical count of items in an annual exercise, or by a 'continuous' inventory count.

Business trading is a continuous activity, but accounting statements must be drawn up at a particular date. In preparing a statement of financial position it is necessary to 'freeze' the activity of a business so as to determine its assets and liabilities at a given moment. This includes establishing the **quantities of inventories** on hand, which can create problems.

A business buys goods continually during its trading operations and either sells the goods onwards to customers or incorporates them as raw materials in manufactured products. This constant movement of inventories makes it difficult to establish what exactly is held at any precise moment.

In simple cases, when a business holds easily counted and relatively small amounts of inventory, quantities of goods on hand at the reporting date can be determined by **physically counting** them.

The continuous nature of trading activity may cause a problem in that inventory movements will not necessarily cease during the time that the physical count is in progress. Two possible solutions are:

(a) To **close down the business** while the count takes place.

(b) To keep detailed **records of inventory movements** during the course of the count.

Closing down the business for a short period for an inventory count (say over a weekend or at Christmas) is considerably easier than trying to keep detailed records of movements during the count. So most businesses prefer that method unless they keep detailed records of inventory movements to keep control on inventory movements.

In more complicated cases, where a business holds considerable quantities of varied inventory, an alternative approach to establishing quantities is to maintain **continuous inventory records**. This means that a card is kept for every item, showing receipts and issues from the stores, and a running total. (Alternatively, the records may be computerised – quite likely in a large company.) A few inventory items are counted each day to make sure their record cards are correct. This is called a 'continuous' inventory count because it is spread out over the year rather than completed for the entire inventory at a designated time.

3.1 Inventory accruals

In Chapter 7 we looked at accruals and we mentioned **purchase accruals** (which are sometimes called **inventory accruals**). These arise where goods have been received before the year end and included in inventory, but no invoice has yet been received. Without an invoice, it will not have been possible to record the liability to the supplier. It is therefore necessary to determine those items of inventory which have not been recorded as a liability.

The procedure for determining those items of inventory for which no liability has been recorded is as follows.

(a) Match all invoices and Goods Received Notes (GRNs) received in the last month of the year.

(b) All unmatched GRNs should be listed.

(c) The goods on the GRNs must be costed at their purchase price. Delivery notes (which should be kept with the GRNs) received from suppliers will sometimes show the prices of the goods delivered. Where this is not the case, it will be necessary to price the inventory using current order forms or pricing lists.

The **double entry** once inventory accruals are identified is:

DEBIT   Purchases
CREDIT   Trade payables

One obstacle is overcome once a business has established how much inventory is on hand. But another of the problems noted earlier immediately arises. What **value** should the business place on those inventories? IAS 2 *Inventories* contains the rules governing the valuation of inventory.

4 Valuing inventories

> The value of inventories is calculated by taking the **lower of cost and NRV** (net realisable value) for each item or group of items.
>
> - **NRV** is the selling price less all estimated costs to completion and less estimated selling costs.
> - **Cost** comprises purchase costs, costs of conversion and other costs incurred to-date.
>
> *(IAS 2, para.6)*

4.1 The basic rule

There are several methods which, **in theory,** might be used for the valuation of inventory items.

(a) Inventories might be valued at their **expected selling price**.

(b) Inventories might be valued at their expected selling price, less any costs still to be incurred in getting them ready for sale and then selling them. This amount is referred to as the **net realisable value** (NRV) of the inventories.

(c) Inventories might be valued at their **historical cost** (ie the cost at which they were originally bought).

(d) Inventories might be valued at the amount it would cost to replace them. This amount is referred to as the **current replacement cost** of inventories.

IAS 2 defines the cost of inventories as 'all costs of purchase, costs of conversion and other costs incurred in bringing the inventories to their present location and condition'.

Net realisable value is defined as 'the estimated selling price in the ordinary course of business less the estimated costs of completion and the estimated costs necessary to make the sale'.

Inventory items that cost $90 to purchase, $15 to transport and $5 to store would have a total cost of $110.

Inventory items that are expected to sell for $80 and would cost $10 to complete and a further $5 in selling expenses would have an NRV of $65.

Current replacement costs are not used in the type of accounts dealt with in this Interactive Text, and so are not considered further.

4.2 Use of selling price

The use of selling prices in inventory valuation is ruled out because this would create a profit for the business before the inventory has been sold.

A simple example might help to explain this. Suppose that a trader buys two items of inventory, each costing $100. They can sell them for $140 each, but in the accounting period we shall consider, they have only sold one of them. The other is closing inventory in hand.

Since only one item has been sold, you might think it is common sense that profit ought to be $40. But if closing inventory is valued at selling price, profit would be $80, ie profit would be taken on the closing inventory as well.

BPP
LEARNING MEDIA

	$	$
Revenue		140
Opening inventory		
Purchases (2 × $100)	200	
	200	
Less closing inventory (at selling price)	(140)	
Cost of sales		(60)
Profit		80

4.3 Use of net realisable value

The same objection **usually** applies to the use of NRV in inventory valuation. Say that the item purchased for $100 requires $5 of further expenditure in getting it ready for sale and then selling it (eg $5 of processing costs and distribution costs). If its expected selling price is $140, its NRV is $(140 − 5) = $135. To value it at $135 in the statement of financial position would still be to anticipate a $35 profit.

4.4 Use of historical cost

We are left with historical cost as the normal basis of inventory valuation. **The only time when historical cost is not used is in the exceptional cases where a lower value is used**.

Staying with the example in Paragraph 4.3, suppose that the market in this kind of product suddenly slumps and the item's expected selling price is only $90. The item's NRV is then $(90 − 5) = $85 and the business has in effect made a loss of $15 ($100 − $85). Losses should be recognised as soon as they are foreseen. This can be achieved by valuing the inventory item in the statement of financial position at its NRV of $85.

The argument developed above suggests that the rule to follow is that inventories should be valued at cost, or if lower, net realisable value. The accounting treatment of inventory is governed by an accounting standard, IAS 2 *Inventories*. IAS 2 states that **inventory should be valued at the lower of cost and net realisable value** as we will see below. This is an important rule and one which you should learn by heart.

IMPORTANT

Inventory should be valued at the lower of cost and net realisable value, analysed on a **line by line** basis.

EXAM FOCUS POINT

Make sure that you understand this rule and can apply it. In the examiner's report from June 2016, it was identified that many students were not able to apply the fundamental principles of the valuation of inventory at the lower of cost and net realisable value. Students were noted to be applying the rule, if at all, on a total inventory basis. It is important that you compare the cost and NRV of each line of inventory.

4.5 Applying the basic valuation rule

If a business has many inventory items on hand the comparison of cost and NRV should theoretically be carried out for each item separately. It is not sufficient to compare the total cost of all inventory items with their total NRV, but instead **each line of inventory should be analysed** in turn. An example will show why.

Suppose a company has four items of inventory on hand at the end of its accounting period. Their cost and NRVs are as follows.

Inventory item	Cost	NRV	Lower of cost/NRV
	$	$	$
1	27	32	27
2	14	8	8
3	43	55	43
4	29	40	29
	113	135	107

It would be incorrect to compare total costs ($113) with total NRV ($135) and to state inventories at $113 in the statement of financial position. The company can foresee a loss of $6 on item 2 and this should be recognised. If the four items are taken together in total the loss on item 2 is masked by the anticipated profits on the other items. By performing the cost/NRV comparison for each item separately the prudent valuation of $107 can be derived. This is the value which should appear in the statement of financial position.

However, for a company with large amounts of inventory this procedure may be impracticable. In this case it is acceptable to group similar items into categories and perform the comparison of cost and NRV category by category, rather than item by item.

QUESTION

The following figures relate to inventory held by Dean at the year end.

	A	B	C
	$	$	$
Cost	20	9	12
Selling price	30	12	22
Modification cost to enable sale	-	2	8
Marketing costs	7	2	2
Units held	200	150	300

Required

Calculate the value of inventory held.

ANSWER

Item	Cost	NRV	Valuation	Quantity	Total value
	$	$	$	Units	$
A	20	23	20	200	4,000
B	9	8	8	150	1,200
C	12	12	12	300	3,600
					8,800

QUESTION   Brian

The following figures relate to inventory held by Brian at the year end.

	X	Y	Z
	$	$	$
Purchase cost	12	14	8
Modification costs (before year end)	1	1	2
Further modification needed before sale (post year end)	1	0	5
Selling price	22	24	20
Marketing costs	3	2	6

Required

Calculate the value per unit of inventory held.

BPP
LEARNING MEDIA

ANSWER

Item		Cost $		NRV $	Valuation $
X	(12 + 1)	13	(22 – 1 – 3)	18	13
Y	(14 + 1)	15	(24 – 2)	22	15
Z	(8 + 2)	10	(20 – 5 – 6)	9	9

Note that cost includes costs incurred in bring the inventory into its present state and condition (ie at the year end), not the expected costs after the year end.

So have we now solved the problem of how a business should value its inventories? It seems that all the business has to do is to choose the lower of cost and net realisable value. This is true as far as it goes, but there is one further problem, perhaps not so easy to foresee: for a given item of inventory, **what was the cost**?

5 Determining the purchase cost

In order to value the inventory, some pricing method must be adopted. This can be **FIFO** or **average cost**.

A business may be continually purchasing consignments of a particular component. As each consignment is received from suppliers they are stored in the warehouse on the appropriate shelf or pallet, where they will be mingled with previous consignments. When the storekeeper issues components to production they will simply pull out from the bin the nearest components to hand, which may have arrived in the latest consignment or in an earlier consignment or in several different consignments. Our concern is to devise a pricing technique, a rule of thumb which we can use to attribute a cost to each of the components issued from stores.

There are several techniques which are used in practice. Your syllabus specifies the following techniques.

FIFO (first in, first out). Using this technique, we assume that components are used in the order in which they are received from suppliers. The components issued are deemed to have formed part of the oldest consignment still unused and are costed accordingly.

Weighted average cost. As purchase prices change with each new consignment, the average price of components in the bin is constantly changed. Each component in the bin at any moment is assumed to have been purchased at the average price of all components in the bin at that moment. The weighted average cost can be applied as **continuous** or **periodic**.

Either of these methods might provide a suitable basis for valuing inventories. Remember that terms such as weighted average and FIFO refer to **pricing techniques** only. The **actual** components can be used in any order.

5.1 Example: valuation methods

To illustrate the various valuation methods, the following transactions will be used in each case.

TRANSACTIONS DURING MAY 20X7

	Quantity Units	Unit cost $	Total cost $	Market value per unit on date of transactions $
Opening balance 1 May	100	2.00	200	
Receipts 3 May	400	2.10	840	2.11
Issues 4 May	200			2.11

	Quantity Units	Unit cost $	Total cost $	Market value per unit on date of transactions $
Receipts 9 May	300	2.12	636	2.15
Issues 11 May	400			2.20
Receipts 18 May	100	2.40	240	2.35
Issues 20 May	100			2.35
Closing balance 31 May	200			2.38
			1,916	

Receipts mean goods are received into store (goods purchased) and issues represent the issue of goods from store. The problem is to put a valuation on:

(1)   The issues of materials;
(2)   The closing inventory.

The closing inventory cost becomes the opening inventory for the next period. Therefore the opening inventory is valued using the same principles.

How would opening inventory, issues and closing inventory be valued for May 20X7 using each of the following in turn?

(a)   FIFO
(b)   Weighted average cost (continuous)

There were no receipts into stores during the first half of June. The following **issues** took place in early June 20X7:

	Quantity Units
Issues 3 June	75
Issues 9 June	75

Show the value of these issues and the value of closing inventory following these issues using:

(a)   FIFO
(b)   Weighted average cost (continuous)

Solution

(a)   **FIFO (first in, first out) – May 20X7**

FIFO assumes that materials are **issued out of inventory in the order in which they were delivered into inventory**, ie issues are priced at the **cost** of the earliest delivery remaining in inventory.

The cost of opening inventory, issues and closing inventory value (at the end of May) in the example, using FIFO, would be as follows.

Opening inventory

	Quantity Units	Valuation	Total Cost
Inventory at 1 May 20X7	100	100 at $2	$200

Cost of issues in May 20X7

Date of issue	Quantity Units	Valuation	Cost of issues $	$
4 May	200	100 at $2	200	
		100 at $2.10	210	
				410
11 May	400	300 at $2.10	630	
		100 at $2.12	212	
				842
20 May	100	100 at $2.12		212
				1,464

Closing inventory

	Quantity Units	Valuation	Cost	Total
Closing inventory value	200	100 at $2.12	212	
		100 at $2.40	240	
				452

Note that the cost of materials issued ($1,464) plus the value of closing inventory ($452) equals the cost of purchases plus the value of opening inventory ($1,916).

FIFO (first in, first out) – valuation following issues of inventory in June 20X7

Here it is important to note that the same principles are applied to opening inventory as to purchases. Of those units making up opening inventory on 1 June, the 100 valued at $2.12 each were received into stores (purchased) first, so those are the ones assumed to be issued first.

Opening inventory

	Quantity Units	Valuation	Cost	Total
Opening inventory value 1 June	200	100 at $2.12	212	
		100 at $2.40	240	
				452

Cost of issues in June 20X7

Date of issue	Quantity Units	Valuation	Cost of issues $	$
3 June	75	75 at $2.12	159	
				159
9 June	75	25 at $2.12	53	
		50 at $2.40	120	
				173
				332

Closing inventory

	Quantity Units	Valuation	Total Cost
Inventory following June issues	50	50 at $2.40	$120

(b) **Weighted average cost – May 20X7**

There are various ways in which average costs may be used in pricing inventory issues. The most common (cumulative weighted average pricing) is illustrated below.

The **cumulative or continuous weighted average pricing method** calculates a weighted average price for all units in inventory. Issues are priced at this average cost, and the balance of inventory remaining would have the same unit valuation.

A new weighted average price is calculated whenever a new delivery of materials into store is received. This is the key feature of cumulative weighted average pricing.

In our example, issue costs and closing inventory values for May would be as follows.

Date	Received Units	Issued Units	Balance Units	Total inventory value $	Unit cost $	Price of issue $
Opening inventory			100	200	2.00	
3 May	400			840	2.10	
			500	1,040	2.08 *	
4 May		200		(416)	2.08 **	416
			300	624	2.08	
9 May	300			636	2.12	

Date	Received Units	Issued Units	Balance Units	Total inventory value $	Unit cost $	Price of issue $
			600	1,260	2.10 *	
11 May		400		(840)	2.10 **	840
			200	420	2.10	
18 May	100			240	2.40	
			300	660	2.20 *	
20 May		100		(220)	2.20 **	220
						1,476
Closing inventory value			200	440	2.20	440
						1,916

* A new unit cost of inventory is calculated whenever a new receipt of materials occurs.

** Whenever inventories are issued, the unit value of the items issued is the current weighted average cost per unit at the time of the issue.

For this method too, the cost of materials issued plus the value of closing inventory equals the cost of purchases plus the value of opening inventory ($1,916). However you can see that the closing inventory value is different from that found when using the FIFO method.

Weighted average cost – valuation following issues of inventory in June 20X7

Again, the same principle is applied in the next period. The opening inventory in June is the closing inventory at the end of May. Each issue in June is therefore valued at the average cost so it is not necessary to look back at when the units making up opening inventory were received into inventory (purchased).

Date	Received Units	Issued Units	Balance Units	Total inventory value $	Unit cost $	Price of issue $
Opening inventory			200	440	2.20	
4 May		75		(165)	2.20	165
11 May		75		(165)	2.20	165
						330
Closing inventory value			50	110	2.20	110
						440

5.1.1 Periodic weighted average

You should be aware of another simple method of calculating closing inventory valuation based on average cost. This method is called **periodic weighted average**, and it calculates the average cost of units received (and includes the units in opening inventory if applicable) during an accounting period. To use the example above, the calculation for May 20X7 would look like this.

	Quantity Units	Price per unit $	Total cost $
Opening inventory	100	2.00	200
3 May	400	2.10	840
9 May	300	2.12	636
18 May	100	2.40	240
	900		1,916

- Thus average cost for the period $= \dfrac{\$1,916}{900} = \$2.13$

- Thus closing inventory value $= 200 \times \$2.13 = \$426$ (to the nearest $)

Note that in the next period, the calculation is re-performed and the average will take account of both units purchased and the cost of units in opening inventory.

The formula for calculating the periodic weighted average can therefore be summarised as follows:

$$\text{Periodic weighted average} = \frac{\text{Cost of opening inventory} + \text{total cost of receipts}}{\text{Units of opening inventory} + \text{total units received}}$$

6 Inventory valuations and profit

In the previous descriptions of FIFO, and weighted average costing, the example used raw materials as an illustration. Each method of valuation produced different costs both of closing inventories and also of material issues. Since raw material costs affect the cost of production, and the cost of production works through eventually into the cost of sales, it follows that different methods of inventory valuation will provide different profit figures. An example may help to illustrate this point.

6.1 Example: inventory valuations and profit

On 1 November 20X2 a company held 300 units of finished goods item No 9639 in inventory. These were valued at $12 each. During November 20X2 three batches of finished goods were received into store from the production department, as follows.

Date	Units received	Production cost per unit
10 November	400	$12.50
20 November	400	$14
25 November	400	$15

Goods sold out of inventory during November were as follows.

Date	Units sold	Sale price per unit
14 November	500	$20
21 November	500	$20
28 November	100	$20

What was the profit from selling inventory item 9639 in November 20X2, applying the following principles of inventory valuation?

(a)   FIFO
(b)   Cumulative (continuous) weighted average costing
(c)   Periodic weighted average

Ignore administration, sales and distribution costs.

Solution

(a)   *FIFO*

Date	Issue costs	Issue cost total $	Closing inventory $
14 November	300 units × $12 plus		
	200 units × $12.50	6,100	
21 November	200 units × $12.50 plus		
	300 units × $14	6,700	
28 November	100 units × $14	1,400	
Closing inventory	400 units × $15		6,000
		14,200	6,000

(b) *Cumulative (continuous) weighted average cost*

			Unit cost $	Balance in inventory $	Total cost of issues $	Closing inventory $
1 November	Opening inventory	300	12.000	3,600		
10 November	400		12.500	5,000		
	700		12.286	8,600		
14 November	500		12.286	6,143	6,143	
	200		12.286	2,457		
20 November	400		14.000	5,600		
	600		13.428	8,057		
21 November	500		13.428	6,714	6,714	
	100		13.428	1,343		
25 November	400		15.000	6,000		
	500		14.686	7,343		
28 November	100		14.686	1,469	1,469	
30 November	400		14.686	5,874	14,326	5,874

(c) Periodic weighted average

	Quality Units	Price per unit $	Total cost $
Opening inventory	300	12.00	3,600
10 November	400	12.50	5,000
20 November	400	14.00	5,600
25 November	400	15.00	6,000
	1500		20,200

- Thus average cost for the period $= \dfrac{\$20,200}{1,500} = \$13.47$

- Thus closing inventory value $= 400 \times \$13.47 = \$5,388$ (to the nearest $)

Summary: profit

	FIFO $	Weighted average- continuous $	Weighted average- periodic
Opening inventory	3,600	3,600	3,600
Cost of production	16,600	16,600	16,600
	20,200	20,200	20,200
Closing inventory	(6,000)	(5,874)	(5,388)
Cost of sales	14,200	14,326	14,812
Sales (1,100 × $20)	22,000	22,000	22,000
Profit	7,800	7,674	7,188

Different inventory valuations have produced different cost of sales figures, and therefore different profits. In our example opening inventory values are the same, therefore the difference in the amount of profit under each method is the same as the difference in the valuations of closing inventory.

The profit differences are only temporary. In our example, the opening inventory in December 20X2 will be $6,000, $5,874 or £5,388, depending on the inventory valuation used. Different opening inventory values will affect the cost of sales and profits in December, so that in the long run inequalities in cost of sales each month will even themselves out.

QUESTION

Product R

A firm has the following transactions with its product R

Year 1
Opening inventory: nil
Buys 10 units at $300 per unit
Buys 12 units at $250 per unit
Sells 8 units at $400 per unit
Buys 6 units at $200 per unit
Sells 12 units at $400 per unit

Year 2
Buys 10 units at $200 per unit
Sells 5 units at $400 per unit
Buys 12 units at $150 per unit
Sells 25 units at $400 per unit

Required

Calculate on an item by item basis for both year 1 and year 2 using FIFO:

(a)   The closing inventory
(b)   The sales
(c)   The cost of sales
(d)   The gross profit

ANSWER

FIFO
Year 1

Purchases Units	Sales Units	Balance Units	Inventory value $	Unit cost $	Cost of sales $	Sales $
10		10	3,000	300		
12			3,000	250		
		22	6,000			
	8		(2,400)		2,400	3,200
		14	3,600			
6			1,200	200		
		20	4,800			
	12		(3,100)*		3,100	4,800
		8	1,700		5,500	8,000

* 2 @ $300 + 10 @ $250 = $3,100

Year 2

Purchases Units	Sales Units	Balance Units	Inventory value $	Unit cost $	Cost of sales $	Sales $
B/f		8	1,700			
10			2,000	200		
		18	3,700			
	5		(1,100)*		1,100	2,000
		13	2,600			
12		25	1,800	150		
			4,400			
	25		(4,400)**		4,400	10,000
		0	0		5,500	12,000

* 2 @ $250 + 3 @ $200 = $1,100
** 13 @ $200 + 12 @ $150 = $4,400

Trading accounts	FIFO	
	$	$
Year 1		
Sales		8,000
Opening inventory	0	
Purchases	7,200	
	7,200	
Closing inventory	(1,700)	
Cost of sales		(5,500)
Gross profit		2,500
Year 2		
Sales		12,000
Opening inventory	1,700	
Purchases	3,800	
	5,500	
Closing inventory	(0)	
Cost of sales		(5,500)
Gross profit		6,500

QUESTION

Hudson

Hudson specialises in retailing one product. The firm purchases its inventory from a regional wholesaler and sells through a catalogue. Details of Hudson purchases and sales for the three month period 1 January to 31 March 20X2 are as follows.

Purchases

Date	Quantity in units	Price per unit
		$
14 January	280	24
30 January	160	24
15 February	300	25
3 March	150	26
29 March	240	26

Sales

Date	Quantity in units	Price per unit
		$
22 January	170	60
4 February	140	60
18 February	90	63
26 February	70	64
4 March	110	64
19 March	200	66
30 March	80	66

Note. Hudson had no inventory in hand at 1 January 20X2.

Required

(a)   Record the company's inventory movements for the period 1 January to 31 March by the preparation of a stores card applying FIFO.

(b)   Prepare the opening section of the statement of profit or loss for the three month period applying FIFO.

(c)   Note how IAS 2 affects the valuation of a company's inventory.

ANSWER

(a) **FIFO**

		Quantity		Movement		
		Movement	Balance	Unit cost		Total value
				$		$
14 Jan	Receipt	280	280	24		6,720
22 Jan	Issue	(170)	110	24		(4,080)
30 Jan	Receipt	160	270	24		3,840
4 Feb	Issue	(140)	130	24		(3,360)
15 Feb	Receipt	300	430	25		7,500
18 Feb	Issue	(90)	340	24		(2,160)
				40	24	(1,710)
				30	25	
26 Feb	Issue	(70)	270			
3 Mar	Receipt	150	420	26		3,900
4 Mar	Issue	(110)	310	25		(2,750)
				160	25	(5,040)
				40	26	
19 Mar	Issue	(200)	110			
29 Mar	Receipt	240	350	26		6,240
30 Mar	Issue	(80)	270	26		(2,080)
		Total receipts				28,200
		Total issues				(21,180)
						7,020

(b) HUDSON
STATEMENT OF PROFIT OR LOSS FOR THE 3 MONTH PERIOD TO 31 MARCH 20X2

	FIFO	
	$	$
Sales		54,270
Opening inventory		
Purchases	28,200	
	28,200	
Closing inventory	(7,020)	
Cost of sales		(21,180)
Gross profit		33,090

Workings: sales 1 Jan to 31 Mar X2

	Units	Selling price	Sales value
		$	$
22 Jan	170	60	10,200
4 Feb	140	60	8,400
18 Feb	90	63	5,670
26 Feb	70	64	4,480
4 Mar	110	64	7,040
19 Mar	200	66	13,200
30 Mar	80	66	5,280
			54,270

(c) IAS 2 states that inventories should be stated at the lower of cost and net realisable value. Cost is defined as the expenditure which has been incurred in the normal course of business in bringing the product or service to its present location and condition.

Net realisable value is the actual or estimated selling price less all further costs to be incurred to make the sale.

EXAM FOCUS POINT

The Examiner's report September 2019 – August 2020 included a question where candidates were told about errors to opening and closing inventory and asked to calculated the adjusted profit.

This proved to be a challenging question for many candidates. The question required an adjustment to profit based on errors in both the opening and the closing inventory balances. In this question it is useful to first think logically about how the opening and closing inventory balances impact cost of sales, and therefore the profit, in the statement of profit or loss. From this it can be seen that typically opening inventory will increase cost of sales (therefore reducing profit) and closing inventory will reduce cost of sales (and therefore increase profit).

CHAPTER ROUNDUP

↳ The **cost of goods sold** is calculated by applying the formula:

	$
Opening inventory value	X
Add cost of purchases (net of returns)	X
Less closing inventory value	(X)
Equals cost of goods sold	X

↳ The value of **closing inventory** is accounted for in the general ledger by debiting the inventory account and crediting the statement of profit or loss. The inventory account will therefore always have a debit balance at the end of a period, and this balance will be shown in the statement of financial position as a **current asset** for inventories.

↳ **Opening inventories** brought forward in the inventory account are transferred to the **statement of profit or loss**, so the closing balance on the inventory account is the closing inventory value carried forward.

↳ An **inventory ledger account** is kept which is only ever used at the end of an accounting period, when the business counts up and values inventory in hand. The quantity of inventory held at the year end is established by means of a physical count of items in an annual exercise, or by a 'continuous' inventory count.

↳ The value of inventories is calculated by taking the **lower of cost and NRV (net realisable value)** for **each item or group of items.** Analyse each line of inventory, comparing cost and NRV. Some inventory items may be held at cost and others at NRV.

  – **NRV** is the selling price less all estimated costs to completion and less estimated selling costs.
  – **Cost** comprises purchase costs, costs of conversion and other costs incurred to-date.

↳ In order to value the inventory, some pricing method must be adopted. This can be **FIFO** or **average cost**.

QUICK QUIZ

1 How is the cost of goods sold calculated?

2 Distinguish between carriage inwards and carriage outwards.

3 How is carriage inwards treated in the statement of profit or loss?

4 Give three reasons why goods purchased might have to be written off.

5 When is an inventory account used?

6 How is closing inventory incorporated in financial statements?

7 What is 'continuous' inventory counting?

8 Define net realisable value.

9 Why is inventory not valued at expected selling price?

10 Give three methods of pricing an inventory item at historical cost.

1   Cost of goods sold = opening inventory value *plus* purchases *less* closing inventory value.

2   (a)   Carriage inwards is cost of delivering goods purchased
     (b)   Carriage outwards is cost of delivering goods sold to customers

3   Carriage inwards is treated as an addition to the cost of sales when calculating gross profit.

4   Goods might be lost or stolen; damaged; or obsolete or out of fashion.

5   An inventory account is only used at the end of the accounting period.

6   DEBIT   Inventory account (statement of financial position)
     CREDIT   Statement of profit or loss

7   Continuous inventory counting is where permanent records are kept of inventory movements and random
     counts carried out as a check, spread out over the year.

8   NRV is the expected selling price of inventories less any costs still to be incurred in getting them ready
     for sale and then selling them.

9   Valuation at selling price would create a profit for the business before the inventory was sold.

10   FIFO, continuous weighted average, periodic weighted average

Now try ...

Attempt the questions below from the **Practice Question Bank**

Number	Level	Marks	Time
Q42	Examination	2	2.4 mins
Q43	Examination	2	2.4 mins
Q44	Examination	2	2.4 mins
Q45	Examination	2	2.4 mins
Q46	Examination	2	2.4 mins

CHAPTER

09

In this chapter we look at **non-current assets.**
These are assets acquired and retained in the
business with a view to earning profits and not
merely being turned into cash.

The cost of a non-current asset is spread over its
useful life using **depreciation**. This should result in
the cost of the asset being matched against the full
period during which it earns profits for the
business.

Non-current assets and depreciation

Study Guide	Intellectual level
D **Recording transactions and events**	
4 **Tangible non-current assets and depreciation**	
(a) Define non-current assets	K
(f) Prepare journal and ledger entries to record the acquisition and disposal of non-current assets (including part exchange)	S
(g) Calculate and record profits or losses on disposal of non-current assets in the statement of profit or loss including part exchange transactions and scrapping of assets	S
(h) Explain the purpose of depreciation	K
(i) Calculate the charge for depreciation using straight line and reducing balance methods	S
(j) Identify the circumstances where different methods of depreciation would be appropriate	K
(k) Illustrate how depreciation expense and accumulated depreciation are recorded in ledger accounts	S
(l) Explain the purpose and function of an asset register	K
(m) Prepare the non-current asset register accounting for all or part of the following:	S
(i) Acquisition including authorisation	
(ii) Part exchange and cash non-current asset purchases	
(iii) Depreciation	
(n) Identify and resolve any discrepancies relating to the accounting records for non-current assets	S
(o) Report non-current assets and depreciation in the final accounts	S

1 Non-current assets: the basics

Asset expenditure results in the acquisition of non-current assets or an improvement in their earning capacity. **Expenses charged to profit or loss** is expenditure which is incurred for the purpose of the trade of the business or to maintain the existing earning capacity of non-current assets.

Recording asset expenditure as a non-current asset is also known as **capitalisation.** Only **material items** should be capitalised.

A **non-current asset** is one which is acquired and retained in the business with a view to earning profits and not merely being turned into cash. It is normally used over more than one accounting period. The process of creating a non-current asset is called **capitalisation.**

Here are some examples of non-current assets.

- Motor vehicles
- Plant and machinery
- Fixtures and fittings
- Land and buildings

Technical Performance Objective 8 requires you to demonstrate you are competent in keeping records dealing with acquisition, disposal and depreciation of assets. The knowledge you gain in this chapter will help you to demonstrate your competence in this area.

Non-current assets are to be distinguished from **inventories** which we buy or make in order to sell. Inventories are **current assets**, along with cash and receivables.

The distinction between asset expenditure and expenses charged to profit or loss is an extremely important one. We looked at this in detail in Chapter 2 (Section 7) and you should go back and read through it again. In particular, revise these key terms.

Asset expenditure is expenditure which results in the acquisition of non-current assets, or an improvement in their earning capacity.

- Asset expenditure on non-current assets results in the appearance of a non-current asset in the **statement of financial position** of the business.

- Asset expenditure is not charged as an expense in the **statement of profit or loss**.

Expenses charged to profit or loss is expenditure which is incurred:

- For the purpose of the trade of the business, including expenditure classified as selling and distribution expenses, administration expenses and finance charges

- To maintain the **existing** earning capacity of non-current assets, eg repairs to non-current assets

Expenses charged to profit or loss are shown in the statement of profit or loss of a period, provided that they relate to the trading activity and sales of that particular period. If they carry over into the next period, the expenditure would appear as a current asset in the statement of financial position.

1.1 Materiality

Many **small value assets**, although purchased for continuing use in the business, will not be recorded as assets but will instead be written off directly as an expense when purchased. An obvious example would be a box of pencils or a set of file dividers. Clearly you would not bother to capitalise such items and then calculate depreciation on them at the year end!

The decision as to whether such items are 'small enough' to be written off or 'large enough' to be capitalised is generally clear cut. However, what about **borderline items**, such as a waste paper basket, a set of 'in-trays', or some software for the computer?

The decision taken has to depend on whether or not the amount is **material**, that is whether it has a significant effect on the financial statements. Something that is material to a small organisation may not be material to a large one. Also remember that sometimes a lot of 'immaterial' items may add up to a material amount.

1.2 Self-constructed assets

Where a business **builds it own non-current asset** (eg a builder might build their own office), then all the costs involved in building the asset should be included in the recorded cost of the non-current asset. These costs will include raw materials, but also labour costs and related overhead costs. This treatment means that assets which are self-constructed are treated in a similar way as purchased non-current assets (where all such costs are included in the purchase price of the asset).

1.3 Acquisition of non-current assets

There are three methods of purchasing large non-current assets:

(a) **Cheque payment**

The entry will be:

DEBIT   Non-current asset
CREDIT   Bank

The business has now paid the total amount and has nothing further to pay. Its cash flow is reduced by the total amount.

(b) **Loan**

The entry will be:

DEBIT   Non-current asset
CREDIT   Loan payable

The business owns the asset and will now make loan repayments to the bank or other lender, plus interest.

(c) **Finance lease**

The entry will be:

DEBIT   Non-current asset
CREDIT   Lease payable

In this case, the leasing company legally owns the asset, but the business has acquired the asset for use. Please note that lease transactions are outside the scope of the FA2 sylabus.

---

2   Depreciation

> Since a non-current asset has a cost and a limited useful life and its value eventually declines, it follows that a charge should be made in the statement of profit or loss to reflect the use that is made of the asset by the business. This charge is called **depreciation**.

2.1 Introduction

Nearly every non-current asset eventually **wears out over time**, the only exception being freehold land. Machines, cars and other vehicles, fixtures and fittings and even buildings do not last forever.

When a business acquires a non-current asset, it will have some idea about how long its **useful life** will be, and might decide to do one of two things.

(a) It may keep on using the non-current asset until it becomes **completely worn out**, useless and worthless.

(b) Alternatively, the business might decide to **sell off** the asset at the end of its useful life either by selling it as a second-hand item or as scrap.

Since a non-current asset has a cost, and a limited useful life, and its value eventually declines, it follows that a charge should be made in the statement of profit or loss to reflect the use that is made of the asset by the business. This charge is called **depreciation**.

Suppose that a business buys a machine for $40,000. Its expected life is four years, and at the end of that time it is expected to be worthless. Since the asset is used to make profits for four years, it would be reasonable to charge the cost of the asset over those four years (perhaps by charging $10,000 per annum) so that at the end of the four years the total cost of $40,000 would have been charged against profits.

Indeed, one way of defining depreciation is to describe it as a means of spreading the cost of a non-current asset over its useful life, thereby matching the cost against the full period during which it earns profits for the business.

Here are some definitions from IAS 16 *Property, Plant and Equipment.*

'**Depreciation** is the systematic allocation of the depreciable amount of an asset over its useful life.

Depreciable amount is the cost of an asset, or other amount substitute for cost, less its residual value.

Property, plant and equipment are tangible assets that:

– Are held by an entity for use in the production or supply of goods and services, for rental to others, or for administrative purposes; and

– Are expected to be used during more than one period.

Useful life is:

– The period over which an asset is expected to be available for use by the entity; or

– The number of production or similar units expected to be obtained from the asset by the entity.'

(IAS 16, para.6)

2.2 The total charge for depreciation

The total amount to be charged over the life of a non-current asset (the **depreciable amount**) is usually its **cost less any expected 'residual' sales value** or disposal value at the end of the asset's life. IAS 16 defines an asset's **residual value** to be 'the estimated amount that an entity would currently obtain from disposal of the asset, after deducting the estimated costs of disposal. *(IAS 16, para.6)*

(a) A non-current asset costing $20,000 which has an expected life of five years and an expected residual value of nil should be depreciated by $20,000 in total over the five year period.

(b) A non-current asset costing $20,000 which has an expected life of five years and an expected residual value of $3,000 should be depreciated by $17,000 in total over the five year period.

2.3 Depreciation in the accounts of a business

When a non-current asset is depreciated, two things must be accounted for, one in the statement of profit or loss and one in the statement of financial position.

(a) The charge for depreciation is a **cost or expense** of the accounting period. For the time being, we shall charge depreciation as an expense in the **statement of profit or loss**.

(b) At the same time, the non-current asset is wearing out and diminishing in value, and so the value of the non-current asset must be reduced by the amount of depreciation charged. The value of the non-current asset will be its **carrying amount** (or 'net book value') which is the value net of depreciation in the books of account of the business. Note that the carrying amount is *not* the same as the 'market value' of the asset.

The amount of depreciation deducted from the cost of a non-current asset to arrive at its carrying amount will build up (or 'accumulate') over time, as more depreciation is charged in each successive accounting period. This **accumulated depreciation** is an allowance to provide for the fall in value of the non-current asset.

2.4 What is depreciation?

You may have no difficulty understanding what depreciation is, but there are frequent misconceptions about its **purpose**.

2.4.1 Depreciation is not a cash-expense

Depreciation spreads the cost of a non-current asset (less its residual value) over the asset's life. The cash payment for the asset will be made when, or soon after the asset is purchased. Annual depreciation of the asset in subsequent years is not a cash expense; rather, it **allocates costs** under the matching concept to those later years for a cash payment that has occurred previously.

2.4.2 Depreciation isn't a fund set aside for future replacement of non-current assets

The concept of depreciation as such a fund could not be applied, for instance, if the asset was **not replaced** or was replaced with a very **different asset**, at a different cost, due to technological advances. Depreciation, then, allocates the cost of the **existing asset** to future periods; it does not anticipate the purchase of non-current assets in the future.

2.4.3 Depreciation is not a way to reflect the revised value of an asset

Depreciation is **not** a tool used to revise the perceived value of an asset. Therefore the depreciation charged on an asset should not be the amount needed to reduce its carrying amount down to its estimated present value.

Remember, depreciation is the allocation of the depreciable amount of an asset over its estimated useful life. It is not a tool used to reflect the falling realisable value of an asset.

2.4.4 Subjectivity and consistency

The way in which an asset is depreciated is a subjective matter. The business can make a choice in three areas.

- Estimated useful life
- Method and rate of depreciation
- Residual value

Judgement based on experience of similar assets and known conditions should be used when determining all of these, but there can easily be arbitrary elements.

Consequently, once the decisions on these three aspects have been made, the **consistency concept** demands that they continue to be applied, particularly in the case of the method of depreciation. New information or changes in the business's market may require changes to the estimated useful life and the expected residual value. The depreciation method should only be changed, however, if it became clear that the existing method does not reflect the way the asset is being used up by the business. A business cannot change the method every year just to give a more favourable depreciation figure in the accounts.

EXAM FOCUS POINT

It is very important that you understand the **purpose** of depreciation. This will help you in determining which rates and methods might be appropriate for different non-current assets. Make sure you take careful note of the answer to the question below.

QUESTION

Depreciation

What does depreciation do and why is it necessary?

ANSWER

Depreciation is the allocation of the depreciable amount of an asset over its estimated useful life. It is charged in order to match revenue and expenses with one another in the same accounting period so that profits are fairly and consistently calculated. If the cost of non-current assets was not written off over time, there would be incomplete matching of revenue and expenses.

2.5 Example: Depreciation

A non-current asset costing $40,000 has an expected life of four years and an estimated residual value of nil. It might be depreciated by $10,000 per annum.

	Depreciation charge for the year (SPL) (A)	Accumulated depreciation at end of year (B)	Cost of the asset (C)	Carrying amount at end of year (C–B)
	$	$	$	$
At beginning of its life			40,000	40,000
Year 1	10,000	10,000	40,000	30,000
Year 2	10,000	20,000	40,000	20,000
Year 3	10,000	30,000	40,000	10,000
Year 4	10,000	40,000	40,000	0
	40,000			

At the end of Year 4, the full $40,000 of depreciation charges have been made in the statement of profit or loss of the four years. The carrying amount of the asset is now nil. In theory (although perhaps not in practice) the business will no longer use the asset, which would now need replacing.

3 Methods of depreciation

The most common methods of depreciation are:

– The straight line method
– The reducing balance method

EXAM FOCUS POINT

You will certainly be required to use one or both of these methods in your exam.

3.1 The straight line method

This is the most commonly used method of all. The total depreciable amount is charged in **equal instalments** to each accounting period over the expected useful life of the asset. In this way, the carrying amount of the asset declines at a steady rate, or in a 'straight line' over time.

The annual depreciation charge is calculated as:

$$\frac{\text{Cost of asset minus residual value}}{\text{Expected useful life of the asset}}$$

3.2 Examples: straight line depreciation

Examples of straight line depreciation are as follows.

(a) A non-current asset costing $20,000 with an estimated life of ten years and no residual value would be depreciated at the rate of:

$$\frac{\$20,000}{10\,\text{years}} = \$2,000 \text{ per annum}$$

(b) A non-current asset costing $60,000 has an estimated life of five years and a residual value of $7,000. The annual depreciation charge using the straight line method would be calculated as follows.

$$\frac{\$(60,000-7,000)}{5\,\text{years}} = \$10,600 \text{ per annum}$$

The carrying amount of the non-current asset would reduce each year as follows.

	After 1 year $	After 2 years $	After 3 years $	After 4 years $	After 5 years $
Cost of the asset	60,000	60,000	60,000	60,000	60,000
Accumulated depreciation	10,600	21,200	31,800	42,400	53,000
Carrying amount	49,400	38,800	28,200	17,600	7,000*

* ie its estimated residual value.

Since the depreciation charge per annum is the same amount every year with the straight line method, it is often convenient to state that depreciation is charged at the rate of x% per annum on the cost of the asset. In the example in Paragraph 3.4(a) above, the depreciation charge per annum is 10% of cost (ie 10% of $20,000 = $2,000).

The straight line method of depreciation is a fair allocation of the total depreciable amount between the different accounting periods, provided that it is reasonable to assume that the business enjoys **equal benefits** from the use of the asset in every period throughout its life.

3.3 The reducing balance method

The reducing balance method of depreciation calculates the annual depreciation charge as a **fixed percentage of the carrying amount** of the asset, as at the end of the previous accounting period.

Note that no residual value is deducted initially to calculate a depreciable amount of the asset, because the percentage chosen by the business will already have taken into account this estimated residual value.

3.4 Example: reducing balance method

A business purchases a non-current asset at a cost of $10,000. Its expected useful life is three years. The business wishes to use the reducing balance method to depreciate the asset, and calculates that the rate of depreciation should be 40% of the reducing carrying amount of the asset. (The method of deciding that 40% is a suitable percentage is a problem of mathematics and is not described here.)

The depreciation charge per annum and the carrying amount of the asset as at the end of each year will be as follows.

	$	Accumulated depreciation $
Asset at cost	10,000	
Depreciation in Year 1 (40%)	(4,000)	4,000
Carrying amount at end of year	6,000	
Depreciation in Year 2		
(40% of reducing balance)	(2,400)	6,400 (4,000 + 2,400)
Carrying amount at end of year	3,600	
Depreciation in Year 3 (40%)	(1,440)	7,840 (6,400 + 1,440)
Carrying amount at end of Year 3	2,160	

You should be able to see that with the reducing balance method, the annual charge for depreciation is higher in the earlier years of the asset's life, and lower in the later years. In the example above, the annual charges for Years 1, 2 and 3 are $4,000, $2,400 and $1,440 respectively.

The reducing balance method might be used when it is considered fair to allocate a **greater proportion** of the total depreciable amount to the earlier years and a lower amount in the later years, on the assumption that the benefits obtained by the business from using the asset decline over time.

QUESTION

Laser printer

On 1 January 20X1 a business purchased a laser printer costing $1,800. The printer has an estimated life of four years after which it will have no residual value.

Required

Calculate the annual depreciation charges for 20X1, 20X2, 20X3 and 20X4 on the laser printer on the following bases.

(a)   The straight line basis
(b)   The reducing balance method at 60% per annum

Note. Your workings should be to the nearest $.

ANSWER

(a)   **Straight line depreciation** will give the same charge each year for the four years of economic life, as follows.

$$\text{Annual depreciation} = \frac{\text{Cost minus residual value}}{\text{Estimated economic life}}$$

$$\text{Annual depreciation} = \frac{\$1,800 - \$0}{4 \text{ years}}$$

$$\text{Annual depreciation} = \underline{\$450}$$

Annual depreciation charges are therefore $450 for each year from 20X1 to 2004 inclusive.

(b)   The **reducing balance method** at 60% per annum involves the following calculations.

	$	
Cost at 1.1.20X1	1,800	
Depreciation 20X1	(1,080)	60% × $1,800
Book value 1.1.20X2	720	
Depreciation 20X2	(432)	60% × $720
Book value 1.1.20X3	288	
Depreciation 20X3	(173)	60% × $288
Book value 1.1.20X4	115	
Depreciation 20X4 (Note)	(115)	(balance remaining)
Residual value at end of estimated economic life	–	

Annual depreciation charges are therefore 20X1: $1,080, 20X2: $432, 20X3: $173, 20X4: $115.

Note. At some point it will usually be considered a waste of time to carry on the depreciation calculations as the amounts involved will be immaterial. (Sometimes the asset is maintained in the books at $1.)

3.5 Which method of depreciation should be used?

A business is faced with a choice between the various methods of depreciation for its different types of non-current assets. A **different method** can be used for each type of asset, such as buildings, machinery, motor vehicles and so on. The method chosen must, however, **be fair in allocating the charges between different accounting periods.**

The following needs to be taken into consideration when selecting a method of depreciation.

(a)   The method should **allocate costs in proportion to the economic benefits** consumed during each accounting period by the asset. These profits almost certainly cannot be calculated exactly, but the business should be able to decide whether:

   (i)   The asset provides greater benefits in the earlier years of its life, in which case the reducing balance method would be suitable.

   (ii)   The asset provides equal benefits to each period throughout its life, in which case the straight line method would be suitable.

(b) The method of depreciation used by a business for any non-current asset should be the same as the method used for **similar assets** (consistency concept).

(c) The method used should be one which is **easy to apply** in practice. There is no point in creating unnecessary complications.

The straight line method is by far the most common method used in practice. It is easy to use and it is generally fair to assume that all periods benefit more or less equally from the use of a non-current asset throughout its useful life.

3.6 Assets acquired in the middle of an accounting period

A business may purchase new non-current assets at any time during the course of an accounting period, and so it might seem fair to charge an amount for depreciation in the period when the purchase occurs which reflects the limited amount of use the business has had from the asset in that period.

3.7 Example: Assets acquired during an accounting period

Suppose that a business which has an accounting year which runs from 1 January to 31 December purchases a new non-current asset on 1 April 20X1, at a cost of $24,000. The expected life of the asset is four years, and its residual value is nil.

What should be the depreciation charge for 20X1?

Solution

The annual depreciation charge will be $\dfrac{\$24,000}{4 \text{ years}} = \$6,000$ per annum.

However, since the asset was acquired on 1 April 20X1, the business has only benefited from the use of the asset for nine months instead of a full 12 months. It would therefore seem fair to charge nine months' depreciation in 20X1 as follows.

$^{9}/_{12} \times \$6,000 = \$4,500$

EXAM FOCUS POINT

In this example, the purchase date of the non-current asset is in the middle of an accounting period, and depreciation for the first year has been calculated as a 'part-year' amount.

However, you should be aware that in practice, many businesses ignore the niceties of part-year depreciation, and charge a full year's depreciation on assets in the year of their purchase, regardless of the time of year they were acquired. In the exam the question will make it clear whether or not depreciation for the first year is to be calculated only for the period since it was purchased or for the full year.

3.8 Labour costs in the installation of non-current assets

When a business uses its **own work force** to install some non-current assets, the cost of the labour may be added to the cost of the asset. The ledger accounting entries are simply:

DEBIT   Non-current asset account
CREDIT   Wages/salaries account

with the labour cost of the installation.

4 Recording depreciation in the accounts

The **accounting entries** to record depreciation are:

DEBIT   Depreciation expense (statement of profit or loss)
CREDIT   Accumulated depreciation (statement of financial position)

We must now consider how to record depreciation in the ledger accounts. There are two basic aspects of depreciation to remember.

(a)   A **depreciation charge** is made in the statement of profit or loss of each accounting period for every depreciable asset.

(b)   The total **accumulated depreciation** on an asset builds up as the asset gets older. The total accumulated depreciation is always getting larger, until the asset is fully depreciated.

The ledger accounting period entries for accumulated depreciation are as follows.

(a)   There is an **accumulated depreciation account** for each separate category of non-current assets.

(b)   The **depreciation charge** for an accounting period is accounted for as follows.

DEBIT   Depreciation expense (in the statement of profit or loss)
CREDIT   Accumulated depreciation (statement of financial position)

(c)   The balance on the accumulated depreciation account is the total accumulated depreciation. This is always a **credit balance** brought forward in the ledger account for depreciation.

(d)   The non-current asset accounts are **unaffected by depreciation**. Non-current assets are recorded in these accounts at cost.

(e)   In the **statement of financial position** of the business, the total balance on the accumulated depreciation account is set against the value of non-current asset accounts to derive the carrying amount of the non-current assets.

4.1 Example: Ledger entries for depreciation

Brian Box set up his own computer software business on 1 March 20X6. He purchased a computer system on credit from a manufacturer, at a cost of $16,000. The system has an expected life of three years and a residual value of $2,500.

Using the straight line method of depreciation, show the non-current asset account, accumulated depreciation account and statement of profit or loss (extract) and statement of financial position (extract) for each of the next three years, 28 February 20X7, 20X8 and 20X9.

Solution

COMPUTER EQUIPMENT – COST

	Date		$	Date		$
(a)	1 Mar 20X6	Suppliers	16,000	28 Feb 20X6	Balance c/d	16,000
(b)	1 Mar 20X7	Balance b/d	16,000	28 Feb 20X7	Balance c/d	16,000
(c)	1 Mar 20X8	Balance b/d	16,000	28 Feb 20X8	Balance c/d	16,000
(d)	1 Mar 20X9	Balance b/d	16,000			

In theory, the asset has now lasted out its expected useful life. However, until it is sold off or scrapped, the asset will still appear in the statement of financial position at cost, less accumulated depreciation, and it should remain in the ledger account for computer equipment until it is eventually disposed of.

COMPUTER EQUIPMENT – ACCUMULATED DEPRECIATION

	Date		$	Date		$
(a)	28 Feb 20X7	Balance c/d	4,500	28 Feb 20X7	Dep'n expense	4,500
(b)	28 Feb 20X8	Balance c/d	9,000	1 Mar 20X7	Balance b/d	4,500
				28 Feb 20X8	Dep'n expense	4,500
			9,000			9,000
(c)	28 Feb 20X9	Balance c/d	13,500	1 Mar 20X8	Balance b/d	9,000
				28 Feb 20X9	Dep'n expense	4,500
			13,500			13,500
				1 Mar 20X9	Balance b/d	13,500

The annual depreciation charge is $\dfrac{\$(16,000 - 2,500)}{3 \text{ years}} = \$4,500$

At the end of three years, the asset is fully depreciated down to its residual value of $2,500. If it continues to be used by Brian Box, it will not be depreciated any further (unless its estimated residual value is reduced).

DEPRECIATION EXPENSE ACCOUNT (EXTRACT)

	Date		$
(a)	28 Feb 20X7	Accumulated depreciation	4,500
(b)	28 Feb 20X8	Accumulated depreciation	4,500
(c)	28 Feb 20X9	Accumulated depreciation	4,500

STATEMENT OF FINANCIAL POSITION (EXTRACT) AS AT 28 FEBRUARY

	20X7(a)	20X8(b)	20X9(c)
	$	$	$
Computer equipment at cost	16,000	16,000	16,000
Less accumulated depreciation	(4,500)	(9,000)	(13,500)
Carrying amount	11,500	7,000	2,500

QUESTION

Brian Box

Brian Box prospers in his computer software business, and before long he purchases a car for himself, and later for his chief assistant Bill Ockhead. Relevant data is as follows.

	Date of purchase	Cost	Estimated life	Estimated residual value
Brian Box car	1 June 20X6	$20,000	3 years	$2,000
Bill Ockhead car	1 June 20X7	$8,000	3 years	$2,000

The straight line method of depreciation is to be used.

Required

Prepare the motor vehicles cost account and accumulated depreciation of motor vehicles account for the years to 28 February 20X7 and 20X8. (You should allow for the part-year's use of a car in computing the annual charge for depreciation.) Calculate the carrying amount of the motor vehicles as at 28 February 20X8.

ANSWER

Workings

1	Brian Box car	Annual depreciation $\dfrac{\$(20,000 - 2,000)}{3 \text{ years}} = \$6,000$ pa	
	Depreciation	Monthly depreciation	$500
		1 June 20X6 to 28 February 20X7 (9 months)	$4,500
		1 March 20X7 to 28 February 20X8	$6,000

BPP
LEARNING MEDIA

2   *Bill Ockhead car*   Annual depreciation $\dfrac{\$8,000-2,000}{3\ \text{years}} = \$2,000$ pa

Depreciation 1 June 20X7 to 28 February 20X8 (9 months) $1,500

MOTOR VEHICLES – COST

Date		$	Date		$
1 June 20X6	Payables (or cash) (car purchase)	20,000	28 Feb 20X7	Balance c/d	20,000
1 March 20X7	Balance b/d	20,000			
1 June 20X7	Payables (or cash) (car purchase)	8,000	28 Feb 20X8	Balance c/d	28,000
		28,000			28,000
1 Mar 20X8	Balance b/d	28,000			

MOTOR VEHICLES – ACCUMULATED DEPRECIATION

Date		$	Date		$
28 Feb 20X7	Balance c/d	4,500	28 Feb 20X7	Dep'n expense	4,500
			1 Mar 20X7	Balance b/d	4,500
28 Feb 20X7	Balance c/d	12,000	28 Feb 20X8	Dep'n expense $(6,000+1,500)$	7,500
		12,000			12,000
			1 Mar 20X8	Balance b/d	12,000

STATEMENT OF FINANCIAL POSITION (WORKINGS) AS AT 28 FEBRUARY 20X8

	Brian Box car		Bill Ockhead car		Total
	$	$	$	$	$
Asset at cost		20,000		8,000	28,000
Accumulated depreciation					
Year to:					
28 Feb 20X7	4,500				
28 Feb 20X8	6,000		1,500		
		(10,500)		(1,500)	(12,000)
Carrying amount		9,500		6,500	16,000

4.2 Posting to the ledger from a book of prime entry

The book of prime entry from which postings are made relating to purchases, sales and depreciation of non-current assets is the **journal**.

So far we have discussed entries for capital transactions in asset accounts, depreciation accounts and provision accounts without any mention of the fact that they are first recorded in a **book of prime entry**.

Cash transactions are recorded in the cash day books. You will have come across the journal in your earlier studies and we discussed it again in Chapter 4. It is used to record those transactions which take place only infrequently. Purchases and sales of non-current assets do not normally take place very often and depreciation transfers will only take place at the end of an accounting period.

4.3 Example of journal entries for year end depreciation transfer

Suppose depreciation on motor vehicles which cost $100,000 is to be calculated at 20% on cost for the year ended 30 September. The journal entries required are as follows.

<table>
<tr><td colspan="2"></td><td>JOURNAL</td><td colspan="2">Page 142</td></tr>
<tr><td>Date</td><td>Details</td><td>Ref</td><td>$</td><td>$</td></tr>
<tr><td>30 Sept</td><td>Motor vehicles depreciation a/c

Motor vehicles accumulated depreciation a/c

Being year-end accumulated depreciation</td><td>NLD2

NLP3</td><td>20,000</td><td>
20,000</td></tr>
</table>

5 Acquisition of non-current assets

As we have seen earlier in the chapter, **asset expenditure** results in the **acquisition of non-current assets**, which are assets that will provide benefits to the business in more than one accounting period and which are not acquired with a view to being resold in the normal course of trade. The cost of acquiring non-current assets is therefore not charged in full to the statement of profit or loss of the period in which the purchase occurs. Instead as we have seen in section 3, the non-current asset is gradually depreciated over a number of accounting periods.

The accounting entries on the acquisition (or capitalisation) of non-current assets will be:

		$	$
DEBIT	Non-current asset	X	
CREDIT	Cash/payable		X

For proper monitoring and control, the non-current asset, in addition to the above general ledger journal entry, will be entered in memorandum in the **non-current asset register**. This is kept for **internal control purposes** explained in section 8.

6 The disposal of non-current assets

> The **profit or loss on disposal of non-current assets** is the difference between the sale price of the asset and the carrying amount of the asset at the time of sale.

Non-current assets are not purchased by a business with the intention of reselling them in the normal course of trade. However, they might be sold off at some stage during their life, either when their useful life is over, or before then. A business might decide to sell off a non-current asset long **before its useful life has ended**.

Whenever a business sells something, it will make a **profit or a loss**, therefore when non-current assets are disposed of, there will be a profit or loss on disposal. These gains or losses are reported in the statement of profit or loss of the business as '**profit on disposal of non-current assets**' or '**loss on disposal of non-current assets**'.

Before we look at the ledger accounting for disposing of assets, we will first look at the principles behind calculating the profit (or loss) on disposing of assets.

6.1 The principles behind calculating the profit or loss on disposal

The profit or loss on the disposal of a non-current asset is the **difference** between:

- The **carrying amount** of the asset at the time of its sale
- Its **net sale price**, which is the price minus any costs of making the sale

A profit is made when the sale price exceeds the carrying amount, and a loss is made when the sale price is less than the carrying amount.

6.2 Example: disposal of a non-current asset

A business purchased a non-current asset on 1 January 20X6 for $25,000. It had an estimated life of six years and an estimated residual value of $7,000. The asset was eventually sold after three years on 1 January 20X9 to another trader who paid $17,500 for it.

What was the profit or loss on disposal, assuming that the business uses the straight line method for depreciation?

Solution

Annual depreciation $= \dfrac{\$(25,000 - 7,000)}{6 \text{ years}}$

$= \$3,000$ per annum

	$
Cost of asset	25,000
Less accumulated depreciation (three years)	(9,000)
Carrying amount at date of disposal	16,000
Sale price	17,500
Profit on disposal	1,500

This profit will be shown in the statement of profit or loss of the business where it will be an item of other income added to the gross profit.

6.3 Second example: disposal of a non-current asset

A business purchased a machine on 1 July 20X6 at a cost of $35,000. The machine had an estimated residual value of $3,000 and a life of eight years. The machine was sold for $18,600 on 31 December 20X9, the last day of the accounting year of the business. To make the sale, the business had to incur dismantling costs and costs of transporting the machine to the buyer's premises. These amounted to $1,200.

The business uses the straight line method of depreciation. What was the profit or loss on disposal of the machine?

Solution

Annual depreciation $\dfrac{\$(35,000 - 3,000)}{8 \text{ years}} = \$4,000$ per annum

It is assumed that in 20X6 only one-half year's depreciation was charged, because the asset was purchased six months into the year.

	$	$
Non-current asset at cost		35,000
Depreciation in 20X6 (half year)	2,000	
20X7, 20X8 and 20X9	12,000	
Accumulated depreciation		(14,000)
Carrying amount at date of disposal		21,000
Sale price	18,600	
Costs incurred in making the sale	(1,200)	
Net sale price		17,400
Loss on disposal		(3,600)

This loss will be shown as an expense in the statement of profit or loss of the business, but not brought into the calculation of gross profit.

6.4 Accounting for the disposal of non-current assets

It is customary in ledger accounting to record the disposal of non-current assets in a **disposal of non-current assets account**.

Step 1	As noted above, the profit or loss on disposal is the difference between:
	(a) The **sale price** of the asset (if any)
	(b) The **carrying amount** of the asset at the time of sale

Step 2	The **relevant items** which must appear in the disposal of non-current assets account are as follows.
	(a) The original value of the asset at cost
	(b) The accumulated depreciation up to the date of sale
	(c) The sale price of the asset

Step 3	The ledger accounting entries are therefore as follows.
	(a) DEBIT Disposal of non-current asset account
	CREDIT Non-current asset account
	with the cost of the asset disposed of.
	(b) DEBIT Accumulated depreciation account
	CREDIT Disposal of non-current asset account
	with the accumulated depreciation on the asset as at the date of sale.
	(c) DEBIT Receivable account or bank account
	CREDIT Disposal of non-current asset account
	with the sale price of the asset. The sale is therefore not recorded in a sales account, but in the disposal of non-current asset account.

Step 4	The balance on the disposal account is the **profit or loss on disposal** and the corresponding double entry is recorded in the statement of profit or loss.

6.5 Example: Ledger entries for the disposal of non-current assets

A business has $110,000 worth of machinery at cost. Its policy is to charge depreciation at 20% per annum straight line. The total accumulated depreciation now stands at $70,000. The business now sells for $19,000 a machine which it purchased exactly two years ago for $30,000.

Show the relevant ledger entries.

Solution

PLANT AND MACHINERY ACCOUNT

	$		$
Balance b/d	110,000	Plant disposals account	30,000
		Balance c/d	80,000
	110,000		110,000
Balance b/d	80,000		

PLANT AND MACHINERY ACCUMULATED DEPRECIATION

	$		$
Plant disposals (20% of $30,000 for 2 years)	12,000	Balance b/d	70,000
Balance c/d	58,000		
	70,000		70,000
		Balance b/d	58,000

PLANT DISPOSALS

	$		$
Plant and machinery account	30,000	Depreciation	12,000
Statement of P/L (profit on sale)	1,000	Cash	19,000
	31,000		31,000

Check

	$
Asset at cost	30,000
Accumulated depreciation at time of sale	(12,000)
Carrying amount at time of sale	18,000
Sale price	19,000
Profit on sale	1,000

6.6 Further example: Ledger entries for the disposal of non-current assets

A business purchased two bolt-making machines on 1 January 20X6 at a cost of $15,000 each. Each had an estimated life of five years and a nil residual value. The straight line method of depreciation is used.

On 31 March 20X8, one bolt-making machine was sold (on credit) to a buyer for $8,000. Later in the year, however, it was decided to upgrade their machinery and the second machine was sold on 1 December 20X8 for $2,500 cash.

Prepare the machinery account, accumulated depreciation of machinery account and disposal of machinery account for the accounting year to 31 December 20X8.

Solution

Workings

1   At 1 January 20X5, accumulated depreciation on the machines will be:

2 machines $\times$ 2 years $\times \dfrac{\$15,000}{5}$ = $12,000, or $6,000 per machine

2   Monthly depreciation is $\dfrac{\$3,000}{12}$ = $250 per machine per month

3   The machines are disposed of in 20X5.

    (i)   *On 31 March:* after three months of the year
        Depreciation for the year on the machine = 3 months $\times$ $250 = $750

    (ii)   *On 1 December:* after 11 months of the year
        Depreciation for the year on the machine = 11 months $\times$ $250 = $2,750

MACHINERY: COST ACCOUNT

Date 20X8		$	Date 20X8		$
1 Jan	Balance b/d	30,000	31 Mar	Disposal of machinery account	15,000
			1 Dec	Disposal of machinery account	15,000
		30,000			30,000

MACHINERY: ACCUMULATED DEPRECIATION

Date		$	Date		$
20X8			20X8		
31 Mar	Disposal of machinery account*	6,750	1 Jan	Balance b/d	12,000
1 Dec	Disposal of machinery account**	8,750	31 Dec	Statement of P/L***	3,500
		15,500			15,500

*Depreciation at date of disposal = $6,000 + $750
**Depreciation at date of disposal = $6,000 + $2,750
***Depreciation charge for the year = $750 + $2,750

MACHINERY: DISPOSAL

		$	Date		$
Date					
20X8			20X8		
31 Mar	Machinery account	15,000	31 Mar	Receivables account (sale price)	8,000
			31 Mar	Accumulated depreciation	6,750
1 Dec	Machinery account	15,000	1 Dec	Cash (sale price)	2,500
			1 Dec	Accumulated depreciation	8,750
			31 Dec	Statement of P/L (loss on disposal)	4,000
		30,000			30,000

You should be able to calculate that there was a loss on the first disposal of $250, and on the second disposal a loss of $3,750, giving a total loss of $4,000.

QUESTION   Holloway

The financial year of Holloway ended on 31 May 20X2.

At 1 June 20X1 the company owned motor vehicles costing $124,000 which had been depreciated by a total of $88,000.

On 1 August 20X1 Holloway sold motor vehicles, which had cost $54,000 and which had been depreciated by $49,000, for $3,900 and purchased new motor vehicles costing $71,000.

It is the policy of Holloway to depreciate its motor vehicles at 35% per annum using the reducing balance method. A full year's depreciation is charged on all motor vehicles in use at the end of each year. No depreciation is charged for the year on assets disposed of during that year.

Required

Show the following accounts as they would appear in the ledger of Holloway for the year ended 31 May 20X2 only.

(a)   The motor vehicles account
(b)   The allowance for depreciation: motor vehicles account
(c)   The assets disposals account

ANSWER

MOTOR VEHICLES: COST

		$			$
1.6.X1	Balance b/d	124,000	1.8.X1	Disposals	54,000
1.8.X1	Bank	71,000	31.5.X2	Balance c/d	141,000
		195,000			195,000

MOTOR VEHICLES: ACCUMULATED DEPRECIATION

		$			$
1.8.X1	Disposals	49,000	1.6.X1	Balance b/d	88,000
31.5.X2	Balance c/d	74,700	31.5.X2	Depreciation	
				(Statement of P/L) (W)	35,700
		123,700			123,700

DISPOSAL OF NON-CURRENT ASSETS

		$			$
1.8.X1	Motor vehicles: cost	54,000	1.8.X1	Motor vehicles: depreciation	49,000
			1.8.X1	Bank	3,900
			31.5.X2	Loss on disposal (Statement of P/L)	1,100
		54,000			54,000

Working: Depreciation charge

	$
Assets bought in earlier years:	
Cost b/f	124,000
Less assets sold in year	(54,000)
Still owned at year end	70,000
Depreciation b/f	88,000
Less assets sold in year	(49,000)
	39,000
Carrying amount at 31.5.X2	31,000
Assets acquired in the year	71,000
	102,000
Depreciation for the year at 35%	35,700

6.7 Scrapping of non-current assets

Note that if non-current assets are **scrapped** the same entries are made as for a disposal. The only difference is that the proceeds of disposal are NIL. The amount of the loss will therefore be equal to the carrying amount of the scrapped asset.

6.8 Part exchange of non-current assets

Non-current assets are sometimes exchanged for replacements as part of the **same deal**. The most common form of **part exchange** or trade in as it is also known, is found in the motor trade. You may have seen part exchange deals in operation. The new asset is exchanged for the existing asset, the remaining balance is paid in cash (or by finance).

6.9 Example: part exchange

Larkin's Launderette needs a new van. The van costs $10,000. Lain pays $6,000 and exchanges its existing van on the last day of the accounting period. The existing van had cost $8,000 exactly three years ago. Depreciation on motor vehicles is 20% on the straight line basis.

Solution

VAN ACCOUNT

	$		$
Balance b/d	8,000	Van disposals account	8,000
New van – trade in allowance	4,000	Balance c/d	10,000
– cash paid	6,000		
	18,000		18,000
Balance b/d	10,000		

VAN DEPRECIATION ACCOUNT

	$		$
Van disposals account	4,800	Balance b/d (20% of $8,000 for three years)	4,800
	4,800		4,800

VAN DISPOSALS ACCOUNT

	$		$
Van account	8,000	Van depreciation account	4,800
		Trade-in allowance	
Statement of P/L (profit on sale)	800	($10,000 – $6,000)	4,000
	8,800		8,800

Check

	$
Asset at cost	8,000
Accumulated depreciation at time of sale	(4,800)
Carrying amount at time of sale	3,200
Part exchange allowance	4,000
Profit on sale	800

It is important to note that the exchange is treated in the same way as a sale. The profit or loss on sale is calculated at the time of the part exchange.

7 The non-current assets register

Discrepancies between the register and the actual assets, and between the register and the general ledger must be investigated and resolved.

Capital transactions represent considerable sums spent by a company. There could be many **valuable non-current assets** kept in various departments or on factory floors. Occasionally some of these would be scrapped or sold off and replaced by new ones. With such a large amount of investment capital tied up in non-current assets, **tight control** of the details concerning each non-current asset is required. As mentioned above, the journal is used as a book of prime entry to record the purchase and sale of non-current assets, but this is not sufficient to record and control what happens to them.

Nearly all but the smallest organisations keep a **non-current assets register**.

A **non-current assets register** is a listing of all non-current assets owned by the organisation, broken down perhaps by department, location or asset type.

A non-current assets register is kept mainly for internal purposes. It is **not part of the double entry system** and does not record rights over or obligations towards third parties but shows an organisation's investment in capital equipment. A non-current asset register is also part of the **internal control system**. This is discussed further in Section 9 below.

The main function of the non-asset register is to provide a **system of internal control** for the non-current assets of the business.

The non-current asset register facilitates such control by:

(i)   Enabling reconciliation to be made to the manual ledger

(ii) Enabling depreciation charges to be posted to the general ledger

(iii) Enabling profit or loss on disposal to be easily and accurately calculated by providing detailed records of individual non-current asset

(iv) Enabling physical verification/existence of non-current assets

7.1 Data kept in a non-current assets register

Details held about each non-current asset **might** include the following.

- The organisation's internal reference number (for physical identification purposes)
- Manufacturer's serial number (for maintenance purposes)
- Description of asset
- Location of asset
- Insurance details (sometimes)
- Department which 'owns' asset

However, the **most important details** from an accounting point of view will be as follows.

- Purchase date (for calculation of depreciation)
- Cost
- Depreciation method and estimated useful life (for calculation of depreciation)
- Accumulated depreciation brought forward and carried forward
- Disposal proceeds
- Profit/loss on disposal

The **main events** giving rise to entries in a non-current asset register or 'inputs' in the case of a computerised one, would be the following.

- Purchase of an asset
- Sale of an asset
- Loss or destruction of an asset
- Transfer of assets between departments
- Revision of estimated useful life of an asset
- Scrapping of an asset

Outputs from a non-current assets register would be made:

(a) To enable reconciliations to be made to the general ledger
(b) To enable depreciation charges to be posted to the general ledger
(c) For physical verification/audit purposes
(d) To enable profit or loss on disposals and part exchange of assets to be easily calculated

Layout of non-current assets register

The layout of a non-current assets register and the degree of detail included will depend on the organisation in question. Some may have an individual page devoted to each type of non-current asset. Others may have columns across the page for various headings and list the assets in an organised way, for example by department or by the type of asset it is. Below is a fairly typical layout from a non-current assets register which is maintained **manually**.

Date of purchase	Invoice number	Ref	Item	Cost	Accum'd dep'n b/d	Dep'n expense	Accum'd dep'n c/d	Date of disposal	Disposal proceeds	(Loss)/ gain	Code number	Location

Most non-current assets registers will be **computerised**. Here is an extract from a non-current asset register showing one item as it might appear when the details are printed out.

FASSET HOLDINGS

Asset Code: 938

Next depreciation: 539.36

A	Description:	1 × Seisha Laser printer YCA40809 office publisher
B	Date of purchase:	25/05/X4
C	Cost:	1618.25
D	Accumulated depreciation:	584.35
E	Depreciation %:	33.33%
F	Depreciation type:	straight line
G	Date of disposal:	NOT SET
H	Sale proceeds:	0.00
I	Accumulated depreciation amount:	55Q O/EQPT DEP CHARGE
J	Depreciation expense account:	34F DEPN O/EQPT
K	Depreciation period:	standard
L	Comments:	Electronic office
M	Residual value:	0.00
N	Cost account:	65C O/E ADDITIONS
O	Location	Office C13
P	Code number	0/16/3

7.2 Data recorded in the non-current asset register

The data recorded about each non-current asset in the register serves a purpose in the control, identification and reconciliation process. The purpose served by some of the items of information are discussed below. The **identification number** or **asset code** is the organisations internal **reference number** and will refer to the type of asset, possibly signifying the category and subcategory and possibly even the location.

Example:

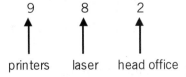

9	8	2
↑	↑	↑
printers	laser	head office

The identification number may also be constructed so as to incorporate a sequential number of assets in a particular category.

The manufacturer's serial number may also be included to enable the unique identification of each asset, for maintenance purposes and to minimise fraud.

From an accounting point of view the most important details are those relating to purchase date, cost, depreciation method, accumulated depreciation and depreciation charge.

These details will provide the outputs for the depreciation charge to be posted to the general ledger, and will enable the correct calculation of profit and loss on disposal.

8 Authorisation and control

8.1 Authorisation

Additions and disposals over a certain amount must be **authorised** on a capital expenditure authorisation form and a disposal authorisation form respectively.

Capital expenditure over a certain amount must normally be authorised by directors of a company and major projects will be noted in the minutes of board meetings. Generally, a document called a **capital expenditure authorisation form** (or some similar name) is used.

The capital expenditure authorisation form should show the prior authority for capital expenditure and indicate the approved method of funding, ie outright purchase or lease. Below is an example of a capital expenditure authorisation form.

**CAPITAL EXPENDITURE
AUTHORISATION FORM**

Company/Division...

Description of item and reason for purchase...

....

....

Supplier...

Cost...

Was this the cheapest quote obtained (if not state reason)?

....

....

Authorised by:..

Counter-authorised (if over $1,000) by:...

Purchase/lease*...

Terms of lease..

PLEASE RETURN TO PENNY WISE, FINANCIAL CONTROLLER

* delete as applicable

A **disposal** (ie sale or scrapping of an asset) over a certain amount must also be authorised. Below is an asset disposal authorisation form. You should note that the form contains a space to insert the reason for disposal. This will generally be that the asset has become obsolete or worn out but it could be that the asset was not present at the last physical count, in which case the 'sale proceeds' would obviously be nil.

**ASSET DISPOSAL
AUTHORISATION FORM**

Company/Division ....

Description and location of asset ....

....

....

Date of purchase...

Date of disposal..

Original cost...

....

Accumulated depreciation..

Carrying amount...

Sale/scrap proceeds..

Profit/loss to statement of profit or loss...

Reason for disposal...

....

....

Authorised by:..

Counter-authorised (if original cost over $1,000) by:...

PLEASE RETURN TO PENNY WISE, FINANCIAL CONTROLLER

8.2 Control

It is important, both from the point of view of external reporting (ie the audit) and for internal purposes, that there are **controls over non-current assets**. The non-current assets register has already been mentioned. Two further points should be made in this context.

(a)   The non-current assets register might not reconcile with the **general ledger**.

(b)   The non-current assets register might not reconcile with the **physical presence** of capital items.

8.2.1 The non-current assets register and the general ledger

Generally, the non-current assets register is **not integrated** with the general ledger. If you look at our example of a non-current assets register above, you will see that the entry lists the general ledger accounts (cost account, accumulated depreciation account and depreciation expense account) to which the relevant amounts must be posted and also contains other details not required in those general accounts. In other words, the non-current assets register is not part of the double entry and is there for **memorandum and control purposes**.

The non-current asset register must therefore be **reconciled to the general ledger** to make sure that all additions, disposals and depreciation provisions and charges have been posted. For example, the total of all the 'cost' figures in the non-current assets register for motor vehicles should equal the balance on the 'motor vehicles cost' account in the general ledger, and the same goes for accumulated depreciation.

If an asset is **sold off**, this should be properly authorised, the asset released, the register completed and the necessary entries made in the journal and ledger accounts.

If discrepancies arise between the register and the general ledger, these must be **investigated**. It could be, for example, that there is a delay in sending the appropriate authorisation form where an asset has been disposed of.

8.2.2 The non-current assets register and the non-current assets

It is possible that the non-current assets register may not reconcile with the non-current assets actually present. This may be for the following reasons.

(a)   An asset has been **stolen** and this has not been noticed or not recorded.

(b)   An asset may have become **obsolete or damaged** and needs to be written down but the appropriate entries have not been made.

(c)   New assets have been **purchased** but not yet recorded in the register because the register has not been kept up to date.

(d)   **Errors** have been made in entering details in the register.

It is important therefore that the company:

(a)   **Physically inspects** all the items in the non-current assets register

(b)   Keeps the register **up to date**.

The nature of the inspection will obviously vary between organisations. A large company might carry out a non-current asset inspection of, for example, 25% of assets by value each year, aiming to cover all categories every four years. A small company might be able to inspect all its non-current assets each day, although this 'inspection' will probably not be formally recorded.

It is important that acquisition, disposal and part exchange of non-current assets is properly authorised, at the appropriate level of seniority and monitored via the non-current asset register. The amounts involved are potentially high and proper authorisation and control will minimise the likelihood of fraud or error.

8.3 Dealing with discrepancies

As mentioned above, some assets may require an adjustment in their **expected life** due to excessive wear and tear. The proper authority to change any estimations to the life of an asset must have the correct authorisation, and the information should be communicated to the accounts department who will need to make adjustments in the journal, the register and the ledger.

When discrepancies are discovered, the **appropriate action** must be taken. It may be possible to resolve the discrepancy by updating the register and/or general ledger to reflect the new position. It may not be possible for the person who discovers the discrepancy to resolve it themselves. For example, if an asset has to be revalued downwards due to wear and tear or obsolescence, they may have to refer the matter to their superior who has more experience and judgement in such matters.

8.4 Computer-based asset management systems

Very large companies can now use computer-based asset management systems which work on **barcodes**, ie all assets have a barcode affixed on purchase and hand-held barcode readers can be used to check assets to the register automatically. This makes the management of assets much easier, but it is expensive to install. Barcodes do combat theft, however, and the subsequent savings for large companies can be substantial.

QUESTION

Annette

The following information has been taken from the ledger of Annette as at 31 May 20X6.

	$
Land	80,000
Buildings	160,000
Fixtures and fittings	176,000
Motor vehicles	90,000
Accumulated depreciation	
Land and buildings	32,000
Fixtures and fittings	88,000
Motor vehicles	54,000

The above information is before taking the following into account.

(a) During the year ended 31 May 20X6 motor vehicles which had cost $30,000 and which had a carrying amount of $6,000 were sold for $9,000.

(b) Depreciation has yet to be provided for as follows.

On buildings	2% straight line method
On fixtures and fittings	25% reducing balance method
On motor vehicles	20% straight line method

No depreciation is charged on land.

Required

Prepare in so far as the above information permits the following ledger accounts for the year ended 31 May 20X6.

(a) Assets disposals
(b) Accumulated depreciation: land and buildings
(c) Accumulated depreciation: fixtures and fittings
(d) Accumulated depreciation: motor vehicles

ANSWER

(a)

ASSET DISPOSALS

		$			$
31.5.X6	Motor vehicles	30,000	31.5.X6	Accumulated	
31.5.X6	Statement of P/L	3,000		Depreciation	24,000
			31.5.X6	Cash	9,000
		33,000			33,000

(b)

LAND AND BUILDINGS: ACCUMULATED DEPRECIATION

		$			$
31.5.X6	Balance c/d	35,200	1.6.X5	Balance b/d	32,000
			31.5.X6	Statement of P/L	3,200
		35,200			35,200

(c)

FIXTURES AND FITTINGS: ACCUMULATED DEPRECIATION

		$			$
31.5.X6	Balance c/d	110,000	1.6.X5	Balance b/d	88,000
			31.5.X6	Statement of P/L*	22,000
		110,000			110,000

* Depreciation is calculated using the reducing balance method, ie 25% × $(176,000 − 88,000) = $22,000.

(d)

MOTOR VEHICLES: ACCUMULATED DEPRECIATION

		$			$
31.5.X6	Assets disposals	24,000	1.6.X6	Balance b/d	54,000
31.5.X6	Balance c/d	42,000	31.5.X6	Statement of P/L	12,000
		66,000			66,000

EXAM FOCUS POINT

It is important that you fully understand the reasons for and methods of calculating depreciation. Also ensure that this chapter is revised carefully, including the impact of calculations on the statement of financial position and on the statement of profit or loss. In their report from the June 2016 sitting, the ACCA examining team identified the understanding and calculation of depreciation as an area for improvement.

CHAPTER ROUNDUP

- **Asset expenditure** (or capitalisation) results in the acquisition of non-current assets or an improvement in their earning capacity. **Expenses charged to profit or loss** is expenditure which is incurred for the purpose of the trade of the business or to maintain the existing earning capacity of non-current assets.

- Only **material items** should be capitalised.

- Since a non-current asset has a cost and a limited useful life and its value eventually declines, it follows that a charge should be made in the statement of profit or loss to reflect the use that is made of the asset by the business. This charge is called **depreciation**.

- The most common **methods of depreciation** are:
  - The straight line method
  - The reducing balance method

- The **accounting entries** to record depreciation are:

  DEBIT   Depreciation expense (in the statement of profit or loss)
  CREDIT   Accumulated depreciation (in the statement of financial position)

- The book of prime entry from which postings are made relating to purchases, sales and depreciation of non-current assets is the **journal**.

- The **profit or loss on disposal of non-current assets** is the difference between the sale price of the asset and the carrying amount of the asset at the time of sale.

- **Discrepancies** between the register and the actual assets, and between the register and the general ledger must be investigated and resolved.

- Additions and disposals over a certain amount must be **authorised** on a capital expenditure authorisation form and a disposal authorisation form respectively.

QUICK QUIZ

1. Define a non-current asset.

2. Under which concept should small value assets not be capitalised?

3. What does depreciation measure?

4. What is an asset's carrying amount?

5. Depreciation is a cash expense. True or false?

6. When would it be appropriate to use the reducing balance method of deprecation?

7. What considerations should apply when deciding which method of depreciation to use?

8. How is the profit or loss on the sale of a non-current asset calculated?

9. The non-current asset register is part of the double entry system. True or false?

10. What types of checks should be made over non-current assets and the register?

ANSWERS TO QUICK QUIZ

1   A non-current asset is one which is bought and kept by a business with a view to earning profits and not merely turning into cash.

2   The materiality concept.

3   Depreciation is the allocation of the depreciable amount of an asset over its estimated useful life.

4   The carrying amount is the value (usually cost) of the asset less accumulated depreciation to date.

5   False. Depreciation allocates costs to future periods under the matching concept.

6   When it is fair to allocate a greater proportion of depreciation in the early years of ownership and a lower amount towards the end.

7   (a)   Allocation of costs to benefits (matching)
    (b)   Method used for similar assets (consistency)
    (c)   Ease of application

8   The profit or loss is the difference between the sale price of the asset (if any) and the carrying amount of the asset at the time of sale.

9   False. The non-current asset register is separate from the double entry system.

10 The register should be reconciled with the physical assets and with the non-current asset accounts in the general ledger at intervals.

Now try ...

Attempt the questions below from the **Practice Question Bank**

Number	Level	Marks	Time
Q47	Examination	2	2.4 mins
Q48	Examination	2	2.4 mins
Q49	Examination	2	2.4 mins
Q50	Examination	2	2.4 mins
Q51	Examination	2	2.4 mins

10

In this chapter we look at the preparation of final accounts for a sole trader directly from the ledger accounts. If the complexity of the underlying records warrant it, it may be necessary to introduce an intermediate step in which a trial balance is drawn up.

The accounts of sole traders

TOPIC LIST	SYLLABUS REFERENCE
1 Closing off ledger accounts	B2(b)
2 The statement of profit or loss	B2(c), G2(a)
3 The statement of financial position	B2(c), D7(c), G2(a)
4 Balancing accounts and preparing financial statements	D7(c), G2(a), G2(c)
5 The opening trial balance	G1(e), G2(c)

Study Guide	Intellectual level
B **The principles and process of basic bookkeeping**	
2 **Books of prime entry and the flow of accounting information in the production of financial statements**	
(b) Identify reasons for closing off accounts and producing a trial balance	K
(c) Explain the process of preparing a set of final accounts from a trial balance	K
D **Recording transactions and events**	
7 **Capital and finance costs**	
(c) Prepare the capital ledger account for an unincorporated business	S
G **The trial balance and the extended trial balance**	
1 **Preparation of the trial balance/extended trial balance**	
(e) Prepare the opening trial balance for the next accounting period	S
2 **Preparation of the final accounts including incomplete records**	
(a) Explain the process of preparing a set of final accounts from a trial balance	K
(c) Prepare the final accounts for a sole trader from	S
(ii) Directly from ledger accounts	
(iii) Trial balance	

Technical Performance Objective 9 requires you to demonstrate you are competent in preparing the final accounts of unincorporated entities, such as sole traders and partnerships. The knowledge you gain in this chapter (along with that you will gain from Chapter 13 on Partnerships) will help you to demonstrate your competence in this area.

1 Closing off ledger accounts

At suitable intervals, the entries in each ledger account are totalled and a balance is struck. Balances are usually collected in a **trial balance** which is then used as a basis for preparing a statement of profit or loss and a statement of financial position. A trial balance checks the accuracy of the accounting records. Debits and credits should be equal.

We will now look at the preparation of final accounts for a sole trader. There are essentially two methods for preparing these final accounts:

(a)   An **extended trial balance** is used (this method is covered in Chapter 11).

(b)   A **trial balance** is used that has been **extracted directly from the ledger accounts** (this method is covered in the remainder of this chapter).

You learned in Chapter 4 how ledger accounts are closed off and the balances brought together in a trial balance. This will show up certain errors, but not others. If an error does not cause an imbalance between the accounts, it will not be detected by a trial balance.

The balances on income and expense accounts will now be transferred to the statement of profit or loss, while the balances on statement of financial position accounts, such a cash, receivables and payables will be carried forward.

Most sole proprietors will be drawing income from the business to live on throughout the year. These amounts will be debited to **drawings**. At the end of the year, the balance on the drawings account will be debited against the proprietors capital. If the trader takes any goods out of stock (inventory) for their own use, these are debited to their drawings account at cost price.

We will now look an example which involves preparing **final accounts**. Final accounts are also often referred to as **financial statements**. Although 'final accounts' or 'year end accounts' are normally used to refer to the statement of profit or loss and statement of financial position of unincorporated entities (sole traders and partnerships), while 'financial statements' is normally used in the context of incorporated entities (limited companies), **the terms are interchangeable**.

We will be preparing final accounts for Norman Archer. His trial balance is as follows.

NORMAN ARCHER (TRIAL BALANCE)

	DEBIT	CREDIT
	$	$
Cash at bank	6,500	
Capital		7,000
Bank loan		1,000
Purchases	5,000	
Trade payables		
Rent	3,500	
Shop fittings	2,000	
Revenue		12,500
Receivables		
Bank loan interest	100	
Other expenses	1,900	
Drawings	1,500	
	20,500	20,500

2 The statement of profit or loss

An **income and expense ledger account** is opened up to gather all items relating to income and expenses. When rearranged, the items make up the **statement of profit or loss**.

The first step in preparing the financial statements is to look through the ledger accounts and identify which ones relate to income and expenses. In the case of Norman Archer, the income and expense accounts consist of purchases, rent, revenue, bank loan interest, and other expenses.

The balances on these accounts are transferred to the **statement of profit or loss**. For example, the balance on the purchases account is $5,000 DR. To balance this to zero, we write in $5,000 CR. But to comply with the rule of double entry, there has to be a debit entry somewhere, so we write $5,000 DR in the statement of profit or loss. Now the balance on the purchases account has been moved to the statement of profit or loss.

If we do the same thing with all the income and expense accounts of Norman Archer, the result is as follows.

PURCHASES

	$		$
Trade payables	5,000	Statement of profit or loss	5,000

RENT

	$		$
Cash	3,500	Statement of profit or loss	3,500

REVENUE

	$		$
Statement of profit or loss	12,500	Cash	10,000
		Receivables	2,500
	12,500		12,500

BANK LOAN INTEREST

	$		$
Cash	100	Statement of profit or loss	100

OTHER EXPENSES

	$		$
Cash	1,900	Statement of profit or loss	1,900

STATEMENT OF PROFIT OR LOSS

	$		$
Purchases	5,000	Revenue	12,500
Rent	3,500		
Bank loan interest	100		
Other expenses	1,900		

If you look at the items we have gathered together in the statement of profit or loss, they should strike a chord in your memory. They are the same items that we need to draw up the statement of profit or loss in the form of a financial statement. With a little rearrangement they could be presented as follows.

NORMAN ARCHER: STATEMENT OF PROFIT OR LOSS

	$	$
Revenue		12,500
Cost of sales (= purchases in this case)		(5,000)
Gross profit		7,500
Expenses		
Rent	3,500	
Bank loan interest	100	
Other expenses	1,900	
		(5,500)
Net profit		2,000

3 | The statement of financial position

> The balances on all remaining ledger accounts (including the income and expense account) can be listed and rearranged to form the **statement of financial position.**

Look back at the ledger accounts of Norman Archer. Now that we have dealt with those relating to income and expenses, which ones are left? The answer is that we still have to find out what to do with cash, capital, bank loan, trade payables, shop fittings, receivables and the drawings account.

Are these the only ledger accounts left? No: don't forget there is still the last one we opened up, called the **income and expenses account**. The balance on this account represents the profit earned by the business, and if you go through the arithmetic, you will find that it has a credit balance – a profit – of $2,000. (Not surprisingly, this is the figure that is shown in the statement of profit or loss.)

These remaining accounts must also be balanced and ruled off, but since they represent assets and liabilities of the business (not income and expenses) their balances are not transferred to the income and expenses account. Instead they are **carried forward** in the books of the business. This means that they become opening balances for the next accounting period and indicate the value of the assets and liabilities at the end of one period and the beginning of the next.

The conventional method of ruling off a ledger account at the end of an accounting period is illustrated by the bank loan account in Norman Archer's books.

BANK LOAN ACCOUNT

	$		$
Balance carried forward (c/f)	1,000	Cash received	1,000
		Balance brought forward (b/f)	1,000

Norman Archer therefore begins the new accounting period with a credit balance of $1,000 on this account. A **credit balance brought forward** denotes a **liability**. An **asset** would be represented by a **debit balance brought forward**.

One further point is worth noting before we move on to complete this example. You will remember that a proprietor's capital comprises any cash introduced by them, plus any profits made by the business, less any drawings made by them. At the stage we have now reached these three elements are contained in different ledger accounts: cash introduced of $7,000 appears in the capital account; drawings of $1,500 appear in the drawings account; and the profit made by the business is represented by the $2,000 credit balance on the income and expenses account. It is convenient to gather together all these amounts into one **capital account**, in the same way as we earlier gathered together income and expense accounts into one income and expenses account.

If we go ahead and gather the three amounts together, the results are as follows.

DRAWINGS

	$		$
Cash	1,500	Capital a/c	1,500

INCOME AND EXPENSES ACCOUNT

	$		$
Purchases	5,000	Revenue	12,500
Rent	3,500		
Bank loan interest	100		
Other expenses	1,900		
Capital a/c	2,000		
	12,500		12,500

CAPITAL

	$		$
Drawings	1,500	Cash	7,000
Balance c/f	7,500	Statement of profit or loss	2,000
	9,000		9,000
		Balance b/f	7,500

A re-arrangement of these balances will complete Norman Archer's simple statement of financial position:

NORMAN ARCHER
STATEMENT OF FINANCIAL POSITION AT END OF FIRST TRADING PERIOD

	$
Non-current assets	
Shop fittings	2,000
Current assets	
Cash	6,500
Total assets	8,500
Capital	7,500
Liabilities	
Bank loan	1,000
Total capital and liabilities	8,500

When a statement of financial position is drawn up for an accounting period which is not the first one, then it ought to show the capital at the start of the accounting period and the capital at the end of the accounting period. This will be illustrated in the next example.

4 Balancing accounts and preparing financial statements

Now work through the following example which goes from transactions to final accounts.

4.1 Example

A business is established with capital of $2,000, and this amount is paid into a business bank account by the proprietor. During the first year's trading, the following transactions occurred:

	$
Purchases of goods for resale, on credit	4,300
Payments to trade payables	3,600
Sales, all on credit	5,800
Payments from receivables	3,200
Non-current assets purchased for cash	1,500
Other expenses, all paid in cash	900

The bank has provided an overdraft facility of up to $3,000.

Required

Prepare the ledger accounts, a statement of profit or loss for the year and a statement of financial position as at the end of the year.

Solution

The first thing to do is to open ledger accounts so that the transactions can be entered up. The relevant accounts which we need for this example are: cash; capital; trade payables; purchases; non-current assets; revenue and receivables; other expenses.

The next step is to work out the double entry bookkeeping for each transaction. Normally you would write them straight into the accounts, but to make this example easier to follow, they are first listed below.

(a)	Establishing business ($2,000)	DEBIT	Cash;	CREDIT	Capital
(b)	Purchases ($4,300)	DEBIT	Purchases;	CREDIT	Payables
(c)	Payments to payables ($3,600)	DEBIT	Payables;	CREDIT	Cash
(d)	Sales ($5,800)	DEBIT	Receivables;	CREDIT	Revenue
(e)	Payments by receivables ($3,200)	DEBIT	Cash;	CREDIT	Receivables
(f)	Non-current assets ($1,500)	DEBIT	Non-current assets;	CREDIT	Cash
(g)	Other (cash) expenses ($900)	DEBIT	Other expenses;	CREDIT	Cash

So far, the ledger accounts will look like this.

CASH AT BANK

	$		$
Capital	2,000	Payables	3,600
		Non-current assets	1,500
Receivables	3,200	Other expenses	900

CAPITAL

	$		$
		Cash	2,000

PAYABLES

	$		$
Cash	3,600	Purchases	4,300

PURCHASES

	$		$
Payables	4,300		

NON-CURRENT ASSETS

	$		$
Cash	1,500		

REVENUE

	$		$
		Receivables	5,800

RECEIVABLES

	$		$
Revenue	5,800	Cash	3,200

OTHER EXPENSES

	$		$
Cash	900		

The next thing to do is to balance all these accounts. It is at this stage that you could, if you wanted to, draw up a trial balance to make sure the double entries are accurate. There is not very much point in this simple example, but if you did draw up a trial balance, it would look like this.

	DEBIT $	CREDIT $
Cash at bank		800
Capital		2,000
Payables		700
Purchases	4,300	
Non-current assets	1,500	
Revenue		5,800
Receivables	2,600	
Other expenses	900	
	9,300	9,300

After balancing the accounts, the income and expenses account should be opened. Into it should be transferred all the balances relating to income and expenses (ie purchases, other expenses, and sales). At this point, the ledger accounts will be:

CASH AT BANK

	$		$
Capital	2,000	Trade payables	3,600
Receivables	3,200	Non-current assets	1,500
Balance c/f	800	Other expenses	900
	6,000		6,000
		Balance b/f	800*

* A credit balance b/f means that this cash item is a liability, not an asset. This indicates a bank overdraft of $800, with cash income of $5,200 falling short of payments of $6,000 by this amount.

CAPITAL

	$		$
Balance c/f	2,600	Cash	2,000
		P & L a/c	600
	2,600		2,600

PAYABLES

	$		$
Cash	3,600	Stores (purchases)	4,300
Balance c/f	700		
	4,300		4,300
		Balance b/f	700

PURCHASES ACCOUNT

	$		$
Trade payables	4,300	Trading a/c	4,300

NON-CURRENT ASSETS

	$		$
Cash	1,500	Balance c/f	1,500
Balance b/f	1,500		

REVENUE

	$		$
Trading a/c	5,800	Receivables	5,800

RECEIVABLES

	$		$
Revenue	5,800	Cash	3,200
		Balance c/f	2,600
	5,800		5,800
Balance b/f	2,600		

OTHER EXPENSES

	$		$
Cash	900	P & L a/c	900

INCOME AND EXPENSE ACCOUNT

	$		$
Purchases account	4,300	Revenue	5,800
Gross profit c/f	1,500		
	5,800		5,800
Other expenses	900	Gross profit b/f	1,500
Net profit (transferred to capital account)	600		
	1,500		1,500

So the statement of profit or loss will be:

STATEMENT OF PROFIT OR LOSS FOR THE ACCOUNTING PERIOD

	$
Revenue	5,800
Cost of sales (purchases)	(4,300)
Gross profit	1,500
Expenses	(900)
Net profit	600

Listing and then rearranging the balances on the ledger accounts gives the statement of financial position as:

STATEMENT OF FINANCIAL POSITION AS AT THE END OF THE PERIOD

	$	$
Non-current assets		1,500
Current assets		
Trade receivables	2,600	
		2,600
		4,100
Capital		
At start of period	2,000	
Net profit for period	600	
At end of period		2,600
Current liabilities		
Trade payables	700	
Bank overdraft	800	
		1,500
		4,100

5 The opening trial balance

The final point to look at regarding financial statements is the balances brought forward to the next period.

At the end of the accounting period, usually the financial year, all of the income and expense accounts are balanced off and the balances transferred to the income and expense account. The income and expense account balance is transferred to the statement of financial position where it is added, in the case of a sole trader, to the proprietor's capital.

So, after the year end, all of the ledger accounts which form part of the statement of profit or loss will have nil balances. This makes sense. All those income and expense items were part of the trading results for the year just gone. The statement of financial position accounts, on the other hand, will have cumulative balances. The business will still have receivables, payables and cash in the bank.

So the opening trial balance for the new period, before any posting takes place, will show only statement of financial position accounts.

To take a very simple example, Norman Archer's opening trial balance for the next period will be as follows:

	DEBIT	CREDIT
	$	$
Shop fittings	2,000	
Cash at bank	6,500	
Bank loan		1,000
Capital		7,500
	8,500	8,500

The statement of financial position we completed in the last example will give the following opening trial balance:

	DEBIT	CREDIT
	$	$
Non-current assets	1,500	
Trade receivables	2,600	
Bank overdraft		800
Trade payables		700
Capital		2,600
	4,100	4,100

QUESTION

This is longer and more difficult than anything you will meet in the exam, but it brings together everything you have studied so far.

STEPHEN CHEE
TRIAL BALANCE AS AT 31 MAY 20X1

	DEBIT	CREDIT
	$	$
Property, at cost	120,000	
Equipment, at cost	80,000	
Accumulated depreciation (as at 1 June 20X0)		
– on property		20,000
– on equipment		38,000
Purchases	250,000	
Revenue (net of settlement discounts)		384,200
Inventory, as at 1 June 20X0	50,000	
Discounts received		4,800
Returns out		15,000
Wages and salaries	58,800	
Receivables expense	4,600	
Loan interest	5,100	
Other operating expenses	17,700	
Trade payables		36,000
Trade receivables	38,000	
Cash in hand	300	
Bank	1,300	
Drawings	24,000	
Allowance for receivables		500
17% long term loan		30,000
Capital, as at 1 June 20X0		121,300
	649,800	649,800

The following additional information as at 31 May 20X1 is available.

(a)   Inventory as at the close of business has been valued at cost at $42,000.

(b)   Wages and salaries need to be accrued by $800.

(c)   Other operating expenses are prepaid by $300.

(d)   The allowance for receivables is to be adjusted so that it is 2% of trade receivables.

(e)   Depreciation for the year ended 31 May 20X1 has still to be charged as follows.

Property: 1.5% per annum using the straight line method; and
Equipment: 25% per annum using the reducing balance method.

Required

To begin with, calculate the posting for (d) and (e).

ANSWER

Workings

1   *Allowance for receivables*

	$
Previous allowance	500
New allowance (2% × 38,000)	760
Increase	260
Per trial balance – receivables expense	4,600
Income and expenses – receivables expense	4,860

2   *Depreciation*

	$
Property	
Opening accumulated depreciation	20,000
Allowance for the year (1.5% × 120,000)	1,800
Closing accumulated depreciation	21,800
Equipment	
Opening accumulated depreciation	38,000
Allowance for the year (25% × 42,000)	10,500
Closing accumulated depreciation	48,500

QUESTION   Stephen Chee

Prepare Stephen Chee's statement of profit or loss for the year ended 31 May 20X1.

ANSWER

STEPHEN CHEE

STATEMENT OF PROFIT OR LOSS FOR THE YEAR ENDED 31 MAY 20X1

	$	$
Revenue		384,200
Cost of sales		
Opening inventory	50,000	
Purchases	250,000	
Purchases returns	(15,000)	
	285,000	
Closing inventory	(42,000)	
		(243,000)
Gross profit		141,200
Other income – discounts received		4,800
		146,000
Expenses		
Operating expenses		
Wages and salaries ($58,800 + $800)	59,600	
Receivables expense (W1)	4,860	
Loan interest	5,100	
Depreciation (W2)	12,300	
Other operating expenses ($17,700 – $300)	17,400	
		(99,260)
Net profit for the year		46,740

QUESTION

Statement of financial position

Prepare Stephen Chee's statement of financial position at 31 May 20X1.

ANSWER

STEPHEN CHEE
STATEMENT OF FINANCIAL POSITION AS AT 31 MAY 20X0

	Cost $	Accumulated depn. $	Carrying amount $
Non-current assets			
Property	120,000	21,800	98,200
Equipment	80,000	48,500	31,500
	200,000	70,300	129,700
Current assets			
Inventory		42,000	
Trade receivables net of allowance for receivables (38,000 – 760)		37,240	
Prepayments		300	
Bank		1,300	
Cash in hand		300	
			81,140
			210,840

	Cost $	Accumulated depn. $	Carrying amount $
Capital			
Balance at 1 June 20X0		121,300	
Net profit for the year		46,740	
		168,040	
Drawings		(24,000)	144,040
Non-current liabilities			
17% loan			30,000
Current liabilities			
Trade payables		36,000	
Accruals		800	
			36,800
Total capital and liabilities			210,840

CHAPTER ROUNDUP

↳ At suitable intervals, the entries in each ledger account are totalled and a balance is struck. Balances are usually collected in a **trial balance** which is then used as a basis for preparing a statement of profit or loss and a statement of financial position. A trial balance checks the accuracy of the accounting records. Debits and credits should be equal.

↳ An **income and expense ledger account** is opened up to gather all items relating to income and expenses. When rearranged, the items make up the **statement of profit or loss.**

↳ The balances on all remaining ledger accounts (including the income and expense account) can be listed and rearranged to form the **statement of financial position.**

QUICK QUIZ

1 What is the purpose of a trial balance?

2 Give four circumstances in which a trial balance might balance although some of the balances are wrong.

3 In a period, sales are $140,000, purchases $75,000 and other expenses $25,000. What is the figure for net profit to be transferred to the capital account?

A $40,000
B $65,000
C $75,000
D $140,000

4 What is the difference between balancing off an expense account and balancing off a liability account?

5 Fill in the blanks in the sentence below.

The opening trial balance for the new period, before any posting takes place, will show only the .... account balances.

1   To test the accuracy of the double entry bookkeeping.

2   • An omitted transaction
     • A transaction posted to the wrong account
     • A compensating error
     • An error of principle (eg posting made the wrong way round)

3   A

INCOME AND EXPENSE ACCOUNT

	$		$
Purchases	75,000	Revenue	140,000
Gross profit c/d	65,000		
	140,000		140,000
Other expenses	25,000	Gross profit b/d	65,000
Net profit – to capital a/c	40,000		
	65,000		65,000

4   When an expense account is balanced off, the balance is transferred to the income and expense account. When a liability account is balanced off, the balance is carried forward to the next trading period.

5   The opening trial balance for the new period, before any posting takes place, will show only show the **statement of financial position** account balances.

Now try ...

Attempt the questions below from the **Practice Question Bank**

Number	Level	Marks	Time
Q52	Examination	2	2.4 mins
Q53	Examination	2	2.4 mins
Q54	Examination	2	2.4 mins
Q55	Examination	2	2.4 mins

Drawing up the final accounts from the trial balance almost always involves adjusting a few of the balances in some way.

In order to keep track of such adjustments and set out the necessary figures neatly, an **extended trial balance (ETB)** may be used.

Extended trial balance

Study Guide	Intellectual level
D **Recording transactions and events**	
5 **Accruals and prepayments**	
(c) Illustrate the process of adjusting for accruals and prepayments when preparing final accounts.	S
6 **Receivables, payables and provisions**	
(k) Account for provisions and liabilities	S
G **The trial balance and the extended trial balance**	
1 **Preparation of the trial balance/extended trial balance**	
(a) Explain the process of extending the trial balance	K
(b) Record the correction of errors on the extended trial balance	S
(c) Explain and record post trial balance adjustments on the extended trial balance	S
(i) Accruals and prepayments	
(ii) Depreciation	
(iii) Provisions	
(iv) Closing inventory	
(v) Allowance for receivables	
(vi) Irrecoverable debts	
(vii) Non-current asset transactions	
(d) Extend and complete the extended trial balance including calculating the final reported profit and loss	S
2 **Preparation of the final accounts including incomplete records**	
(c) Prepare the final accounts for a sole trader from	S
(i) The extended trial balance	

1   The extended trial balance and its purpose

An **extended trial balance** is used to adjust trial balance figures for:

- Errors
- Accruals and prepayments
- Depreciation
- Irrecoverable debts written off
- Adjustments to the receivables allowance
- Closing inventory figures

EXAM FOCUS POINT

All the activities for this chapter are grouped together at the end of the chapter, so that you can go through the preparation of an ETB step by step and then attempt one on your own in one go.

The knowledge you gain in this chapter will help you demonstrate the experience and competence needed for Technical Performance Objective 7, correct errors and process accounting adjustments in an extended trial balance.

We have already seen what a **trial balance** is: it is a list of all the balances in the ledger accounts, made up before the preparation of the financial statements to check the accuracy of the double entry accounting. The financial statements (the statement of profit or loss and the statement of financial position) are drawn up using the balances in the trial balance. We also saw in Chapter 10 that final accounts can be drawn up directly from the trial balance extracted from the ledger accounts.

Usually this step of drawing up the final accounts (or financial statements) from the trial balance involves adjusting a few of the balances in some way. For example:

- Correction of errors
- Recognition of accruals and prepayments
- Calculating and recording depreciation
- Writing off irrecoverable debts
- Adjusting and recording the allowance for receivables
- Adding in the closing inventory figure

In order to keep track of such adjustments and set out the necessary figures neatly, an **extended trial balance** may be used. The overall principles involved when drawing up final accounts using an ETB are the same as those we saw applied in Chapter 10 for drawing up accounts directly from the ledger accounts. However, in this chapter we will show how an ETB is used to keep track of any adjustments.

An extended trial balance is a worksheet, used to keep track of adjustments between the trial balance and the final accounts.

1.1 Format of an extended trial balance

The extended trial balance gives a vertical list of all the ledger account balances (the trial balance) with four further columns (for adjustments, accruals and prepayments) and then two pairs of further columns which show whether figures go to the statement of profit or loss or the statement of financial position.

Its columns headings will look something like this:

Ledger account	Trial balance figure		Adjustments		Accruals	Prepayments	Statement of profit or loss		Statement of financial position	
	DEBIT	CREDIT	DEBIT	CREDIT			DEBIT	CREDIT	DEBIT	CREDIT
	$	$	$	$	$	$	$	$	$	$

Sometimes, instead of the above 10 column format, you may well encounter an 8 column format, which dispenses with accruals and prepayments columns, so these items would have to be processed via the adjustment columns.

The preparation of the ETB draws on all the knowledge and skills you have gained in the first nine chapters of this text.

2 Preparing the extended trial balance

The extended trial balance is basically a **worksheet** representing all the ledger account balances and adjustments to them. It produces balances which can be taken directly to the statement of financial position and statement of profit or loss.

The best way to see how the extended trial balance works is to follow through an example. If you have access to a spreadsheet you may like to practice this on screen.

2.1 Example: Extended trial balance

The ledger accounts of Janey Lee, a trader, as at 31 December 20X8 before any adjustments have been made to them, are as follows.

	$
Shop fittings: at cost	9,000
depreciation allowance at 1.1.X8	450
Leasehold premises: at cost	56,000
depreciation allowance at 1.1.X8	2,800
Inventory at 1.1.X8	117,000
Receivables at 31.12.X8	240,750
Allowance for receivables at 1.1.X8	4,320
Cash in hand	120
Cash at bank	18,300
Payables for supplies	292,500
Proprietor's capital at 1.1.X8	120,000
Purchases	459,000
Revenue	580,000
Wages	81,900
Advertising	10,350
Local taxes for 15 months to 31.3.X9	6,750
Bank charges	900

The adjustments Janey Lee needs to make to her accounts are as follows.

(a) A bonus payment to an employee of $500 had been incorrectly posted to the purchases account

(b) Depreciation of shop fittings $450

(c) Depreciation of leasehold $2,800

(d) A debt of $2,250 is irrecoverable and is to be written off and the receivables allowance is to be increased to 2% of the year end receivables figure

(e) The inventory at 31 December 20X8 is valued at $135,000

(f) On 31 December 20X8, $540 was owed for advertising expenses but an invoice has not yet been received

(g) Local taxes have been paid up to 31.3.X9

You are required to give effect to these adjustments by using an extended trial balance and to prepare a statement of profit or loss for the year ended 31 December 20X8 and a statement of financial position as at that date.

Solution

The first step is to draw up a **trial balance** from this list of balances and insert it in the first two columns of the extended trial balance. These are the debit and credit columns, and so first you must sort out the credit balances in the ledger accounts from the debit balances.

If there are no errors in the accounts, the total of the debit and credit balances should be equal. The result of this process is shown on the next page.

Folio	Account	Trial balance		Adjustment		Accrued	Prepaid	Statement of profit or loss		Statement of financial position	
		DEBIT	CREDIT	DEBIT	CREDIT			DEBIT	CREDIT	DEBIT	CREDIT
		$	$	$	$	$	$	$	$	$	$
1	Shop fittings: cost all.	9,000									
2	Shop fittings: accumulated dep'n		450								
3	Leasehold premises: cost	56,000									
4	Leasehold premises: accum. dep'n		2,800								
5	Inventory at 1.1.X8	117,000									
6	Receivables ledger control	240,750									
7	Allowance for receivables		4,320								
8	Petty cash	120									
9	Bank	18,300									
10	Payables ledger control		292,500								
11	Proprietor's capital at 1.1.X8		120,000								
12	Purchases	459,000									
13	Revenue		580,000								
14	Wages	81,900									
15	Advertising	10,350									
16	Local taxes	6,750									
17	Bank charges	900									
	Accruals										
	Prepayments										
	SUB-TOTAL	1,000,070	1,000,070								
	Profit for the year										
	Total	1,000,070	1,000,070								

The next step is to make all the various adjustments. Remember that each adjustment has to be put in twice, in accordance with the rule of double entry (because the extended trial balance, in effect, is like a handy listing of all the ledger accounts). The adjustments fall into two main types.

- Journal entries
- Post trial balance adjustments

2.2 Journal entries

Any correcting entries which are required will be made here. For example, a transaction that had been posted to the wrong account would be corrected in these columns. In our example, we have one entry to make here, to reverse an incorrect posting of a $500 employee bonus to the purchases account.

(a)   DEBIT   Wages
      CREDIT   Purchases

2.3 Post trial balance adjustments

This pair of columns is used for adjustments which will convert the trial balance into the final accounts. Typical items are:

- Closing inventory
- Accruals
- Prepayments
- Depreciation
- Irrecoverable debts written off
- Adjustments to the receivables allowance
- Provisions

Provisions include matters such as outstanding legal costs. Perhaps it is not known exactly what the cost will be, but an estimate may be made. This will be posted as:

DEBIT   Legal costs (statement of profit or loss)
CREDIT   Provision for legal costs (statement of financial position)

In our example, there are the following adjustments to be made.

(b)   *Shop fittings depreciation of $450*

      DEBIT   Depreciation expense (eventually a deduction in the statement of profit or
                         loss)
      CREDIT   Accumulated depreciation: shop fittings

      The depreciation expense account does not yet appear in the list of ledger accounts, so we will have to add it on; the credit increases the accumulated depreciation in the statement of financial position.

(c)   *Leasehold depreciation of $2,800*

      DEBIT   Depreciation expense
      CREDIT   Accumulated depreciation: leasehold

(d)   (i)   *Write off debt of $2,250*

             DEBIT   Irrecoverable debts (expense)
             CREDIT   Receivables control a/c

      The irrecoverable debts expense account does not yet appear in the list of ledger accounts, so we will have to add it on.

      (ii)   *Increase receivables allowance to 2% of receivables*

             2% of receivables = 2% of $(240,750 – 2,250) = $4,770
             Increase is therefore $4,770 – $4,320 = $450

             DEBIT   Irrecoverable debt expense
             CREDIT   Allowance for receivables

(e)   *The closing inventory figure of $135,000 is entered into the extended trial balance.*

DEBIT   Inventory account (statement of financial position)
CREDIT   Inventory account (statement of profit or loss)

(The inventory account is drawn up specially for the preparation of financial statements.)

(f)   *Accrued advertising expenses $540*

Advertising expenses of $540 are owed, but have not yet been recorded in the accounts because an invoice has not yet been received. The $540 is an accrued expense, and it is necessary to increase advertising expenses (debit advertising expenses) so that the $540 is debited in the statement of profit or loss just like any other expenses. The 'other side' of the entry is an accrual of $540.

DEBIT   Advertising expenses
CREDIT   Accruals

(g)   *Prepaid rates*

From the information in the list of ledger accounts, it can be seen that there is a prepayment adjustment that has to be made as well. Local taxes to 31 March 20X9 have been paid, so there is a prepayment of $3/15 \times \$6,750 = \$1,350$ that will be credited to the local taxes account. The 'other side' of the entry should be a prepayment.

DEBIT   Prepayments
CREDIT   Local taxes expense

The results of entering these adjustments are shown on the spreadsheet set out on the next page. The total figures for depreciation, irrecoverable debts and movements on the allowance for receivables have been entered, to make the workings neater.

Folio	Account	Trial balance DEBIT $	Trial balance CREDIT $	Journal entries DEBIT $	Journal entries CREDIT $	Post TB adjustment DEBIT $	Post TB adjustment CREDIT $	Statement of profit or loss DEBIT $	Statement of profit or loss CREDIT $	Statement of financial position DEBIT $	Statement of financial position CREDIT $
1	Shop fittings: cost all.	9,000									
2	Shop fittings: accumulated dep'n		450				450				
3	Leasehold premises: cost	56,000									
4	Leasehold premises: accum. dep'n		2,800				2,800				
5	Inventory at 1.1.X8	117,000									
6	Receivables ledger control	240,750					2,250				
7	Allowance for receivables		4,320				450				
8	Petty cash	120									
9	Bank	18,300									
10	Payables ledger control		292,500								
11	Proprietor's capital at 1.1.X8		120,000								
12	Purchases	459,000			500						
13	Revenue		580,000								
14	Wages	81,900		500		540					
15	Advertising	10,350									
16	Local taxes	6,750					1,350				
17	Bank charges	900									
18	Depreciation expense					3,250					
19	Irrecoverable debts					2,700					
20	Inventory (SPL) 31.12.X8					135,000					
21	Inventory (SOFP) 31.12.X8						135,000				
	Accruals										
	Prepayments										
	SUB-TOTAL	1,000,070	1,000,070								
	Profit for the year										
	Total	1,000,070	1,000,070								

264

Now there is very little left to do.

(a)   **Add up the accruals figures and the prepayments figures** (simple in this case as there is only one of each!) and **transfer them to the statement of financial position columns**. Accruals become a liability (a credit entry) in the statement of financial position; prepayments are an asset (a debit entry). This completes the double entry for the accruals and prepayments, ie the columns show the 'expense' side of the double entry, so the statement of financial position entry of the receivable (prepayment) or payable (accrual) must still be made.

(b)   **Add up the other adjustments column,** just to make sure that debits equal credits and that you have filled in the adjustments correctly.

(c)   **Add the figures across the extended trial balance**. For example, shop fittings is just $9,000 and will be a statement of financial position figure (non-current asset). Allowance for depreciation will become $900 ($450 + $450) and is also a statement of financial position figure.

(d)   **Add up the statement of profit or loss debits and credits**. The difference between them is the profit (or loss) for the year. If the total of the debits is less than the total of the credits, the result is a profit. If the total of the debits is more than the total of the credits, the result is a loss.

(e)   **Take the profit (or loss) into the statement of financial position** (a profit is entered in the credit column, a loss is entered in the debit column). Then **add up the debits and credits in the statement of financial position** to make sure that they do, in fact, balance.

The results of these procedures are shown on the next page.

Folio	Account	Trial balance		Journal entries		Post TB adjustment		Statement of profit or loss		Statement of financial position	
		DEBIT $	CREDIT $	DEBIT $	CREDIT $	DEBIT $	CREDIT $	DEBIT $	CREDIT $	DEBIT $	CREDIT $
1	Shop fittings: cost all.	9,000								9,000	
2	Shop fittings: accumulated dep'n		450				450				900
3	Leasehold premises: cost	56,000								56,000	
4	Leasehold premises: accum. dep'n		2,800				2,800				5,600
5	Inventory at 1.1.X8	117,000						117,000			
6	Receivables ledger control	240,750					2,250			238,500	
7	Allowance for receivables		4,320				450				4,770
8	Petty cash	120								120	
9	Bank	18,300								18,300	
10	Payables ledger control		292,500								292,500
11	Proprietor's capital at 1.1.X8		120,000								120,000
12	Purchases	459,000			500	458,500		458,500			
13	Revenue		580,000						580,000		
14	Wages	81,900		500		82,400		82,400			
15	Advertising	10,350				540		10,890			
16	Local taxes	6,750					1,350	5,400			
17	Bank charges	900						900			
18	Depreciation expense					3,250		3,250			
19	Irrecoverable debts					2,700		2,700			
20	Inventory (SOFP) 31.12.X8					135,000				135,000	
21	Inventory (SPL) 31.12.X8						135,000		135,000		
	Accruals						540				
	Prepayments					1,350					
	SUB-TOTAL	1,000,070	1,000,070	500	500	142,840	142,840	681,040	715,000	458,270	424,310
	Profit for the year							33,960			33,960
	Total	1,000,070	1,000,070	500	500	142,840	142,840	715,000	715,000	458,270	458,270

So how do we get from the trial balance to the financial statements? The final step is to use the figures in the last two columns of the extended trial balance to draw up the statement of financial position and statement of profit or loss. For this example, the result would be as follows.

JANEY LEE
STATEMENT OF PROFIT OR LOSS FOR THE YEAR ENDED 31 DECEMBER 20X8

	$	$
Revenue		580,000
Less cost of sales		
Opening inventory	117,000	
Purchases	458,500	
	575,500	
Less closing inventory	(135,000)	
		(440,500)
Gross profit		139,500
Less expenses		
Wages	82,400	
Advertising	10,890	
Local taxes	5,400	
Bank charges	900	
Depreciation: fixtures	450	
fittings	2,800	
Irrecoverable debt written off	2,250	
Increase in receivables allowance	450	
		(105,540)
Net profit		33,960

JANEY LEE
STATEMENT OF FINANCIAL POSITION AS AT 31 DECEMBER 20X8

	$	$
Non-current assets		
Leasehold		50,400
Fixtures		8,100
		58,500
Current assets		
Inventories		135,000
Trade receivables	238,500	
Less allowance for receivables	(4,770)	
		233,730
Prepayments	1,350	
Cash at bank	18,300	
Cash in hand	120	
		388,500
		447,000
Capital		
At 1 January 20X8		120,000
Profit for year		33,960
At 31 December 20X8		153,960
Current liabilities		
Trade payables	292,500	
Accruals	540	
		293,040
		447,000

2.4 Computerising the extended trial balance

Like other accounting activities, the extended trial balance can be **computerised**.

(a)   **The computer could be programmed to do all the work itself**. The trial balance would be input (or the computer might already have drawn it up from the ledger accounts) and then the individual corrections would be input. The computer would go ahead and produce the financial statements by itself.

(b)   **The extended trial balance could be prepared using a spreadsheet package**. That is, it would look just like the example in this chapter, but it would be on a screen instead of paper. It would be used just as a handwritten version would be used, except that numbers would be keyed in rather than written down. In this sort of 'computerised' extended trial balance, the computer would do some of the arithmetic, but the human operator would still be doing a lot of the work.

2.5 The extended trial balance and the journal

Normally, when an error is found, it is entered into the journal and then the correcting entries are made in the relevant ledger accounts. So in an ideal world, when the trial balance and the extended trial balance are drawn up, corrections of errors have already been incorporated into the ledger account balances.

In practice, some errors are not discovered until the last minute (for example, perhaps the auditors of the accounts, who often carry out their work at year-end, discover some errors). When this happens, the corrections are entered in the journal, and their effect must be noted on the extended trial balance, in the 'other adjustments' column.

Now try an ETB preparation yourself. The blank ETB given on page 269 can be used for your solution. This is in the simplified form, so you will have to process your accruals and prepayments via the adjustments columns.

QUESTION

Hassan & Co

You are assisting the accountant of Hassan & Co in the preparation of the accounts for the year ending 31 December 20X8. The following list of balances has been extracted from the ledgers.

	$
Land and buildings	120,000
Proprietor's capital at 1.1.X8	208,000
Revenue	466,000
Purchases	246,000
Inventory at 1.1.20X8	79,500
Returns in	400
Returns out	1,800
Discounts received	2,100
Local tax	27,450
Motor expenses	12,250
Salaries	103,500
Insurance	9,500
Trade receivables	32,300
Trade payables	17,800
Carriage in	4,200
Carriage out	2,550
Motor vehicles	65,150
Bank balance (in credit at the bank)	7,800
Accumulated depreciation	
Buildings	4,000
Motor vehicles	21,370
Irrecoverable debts	600

Required

Enter the trial balance on the ETB below and add it up.

ANSWER

The full completed ETB is shown on page 273. You should attempt the question above and those that follow before looking at the completed ETB for Hassan & Co.

Folio	Account	Trial balance DEBIT $	Trial balance CREDIT $	Adjustments DEBIT $	Adjustments CREDIT $	Accured $	Prepaid $	Statement of profit or loss DEBIT $	Statement of profit or loss CREDIT $	Statement of financial position DEBIT $	Statement of financial position CREDIT $
	SUB-TOTAL										
	Profit for the year										
	TOTAL										

QUESTION

Difference

You should have realised by now that there is a difference on the trial balance you created in the previous question. You should enter the difference in a suspense account.

On investigation, the following errors and omissions are found to have occurred.

(a) An invoice for $3,300 for general insurance has been posted to cash but not to the ledger account.

(b) A customer went into liquidation just before the year end, owing Hassan & Co $1,300. The amount was taken off receivables but the corresponding entry to irrecoverable debt expense has not been made.

(c) A cheque paid for cash purchases has been posted to the purchases account as $4,595, when the cheque was made out for $4,955.

(d) A van was purchased during the year for $2,455, but this amount was credited to the motor vehicles account.

Required

Show the journal which will clear the suspense account, by dealing with the points noted above. Enter the journal on to the ETB.

ANSWER

Journal 1

		$	$
DEBIT	Insurance	3,300	
	Irrecoverable debt expense	1,300	
	Purchases ($4,955 – $4,595)	360	
	Motor vehicles ($2,455 × 2)	4,910	
CREDIT	Suspense account		9,870

In ledger account form:

SUSPENSE ACCOUNT

	$		$
Balance b/f	9,870	Insurance	3,300
		Irrecoverable debt expense	1,300
		Purchases	360
		Motor vehicles	4,910
	9,870		9,870

QUESTION

Adjustments

No adjustments have yet been made for accruals or prepayments. The accountant asks you to search for any required accruals and prepayments and you find the following information.

(a) The bill for the local taxes was received and paid on 1 April 20X8. The bill covers the period 1 April 20X1 to 31 March 20X9 and amounts to $21,600.

(b) The insurance bill ($3,300) which had originally been posted to the suspense account was for motor insurance, for the period 1 December 20X8 to 30 November 20X9.

(c) An invoice for carriage outwards was received after the year end for the period 1 November 20X8 to 31 January 20X9, amounting to $720 plus sales tax of $126.

Required

Calculate the necessary accruals or prepayments and enter them on the ETB.

ANSWER

(a)   Local taxes: prepaid 1 January to 31 March 20X9

$= {}^{3}/_{12} \times \$21,600 = \$5,400$

(b)   Insurance: prepaid 1 January to 30 November 20X9

$= {}^{11}/_{12} \times \$3,300 = \$3,025$

(c)   Carriage outwards: accrue 1 November to 31 December 20X8

$= {}^{2}/_{3} \times \$720 = \$480$

QUESTION

More adjustments

The accountant tells you that the following adjustments need to be made.

(a)   Depreciation is to be charged as follows.

Freehold buildings	2% on cost
Motor vehicles	20% on cost

The buildings element of the figure for land and buildings is $40,000. A full year of depreciation is charged in the year of acquisition of any asset.

(b)   An allowance for receivables is to be made, at 1% of net trade receivables.

(c)   The closing inventory figure was agreed at $82,000.

Required

Enter the necessary adjustments for the above items on to the ETB.

ANSWER

Tutorial note. When calculating the receivables allowance in (b) you do not need to deduct the irrecoverable debts written off from the year end receivables figure. This adjustment has already been made. The suspense account balance arose because the irrecoverable debt expense entry had not been made.

(a)   *Depreciation*

Buildings: 2% × $40,000 = $800
Motor vehicles: 20% × $(65,150 + 4,910) = $14,012

Journal 2

DEBIT	Depreciation expense	$14,812	
CREDIT	Accumulated depreciation		
	Buildings		$800
	Motor vehicles		$14,012

(b)   *Receivables allowance*

Trade receivables	$32,300
Allowance @ 1%	$323

Journal 3

DEBIT	Irrecoverable debt expense	$323	
CREDIT	Accumulated receivables		$323

(c)   *Journal 4*

DEBIT	Closing inventory (statement of financial position)	$82,000	
CREDIT	Closing inventory (statement of profit or loss)		$82,000

QUESTION

ETB

Extend and total the ETB.

ANSWER

See ETB on the following page.

QUESTION

Accounts

Just to finish off the scenario in this chapter, you may want to attempt to produce a basic statement of financial position and a statement of profit or loss from the ETB.

ANSWER

HASSAN & CO
STATEMENT OF PROFIT OR LOSS FOR THE YEAR ENDED 31 DECEMBER 20X8

	$	$
Revenue ($466,000 – $400)		465,600
Cost of sales		
Opening inventory	79,500	
Purchases ($246,360 – $1,800)	244,560	
Carriage inwards	4,200	
	328,260	
Closing inventory	(82,000)	
		(246,260)
Gross profit		219,340
Expenses		
Carriage outwards	3,030	
Discounts received	(2,100)	
Local taxes	22,050	
Motor expenses	12,250	
Salaries	103,500	
Insurance	9,775	
Irrecoverable debt expense	2,223	
Depreciation expense	14,812	
		(165,540)
		53,800

Note. The answer for the statement of financial position follows the completed ETB.

Hassan & Co

Account	Trial balance DEBIT $	Trial balance CREDIT $	Ref	Adjustments DEBIT $	Adjustments CREDIT $	Statement of profit or loss DEBIT $	Statement of profit or loss CREDIT $	Statement of financial position DEBIT $	Statement of financial position CREDIT $
Land and buildings	120,000							120,000	
Proprietor's capital at 1.1.X8		208,000							208,000
Revenue		466,000					466,000		
Purchases	246,000		1	360		246,360			
Inventory at 1.1.X8	79,500					79,500			
Returns in	400					400			
Returns out		1,800					1,800		
Discounts received		2,100					2,100		
Local tax	27,450		6		5,400	22,050			
Motor expenses	12,250					12,250			
Salaries	103,500					103,500			
Insurance	9,500		1,6	3,300	3,025	9,775			
Trade receivables	32,300							32,300	
Trade payables		17,800							17,800
Carriage in	4,200					4,200			
Carriage out	2,550		5	480		3,030			
Motor vehicles	65,150		1	4,910				70,060	
Bank	7,800							7,800	0
Accumulated depreciation: buildings		4,000	2		800				4,800
Accumulated depreciation: motor vehicles		21,370	2		14,012				35,382
Receivables expense	600		1,3	1,623		2,223			
Allowance for receivables			3		323				323
Depreciation expense			2	14,812		14,812			
Suspense accounts	9,870		1		9,870				
Inventory at 31.12.X8 (SPL)			4		82,000		82,000		
Inventory at 31.12.X8			4	82,000				82,000	
Prepayments			6	8,425				8,425	
Accruals			5		480				480
SUB-TOTAL	721,070	721,070		115,910	115,910	498,100	551,900	320,858	266,785
Profit for the year						53,800			53,800
TOTAL	721,070	721,070		115,910	115,910	551,900	551,900	320,585	320,585

HASSAN & CO
STATEMENT OF FINANCIAL POSITION AS AT 31 DECEMBER 20X8

	Cost $	Dep'n $	Carrying amount $
Non-current assets			
Land and buildings	120,000	4,800	115,200
Motor vehicles	70,060	35,382	34,678
	190,060	40,182	149,878
Current assets			
Inventories		82,000	
Trade receivables ($32,300 – $323)		31,977	
Prepayments		8,425	
Bank		7,800	
			130,202
			280,080
Capital			
Proprietor's capital at 1.1.X8			208,000
Profit for the year			53,800
Proprietor's capital at 31.12.X8			261,800
Current liabilities			
Trade payables		17,800	
Accruals		480	
			18,280
			280,080

2.6 Summary of steps to complete an ETB

These are the steps to complete an extended trial balance.

Step 1	Draw up the trial balance, enter it on the ETB and add it up.
Step 2	If debits and credits are unequal in the trial balance, check all the entries are correct, then insert a suspense account.
Step 3	Make the various adjustments required in the question. • Accruals and prepayments • Adjustments to inventory figures • Other adjustments
Step 4	Check that the suspense account has been cleared by the adjustments you have made.
Step 5	Add up the accruals and prepayments columns and transfer the totals to the statement of financial position . • **Accruals** = liability = CREDIT • **Prepayments** = asset = DEBIT **Note.** Where you have a simplified ETB, there will be no accruals or prepayments columns and you will have to process the self-balancing adjustments for accruals and prepayments via the adjustments columns.
Step 6	Add up the adjustments columns and check all the entries are correct and debits equal credits.

Step 7	Add the figures across the ETB.
Step 8	Add up the statement of profit or loss debits and credits.
Step 9	Take the profit or loss for the year to the statement of financial position columns • **Profit** = DEBIT in statement of profit or loss = CREDIT in SOFP • **Loss** = CREDIT in statement of profit or loss = DEBIT in SOFP
Step 10	Add up the debits and credits in the statement of financial position and make sure they are equal. Investigate any differences.

The following table shows the items that are commonly included in the trial balance and indicates whether each item is transferred to the statement of profit or loss at the end of the accounting period or carried forward in the statement of financial position.

Item	Statement of profit or loss $	Statement of financial position $
Revenue	✓	
Purchases	✓	
Inventory	Opening and closing	Closing
Discounts	✓	
Rent and rates	✓	
Electricity	✓	
Wages	✓	
Depreciation charge	✓	
Bank charges	✓	
Property		✓
Equipment		✓
Accumulated depreciation		✓
Tax receivables		✓
Bank and cash		✓
Trade payables		✓
Drawings		✓
Capital		✓

2.7 Remember its still double entry!

The CBT format of the exam means you will be tested on various aspects of ETB preparation rather than having to extend a trial balance in full. It is important you always remember the ETB is just a means of tracking adjustments and these adjustments follow the same basic principles of double entry we have looked at throughout this Text.

EXAM FOCUS POINT

It is very important that you realise any adjustments made via the ETB still contain equal and opposite debit and credit entries, just like, for example, adjustments made using a journal.

QUESTION

Maxine

Maxine was extending her trial balance for the year ended 31 December 20X1. In her eight column ETB she recorded only three post trial balance adjustments. These were an accrual for $8,120, writing off an irrecoverable debt of $1,225 and recording a depreciation charge of $5,340.

What is the total value of the credit column for the post trial balance adjustments?

ANSWER

The correct answer is **$14,685**.

Any adjustment to the trial balance requires both a debit and a credit entry, whether made as part of the trial balance extension or otherwise. The debit and credit column of the adjustments column will have the same value which will be equal to the sum of each adjustment.

Therefore the CREDIT column (and the DEBIT column) will total $14,685 (= $8,120 + $1,225 + $5,340).

CHAPTER ROUNDUP

↻ An **extended trial balance** is used to adjust trial balance figures for:

- Errors
- Accruals and prepayments
- Depreciation
- Irrecoverable debts written off
- Adjustments to the receivables allowance
- Closing inventory figures

↻ The extended trial balance is basically a **worksheet** showing all the ledger account balances and adjustments to them. It produces **balances** which can be taken directly to the statement of financial position and statement of profit or loss.

QUICK QUIZ

1   Why is an ETB necessary?

2   What is the double entry to record closing inventory on the ETB?

3   The accruals and prepayments columns should always add up to the same amount. True or false?

4   If the debit column total of the statement of profit or loss in the ETB is greater than the credit column, has the business made a profit or a loss?

5   In what ways can a computer help in the preparation of the ETB?

1 An ETB helps to keep track of adjustments between the trial balance and the final accounts.

2 DEBIT   Inventory a/c (statement of financial position)

     CREDIT   Inventory a/c (statement of profit or loss)

3 False. These are only the statement of profit or loss entries; the other side of the double entry for each is in the statement of financial position columns.

4 A loss.

5 (a) The computer can automatically extract the ledger balances.

     (b) A spreadsheet package can be used for the ETB and will aid with casting the various columns.

Now try ...

Attempt the questions below from the **Practice Question Bank**

Number	Level	Marks	Time
Q56	Examination	2	2.4 mins
Q57	Examination	2	2.4 mins
Q58	Examination	2	2.4 mins

part

C

Incomplete records and other accounts

CHAPTER

12

In this chapter we look at methods for drawing up accounts when a business does not have a full set of accounting records.

The records may be incomplete as a result of the trader not maintaining a ledger or it may be that some accounting records have been accidentally destroyed.

Incomplete records

Study Guide
Intellectual level

G **The trial balance and the extended trial balance**

2 **Preparation of the final accounts including incomplete records**

(d) Describe the circumstances which lead to incomplete records — K

(e) Describe the methods of constructing accounts from incomplete records — K

(f) Prepare the final accounts or elements thereof using incomplete record techniques such as — S

    (i) Mark ups and margins

    (ii) Ledger accounts to derive missing figures

    (iii) Manipulation of the accounting equation

Technical Performance Objective 7 requires you to be able to reconstruct ledger accounts from incomplete records and prepare an initial trial balance. The knowledge you gain in this chapter will help you to demonstrate your competence in this area.

1 Preparing accounts from incomplete records

Incomplete records questions may test your ability to prepare accounts in the following situations.

- A trader **does not maintain a ledger** and therefore has no continuous double entry record of transactions.
- Accounting records are **destroyed** by accident, such as fire.
- Some essential figure is **unknown** and must be calculated as a balancing figure.

Incomplete records problems occur when a business does not have a full set of accounting records, either because:

- The proprietor of the business does not keep a full set of accounts; or
- Some of the business accounts are accidentally lost or destroyed.

The problem for the accountant is to prepare a set of year-end accounts for the business; ie a statement of profit or loss, and a statement of financial position. Since the business does not have a full set of accounts, preparing the final accounts is not a simple matter of closing off accounts and transferring balances to the trading, income and expense account, or showing outstanding balances in the statement of financial position. The task of preparing the final accounts involves:

(a) Establishing the **cost of purchases** and other expenses

(b) Establishing the **total amount of sales**

(c) Establishing the amount of **trade payables, accruals, trade receivables and prepayments** at the end of the year

Examination questions often take incomplete records problems a stage further, by introducing an 'incident', such as fire or burglary which leaves the owner of the business uncertain about how much inventory has been destroyed or stolen.

The great merit of incomplete records problems is that they focus attention on the relationship between cash received and paid, sales and accounts receivable, purchases and accounts payable, and inventory, as well as calling for the preparation of final accounts from basic principles.

BPP
LEARNING MEDIA

To understand what incomplete records are about, it will obviously be useful now to look at what exactly might be incomplete. The items we shall consider in turn are:

(a)   The opening statement
(b)   Credit sales and trade receivables
(c)   Purchases and trade payables
(d)   Purchases, inventory and the cost of sales

(e)   Stolen goods or goods destroyed
(f)   The cash day books
(g)   Accruals and prepayments
(h)   Drawings

EXAM FOCUS POINT

Incomplete records questions are a good test of whether you have a really thorough grasp of double entry.

2   The opening statement

In practice there should not be any missing item in the opening statement of financial position of the business, because it should be available from the preparation of the previous year's final accounts. However, an examination problem might provide information about the assets and liabilities of the business at the beginning of the period under review, but then leave the balancing figure (ie the proprietor's business capital) unspecified.

2.1 Example: opening statement of financial position

Suppose Joe Han's business has the following assets and liabilities as at 1 January 20X3.

	$
Fixtures and fittings at cost	7,000
Accumulated depreciation, fixtures and fittings	4,000
Motor vehicles at cost	12,000
Accumulated depreciation, motor vehicles	6,800
Inventory	4,500
Trade receivables	5,200
Cash at bank and in hand	1,230
Trade payables	3,700
Prepayment	450
Accrued rent	2,000

You are required to prepare a statement of financial position for the business, inserting a balancing figure for proprietor's capital.

Solution

STATEMENT OF FINANCIAL POSITION AS AT 1 JANUARY 20X3

	$	$
Assets		
Non-current assets		
Fixtures and fittings at cost	7,000	
Less accumulated depreciation	(4,000)	
		3,000
Motor vehicles at cost	12,000	
Less accumulated depreciation	(6,800)	
		5,200
Current assets		
Inventories	4,500	
Trade receivables	5,200	
Prepayment	450	
Cash	1,230	
		11,380
Total assets		19,580

	$	$
Capital and liabilities		
Proprietor's capital as at 1 January 20X3 (balancing figure)		13,880
Current liabilities		
Trade payables	3,700	
Accruals	2,000	
		5,700
Total capital and liabilities		19,580

Remember the use of the **business equation** to calculate profit when you have a figure for opening capital and a figure for year-end closing capital. The difference between the two, adjusting for drawings and any capital deposits will be profit for the year. You may want to look back at Chapter 1.

3 Credit sales and trade receivables

> The approach to incomplete records questions is to build up the information given so as to complete the necessary **double entry**. This may involve reconstructing **control accounts** for:
>
> – Cash and bank
> – Trade receivables and payables

If a business does not keep a record of its sales on credit, the value of these sales can be derived from the opening balance of trade receivables, the closing balance of trade receivables, and the payments received from customers during the period.

FORMULA TO LEARN

	$
Payments from trade receivables	X
Plus closing balance of trade receivables (since these represent sales in the current period for which cash payment has not yet been received)	X
Less opening balance of trade receivables (unless these become irrecoverable debts, they will pay what they owe in the current period for sales in a previous period)	(X)
Credit sales during the period	X

For example, suppose that Joe Han's business had trade receivables of $1,750 on 1 April 20X4 and trade receivables of $3,140 on 31 March 20X5. If payments received from receivables during the year to 31 March 20X5 were $28,490, and if there are no irrecoverable debts, then credit sales for the period would be:

	$
Cash from receivables	28,490
Plus closing receivables	3,140
Less opening receivables	(1,750)
Credit sales	29,880

If there are irrecoverable debts during the period, the value of sales will be increased by the amount of irrecoverable debts written off, no matter whether they relate to opening receivables or credit sales during the current period.

QUESTION   Sales

The calculation above could be made in a T-account, with credit sales being the balancing figure to complete the account. Prepare the T-account.

ANSWER

RECEIVABLES CONTROL ACCOUNT

	$		$
Opening balance b/f	1,750	Cash received	28,490
Credit sales (balancing fig)	29,880	Closing balance c/f	(3,140)
	31,630		31,630

The same interrelationship between credit sales, cash from receivables, and opening and closing receivables balances can be used to derive a missing figure for cash from receivables, or opening or closing receivables, given the values for the three other items. For example, if we know that opening receivables are $6,700, closing receivables are $3,200 and credit sales for the period are $69,400, then cash from receivables during the period would be as follows.

RECEIVABLES CONTROL ACCOUNT

	$		$
Opening balance	6,700	Cash received (balancing figure)	72,900
Sales (on credit)	69,400	Closing balance c/f	3,200
	76,100		76,100

An alternative way of presenting the same calculation would be:

	$
Opening balance of trade receivables	6,700
Credit sales during the period	69,400
Total money owed to the business	76,100
Less closing balance of trade receivables	(3,200)
Equals cash received during the period	72,900

3.1 Control account

Control account reconciliations have been covered earlier in this text and it is possible that you will be asked to **reconcile control accounts** in an incomplete records question or assessment. You should also remember the complications which might arise in a receivables control account, which might include the following.

RECEIVABLES CONTROL ACCOUNT

	$		$
Opening debit balances	X	Opening credit balances (if any)	X
Revenue	X	Cash received	X
Dishonoured bills or cheques	X		
Cash paid to clear credit balances	X	Credit notes*	X
Irrecoverable debts recovered**	X	Irrecoverable debts	X
Closing credit balances	X	Cash from irrecoverable debts recovered**	X
		Contra with P/L control a/c	X
		Closing debit balances	X
	X		X

* Credit notes may be issued to refund customers in the event of goods being returned or allowances on damaged or faulty goods being sent to customers.

** The credit entry for cash from irrecoverable debts recovered and the debit entry for the irrecoverable debt recovered are shown separately in the control account to remind you to include **both** if this issue is included in an exam question. (Refer to Chapter 7 for treatment of irrecoverable debts.)

If you have to find a balancing figure in the receivables control account, you may have to consider all the above items.

QUESTION

Receivables control

A receivables control account contains the following entries:

	$
Balance b/f 1 January	42,800
Bank	204,000
Credit sales	240,200

Assuming there are no other entries into the account, what is the closing balance at 31 December?

ANSWER

The ledger account will look like this.

RECEIVABLES CONTROL ACCOUNT

	$		$
1 January balance b/f	42,800	Bank	204,000
Sales	240,200		
	-	31 December balance c/f	79,000
	283,000		283,000

4 Purchases and trade accounts payable

A similar relationship exists between purchases of inventory during a period, the opening and closing balances for trade payables, and amounts paid to suppliers during the period.

We can calculate an unknown amount for purchases as follows.

FORMULA TO LEARN

	$
Payments to trade payables during the period	X
Plus closing balance of trade payables	X
(since these represent purchases in the current period for which payment has not yet been made)	
Less opening balance of trade payables	(X)
(these debts, paid in the current period, relate to purchases in a previous period)	
Purchases during the period	X

For example, suppose that Joe Han's business had trade payables of $3,728 on 1 October 20X5 and trade payables of $2,645 on 30 September 20X6. If payments to trade payables during the year to 30 September 20X6 were $31,479, then purchases during the year would be:

	$
Payments to trade payables	31,479
Plus closing balance of trade payables	2,645
Less opening balance of trade payables	(3,728)
Purchases	30,396

QUESTION

Trade accounts payable

Again, the calculation above could be made in a T-account, with purchases being the balancing figure to complete the account. Prepare the T-account.

ANSWER

PAYABLES CONTROL ACCOUNT

	$		$
Cash payments	31,479	Opening balance b/f	3,728
Closing balance c/f	2,645	Purchases (balancing figure)	30,396
	34,124		34,124

4.1 Control account

Once again, various complications can arise in the trade payables control account which you may have to consider.

PAYABLES CONTROL ACCOUNT

	$		$
Opening debit balances (if any)	X	Opening credit balances	X
Cash paid	X	Purchases and other expenses	X
Returns outwards	X	Cash received clearing debit	
Contras with P/L control a/c	X	balances	X
Allowances on goods damaged	X	Closing debit balances	X
Closing credit balances	X		
	X		X

 ## QUESTION

Purchases

Joe Clinton has not kept a proper set of accounting records during 20X1 due to the prolonged illness of his bookkeeper. However, the following information is available.

	$
Cash purchases in year	5,850
Cash paid for goods supplied on credit	41,775
Trade payables at 1 January 20X1	1,455
Trade payables at 31 December 20X1	1,080

Required

Calculate Joe Clinton's purchases figure for the trading account for 20X1.

ANSWER

	$
Trade payables b/f	(1,455)
Cash paid	41,775
Trade payables c/f	1,080
Credit purchases	41,400
Add cash purchases	5,850
Total purchases	47,250

5 Establishing cost of sales

 Where inventory, sales or purchases is the unknown figure, it will be necessary to use information on **gross profit percentages** to construct a trading account in which the unknown figure can be inserted as a balance.

When the value of purchases is not known, a different approach might be required to find out what they were, depending on the nature of the information given to you.

One approach would be to use information about the cost of sales, and opening and closing inventory, in other words, to use the trading account rather than trade accounts payable to find the cost of purchases.

FORMULA TO LEARN

		$
Since	opening inventory	X
	plus purchases	X
	less closing inventory	(X)
	equals the cost of goods sold	X
then	the cost of goods sold	X
	plus closing inventory	X
	less opening inventory	(X)
	equals purchases	X

Suppose that the inventory of Joe Han's business on 1 July 20X6 has a statement of financial position value of $8,400, and an inventory count at 30 June 20X7 showed inventory to be valued at $9,350. Sales for the year to 30 June 20X7 are $80,000, and the business makes a mark-up of $33^1/3\%$ on cost for all the items that it sells. What were the purchases during the year?

The cost of goods sold can be derived from the value of sales, as follows.

		$
Sales	$(133^1/3\%)$	80,000
Gross profit (mark-up)	$(33^1/3\%)$	20,000
Cost of goods sold	(100%)	60,000

The cost of goods sold is 75% of sales value.

	$
Cost of goods sold	60,000
Plus closing inventory	9,350
Less opening inventory	(8,400)
Purchases	60,950

It is worth mentioning here that two different terms may be given to you in the exam for the calculation of profit.

Mark-up is the gross profit as a percentage of **cost**.

Gross profit margin is the gross profit as a percentage of **sales**. This is often referred to as the **margin** on sales.

Looking at the above example:

(a) The **mark-up** on cost is $33^1/_3\%$
(b) The gross profit **margin** (percentage) is 25% (ie $33^1/_3/133^1/_3 \times 100\%$)

EXAM FOCUS POINT

An incomplete records question may require you to use the profit margin and profit mark-up percentages to identify missing values.

QUESTION   Mark up

Harry has budgeted sales for the coming year of $175,000. He achieves a constant gross mark-up of 40% on cost. He plans to reduce his inventory level by $13,000 over the year.

What will Harry's purchases be for the year?

ANSWER

Cost of sales = 100/140 × $175,000
= $125,000

Since the inventory level is being allowed to fall, it means that purchases will be $13,000 less than $125,000.

---

6 Goods stolen or destroyed

A similar type of calculation might be required to derive the value of goods stolen or destroyed. When an unknown quantity of goods is lost, whether they are stolen, destroyed in a fire, or lost in any other way such that the quantity lost cannot be counted, then the cost of the goods lost is the difference between

(a) The **cost of goods sold**; and

(b) **Opening inventory of the goods** (at cost) plus **purchases** less **closing inventory of the goods** (at cost).

In theory (a) and (b) should be the same. However, if (b) is a larger amount than (a), it follows that the difference must be the cost of the goods purchased and neither sold nor remaining in inventory, ie the cost of the goods lost.

6.1 Example: cost of goods destroyed

Orlean Flames is a shop which sells fashion clothes. On 1 January 20X5, it had trade inventory which cost $7,345. During the 9 months to 30 September 20X5, the business purchased goods from suppliers costing $106,420. Sales during the same period were $154,000. The shop makes a gross profit of 40% on cost for everything it sells. On 30 September 20X5, there was a fire in the shop which destroyed most of the inventory in it. Only a small amount of inventory, known to have cost $350, was undamaged and still fit for sale.

How much of the inventory was lost in the fire?

Solution

(a)
	$
Sales (140%)	154,000
Gross profit (40%)	44,000
Cost of goods sold (100%)	110,000

(b)
	$
Opening inventory, at cost	7,345
Plus purchases	106,420
	113,765
Less closing inventory, at cost	(350)
Equals cost of goods sold and goods lost	113,415

(c)
	$
Cost of goods sold and lost	113,415
Cost of goods sold	(110,000)
Cost of goods lost	3,415

6.2 Example: cost of goods stolen

Beau Gullard runs a jewellery shop in the High Street. On 1 January 20X9, his trade inventory, at cost, amounted to $4,700 and his trade payables were $3,950.

During the six months to 30 June 20X9, sales were $42,000. Beau Gullard makes a gross profit margin of 33$\frac{1}{3}$% on the sales value of everything he sells.

On 30 June, there was a burglary at the shop, and all the inventory was stolen.

In trying to establish how much inventory had been taken, Beau Gullard was only able to say that:

(a)   He knew from his bank statements that he had paid $28,400 to trade account payables in the 6 month period to 30 June 20X9;

(b)   He currently had payables due of $5,550.

Required

(a)   Calculate the amount of inventory stolen.
(b)   Prepare a trading account for the 6 months to 30 June 20X9.

Solution

Step 1	The first 'unknown' is the amount of purchases during the period. This is established by the method previously described in this chapter.

TRADE PAYABLES CONTROL ACCOUNT

	$		$
Payments to trade payables	28,400	Opening balance b/f	3,950
Closing balance c/f	5,550	Purchases (balancing figure)	30,000
	33,950		33,950

Step 2	The cost of goods sold is also unknown, but this can be established from the gross profit margin and the sales for the period.

		$
Sales	(100%)	42,000
Gross profit	($33^1/3$%)	14,000
Cost of goods sold	($66^2/3$%)	28,000

Step 3	The cost of the goods stolen is:

	$
Opening inventory at cost	4,700
Purchases	30,000
	34,700
Less closing inventory (after burglary)	0
Cost of goods sold and goods stolen	34,700
Cost of goods sold (see (b) above)	28,000
Cost of goods stolen	6,700

Step 4	The cost of the goods stolen will not be a charge in the trading account, and so the trading account for the period is as follows.

BEAU GULLARD STATEMENT OF PROFIT OR LOSS FOR THE SIX MONTHS TO 30 JUNE 20X9

	$	$
Revenue		42,000
Less cost of goods sold		
Opening inventory	4,700	
Purchases	30,000	
	34,700	
Less inventory stolen	(6,700)	
		(28,000)
Gross profit		14,000

6.3 Accounting for inventory destroyed, stolen or otherwise lost

When inventory is stolen, destroyed or otherwise lost, the loss must be accounted for somehow. The procedure was described briefly in the earlier chapter on inventory accounting. Since the loss is not a trading loss, the cost of the goods lost is not included in the trading account, as the previous example showed. The accounting double entry is therefore:

DEBIT   See below

CREDIT   Statement of profit or loss (although instead of showing the cost of the loss as a credit, it is usually shown as a deduction on the debit side of the statement of profit or loss, which is the same as a 'plus' on the credit side).

The account that is to be debited is one of two possibilities, depending on whether or not the lost goods were insured against the loss.

(a)   If the lost goods were not insured, the business must bear the loss, and the loss is shown in the net profit (income and expenses) part of the statement of profit or loss; ie:

        DEBIT   Statement of profit or loss (expenses)
        CREDIT   Statement of profit or loss (calculation of gross profit)

(b)   If the lost goods were insured, the business will not suffer a loss, because the insurance will pay back the cost of the lost goods. This means that there is no loss at all in the statement of profit or loss, and the appropriate double entry is:

        DEBIT   Insurance claim account (receivables control account)
        CREDIT   Statement of profit or loss (calculation of gross profit)

     with the cost of the loss. The insurance claim will then be a current asset, and shown in the statement of financial position of the business as such. When the claim is paid, the account is then closed by:

        DEBIT   Cash
        CREDIT   Insurance claim account

7   The cash day books

The construction of cash received and cash payments day books, largely from bank statements showing receipts and payments of a business during a given period, is often an important feature of incomplete records problems.

EXAM FOCUS POINT

In an examination, the purpose of incomplete records questions is largely to test the understanding of candidates about how various items of receipts or payments relate to the preparation of a final set of accounts for a business. In both the June 2015 and the June 2016 examining team's reports, it was mentioned that students need to be able to demonstrate their understanding of how reconciliation accounts work, and how they can be used to find missing information.

We have already seen in this chapter that information about cash receipts or payments might be needed to establish:

(a)   The amount of purchases during a period; or
(b)   The amount of credit sales during a period.

Other items of receipts or payments might be relevant to establishing:

(a)   The amount of cash sales;
(b)   The amount of certain expenses in the statement of profit or loss; or
(c)   The amount of drawings by the business proprietor.

It might therefore be helpful, if a business does not keep cash day books day to day, to construct cash day books at the end of an accounting period. A business which typically might not keep day to day cash day books is a shop, where:

(a) Many sales, if not all sales, are cash sales (ie with payment by notes and coins, cheques, or credit cards at the time of sale);

(b) Some payments are made in notes and coins out of the till rather than by payment out of the business bank account by cheque.

Where there appears to be a sizeable volume of receipts and payments in cash (ie notes and coins), then it is also helpful to construct both cash day books and a petty cash book.

An example will illustrate this.

7.1 Example: cash day books

Jonathan Slugg owns and runs a shop selling fishing tackle, making a gross profit of 25% on the cost of everything he sells. He does not keep cash day books.

On 1 January 20X7 the statement of financial position of his business was as follows.

	$	$
Non-current assets		20,000
Current assets		
Inventories	10,000	
Cash in the bank	3,000	
Cash in the till	200	
		13,200
		33,200
Proprietor's capital		32,000
Trade payables		1,200
		33,200

In the year to 31 December 20X7:

(a) There were no sales on credit;

(b) $41,750 in receipts were banked;

(c) The bank statements of the period show the payments:

		$
(i)	To trade payables	36,000
(ii)	Sundry expenses	5,600
(iii)	In drawings	4,400

(d) payments were also made in cash out of the till:

		$
(i)	For trade payables	800
(ii)	Sundry expenses	1,500
(iii)	In drawings	3,700

At 31 December 20X7, the business had cash in the till of $450 and trade payables of $1,400. The cash balance in the bank was not known and the value of closing inventory has not yet been calculated. There were no accruals or prepayments. No further non-current assets were purchased during the year. The depreciation charge for the year is $900.

Required

(a) Prepare cash day books for the period.

(b) Prepare the statement of profit or loss for the year to 31 December 20X7 and the statement of financial position as at 31 December 20X7.

Solution

Here we will show cash received and cheques paid in the form of day books, with a separate petty cash book for actual cash.

Step 1	Enter the opening cash balances.

Step 2	Enter the information given about cash payments (and any cash receipts, if there had been any such items given in the problem).

Step 3	The cash receipts banked can go directly to the cash received day book.

Step 4 Make the entries.

CASH DAY BOOKS

Cash received day book		*Cash payments day book*	
Balance b/f	3,000	Trade payables	36,000
Cash receipts banked	41,750	Sundry expenses	5,600
Balance c/f (overdrawn)	1,250	Drawings	4,400
	46,000		46,000

PETTY CASH BOOK

Receipts		*Payments*	
Balance b/f	200	Trade payables	800
Cash receipts not banked		Sundry expenses	1,500
(balancing figure)	6,250	Drawings	3,700
		Balance c/f	450
	6,450		6,450

EXAM FOCUS POINT

Note that in step 4 above, although the entries are made in records labelled as the cash received and cash payments day books, because we are constructing these at the end of the accounting period, we end up entering totals for payments and receipts. The result is something that looks very similar to (and is the equivalent of) a bank ledger account with b/f balances, totals and c/f balances.

For a business with incomplete records, the day books are only prepared on the last day of the period and actually represent a control account for cash at bank.

It is important to notice that since not all receipts from cash sales are banked, the value of cash sales during the period is:

	$
Receipts banked	41,750
Plus expenses and drawings paid out of the till in cash	
$(800 + 1,500 + 3,700)$	6,000
Plus any cash stolen (here there is none)	0
Plus the closing balance of cash in hand	450
	48,200
Less the opening balance of cash in hand	(200)
Equals cash sales	48,000

The cash day books constructed in this way have enabled us to establish both the closing balance for cash in the bank and also the volume of cash sales. The statement of profit or loss and the statement of financial position can also be prepared, once a value for purchases has been calculated.

TRADE PAYABLES CONTROL ACCOUNT

	$		$
Cash payments day book: payments			
from bank	36,000	Balance b/f	1,200
Petty cash book: payments in cash	800	Purchases (balancing figure)	37,000
Balance c/f	1,400		
	38,200		38,200

The mark-up of 25% on cost indicates that the cost of the goods sold is $38,400, ie:

	$
Sales (125%)	48,000
Gross profit (25%)	9,600
Cost of goods sold (100%)	38,400

The closing inventory is now a balancing figure in the statement of profit or loss.

JONATHAN SLUGG
STATEMENT OF PROFIT OR LOSS
FOR THE YEAR ENDED 31 DECEMBER 20X7

	$	$
Revenue		48,000
Less cost of goods sold		
Opening inventory	10,000	
Purchases	37,000	
	47,000	
Less closing inventory (balancing figure)	(8,600)	
		(38,400)
Gross profit (25/125 × $48,000)		9,600
Expenses		
Sundry $(1,500 + 5,600)	7,100	
Depreciation	900	
		(8,000)
Net profit		1,600

JONATHAN SLUGG
STATEMENT OF FINANCIAL POSITION AS AT 31 DECEMBER 20X7

	$	$
Net non-current assets $ (20,000 – 900)		19,100
Current assets		
Inventory	8,600	
Cash in the till	450	
		9,050
Total assets		28,150
Capital and liabilities		
Proprietor's capital		
Balance b/f	32,000	
Net profit for the year	1,600	
Drawings $(3,700 + 4,400)	(8,100)	
Balance c/f		25,500
Current liabilities		
Trade payables	1,400	
Bank overdraft	1,250	
		2,650
Total capital and liabilities		28,150

7.2 Theft of cash from the till

When cash is stolen from the till, the amount stolen will be a credit entry in the cash day book, and a debit in either the net profit section (income and expenses account) of the statement of profit or loss or insurance claim account, depending on whether the business is insured. The missing figure for cash sales, if this has to be calculated, must not ignore cash received but later stolen – see above.

7.3 Using a receivables account to calculate both cash sales and credit sales

Another point which needs to be considered is how a missing value can be found for **cash sales and credit sales**, when a business has both, but takings banked by the business are not divided between takings from cash sales and takings from credit sales.

7.4 Example: Determining the value of sales during the period

Suppose that a business had, on 1 January 20X1, trade receivables of $2,000, cash in the bank of $3,000, and cash in hand of $300.

During the year to 31 December 20X1 the business banked $95,000 in takings. It also paid out the following expenses in cash from the till.

Drawings	$1,200
Sundry expenses	$800

On 29 August 20X1 a thief broke into the shop and stole $400 from the till.

At 31 December 20X1 trade receivables amounted to $3,500, cash in the bank $2,500 and cash in the till $150.

What was the value of sales during the year?

Solution

If we tried to prepare a receivables account and the cash day books, we would have insufficient information, in particular about whether the takings which were banked related to cash sales or credit sales.

RECEIVABLES CONTROL ACCOUNT

	$		$
Balance b/f	2,000	Payments from customers	
Credit sales	Unknown	(credit sales)	Unknown
		Balance c/f	3,500

	Cash received day book			Cash payments day book	
	Cash	Bank		Cash	Bank
	$	$		$	$
Balance b/f	300	3,000	Drawings	1,200	
			Sundry expenses	800	
Customers: payments		Unknown	Cash stolen	400	
Cash sales		Unknown	Balance c/f	150	2,500

All we do know is that the combined sums from customers and cash takings banked is $95,000. The value of sales can be found instead by using the receivables account, which should be used to record cash takings banked as well as payments by customers. The balancing figure in the receivables account will then be a combination of credit sales and some cash sales. The cash day books only need to have single columns.

RECEIVABLES CONTROL ACCOUNT

	$		$
Balance b/f	2,000	Cash banked	95,000
Revenue	96,500	Balance c/f	3,500
	98,500		98,500

Cash received day book		Cash payments day book	
	$		$
Balance in hand b/f	300	*Payments in cash*	
Balance in bank b/f	3,000	Drawings	1,200
Receivables a/c	95,000	Expenses	800
		Other payments	?
		Cash stolen	400
		Balance in hand c/f	150
		Balance in bank c/f	2,500

The remaining 'undiscovered' amount of cash sales is now found as follows.

	$
Payments in cash out of the till	
Drawings	1,200
Expenses	800
	2,000
Cash stolen	400
Closing balance of cash in hand	150
	2,550
Less opening balance of cash in hand	(300)
Further cash sales	2,250

	$
Total revenue for the year	
From receivables control account	96,500
Further cash sales from working above	2,250
Total revenue	98,750

8 Accruals and prepayments

Where there is an accrued expense or a prepayment, the charge to be made in the statement of profit or loss for the item concerned should be found from the opening balance b/f, the closing balance c/f, and cash payments for the item during the period. The charge in the statement of profit or loss is perhaps most easily found as the balancing figure in a T-account.

For example, suppose that on 1 April 20X6 a business had prepaid rent of $700 which relates to the next accounting period. During the year to 31 March 20X7 it pays $9,300 in rent, and at 31 March 20X7 the prepayment of rent is $1,000. The cost of rent in the I&E account for the year to 31 March 20X7 would be the balancing figure in the following T-account. (Remember that a prepayment is a current asset, and so is a debit balance b/f.)

RENT

	$		$
Prepayment: balance b/f	700	Statement of profit or loss	
Cash	9,300	(balancing figure)	9,000
		Prepayment: balance c/f	1,000
	10,000		10,000
Balance b/f	1,000		

Similarly, if a business has accrued telephone expenses as at 1 July 20X6 of $850, pays $6,720 in telephone bills during the year to 30 June 20X7, and has accrued telephone expenses of $1,140 as at 30 June 20X7, then the telephone expense to be shown in the statement of profit or loss for the year to 30 June 20X7 is the balancing figure in the following T-account. (Remember that an accrual is a current liability, and so is a credit balance b/f.)

TELEPHONE EXPENSES

	$		$
Cash	6,720	Balance b/f (accrual)	850
Balance c/f (accrual)	1,140	Statement of profit or loss a/c	
		(balancing figure)	7,010
	7,860		7,860
		Balance b/f	1,140

9 Drawings

Drawings would normally represent no particular problem at all in preparing a set of final accounts from incomplete records, but it is not unusual for examination questions to contain complicating situations.

(a) The business owner may pay income into their bank account which has nothing whatever to do with the business operations. For example, the owner might pay dividend income, or other income from investments into the bank, from stocks and shares which they own personally, separate from the business itself. (In other words, there are no investments in the business statement of financial position, and so income from investments cannot possibly be income of the business.)

(b) The business owner may pay money out of the business bank account for items which are not business expenses, such as life insurance premiums or a payment for their family's holidays etc.

Where such **personal items of receipts or payments** are made the following adjustments should be made.

(a) Receipts should be set off against drawings. For example, if a business owner receives $600 in dividend income and pays it into their business bank account, although the dividends are from investments not owned by the business, then the accounting entry is:

DEBIT   Bank
CREDIT   Drawings

(b) Payments should be charged to drawings, ie:

DEBIT   Drawings
CREDIT   Bank

9.1 Using simple accounting ratios

An incomplete records exercise may require you to use the profit margin and profit mark-up percentages to identify missing values. These were discussed earlier in this chapter.

10 Dealing with incomplete records problems

A suggested approach to dealing with incomplete records problems brings together the various points described so far in this chapter.

EXAM FOCUS POINT

In the examination you may just be tested on one aspect or step of the process below, but it is necessary to demonstrate using an illustration of the entire process.

The nature of the 'incompleteness' in the records will vary from problem to problem, but the approach, suitably applied, should be successful in arriving at the final accounts whatever the particular characteristics of the problem might be.

The approach is as follows.

Step 1	If possible, and if it is not already known, establish the opening statement of financial position and the proprietor's interest.

Step 2	Open up four accounts.

- Statement of profit or loss
- Cash day books with two columns if cash sales are significant and there are payments in cash out of the till
- A trade receivables account
- A trade payables account

Step 3	Enter the opening balances in these accounts.

Step 4	Work through the information you are given line by line; and each item should be entered into the appropriate account if it is relevant to one or more of these four accounts.

You should also try to recognise each item as an 'income or expense item' or a 'closing statement of financial position item'.

It may be necessary to calculate an amount for drawings and an amount for non-current asset depreciation.

Step 5	Look for the balancing figures in your accounts. In particular you might be looking for a value for credit sales, cash sales, purchases, the cost of goods sold, the cost of goods stolen or destroyed, or the closing bank balance. Calculate these missing figures, and make any necessary double entry (eg to the trading account from trade payables for purchases, to the trading account from the cash received day book for cash sales, and to the trading account from trade receivables for credit sales).

Step 6	Now complete the statement of profit or loss and statement of financial position. Working T-accounts might be needed where there are accruals or prepayments

An example will illustrate this approach.

10.1 Example: an incomplete records problem

John Snow is the sole distribution agent in the Branton area for Diamond floor tiles. Under an agreement with the manufacturers, John Snow purchases the Diamond floor tiles at a trade discount of 20% off list price and annually in May receives an agency commission of 1% of his purchases for the year ended on the previous 31 March.

For several years, John Snow has obtained a gross profit of 40% on all sales. In a burglary in January 20X8 John Snow lost inventory costing $4,000 as well as many of his accounting records. However, after careful investigations, the following information has been obtained covering the year ended 31 March 20X8.

(a) Assets and liabilities at 31 March 20X7 were as follows.

		$
Buildings:	at cost	10,000
	accumulated depreciation	6,000
Motor vehicles:	at cost	5,000
	accumulated depreciation	2,000
Inventory: at cost		3,200
Trade receivables (for sales)		6,300

	$
Agency commission due	300
Prepayments (trade expenses)	120
Balance at bank	4,310
Trade payables	4,200
Accrued wages	230

(b) John Snow has been notified that he will receive an agency commission of $440 on 1 May 20X8.

(c) Inventory, at cost, at 31 March 20X8 was valued at an amount $3,000 more than a year previously.

(d) In October 20X7 inventory costing $1,000 was damaged by dampness and had to be scrapped as worthless.

(e) Trade payables at 31 March 20X8 related entirely to goods received whose list prices totalled $9,500.

(f) Settlement discounts received were $1,200.

(g) Trade expenses prepaid at 31 March 20X8 totalled $80.

(h) Wages for the year ended 31 March 20X8 amounted to $7,020.

(i) Trade receivables (for sales) at 31 March 20X8 were $6,700.

(j) All receipts are passed through the bank account.

(k) Depreciation is provided annually at the following rates.

Buildings 5% on cost
Motor vehicles 20% on cost.

(l) Commissions received are paid directly to the bank account.

(m) In addition to the payments for purchases, the bank payments were:

	$
Wages	6,720
Drawings	4,300
Trade expenses	7,360

(n) John Snow is not insured against loss of inventory owing to burglary or damage to inventory caused by damp.

Required

Prepare John Snow's statement of profit or loss for the year ended 31 March 20X8 and a statement of financial position on that date.

Solution

This is an incomplete records problem because we are told that John Snow has lost many of his accounting records. In particular we do not know sales for the year, purchases during the year, or all the cash receipts and payments.

The first step is to find the opening position, if possible. In this case, it is. The proprietor's capital is the balancing figure.

JOHN SNOW
STATEMENT OF FINANCIAL POSITION AS AT 31 MARCH 20X7

		$	$
Assets			
Non-current assets			
Buildings:	cost	10,000	
	accumulated depreciation	6,000	
			4,000
Motor vehicles:	cost	5,000	
	accumulated depreciation	2,000	
			3,000

	$	$
Current assets		
Inventory	3,200	
Trade receivables	6,300	
Commission due	300	
Prepayments	120	
Balance of cash at hand	4,310	
		14,230
Total assets		21,230
Capital and liabilities		
Proprietor's capital (balance)		16,800
Current liabilities		
Trade payables	4,200	
Accrued wages	230	
		4,430
Total capital and liabilities		21,230

The next step is to open up a statement of profit or loss, bank ledger account, a trade receivables account and a trade payables account and to insert the opening balances, if known.

The problem should then be read line by line, identifying any transactions affecting those accounts. (Notes refer to notes (a)–(h) given after the statement of financial position)

STATEMENT OF PROFIT OR LOSS

	$	$
Sales (W6)		60,000
Opening inventory	3,200	
Purchases (W1)	44,000	
	47,200	
Less: Damaged inventory written off (W3)	(1,000)	
Inventory stolen (W5)	(4,000)	
	42,200	
Less closing inventory (W2)	(6,200)	
Cost of goods sold		(36,000)
Gross profit (W6)		24,000

BANK ACCOUNT

	$		$
Opening balance	4,310	Trade payables	
Trade receivables (see below)	57,980	(see trade payables)	39,400
Agency commission (W7)	300	Trade expenses	7,360
		Wages	6,720
		Drawings	4,300
		Balance c/f	4,810
	62,590		62,590

TRADE ACCOUNTS RECEIVABLE

	$		$
Opening balance b/f	6,300		
Sales (W7)	60,000	Cash received (balancing figure)	59,600
		Closing balance c/f	6,700
	66,300		66,300

TRADE ACCOUNTS PAYABLE

	$		$
Discounts received (W4)	1,200	Opening balance b/f	4,200
Cash paid (balancing figure)	39,400	Purchases (W1)	44,000
Closing balance c/f	7,600		
	48,200		48,200

WAGES

	$		$
Cash	6,720	Accrual b/f	230
Accrual c/f (balancing figure)	530	Statement of profit or loss	7,020
	7,250		7,250

Now the complete statement of profit or loss and statement of financial position can be prepared. Remember not to forget items such as the inventory losses, commission earned on purchases, discounts allowed and discounts received.

JOHN SNOW
STATEMENT OF PROFIT OR LOSS FOR THE YEAR ENDED 31 MARCH 20X8

	$	$
Revenue (W6)		60,000
Opening inventory	3,200	
Purchases (W1)	44,000	
	47,200	
Less: Damaged inventory written off (W3)	(1,000)	
Inventory stolen	(4,000)	
	42,200	
Less closing inventory (W2)	(6,200)	
Cost of goods sold		(36,000)
Gross profit (W6)		24,000
Add: Commission on purchases		440
Discounts received		1,200
		25,640
Expenses		
Trade expenses (W8)	7,400	
Inventory damaged	1,000	
Inventory stolen	4,000	
Wages	7,020	
Discounts allowed	1,620	
Depreciation		
Buildings	500	
Motor vehicles	1,000	
		(22,540)
Net profit (to capital account)		3,100

JOHN SNOW
STATEMENT OF FINANCIAL POSITION AS AT 31 MARCH 20X8

	$	$
Assets		
Non-current assets		
Buildings: Cost	10,000	
Accumulated depreciation	6,500	
		3,500
Motor vehicles: Cost	5,000	
Accumulated depreciation	3,000	
		2,000
Current assets		
Inventory	6,200	
Trade receivables	6,700	
Commission due	440	
Prepayments (trade expenses)	80	
Balance at bank	4,810	
		18,230
Total assets		23,730

	$	$
Capital and liabilities		
Proprietor's capital		
As at 31 March 20X7	16,800	
Net profit for year to 31 March 20X8	3,100	
Less drawings	(4,300)	
As at 31 March 20X8		15,600
Current liabilities		
Trade payables	7,600	
Accrued expenses	530	
		8,130
Total capital and liabilities		23,730

Workings

1   The agency commission due on 1 May 20X8 indicates that purchases for the year to 31 March 20X8 were:

    100%/1% × $440 = $44,000

2   Closing inventory at cost on 31 March 20X8 was $(3,200 + 3,000) = $6,200.

3   Inventory scrapped ($1,000) is accounted for by:

    CREDIT   Statement of profit or loss (gross profit section)
    DEBIT   Statement of profit or loss (expenses section)

4   Discounts received are:

    DEBIT   Trade payables
    CREDIT   Discounts received

    Note. Discounts received represents settlement discounts, not **trade** discounts, which are not usually accounted for as they are given automatically at source.

5   Inventories lost in the burglary are accounted for by:

    CREDIT   Statement of profit or loss (gross profit section)
    DEBIT   Statement of profit or loss (expenses section)

6   The trade discount of 20% has already been deducted in arriving at the value of the purchases. The gross profit is 40% on sales, so with cost of sales = $36,000

		$
Cost	(60%)	36,000
Profit	(40%)	24,000
Sales	(100%)	60,000

    (It is assumed that trade expenses are not included in the trading account, and so should be ignored in this calculation.)

7   The agency commission of $300 due on 1 May 20X7 would have been paid to John Snow at that date.

8   The account for trade expenses is as follows.

TRADE EXPENSES

	$		$
Prepayment	120	Statement of profit or loss (balancing figure)	7,400
Cash	7,360	Prepayment c/f	80
	7,480		7,480

QUESTION

Mary Grimes

Mary Grimes, retail fruit and vegetable merchant, does not keep a full set of accounting records. However, the following information has been produced from the business's records.

(a) *Summary of the bank account for the year ended 31 August 20X8*

	$		$
1 Sept 20X7 balance b/f	1,970	Payments to suppliers	72,000
Cash from trade receivables	96,000	Purchase of motor van (E471 KBR)	13,000
Sale of private yacht	20,000	Rent and local taxes	2,600
Sale of motor van (A123 BWA)	2,100	Wages	15,100
		Motor vehicle expenses	3,350
		Postages and stationery	1,360
		Drawings	9,200
		Repairs and renewals	650
		Insurances	800
		31 August 20X8 balance c/f	2,010
	120,070		120,070
1 Sept 20X8 balance b/f	2,010		

(b) *Assets and liabilities, other than balance at bank*

		1 Sept 20X7	31 Aug 20X8
		$	$
Trade payables		4,700	2,590
Trade receivables		7,320	9,500
Rent and local taxes accrued		200	260
Motor vans:			
A123 BWA:	At cost	10,000	–
	Aggregate depreciation	8,000	–
E471 KBR:	At cost	–	13,000
	Aggregate depreciation	–	To be determined
Inventory		4,900	5,900
Insurance prepaid		160	200

(c) All receipts are banked and all payments are made from the business bank account.

(d) A trade debt of $300 owing by John Blunt and included in the trade receivables at 31 August 20X8 (see (b) above), is to be written off as an irrecoverable debt.

(e) It is Mary Grimes' policy to charge depreciation at the rate of 20% on the cost of motor vans held at the end of each financial year; no depreciation is charged in the year of sale or disposal of a motor van.

(f) Discounts received during the year ended 31 August 20X8 from trade payables amounted to $1,100.

Required

(a) Prepare Mary Grimes' statement of profit or loss for the year ended 31 August 20X8.
(b) Prepare Mary Grimes' statement of financial position as at 31 August 20X8.

ANSWER

(a) STATEMENT OF PROFIT OR LOSS FOR THE YEAR ENDED 31 AUGUST 20X8

	$	$
Sales (W1)		98,180
Opening inventory	4,900	
Purchases (W2)	70,990	
	75,890	
Less closing inventory	(5,900)	
		(69,990)
Gross profit		28,190
Discounts received		1,100
Profit on sale of motor vehicle ($2,100 – $(10,000 – 8,000))		100
		29,390
Rent and local taxes (W3)	2,660	
Wages	15,100	
Motor vehicle expenses	3,350	
Postages and stationery	1,360	
Repairs and renewals	650	
Insurances (W4)	760	
Irrecoverable debt expense	300	
Depreciation of van (20% × $13,000)	2,600	
		(26,780)
		2,610

(b) STATEMENT OF FINANCIAL POSITION AS AT 31 AUGUST 20X8

	$	$
Assets		
Non-current assets		
Motor van: Cost	13,000	
Depreciation	(2,600)	
		10,400
Current assets		
Inventory	5,900	
Trade receivables ($9,500 – $300 irrecoverable debt)	9,200	
Prepayment	200	
Cash at bank	2,010	
		17,310
Total assets		27,710
Capital and liabilities		
Capital account		
Balance at 1 September 20X7 (W5)	11,450	
Additional capital: proceeds on sale of yacht	20,000	
Net profit for the year	2,610	
Less drawings	(9,200)	
Balance at 31 August 20X8		24,860
Current liabilities		
Trade payables	2,590	
Accrual	260	
		2,850
Total capital and liabilities		27,710

Workings

1   *Sales*

	$
Cash received from customers	96,000
Add trade receivables at 31 August 20X8	9,500
	105,500
Less trade receivables at 1 September 20X7	(7,320)
Sales in year	98,180

2   *Purchases*

	$	$
Payments to suppliers		72,000
Add: Trade payables at 31 August 20X8	2,590	
Discounts granted by suppliers	1,100	
		3,690
		75,690
Less trade payables at 1 September 20X7		(4,700)
		70,990

3   *Rent and local taxes*

	$
Cash paid in year	2,600
Add accrual at 31 August 20X8	260
	2,860
Less accrual at 1 September 20X7	(200)
Charge for the year	2,660

4   *Insurances*

	$
Cash paid in year	800
Add prepayment at 1 September 20X7	160
	960
Less prepayment at 31 August 20X8	(200)
	760

Workings 1–4 could also be presented in ledger account format as follow:

RECEIVABLES CONTROL ACCOUNT

	$		$
Balance b/f	7,320	Bank	96,000
∴ Revenue	98,180	Balance c/f	9,500
	105,500		105,500

PAYABLES CONTROL ACCOUNT

	$		$
Bank	72,000	Balance b/f	4,700
Discounts received	1,100	∴ Purchases	70,990
Balance c/f	2,590		
	75,690		75,690

RENT AND LOCAL TAXES

	$		$
Bank	2,600	Balance b/f	200
Balance c/f	260	∴Statement of P/L charge	2,660
	2,860		2,860

INSURANCES

	$		$
Balance b/f	160	∴ Statement of P/L charge	760
Bank	800	Balance c/f	200
	960		960

5 *Capital at 1 September 20X7*

	$	$
Assets		
Bank balance		1,970
Trade receivables		7,320
Motor van $(10,000 – 8,000)$		2,000
Inventory		4,900
Prepayment		160
		16,350
Liabilities		
Trade payables	4,700	
Accrual	200	
		(4,900)
		11,450

CHAPTER ROUNDUP

↳ **Incomplete records** questions may test your ability to prepare accounts in the following situations.

- A trader **does not maintain a ledger** and therefore has no continuous double entry record of transactions.
- Accounting records are **destroyed** by accident, such as fire.
- Some essential figure is **unknown** and must be calculated as a balancing figure.

↳ The approach to incomplete records questions is to build up the information given in order to complete the necessary **double entry**. This may involve reconstructing **control accounts** for:

- Cash and bank
- Trade receivables and payable

↳ Where inventory, sales or purchases is the unknown figure it will be necessary to use information on **gross profit percentages** to construct a trading account in which the unknown figure can be inserted as a balance.

QUICK QUIZ

1   In the absence of a sales account or sales day book, how can a figure of sales for the year be computed?

2   In the absence of a purchases account or purchases day book, how can a figure of purchases for the year be computed?

3   What is the difference between 'mark-up' and 'gross profit margin'?

4   In what circumstances are two-column cash day books useful?

5   If a business proprietor pays their personal income into the business bank account, what is the accounting double entry to record the transaction?

ANSWERS TO QUICK QUIZ

1   By adjusting cash received from customers for opening and closing receivables (and any other relevant items, such as contras, discounts etc)

2   By adjusting cash paid to suppliers for opening and closing payables.

3   Mark-up is gross profit as a percentage of cost.
    Gross profit margin is gross profit as a percentage of sales

4   When there are both cash receipts and payments and bank receipts and payments in a question.

5   DEBIT   Bank
    CREDIT   Drawings

Now try ...

Attempt the questions below from the **Practice Question Bank**

Number	Level	Marks	Time
Q59	Examination	2	2.4 mins
Q60	Examination	2	2.4 mins
Q61	Examination	2	2.4 mins
Q62	Examination	2	2.4 mins

CHAPTER

13

In this chapter we look at accounting for **partnerships**. Partnerships can be formed when two or more persons agree to run a business together.

Partnerships

TOPIC LIST	SYLLABUS REFERENCE
1 Partnership accounts	H1, H2, H3

Study Guide

Intellectual level

H   Partnerships

1   Partnership agreement

(a)   Define a partnership   K

(b)   Explain the purpose and content of a partnership agreement   K

(c)   Explain, calculate and account for appropriations of profit   S

    (i)   Salaries of partners

    (ii)   Interest on drawings

    (iii)   Interest on capital

    (iv)   Share of residual profit (the amount of profit available
                   to be shared between the partners in the profit and
                   loss sharing ratio, after all other appropriations have
                   been made)

2   Partnership accounting records

(a)   Explain the difference between partners' capital and current   K
accounts

(b)   Prepare the partners' capital and current accounts   S

3   Partnership financial statements and change in partnership

(a)   Prepare the final accounts for a partnership   S

(b)   Explain and account for the admission of a new partner   S
including the treatment of any goodwill arising.

Note. Candidates will not be expected to calculate the value of
goodwill.

Technical Performance Objective 9 requires you to demonstrate that you are competent in preparing
the final accounts of unincorporated entities, such as sole traders and partnerships. The knowledge you
gain in this chapter will help you to demonstrate your competence in this area.

1   Partnership accounts

1.1 What is a partnership?

A **partnership** can be defined as the relationship which exists between persons carrying on a business in
common with a view of profit.

In other words, if two or more persons agree to join forces in some kind of business venture, then a
partnership is the usual result. In some countries there is legislation governing partnership. In this
section we consider the normal rules for partnerships.

(a)   Unless the partnership is a limited liability partnership (LLP), the **personal liability** of each
partner for the firm's liabilities is **unlimited**, and so an individual's personal assets may be used to

meet any partnership liabilities in the event of partnership bankruptcy. In this exam we only look at partnerships with unlimited liability, and do not cover limited liability partnerships.

(b) All partners usually **participate in the running of the business**, rather than merely providing the capital.

(c) Adjustments to the partnership's net profit or loss (referred to as appropriations) will normally be made (see Section 1.3). The adjusted profit or loss is referred to as the residual profit or residual loss. This amount is **shared** between the partners in the profit or loss sharing ratio.

(d) A **partnership agreement** is usually (though not always) drawn up detailing the provisions of the contract between the partners.

The **partnership agreement** is likely to specify:

- Any salaries to be paid to partners
- Interest to be paid on any loans made to the partnership by a partner
- Interest (if any) to be paid on partners' capital account balances
- Interest (if any) to be charged on partners' drawings
- The proportion in which any residual profit is to be allocated between the partners

1.2 Partnership capital

In the **partnership statement of financial position**, net assets are financed by **partners' capital and current accounts**. Current accounts must be credited with the profits appropriated to each partner for the year, and debited with partners' drawings. Drawings, salaries and interest on capital are **not** expenses. They appear in the appropriation account.

Just as capital contributed by a sole trader to their business is recorded in their capital account, the capital contributed to a partnership is recorded in a series of **capital accounts, one for each partner**. The amount of each partner's contribution usually depends upon the partnership agreement, and since each partner is ultimately entitled to repayment of their capital it is vital to keep a continuous record of their interest in the firm. Sometimes partners may be required to contribute equally to the capital fund.

With one or two exceptions (dealt with below) each partner's capital account balance normally **remains constant** from year to year.

A **current account** for each partner is maintained to record a wide range of items on a continuous basis, for example, to charge drawings and other personal benefits and to credit salaries, interest on capital, share of profits etc. In effect, a partner's current account is merely an extension of their capital account, its balance representing further funds invested by the partner in the firm.

Sometimes, as in sole traders' accounts, a **drawings account** is kept to record each partner's withdrawals (in money or money's worth) throughout the year.

		$	$
DEBIT	Drawings account (or current account)	X	
CREDIT	Bank account (or other asset accounts)		X
	Purchases (or cost of sales)		X

Being withdrawal of cash (drawings and/or salaries) or other assets (including goods originally purchased for resale) by the partner

The balance on the partner's drawings account is **debited to their current account at the end of the year**. If they have withdrawn more than their profit share the current account may show a debit balance. This disadvantages the other partners who have credit balances and who have to find the excess. To overcome this problem, the partnership agreement could be altered to give partners interest on their current accounts and/or charge interest where debit balances are outstanding at the end of the year.

The partnership agreement may provide for **interest on drawings**. Each partner is charged a fixed percentage on their drawings throughout the year. This will be debited to their current account and added back to the profit available for appropriation.

Where an existing or previous partner makes a **loan to the partnership** they become an account payable of the partnership.

(a) If the partnership is short of cash (which often happens) and the existing partners do not wish to contribute further capital which would be tied up in the business for many years, one or more of them may be prepared to enter into a formal loan agreement for a specified period and at a realistic interest rate.

(b) When a partner retires, if there is insufficient cash to pay the balance owed to them (the total of their capital and current account balances), the amount which they cannot yet be paid is usually transferred to a loan account.

In the partnership statement of financial position a loan is shown separately as a non-current liability (unless repayable within 12 months), whether or not the lender is also an existing partner.

When preparing the partnership accounts, the statement of financial position is presented in the same way as in a sole trader's set of accounts, except for the capital and current accounts, which could be as shown below in place of the single capital account of a sole trader.

	$	$
Capital accounts		
Jill	10,000	
Susan	6,000	
		16,000
Current accounts		
Jill	2,500	
Susan	(1,000)	
		1,500
		17,500

Note that, unlike in a sole trader's statement of financial position, the profit and drawings figures are not shown separately. They have been absorbed into the current accounts and only the balances appear on the final accounts.

1.3 Appropriation of net profits

A statement of profit or loss may be prepared for a partnership in exactly the same way as for a sole trader. In the **appropriation account** the net profit is then apportioned between the partners according to the partnership agreement.

When a sole trader's net profit has been ascertained it is appropriated by them, ie credited to their capital account. They may or may not remove it from the business in the form of drawings. The net profit of a partnership is appropriated by the partners, according to whatever formula they choose, and the sharing out of profit between them is detailed in an **appropriation account**. The following factors have to be taken into consideration.

(a) **Interest**. Partners can agree to credit themselves with interest on capital account balances, and, more rarely, interest may be allowed (or charged) on current accounts. This is a means of compensating partners for funds tied up in the business that could be earning interest if invested elsewhere. However, the rate of interest agreed upon often bears little relation to current market rates.

(b) **Salaries**. Partners can agree to credit one or more partners with fixed salaries. This can be a means of compensating a partner for particularly valuable services rendered, especially if their share of profits is otherwise small. Salaries are an **appropriation of profit**, not a charge against profit.

(c) Partners may draw money out of the business over the course of the accounting period (we looked at how drawings are recorded in Section 1.2. The partnership agreement may stipulate that partners be charged interest on those drawings. The interest is a cost to the partners to reflect the fact that they have benefited by drawing money out of the business before the year end. Interest on drawings is credited to the appropriation account and debited to the partners' current accounts. It is only interest on drawings that is appropriated, not the drawings themselves which, as we have seen, are debited to the partners' current accounts.

(d) **Share of residual profits (or losses).** After allowing any interest and salaries, partners share remaining profits (or losses) according to their profit sharing ratio.

All these appropriations of profit (or loss) are credited (or debited) to the partners' current accounts.

Interest on a loan account represents an expense charged against profit, whereas **interest on a capital account** is an appropriation of profit. Loan interest must therefore be deducted before arriving at the figure of net profit available for appropriation.

1.4 Presentation of partnership accounts

For the purposes of your exam it is preferable to present details of partners' capital and current ledger accounts side by side, in **columnar form**. In practice, of course, a separate ledger account would be maintained for each account for each partner, but in the subsequent examples the columnar format is adopted.

1.5 Example: partnership accounts

Crossly, Steels and Nabs are partners in a music business, sharing profits in the ratio 5:3:2 respectively. Their capital and current account balances on 1 January 20X5 were as follows.

	Capital accounts $	Current accounts $
Crossly	24,000	2,000
Steels	18,000	(1,000) Dr
Nabs	13,000	1,500

Interest at 10% per annum is given on the fixed capital amounts, and salaries of $8,000 per annum are credited to Steels and Nabs.

Expansion of the business was hindered by lack of working capital, so Crossly made a personal loan of $20,000 on 1 July 20X5. The loan was to be repaid in full on 30 June 20X8 and loan interest at the rate of 15% per annum was to be credited to Crossly's account every half year.

The partnership profit (before charging loan interest) for the year ended 31 December 20X5 was $63,000 and the partners had made drawings of: Crossly $16,000; Steels $16,500; Nabs $19,000, during the year. Interest on drawings is charged at 10% of the year-end balance. Prepare the appropriation account, the partners' capital and current accounts in respect of the year ended 31 December 20X5.

Solution

APPROPRIATION ACCOUNT FOR THE YEAR ENDED 31 DECEMBER 20X5

	$	$
Net profit*		61,500
Interest on drawings		
Crossly	1,600	
Steels	1,650	
Nabs	1,900	
		5,150
		66,650
Interest on capital accounts		
Crossly	2,400	
Steels	1,800	
Nabs	1,300	
	5,500	
Salaries		
Steels	8,000	
Nabs	8,000	
	16,000	

	(21,500)
	45,150
	$

Partners' shares of balance

Crossly (5/10)	22,575
Steels (3/10)	13,545
Nabs (2/10)	9,030
	45,150

	$
*Profit per question	63,000
Less loan interest to Crossly: 15% × $20,000 × 6/12	(1,500)
Net profit available for appropriation	61,500

PARTNERS' CAPITAL ACCOUNTS

	Crossly $	Steels $	Nabs $		Crossly $	Steels $	Nabs $
				Balances b/f	24,000	18,000	13,000

PARTNERS' CURRENT ACCOUNTS

	Crossly $	Steels $	Nabs $		Crossly $	Steels $	Nabs $
Balances b/f		1,000		Balances b/f	2,000		1,500
Interest on				Loan interest	1,500		
drawings	1,600	1,650	1,900				
Drawings							
(cash)	16,000	16,500	19,000	Appropriation			
				a/c			
Balances c/d	10,875	4,195		Interest on			
				capital	2,400	1,800	1,300
				Salary		8,000	8,000
				Balance of			
				profit	22,575	13,545	9,030
				Balance c/d			1,070
	28,475	23,345	20,900		28,475	23,345	20,900

It is possible that salaries and interest on capital may **exceed the partnership profit**, or indeed, increase a partnership loss. In such a case the treatment is to credit the partners with their salaries, interest on capital etc and divide the total loss between them in the usual profit sharing ratio.

EXAM FOCUS POINT

When answering questions on partnerships it is very important you take note of dates included in the question. For example, in the illustrative example above you needed to notice the personal loan was made on 1 July, which is 6 months into the year. Therefore you need to multiply by 6/12 when calculating the loan interest at 15%.

The examining team December 2011 report highlighted that students had failed to do this. In a question requiring students to calculate interest on partnership capital, it appeared that only a small number had noted the date the capital was introduced when calculating the interest on capital to be paid. The capital had been introduced part way through the year, but most students seemed to have included interest on capital for a whole year in their answer. It is very important that you always read the question carefully to avoid making a similar mistake.

QUESTION

Shaw and Turner

Shaw and Turner began trading on 1 April 20X1 when P Shaw, an established retailer in a small town north of Manchester, entered into partnership with B Turner.

A colleague in your firm has already produced a draft statement of profit or loss and a draft statement of financial position for the partnership for the year ended 31 March 20X2 but has become unwell and is unable to complete all the entries required and finalise the financial statements. You have been asked to complete the task.

From the file of information left by your colleague you have discovered that a net profit of $52,530 had been made by the partnership according to the draft statement of profit or loss. No appropriation account or partners' current accounts had yet been completed and some adjustment may be necessary to the draft net profit figure.

Your colleague has left a memorandum with the following information which may be relevant.

(a)   P Shaw made a loan of $10,000 to the partnership on 1 April 20X1. Interest on the loan is to be credited to P Shaw at a rate of $12\frac{1}{2}\%$.

(b)   The partners are to be credited with annual salaries as follows.

P Shaw $20,000
B Turner $10,000

(c)   The partners are to be credited with interest on their capital account balances at the rate of 10% per annum.

(d)   The balances of net profits and losses are to be shared between P Shaw and B Turner in the proportions $\frac{3}{5}$ and $\frac{2}{5}$ respectively.

(e)   The partners have made the following drawings during the year.

P Shaw $16,700
B Turner $22,300

(f)   Separate capital accounts and current accounts are to be maintained for each partner. The balances on the capital accounts at 31 March 20X2 as shown in the draft statements are as follows.

P Shaw $34,000
B Turner $24,000

Required

(a)   Draw up the appropriation account for the partnership of Shaw and Turner for the year ended 31 March 20X2.

(b)   Prepare the partners' current accounts for the year ended 31 March 20X2.

ANSWER

(a)   SHAW AND TURNER
APPROPRIATION ACCOUNT FOR THE YEAR ENDED 31 MARCH 20X2

	$	$
Net profit b/d		52,530
Less interest on partner's loan		(1,250)
Adjusted net profit available for appropriation		51,280
Less partners' salaries		
Shaw	20,000	
Turner	10,000	
		(30,000)
Less interest on capital		
Shaw	3,400	
Turner	2,400	
		(5,800)
		15,480
Share of net profit balance		
Shaw 3/5		9,288
Turner 2/5		6,192
		15,480

(b)

PARTNERS' CURRENT ACCOUNTS

	Shaw $	Turner $		Shaw $	Turner $
Drawings	16,700	22,300	Interest on capital	3,400	2,400
			Partners' salaries	20,000	10,000
			Interest on loan	1,250	
			Balance of profit	9,288	6,192
Balance c/d	17,238		Balance c/d		3,708
	33,938	22,300		33,938	22,300

1.6 Admission of a new partner

When a new partner is admitted to the partnership they will introduce funds to share in the ownership of the firm's assets and to purchase a share of the partnership's **goodwill**.

A new partnership agreement is needed to cover the appropriation of profits when a new partner is admitted. When a new partner introduces additional funds into the partnership, the total amount they bring is credited to their capital account. The new partner pays in capital for two reasons:

(a)   To share in the ownership of the firms assets

(b)   To share in the future profits and losses of the firm. In order to do this the new partner must pay for a share of the partnership's **goodwill**.

Goodwill represents the value of the partnership not represented by its tangible assets, for example the reputation the firm enjoys with its clients.

The existing partners' share of the partnership's goodwill is calculated at the date of admission of a new partner. This is then credited to the existing partners in the old profit sharing ratio, with the debit entry posted to a goodwill account.

The new partner will usually need to purchase a share of the firms assets and goodwill by introducing cash (or other assets).

The partners then have a choice as to whether they wish to **maintain** the goodwill in the partnership accounts or to remove it immediately.

If the partners decide not to maintain the goodwill then it is debited to the partners' capital accounts in the new profit sharing ratio and the credit entry results in the removal of the goodwill balance on the goodwill account.

EXAM FOCUS POINT

Admission of a new partner is an area which has been highlighted in recent examiner's reports as one which students can struggle with. Key points from the examiner's report September 2019 – August 2020 for candidates to remember include:

1)   Goodwill is created with a debit entry in the goodwill account with the value shared between the old partners in the old profit sharing ratio (the credit is to the capital accounts).

2)   The question will state whether or not the goodwill will be maintained in the accounts (sometimes referred to as 'carried in the books'). If goodwill is going to be maintained, no further entries are made at this time. If goodwill is not going to be maintained, it is then charged to the new partners in the new profit sharing ratio by debiting their capital accounts and crediting the goodwill account. The goodwill account will then have a zero balance.

The best way to demonstrate this is using an example.

1.6.1 Example: new partner

Ant and Dec share profits in the ratio – Ant 1: Dec: 1 – in a repairs and maintenance business. They agree to Noel becoming a partner on 1 January 20X9. At that date Ant and Dec value the business's goodwill at $5,000 and their capital accounts are Ant – $12,000; Dec – $9,000. Noel agrees to introduce $3,000 in cash. The partners agree to share profits in the ratio – Ant 2: Dec 2: Noel 1.

Initially goodwill will be calculated and allocated to the existing partners in the old profit sharing ratio. A goodwill account will also be opened.

GOODWILL

	$		$
Goodwill	5,000		

PARTNERS' CAPITAL ACCOUNTS

Ratio	1: Ant $	1 Dec $		1: Ant $	1 Dec $
			Balances b/d	12,000	9,000
			Goodwill (old ratio)	2,500	2,500
				14,500	11,500

Noel's cash introduced is then recorded in the capital account.

GOODWILL

	$		$
Goodwill	5,000		

PARTNERS' CAPITAL ACCOUNTS

Ratio	2: Ant $	2: Dec $	1 Noel $		2: Ant $	2: Dec $	1 Noel $
				Balances b/d	12,000	9,000	
				Goodwill (old ratio)	2,500	2,500	
				Cash introduced			3,000
					14,500	11,500	3,000

BANK ACCOUNT

	$		$
Capital account (Cash introduced)	3,000		

The partners now have a choice. They may choose to maintain the goodwill in the accounts and no further entries are made at this time. However, if they decide they will not maintain goodwill in the accounts, the goodwill is debited to the capital accounts in the new profit sharing ratio. The goodwill account and the partners' capital accounts will then be as follows.

GOODWILL

	$		$
Goodwill	5,000	Partners' capital accounts	5,000

PARTNERS' CAPITAL ACCOUNTS

Ratio	2: Ant $	2: Dec $	1 Noel $		2: Ant $	2: Dec $	1 Noel $
Goodwill (new ratio)	2,000	2,000	1,000	Balances b/d	12,000	9,000	
Balances c/d	12,500	9,500	2,000	Goodwill (old ratio)	2,500	2,500	
				Cash introduced			3,000
	14,500	11,500	3,000		14,500	11,500	3,000

This shows that $1,000 of Noel's cash introduced was actually to pay for his proportion of the goodwill. This makes sense as the goodwill is valued at $5,000 and his share in the partnership is 1/5.

EXAM FOCUS POINT

There are two very useful technical articles within the FA2 section of the ACCA website covering partnerships and accounting for them. The articles are targeted at the FA2 Section H learning outcomes and look at the sorts of calculations you will need to perform when answering FA2 exam questions on partnerships. They are essential reading for all students planning to take the FA2 exam and you should carefully work through the examples included in each article.

CHAPTER ROUNDUP

↳ In the **partnership statement of financial position**, net assets are financed by **partners' capital and current accounts**. Current accounts must be credited with the profits appropriated to each partner for the year, and debited with partners' drawings. Drawings, salaries and interest on capital are **not** expenses. They appear in the appropriation account.

↳ A statement of profit or loss may be prepared for a partnership in exactly the same way as for a sole trader. In the **appropriation account** the net profit is then apportioned between the partners according to the partnership agreement.

↳ When a new partner is admitted to the partnership they will introduce funds to share in the ownership of the firms assets and to purchase a share of the partnership's **goodwill**.

QUICK QUIZ

1　Fill in the blanks.

　The salaries due to each of the partners is likely to be specified in the ....

2　In the statement of financial position of a partnership, how is a loan from a partner disclosed?

3　Interest on a loan made by a partner is shown as an appropriation of profit, not as an expense. True or false?

4　How is the balance on a partners' drawings account treated at the year end?

5　When a new partner is admitted to a partnership and introduces funds towards a share of the partnerships goodwill, the goodwill must always be maintained in the partnership accounts. True or false?

1   The salaries due to each of the partners is likely to be specified in the **partnership agreement**.

2   A loan from a partner is shown separately as a non-current liability.

3   False. Interest on a loan is an expense charged against profit.

4   It is debited to their current account.

5   False. The partners may choose not to maintain the goodwill in the accounts.

Now try ...

Attempt the questions below from the **Practice Question Bank**

Number	Level	Marks	Time
Q63	Examination	2	2.4 mins
Q64	Examination	2	2.4 mins
Q65	Examination	2	2.4 mins
Q66	Examination	2	2.4 mins
Q67	Examination	2	2.4 mins

Practice question and answer bank

Questions

1   Sally keeps records identifying those business debts she has met personally and those debts met using business assets.

   By doing this Sally is trying to make sure that when she prepares her accounts she does so in accordance with which principle or concept:

   A   Accruals
   B   Business entity
   C   Going concern
   D   Historical cost

2   Which of the following explains the dual effects when inventory which cost $2,000 is sold for $2,500 (the customer paying immediately with a cheque)?

   A   Assets (cash at bank) increase by $500; assets (inventory) decrease by $2,000; capital (profit earned for the proprietor) increases by $1,500.

   B   Assets (cash at bank) decrease by $2,500; assets (inventory) increase by $2,000; capital (profit earned for the proprietor) increases by $500.

   C   Assets (cash at bank) increase by $500; assets (inventory) decrease by $2,000; capital (profit earned for the proprietor) increases by $2,500.

   D   Assets (cash at bank) increase by $2,500; assets (inventory) decrease by $2,000; capital (profit earned for the proprietor) increases by $500.

3   Which of the following correctly records the dual effects when goods which cost $5,000 are sold on credit for $6,000?

   A   Assets (receivables) increase by $1,000; assets (inventory) decrease by $5,000; capital (profit earned for the proprietor) increases by $4,000.

   B   Assets (receivables) decrease by $6,000; assets (inventory) increase by $5,000; capital (profit earned for the proprietor) decreases by $1,000.

   C   Assets (receivables) increase by $6,000; assets (inventory) decrease by $5,000; capital (profit earned for the proprietor) increases by $1,000.

   D   Assets (cash at bank) increase by $6,000; assets (inventory) decrease by $5,000; capital (profit earned for the proprietor) increases by $1,000.

4   Which of the following correctly records the dual effects when a business purchases goods on credit for $3,000?

   A   Assets (inventory) increase by $3,000; liabilities (payables) remain unchanged; capital (profit earned for the proprietor) increases by $3,000.

   B   Assets (inventory) increase by $3,000; liabilities (payables) increase by $3,000; capital (profit earned for the proprietor) remains unchanged.

   C   Assets (inventory) increase by $3,000; assets (cash at bank) decrease by $3,000; capital (profit earned for the proprietor) remains unchanged.

   D   Assets (cash at bank) decrease by $3,000; liabilities (payables) increase by $3,000; capital (profit earned for the proprietor) remains unchanged.

5   A business had net assets at 1 January and 31 December 20X9 of $75,600 and $73,800 respectively. During the year, the proprietor introduced additional capital of $17,700 and withdrew cash and goods to the value of $16,300.

   What profit or loss was made by the business in 20X9?

   A $3,200 loss
   B $400 loss
   C $400 profit
   D $3,200 profit

6   A business had net assets at 1 January and 31 December 20X9 of $47,100 and $54,200 respectively. During the year the business borrowed $2,000 from the bank and the proprietor introduced additional capital of $22,000. The proprietor also made drawings of $200 per week.

What profit or loss was made by the business in 20X9?

A $18,700 loss
B $4,500 loss
C $4,500 profit
D $18,700 profit

7   The net assets of Kate's business were $15,000 at 1 April 20X3 and $25,000 at 31 March 20X4. During the year Kate paid lottery winnings of $2,500 into the business bank account and withdrew $1,000.

What was her net profit for the year ended 31 March 20X4?

☐

8   Ellie is recording the purchase of a new non-current asset. Which TWO items would be treated as expenses charged to profit and loss?

(1)   Delivery
(2)   Installation
(3)   Maintenance
(4)   Technical support contract

☐   1 and 3
☐   2 and 3
☐   3 and 4
☐   4 and 1

9   In the year to 31 December 20X9, Jason recorded some asset expenditure as expenses charged to profit or loss.

What is the effect on his profit for the year to 31 December 20X9 and his net assets at that date?

	Profit	Net assets
A	Overstated	Overstated
B	Overstated	Understated
C	Understated	Overstated
D	Understated	Understated

10   Which of the following should be included within non-current assets in the accounts of a business?

(1)   The cost of a new delivery van
(2)   The cost of insuring the van
(3)   The cost of a new set of tyres for the van when they need to be replaced
(4)   The wages of a new employee needed to drive the van

A   1 only
B   1 and 3
C   2 and 3
D   2 and 4

11   Which of the following are current assets? (please tick all that apply)

☐   A prepayment
☐   An accrual
☐   An item of inventory
☐   An overdrawn bank balance

12   Which of the following should be included within current liabilities in the accounts of a business?

(1)   A bank overdraft
(2)   A bank loan repayable in five years
(3)   Proprietor's capital
(4)   Trade payables

A   2 and 3
B   1 and 2
C   3 and 4
D   1 and 4

13   James has been asked to supply goods to Paul's business. He is anxious to get hold of a set Paul's latest accounts.

What is the most likely reason for James wanting to look at Paul's accounts?

A   To calculate the amount of tax Paul needs to pay
B   To assess the ability of Paul's business to pay its debts as they fall due
C   To compare the performance of Paul's business with his own
D   To see the level of salary Paul is paying himself from the business

14   Which of the following is a book of prime entry?

A   A cheque received
B   A statement of financial position
C   A bank ledger account
D   A cash payments day book

15   Anna obtains the majority of her inventory from two other businesses, one run by Sophie and another run by Rob.

Sophie has agreed that Anna must pay full price for the first $1,000 of goods ordered, but for any purchases in excess of this she will offer a trade discount of 5%. Rob offers a 10% settlement discount for immediate payment or a 5% settlement discount for all items paid for within 15 days of purchase. There is no discount if items are paid for after 15 days.

In October 20X9, Anna purchases goods as follows (amounts stated are those before discounts have been deducted):

(1)   From Sophie: $1200
(2)   From Rob: $500 (settled in cash immediately)
              $800 (to be paid on 16.10.X9 for goods purchased on 5.10.X9)

What are the total savings by Anna in October 20X9 as a result of discounts:

A $150
B $115
C $100
D $90

16   Which of the following items will affect the gross profit of a business?

(1)   Early settlement discount allowed
(2)   Early settlement discount received

A   1 only
B   2 only
C   1 and 2
D   None of them

17   You return goods that cost $400 to a supplier because they are found to be damaged. Which of the following is the most appropriate day book in which to record this transaction?

A   Sales day book
B   Sales returns day book
C   Purchase day book
D   Purchase returns day book

18 When preparing the sales tax ledger account, which of the following entries will be debit entries? (please tick all that apply)

- [ ] Sales tax on cash purchases
- [ ] Sales tax on cash sales
- [ ] The total input sales tax shown in the purchases day book
- [ ] The total output sales tax shown in the sales day book

19 Karen, who runs her own business, has discovered that she slightly understated the input tax when filling in the sales tax return for the quarter to 31 March 20X0, which has already been submitted. Which of the following is the most appropriate course of action?

A   Karen will fill out another sales tax return for the quarter to 31 March 20X0
B   Karen will decrease the input tax on the return to 30 June 20X0
C   Karen will increase the input tax on the return to 30 June 20X0
D   Karen will take no action in respect of this

20 What transaction is represented by the following journal entry?

DEBIT   Surveyor's fee $600
CREDIT   Payables control $600

A   Payment of surveyor's fee by cheque
B   A credit note received from a surveyor
C   An invoice received from a surveyor
D   An invoice issued to a surveyor

21 'It is an account which keeps a record of a total value of a number of similar but individual items and is regularly agreed with the total of the individual balances. This account therefore helps to provide a check to ensure that all transactions have been recorded correctly.'

What type of account is being described in the above paragraph?

A   A control account
B   A memorandum account
C   A general ledger account
D   An expense account

22 Which of the following is an example of an error of commission?

A   A transaction has not been recorded

B   One side of a transaction has been recorded in the wrong account, and that account is of a different class to the correct account

C   One side of a transaction has been recorded in the wrong account, and that account is of the same class as the correct account

D   A transaction has been recorded using the wrong amount

23 Which of these errors will still cause the trial balance to balance?

A   An error of partial omission
B   An error of transposition made in the credit entry only
C   An error where both entries of a journal are posted as a debit
D   An error of complete omission

24 Mike draws up his accounts on the assumption he will continue in business for the foreseeable future. Which accounting principle is Mike applying?

A   Consistency
B   Historical cost
C   Going concern
D   Accruals

25   Final accounts for different businesses are presented using the same primary statements (the statement of financial position and the statement of profit or loss). The sub-headings within these statements are also the same or similar regardless of the business.

The features described above contribute most to which qualitative characteristic of financial statements?

A   Comparability
B   Relevance
C   Materiality
D   Faithful representation

26   A supplier sends you a statement showing a balance outstanding of $14,350. Your own records show a balance outstanding of $14,500.

Which of the following could be a reason for this difference?

☐   The supplier sent an invoice for $150 which you have not yet received

☐   The supplier has allowed you $150 settlement discount which you had omitted to enter in your ledgers

☐   You have paid the supplier $150 which they have not yet accounted for

☐   You have returned goods worth $150 which the supplier has not yet accounted for

27   Phil is preparing a reconciliation of the balance on the trade payables control account to the total of the list of balances on the accounts in the payables ledger. He has discovered the following:

(1)   A debit balance of $50 on a supplier's account was listed as a credit balance
(2)   An invoice for $989 was entered in the purchase day book as $998

Which of the errors will require an adjustment to the trade payables control account in the general ledger?

A   Neither 1 nor 2
B   1 only
C   2 only
D   Both 1 and 2

28   How should the balance on the payables control account be reported in the final accounts?

A   As an expense
B   As a current asset
C   As a current liability
D   As a non-current asset

29   Alison has prepared the following reconciliation of the balance on the receivables control account in her general ledger to the total of the list of balances on customers' personal accounts:

	$
Balance on receivables control account	75,356
Balance omitted from list of balances	(849)
	74,507
Sales day book undercast	400
Total of list of balances	74,907

What is the correct balance of receivables to be reported on the statement of financial position?

☐

30   A business receives an invoice from a supplier for $2,800 which is mislaid before any entry is made, resulting in the transaction being left out of the books entirely.

This is an example of which type of error?

A   Error of transposition
B   Error of omission
C   Error of principle
D   Error of commission

31   Which of the following is an error of principle?

☐   A gas bill credited to the gas account and debited to the bank account

☐   The purchase of a non-current asset credited to the asset at cost account and debited to the payables control account

☐   The purchase of a non-current asset debited to the purchases account and credited to the payables control account

☐   The payment of wages debited and credited to the correct accounts, but using the wrong amount

32   When posting an invoice received for building maintenance $980 was entered on the building maintenance expense account instead of the correct amount of $890.

What correction should be made to the building maintenance expense account?

▼		▼

Picklist: Picklist:

Debit $890
Credit $980
                       $90

33   Which of the following items reconciling the balance on the bank ledger account to the balance shown on the bank statement are referred to as timing differences?

(1)   Bank charges not recorded in the cash day books
(2)   Interest charged not recorded in the cash day books
(3)   Outstanding lodgements
(4)   Unpresented cheques

☐   1 and 2
☐   3 and 4
☐   2 and 3
☐   1 and 4

34   Mary is preparing her bank reconciliation. The bank balance in her general ledger is $540 credit. There are two items she has yet to deal with.

(1)   A cheque for $620 was sent to a supplier but is not yet showing on the bank statement.
(2)   A bank charge of $28 was charged by the bank, but was not recorded by Mary.

What is the closing balance on Mary's bank statement assuming there are no other errors or adjustments?

A $1,132 overdrawn
B $1,188 overdrawn
C $52 credit
D $108 credit

35 Which of the following is the reason for carrying out a receivables control account reconciliation?

    A   To check that the balance on a customer's ledger account agrees with the supplier account balance in the customer's books

    B   To check for indications that the balance on the general ledger is incorrect

    C   To check that the value of sales is correctly recorded in the general ledger

    D   To check there is no cash outstanding from customers

36 A suspense account was opened when a trial balance failed to balance. When the following errors were corrected, the suspense account was cleared:

- A gas bill for $420 was entered on the correct side of the gas account as $240.

- An invoice of $50 received in respect of telephone costs had been credited to the telephone expense account. The other entry had been made correctly.

- Interest received of $70 was entered correctly in the bank account, but no other entry was made.

What was the balance on the suspense account when it was created?

Picklist:	Picklist:
Debit	$210
Credit	$160

37 Sandy wants to write off a debt due to him from a business that has recently ceased trading. What entries should Sandy make?

    A   DEBIT   Receivables control account
           CREDIT   Irrecoverable debt expense

    B   DEBIT   Revenue
           CREDIT   Irrecoverable debt expense

    C   DEBIT   Irrecoverable debt expense
           CREDIT   Receivables control account

    D   DEBIT   Irrecoverable debt expense
           CREDIT   Revenue

38 At 1 January 20X1 there was an allowance for receivables of $2,000. During the year $1,000 of debt was written off and $800 of irrecoverable debt was recovered. At 31 December 20X1, it was decided to adjust the receivables allowance to 10% of receivables, which were $30,000. What was the irrecoverable debt expense in the statement of profit or loss for the year?

39 Graham prepared his draft end of year accounts, however he has now realised that he did not adjust these for a prepayment of $2,100 and an accrual of $800.

How will Graham's profit and net assets be affected by including the prepayment and accrual?

	Net profit will:	Net assets will
A	Increase by $2,900	Reduce by $2,900
B	Increase by $1,300	Increase by $1,300
C	Reduce by $1,300	Increase by $1,300
D	Reduce by $2,900	Reduce by $2,900

40   On 3 July 20X0 Alex paid rent of $18,000 for the period 1 July 20X0 to 30 June 20X1. He is drawing up accounts for the year to 31 January 20X1.

What entry does Alex need to make in respect of rent in order for the year end figure to be correct?

| ▼ | | ▼ |

Picklist: Picklist:

accrual $7,500
prepayment $10,500

41   Wendy is drawing up accounts for her toy store for the year ended 31 December 20X8. During that year one of the toys she sold was faulty and resulted in an injury to a child. As a result the parents of the child have taken legal action and are demanding a maximum of $6,000 in damages.

Wendy offered compensation of $1,200 which has been turned down. She has now taken advice on the matter from her solicitor who thinks that, although there is a slim chance she will be able to avoid paying damages if the case goes to court, the sensible course of action is to settle out of court. The solicitor has advised that a sum of around $4,500 is likely to be accepted by the parents.

Calculate the amount of the provision to be included in Wendy's accounts.

| |

42   Sarah made a mistake when she calculated the value of her closing inventory. As a result the inventory is undervalued.

How are her net profits for the year and net assets at the end of the year affected by this error?

	Net profit	Net assets
A	Overstated	Understated
B	Overstated	Overstated
C	Understated	Understated
D	Understated	Overstated

43   Fernando runs a clothes shop selling replica football kits and valued all his inventory at 31 March 20X8 at its cost of $15,550.

Inventory includes 50 of last season's football kits which originally cost $30 and were on sale during the year for $50 each. However, now that new kits are out for the coming season, Fernando knows he will have to reduce the old kits to half price in order to sell them.

Calculate the correct value for inventory at 31 March 20X8.

| |

44   The following records were kept for an inventory item in June.

June   1   100 units in inventory at $10 each
           5   50 units bought at $10 each
          12   60 units sold
          20   20 units bought at $8 each
          29   80 units sold

Using the FIFO method, what would be the value of inventory at 30 June?

A $300
B $260
C $340
D $220

45   Adam uses the continuous weighted average cost method of valuing inventories. During May 20X1, he recorded the following inventory details:

Opening balance   50 units valued at $4 each
4 May   purchase of 50 units at $4.40 each
11 May   issue of 80 units
19 May   purchase of 60 units at $4.60 each
24 May   issue of 50 units

What is the value of the inventory held at 31 May 20X1?

A $120.00
B $126.00
C $132.00
D $135.00

46   Jack has recently commenced trading and is unsure how to value his inventory. He needs to decide whether to use First In First Out (FIFO), or continuous weighted average.

One of the raw materials he uses in his business is oil. The price of oil has consistently risen and is expected to continue to rise.

Which of the following statements is correct?

A   Jack's profit will be the same regardless of the method of inventory valuation adopted

B   FIFO will lead to Jack reporting a higher profit than if he uses continuous weighted average

C   Continuous weighted average will lead to a higher reported profit than if he uses FIFO

D   A more accurate profit will be reported if FIFO is used

47   Which of the following statements best describes the purpose of charging depreciation on non-current assets?

A   Put money aside to replace the assets when required
B   Show the assets at their current market value
C   Ensure that the profit is not understated
D   Spread the cost of the assets over their estimated useful life

48   Brook sold a delivery van which originally cost $24,500. The accumulated depreciation on the van was $13,650 at the date it was sold. Sale proceeds of $7,500 were received.

What is the profit or loss on the disposal of the van?

A   A loss of $3,350
B   A loss of $6,150
C   A loss of $17,000
B   A profit of $3,350

The following information relates to questions 49 and 50

Holly bought some equipment for use in her business on 1 May 20X8.

In order to purchase the asset she transferred $15,000 from her bank account to the supplier's bank account and traded in some old equipment which was assigned a part exchange value of $4,450 by the supplier.

Holly depreciates equipment on the reducing balance basis at a rate of 30% per annum. The old equipment had cost $15,000 and had been depreciated by $9,855.

49   What is the depreciation charge on the new equipment for the year to 30 April 20X9?

50   What is the profit or loss on disposal arising on the old equipment that was traded in?

    A $10,550 profit
    B $10,550 loss
    C $695 profit
    D $695 loss

51   An organisation's asset register shows a carrying amount of $145,600. The non current asset account in the general ledger shows a carrying amount of $135,600. The difference is due to a disposal which has not been removed from the asset register. Which of the following disposals is the most likely cause for this difference?

    A   Sale of a car with disposal proceeds of $15,000 and a profit on disposal of $5,000
    B   Sale of a tractor with disposal proceeds of $15,000 and a carrying amount of $5,000
    C   Sale of a machine with disposal proceeds of $15,000 and a loss on disposal of $5,000
    D   Sale of plant with disposal proceeds of $5,000 and a carrying amount of $5,000

52   A sole trader is balancing and ruling off a ledger account at the end of the year. The ledger account shows an overall credit balance. Which of the following could it represent?

    (1)   A liability that should be carried forward to the next year
    (2)   An asset that should be carried forward to the next year
    (3)   An expense to be transferred to the statement of profit or loss
    (4)   Income to be transferred to the statement of profit or loss

    A   1 and 2
    B   3 and 4
    C   2 and 3
    D   1 and 4

53   Which of the following would be included amongst current liabilities in the accounts of a business? (please tick all that apply)

    (1)   An allowance for receivables
    (2)   Accrual for rent
    (3)   Bank overdraft
    (4)   A new bank loan due for repayment in two years' time

    ☐   1 and 2
    ☐   2 and 3
    ☐   1 and 3
    ☐   2 and 4

54   In October 20X0, Brenda took out a bank loan for $20,000. This is to be repaid in five equal instalments. The first instalment is due for repayment on 1 April 20X1. The other payments are due annually on the same date each year.

How should the outstanding balance be reported in Brenda's statement of financial position at 31 March 20X1?

    A $20,000 as a current liability
    B $5,000 as a current liability and $15,000 as a non-current liability
    C $10,000 as a current liability and $10,000 as a non-current liability
    D $20,000 as a non-current liability

55   Luke's trial balance at 31 December 20X9 included the following:

	Dr $	Cr $
Revenue		950,250
Purchases	540,755	
Inventory at 1.1.X9	88,540	
Carriage inwards	14,985	
Discounts received	6,340	
Repairs	14,200	
Advertising and promotions	35,736	
Telephone	24,522	

Luke's inventory at 31 December 20X9 was valued at $93,670.

What figure should Luke show for gross profit on his statement of profit or loss?

        ┌─────────────────┐
        │   │
        └─────────────────┘

56   Harry has just completed his extended trail balance. The totals were as follows:

Statement of profit or loss columns		Statement of financial position columns	
DEBIT $	CREDIT $	DEBIT $	CREDIT $
149,787	156,999	159,219	152,007

What is Harry's profit or loss for the period?

A   A profit of $7,212
B   A loss of $7,212
C   A loss of $7,221
D   A profit of $7,221

57   When the extended trial balance is being completed, in which column should the value for proprietor's capital be entered?

A   Statement of profit or loss debit
B   Statement of profit or loss credit
C   Statement of financial position debit
D   Statement of financial position credit

58   What is the main purpose of the extended trial balance?

A   To keep track of adjustments between the trial balance and the final accounts
B   To comply with laws and regulations for accounting
C   To summarise the balances on the ledger accounts
D   To adjust for inventory

59   Hengist, a sole trader, has calculated that his cost of sales for the year is $144,000. His revenue figure for the year includes an amount of $2,016 being the amount paid by Hengist himself into the business bank account for goods withdrawn for private use. The figure of $2,016 was calculated by adding a mark-up of 12% to the cost of the goods. His gross profit margin on all other goods sold was 20%.

What is the total figure of revenue for the year?

A $172,656
B $177,750
C $179,766
D $180,000

BPP
LEARNING MEDIA

333

60 Barry is a sole trader. He has calculated a cost of sales figure for the year, which is $342,000. Barry paid $8,030 into the business bank account for goods withdrawn for private use and this amount has been included within revenue. The figure of $8,030 was calculated by adding a mark-up of 10% to the cost of the goods. His gross profit margin on all other goods sold was 20% of revenue.

What is the total figure of revenue for the year?

```
┌──────────────────┐
│                  │
│                  │
└──────────────────┘
```

61 Alfred does not keep full accounting records. He has calculated that his assets and liabilities at 30 June 20X1 were:

	$
Non-current assets	51,300
Inventory	7,770
Receivables	5,565
Payables	3,994
Bank overdraft	3,537

On reviewing his calculations, you note that there were no entries made in relation to rent for the month of June 20X1 because rent is paid in arrears, with the payment for June having been made on 1 July 20X1. Rent is $500 per month.

What is the value of Alfred's closing capital at 30 June 20X1?

A $64,678
B $56,604
C $57,604
D $63,678

62 Elizabeth is trying to work out her cost of sales for the year ended 31 December 20X9

She has the following details for supplier and inventory balances:

	At 1 January 20X9	At 31 December 20X9
Suppliers	$15,264	$16,812
Inventory	$6,359	$4,919

In the year to 31 December 20X9, Elizabeth's payments to suppliers totaled $141,324.

What was Elizabeth's cost of sales for the year to 31 December 20X9?

A $149,231
B $144,312
C $142,872
D $141,432

63 Wayne and Kay are in partnership. In the year to 31 May 20X1, Wayne's drawings were $12,000 and the following entries have been made in the partnership appropriation account for Wayne:

	$
Salary	7,500
Interest on drawings	2,800
Share of profit	13,500

At 1 June 20X0, the balance on Wayne's current account was $31,200 (credit).

What is the balance on Wayne's current account at 31 May 20X1?

A $37,400
B $43,000
C $49,400
D $22,400

64   Bill and Ted were in partnership and shared profits and losses equally. On 1 October 20X0 they admitted a new partner, Fred. Bill and Ted had established the goodwill in the partnership at that date was valued at $120,000 and Fred introduced enough cash to ensure his opening capital balance on admission was $10,000.

The three partners now share profits and losses equally and goodwill was not maintained in the partnership accounts.

How much cash did Fred contribute?

A $120,000
B $60,000
C $50,000
D $40,000

65   When preparing partnership accounts, which of the following are treated as an expense of the business?

(1)   A partner's salary
(2)   Loan interest paid to a partner
(3)   A partner's entertaining expenses
(4)   Interest paid on a partner's capital

☐   1
☐   2
☐   3
☐   4

66   Alice and Ann share their partnership profits in the ratio 2:1 after payment of Ann's salary of $10,000. They both owe $500 interest on drawings. Profit for the year is $75,000. What will Alice's profit share be?

A $50,000
B $43,500
C $44,000
D $43,333

67   Bruce and Sheila are in partnership sharing profits and losses in the ratio 5:6. A net profit of $34,100 was reported in the statement of profit or loss for the year to 30 September 20X0. Bruce is entitled to a salary of $12,100 per annum.

What is Sheila's share of the profit for the year to 30 September 20X0?

☐

Answers

1	B		The business entity concept specifies that a business is always treated as a separate entity from its owner for accounting purposes. Keeping track of debts met personally and those met using business assets will mean Sally will be in a better position when it comes to drawing up accounts for the business as a separate entity.
2	D		Assets (cash at bank) increase by $2,500; assets (inventory) decrease by $2,000; capital (profit earned for the proprietor) increases by $500.
3	C		Assets (receivables) increase by $6,000; assets (inventory) decrease by $5,000; capital (profit earned for the proprietor) increases by $1,000.
4	B		Assets (inventory) increase by $3,000; liabilities (payables) increase by $3,000; capital (profit earned for the proprietor) remains unchanged.

5   A P $= I + D - Ci$
             $= -\$1,800 + \$16,300 - \$17,700$
             $= -\$3,200$ (ie a loss of $3,200)

6   B P $= I + D - Ci$
             $= \$7,100 + (52 \times \$200) - \$22,000$
             $= -\$4,500$ (ie a loss of $4,500)

7   $8,500 $10,000 + $1,000 - $2,500 = $8,500

8	3, 4	Delivery and installation costs are included in the capital cost of the non-current asset. Maintenance and support contract costs are revenue items as they are to maintain the performance of the asset rather than to enhance it.
9	D	Non-current assets will be understated, leading to a lower net assets position. Additionally too much will have been charged in the statement of profit or loss resulting in an understatement of profit.
10	A	The cost of the van is the only capital expenditure to be classified within non-current assets. The insurance is an annual cost of running the van, as is the employee's wage and both should be charged to the statement of profit or loss. The cost of tyres is the cost of a repair (a revenue expense) to maintain the existing performance of the asset. This will also be charged to the statement of profit or loss.
11		A prepayment and an item of inventory are both current assets. The accrual and bank overdraft are both current liabilities.
12	D	A bank overdraft and trade payables would both be classified as current liabilities. The bank loan is a long term liability and this would be classified as a non-current liability. Capital is classified separately on the statement of financial position.
13	B	As a potential supplier, James will want to make sure Paul can pay him for any goods he supplies to Paul's business.
14	D	The cash payments day book is a book of prime entry used to record cash, cheques and other bank payments. A cheque received by a business from a customer is a source document. A statement of financial position is the end result of a series of processes to summarise financial records. The bank account is a summary of cash day book entries.

15   C

		$	
From Sophie	($1,200 – $1,000) × 5%	10	Trade
From Rob	$500 × 10%	50	Cash: immediate
	$800 × 5%	40	Cash: prompt
		$\underline{\underline{100}}$	

16   A   Early settlement discounts allowed are deducted from revenue at the time of the sale. If the customer takes advantage of the discount, no further adjustment is made to the accounts. If the customer does not take advantage of the discount, an adjustment to revenue will be made. Discounts received are essentially income (or a reduction in expenses) for the business and are therefore added rather than deducted when arriving at profit for the year.

17   D   This would be recorded in the purchase returns day book.

18   1, 3   The sales tax ledger account is a control account. Sales tax on purchases (input tax) is reclaimed back from the authorities, so input tax from the purchases day book and relating to cash purchases are debit entries. Sales tax charged on sales is due to the authorities, so sales tax on cash and credit sales are entered as credits in the sales tax ledger account.

19   C   If errors are not deemed to be large, tax authorities usually allow adjustment for them to be made on the next sales tax return. In this case Karen will have paid too much to the authorities in the quarter to 31 March 20X0, so she needs to include the additional input tax missed off this return (which should have been set against the output tax due) on the next return to 30 June 20X0.

20   C   This entry represents the posting of an expense item. The total of the invoice is credited to the payables control account and debited to surveyor's fees in the statement of profit or loss.

21   A   The description is of a control account.

22   C   An error of commission is where one side of a transaction has been recorded in the wrong account, and that account is of the same class as the correct account.

23   D   Errors which are picked up by extracting a trial balance are those that cause an imbalance. The complete omission of a transaction, because neither a debit nor a credit is made, would not cause the trial balance to be out of balance.

24   C   The going concern assumption implies that the business will continue in operation for the foreseeable future, and that there is no intention to put the company into liquidation or to make drastic cutbacks to the scale of operations.

25   A   The fact that the final accounts follow similar formats for different businesses aids comparability.

          Relevance and faithful representation are also both qualitative characteristics, but other features contribute to these. Financial information is relevant if it is capable of influencing the economic decisions of users and is provided in time to influence those decisions. Materiality is an accounting principle rather than a qualitative characteristic.

26   The supplier has allowed you $150 settlement discount which you had omitted to enter in your ledgers. All of the other options would make the balance on the supplier's account **higher** than the balance in the accounts.

27   C   Error 1 will affect the list of balances but not the control account. Error 2 will affect the control account.

28   C   As a current liability.

29    $75,756   The correct balance on the control account is $75,756 ($75,356 + $400 undercast).

30   B   An error of omission.

31   The purchase of a non-current asset debited to the purchases account and credited to the trade payables account

      A non-current asset has been debited to the wrong **class** of account (purchases).

32   CREDIT $90 $890 should have been debited to the expense account. Instead, $980 has been debited. To bring this amount down to $890, the expense account should be credited with $90.

33   3, 4   Outstanding lodgements and unpresented cheques are timing differences.

34   C   The ledger balance of $540 credit should be adjusted by a credit entry of $28 for bank charges. Therefore the corrected ledger balance is $568 credit.

           The statement balance will be an overdraft of $568 after the cheque of $620 has been processed.

           Therefore the statement balance must currently be $52 credit.

35   B   To check for indications that the balance on the general ledger is incorrect.

36   DEBIT $210

SUSPENSE ACCOUNT

	$		$
Balance b/d	210	Gas bill (420 – 240)	180
Interest received	70	Telephone expense (2 × 50)	100
	280		280

37   C   The irrecoverable debt expense account is debited with the cost of the irrecoverable debt. The receivables control account is credited to remove the debt from the receivables balance.

38    $1,200

	$
Irrecoverable debt written off	1,000
Irrecoverable debt recovered	(800)
Increase in allowance (3,000 – 2,000)	1,000
Irrecoverable debt expense	1,200

39   B   The prepayment will add $2,100 to profit and net assets.
The accrual will reduce profit and net assets by $800.
The net effect will be to increase both by $1,300.

40   A prepayment of $7,500 for five months (5/12 × $18,000 = $7,500).

41    $4,500 is the best estimate for the provision being the most likely outcome based on the solicitor's advice.

42   C   Closing inventory is a credit in the statement of profit or loss so when it is undervalued it results in an understatement of profit. Closing inventory is also an asset in the statement of financial position, so undervaluing it also understates net assets.

43    $15,300   The kits from last season should be stated at the lower of the cost ($30) and the net realisable value ($25 which is half the original selling price of $50). Therefore the inventory value is $15,550 – ($30 × 50) + ($25 × 50) = $15,300.

44   B

	$
30 units remain in inventory	
20 units @ $8	160
10 units @ $10	100
	260

45   D

	Units	Unit cost $	Total $	Average $
Opening inventory	50	4.00	200	
4 May purchase	50	4.40	220	
	100		420	4.20
11 May issue	(80)	4.20	(336)	
	20		84	
19 May purchase	60	4.60	276	
	80		360	4.50
24 May issue	(50)	4.50	(225)	
	30		135	

46   B   FIFO will lead to higher reported profit because his cost of sales will be based on the earliest (and therefore less expensive) purchases.

47 D To spread the net cost of the assets over their useful life.

48 A Carrying amount of the van is $24,500 – $13,650 = $10,850. This is higher than the proceeds of $7,500. Therefore there is a loss on disposal of $10,850 – $7,500 = $3,350.

49 $5,835

	$
Cost of new equipment	
Bank transfer	15,000
Part exchange	4,450
	19,450
Depreciation ($19,450 × 30%)	5,835

50 D

	$
Carrying amount of old equipment	
Cost	15,000
Depreciation	(9,855)
	5,145
Proceeds	4,450
Carrying amount	(5,145)
Loss on sale	(695)

51 A If disposal proceeds are $15,000 and profit on disposal is $5,000, then carrying amount must be $10,000. This is the difference between the asset register figure and the non current asset account in the general ledger.

52 D An credit balance will be either a liability to be carried forward or income to be transferred to the statement of profit or loss. Expenses and assets are debit balances.

53 2, 3 Accrual for rent and bank overdraft.

The accrual and bank overdraft are current liabilities. The allowance for receivables is deducted from receivables before they are included in current assets. The majority of the new bank loan is likely to be included in non-current liabilities as these are repaid over a number of years.

54 B $5,000 is due within one year of the year end date of 31 March 20X1 so is classified as a current liability. The remainder is due after 31 March 20X2 so is classed as non-current.

55 $399,640

	$	$
Revenue		950,250
Cost of sales		
Opening inventory	88,540	
Purchases	540,755	
Carriage inwards	14,985	
	644,280	
Closing inventory	(93,670)	
		(550,610)
Gross profit		399,640

56 A In the statement of profit or loss, credit entries exceed debit entries. Harry has made a profit of $7,212 ($156,999 – $149,787).

57 D Proprietor's capital is entered in the statement of financial position credit column.

58 A The main purpose of the extended trial balance is to keep track of adjustments between the trial balance and the final accounts.

59 C

	Total $	Ordinary revenue $	Private drawings $
Cost of sales	144,000	142,200	1,800
Mark-up:			
12% on cost	216		216
20% on sales (= 25% on cost)	35,550	35,550	
Revenue	179,766	177,750	2,016

60 $426,405

	Total revenue $	Ordinary revenue $	Private revenue $
Cost of sales	342,000	334,700	7,300
Mark-up:			
10% on cost	730	–	730
20% on sales (= 25% on cost)	83,675	83,675	
Revenue	426,405	418,375	8,030

61 B

	$	$
Non-current assets		51,300
Inventory		7,770
Receivables		5,565
		64,635
Less		
Payables	3,994	
Overdraft	3,537	
Rent accrual	500	
		(8,031)
Closing capital		56,604

62 B Purchases were payments made plus increase in suppliers' balances
ie $141,324 + ($16,812 – $15,264) = $142,872

		$
Thus cost of sales	Opening inventory	6,359
	Purchases	142,872
		149,231
	Less closing inventory	(4,919)
		144,312

63 A Closing balance (37,400) = Opening balance (31,200) + Salary (7,500)

– Interest on drawings (2,800) + Share of profit (13,500)

– Drawings (12,000)

64 C Fred needed to contribute enough to purchase his share of the goodwill plus the amount he wanted to have as opening capital. Therefore he must have contributed $40,000 in relation to the goodwill ($120,000/3) plus the $10,000 of opening capital = $50,000.

65 4 Loan interest paid to a partner and the cost of a partner's entertaining expenses are expenses of the business. Salaries to partners and interest on capital paid to partners are treated as appropriations of profit.

66   C

	Partnership profit $	Ann $	Alice $
	75,000		
Salary	(10,000)	10,000	
Interest	1,000	(500)	(500)
Profit share	(66,000)	22,000	**44,000**
	–	31,500	43,500

67    $12,000   Sheila is entitled to her share of the net profit after deducting Bruce's salary.
$(34,100 – 12,100) \times 6/11) = 12,000$

Bibliography

Bibliography

HM Revenue & Customs (2021) *VAT returns*. [Online]. Available at: https://www.gov.uk/vat-returns/surcharges-and-penalties [Accessed 4 January 2021].

IFRS Foundation (2021) *IFRS* [Online] Available at: http://eifrs.ifrs.org [Accessed 4 January 2021].

International Accounting Standards Board (2021), *Conceptual Framework* [Online]. Available at: http://eifrs.ifrs.org [Accessed 4 January 2021].

Index

Review form

Name: _____   Address: _____
_____
_____

How have you used this Interactive Text?
(Tick one box only)

☐ Distance learning (book only)

☐ On a course: college _____

☐ As a tutor

☐ With 'correspondence' package

☐ Other _____

Why did you decide to purchase this Interactive Text? *(Tick one box only)*

☐ Have used BPP Texts in the past

☐ Recommendation by friend/colleague

☐ Recommendation by a lecturer at college

☐ Saw advertising

☐ Other _____

Which BPP products have you used?

☑ Text ☐ Kit ☐ Passcards

During the past six months do you recall seeing/receiving any of the following?
(Tick as many boxes as are relevant)

☐ Our advertisement in *ACCA Student Accountant*

☐ Our advertisement in *Teach Accounting*

☐ Other advertisement _____

☐ Our brochure

☐ ACCA email

☐ BPP email

☐ Our website www.bpp.com

Which (if any) aspects of our advertising do you find useful?
(Tick as many boxes as are relevant)

☐ Prices and publication dates of new editions

☐ Information on Interactive Text content

☐ Facility to order books off-the-page

☐ None of the above

Your ratings, comments and suggestions would be appreciated on the following areas

	Very useful	Useful	Not useful
Introductory section (How to use this Interactive Text)	☐	☐	☐
Key terms	☐	☐	☐
Examples	☐	☐	☐
Questions and answers	☐	☐	☐
Fast forwards	☐	☐	☐
Quick quizzes	☐	☐	☐
Exam alerts	☐	☐	☐
Practice Question Bank	☐	☐	☐
Practice Answer Bank	☐	☐	☐
Index	☐	☐	☐
Structure and presentation	☐	☐	☐
Icons	☐	☐	☐

	Excellent	Good	Adequate	Poor
Overall opinion of this Interactive Text	☐	☐	☐	☐

Do you intend to continue using BPP products?   ☐ Yes ☐ No

Please visit https://www.bpp.com/request-support to provide your feedback for this material.

Review form (continued)

Please note any further comments and suggestions/errors below